THE REBEL IN THE RED JEEP

THE REBEL
IN THE RED JEEP

Ken Hechler's Life in
West Virginia Politics

CARTER TAYLOR SEATON

WEST VIRGINIA UNIVERSITY PRESS
MORGANTOWN 2017

Copyright 2017 by Carter Taylor Seaton
All rights reserved
First edition published 2017 by West Virginia University Press
Printed in the United States of America

ISBN:
pb   978–1–943665–61–7
epub   978–1–943665–62–4
pdf   978–1–943665–63–1

Library of Congress Cataloging-in-Publication Data is available from
the Library of Congress

Cover design by Than Saffel
Cover photograph courtesy of the author. Photographer unknown.

Prayer

God, though this life is but a wraith,
Although we know not what we use,
Although we grope with little faith,
Give me the heart to fight—and lose.

Ever insurgent let me be,
Make me more daring than devout;
From sleek contentment keep me free,
And fill me with a buoyant doubt.

Open my eyes to visions girt
With beauty, and with wonder lit—
But always let me see the dirt,
And all that spawn and die in it.

Open my ears to music; let
Me thrill with Spring's first flutes and drums—
But never let me dare forget
The bitter ballads of the slums.

From compromise and things half done,
Keep me with stern and stubborn pride;
And after the fight is then won,
Oh, Lord, keep me still unsatisfied.

Louis Untermeyer

CONTENTS

LIST OF PHOTOGRAPHS

ACKNOWLEDGMENTS

I'm indebted to Ken Hechler for our many in-depth conversations and his willingness to answer any question I posed, as well as for the unfettered access he provided to his papers—both personal and at Marshall University. Without the help of Nat deBruin, Marshall's Special Collections archivist, and his predecessor, the late Lisle Brown, and their staffs, the task of researching Hechler's voluminous papers would have been insurmountable. Myrna Sloam, archivist at the Bryant Library in Roslyn, New York, deserves special thanks for her research assistance, as does Judy May of Roslyn for providing her insights into the Hechler family and her tour services. Each of you—former colleagues, students, employees, friends, and a few detractors—who talked freely with me about Hechler gets a gold star. Many were my friends beforehand; others became friends in the process. You know who you are. Russ Barbour's transcripts for the Hechler documentary, *In Pursuit of Justice*, filled in many interview gaps. Finally, bless each of my early readers: Richard Cobb, Eddy Pendarvis, Charles Lloyd, and Gwenyth Hood. You saved me from myself.

INTRODUCTION

In the nineteenth century, two theories on leadership arose. In 1840, Scottish writer Thomas Carlyle proposed his "great men" theory, which held that great men or heroes influenced historical events through their skills, wisdom, or personalities. The counter theory, posed twenty years later by Herbert Spencer, said great men were the product of their circumstances, influenced by social conditions that existed before they were born. Both theories have been dismissed in modern times, but Ken Hechler subscribed to the former after learning it at Swarthmore. However, he was also quick to admit that what he was able to accomplish often flowed from the events and circumstances that confronted him. Regardless of what influenced him most, Hechler stands out as a great man in the history of our nation.

Never deigning to bend to his party's political machinations—and in West Virginia, they were well established—Hechler did it his way. His way often earned him the enmity of the party regulars, but it also earned him the love and respect of the voters—and of his fellow congresspeople. Today, his name still elicits praise and a desire for a similar type of politician now.

Emblematic of his rebellious nature, Hechler drove a bright red Jeep throughout his career. He'd come to admire its workhorse quality in the army and knew instinctively it would draw attention as it plied the campaign trail. However, some saw it as an embarrassment—my Blue Dog Democratic father included. Many thought it unbecoming for a man of his stature. But Hechler eschewed their opinion; instead, he felt the Jeep connected him to his constituents, the regular folk. Plus, it easily traversed West Virginia's often-treacherous back roads.

Before he adopted West Virginia as his home in 1958, he had helped gather and publish the papers of President Franklin D. Roosevelt; taught and introduced innovative classroom techniques at several prestigious universities, including Columbia, Barnard, and Princeton; served as a researcher and speech writer for both President Harry Truman and presidential hopeful Adlai Stevenson; written the histories of the major European battles of World War II; interviewed high-ranking Nazi officers to document their war strategies for future military leaders; and created the Congressional Fellowship Program while working for the American Political Science Association. These accomplishments before age forty-five would have sufficed as an outstanding career for most men. But he didn't stop there.

Once in West Virginia, he served in the United States House of Representatives for eighteen years, served as West Virginia's secretary of state for sixteen more, and later battled for the environment and against the practice of mountaintop removal mining. During these years, he touched and made an impact on some of the most important issues facing the country: the advent of the space age, civil rights, black lung and miners' rights, campaign finance and election reform, and the environment. Regarding each, his fight for justice and the rights of individuals drove his every move. Perhaps his independence as a politician enabled him to take up these causes, as certainly few others were. In so doing, he affected the lives of all of us, not just those in West Virginia.

This biography is arranged both chronologically and thematically. His early life is handled chronologically until his political career begins in earnest. When recounting his time in Congress, I felt it would be more cohesive to deal with each issue as a whole, rather than spreading his work on them year by year. Thus, there are individual chapters on his time on the space committee, on his commitment to civil rights, on his fight for coal miners' health and safety, on his concern for the environment, and on his more minor battles in Congress. Similarly, because he ran for Congress nine times, it seemed more organized to deal with all of those elections in one chapter, rather than interspersing them throughout the book. This also shows more clearly how his once revolutionary person-to-person campaign style waned in effectiveness over the years with the eventual dominance of broadcast media campaigning.

Following his congressional years, the format reverts to the chronology of his life and follows him through his stint as West Virginia's chief election officer and into his retirement. The book is not just a recitation of his accomplishments, though there are many. It's also a look at the personal life of one of America's most remarkable public servants. In telling this story, I wanted to explain what inspired and drove him, and to reveal the personality behind Ken Hechler's public persona.

Carter Taylor Seaton

1

BEHIND THE WROUGHT IRON GATES

A small boy, hair cut in a Dutch bob, wears a determined look as he trudges down a gravel driveway pulling a wooden wagon. It's filled with pots of hyacinths and jonquils in full bloom. From under his straw hat, he looks back at his best friend, Billy Letson. The five-year-old pulling the wagon is Kenneth William Hechler, whose father, Charles Hechler, is the superintendent of Harbor Hill—the 648-acre Clarence Mackay estate in Roslyn, New York, where Billy's father manages the dairy. The two are on their way to peddle the flowers to other families on the estate. The year is 1919, and the estate is the boys' entire world, with acres of woods in which to play, free from worry or traffic. Since the workers' children were to remain unseen, their parents' only rule was, "Don't let the Mackay family see you."

Beyond the estate is the town of Roslyn, about thirty-five miles from New York City, on Long Island, which is often called America's Gold Coast. There, wealthy families built palatial estates in the early part of the twentieth century as a retreat from the stress and bustle of the city. About a mile from the Mackay estate, the Long Island Rail Road ferried the owners of these mansions—William C. Whitney, financier; Henry Phipps, philanthropist; and Clarence Mackay, owner of Postal Telegraph and Commercial Cable company—back to the city for work and for the social season.

On the island, the larger world remained at bay. Back then, the town's weekly paper, the *Roslyn News*, reported primarily

Ken Hechler at age five on the Mackay estate, circa 1919 (Courtesy Ken Hechler)

on parties, town elections, recipes, and the latest fashions.[1] Those interested in the broader issues of world politics or current events had to read about them in the *New York Times*. Although Mrs. Mackay—former debutante Katherine Duer—was a suffragette,[2] it's likely that news of the 1920 passage of the Nineteenth Amendment granting women the right to vote had little impact on others on the Mackay estate. Nor is it likely that news of the Panama Canal's opening in August 1914 made much difference to the Hechlers, whose son, Kenneth, would be born a month later. Although the outbreak of World War I would soon become an intrusion on idyllic Long Island life, when the French and their English Allies declared victory in the first official battle of World War I near Paris on September 12, 1914, life at Harbor Hill rolled on peacefully.

As these larger world events unfolded, Kenneth William Hechler mewled his way into the world at the Hechler home in North Hempstead, New York. With the birth of a third son, September 20, 1914, marked a big day for the Hechler family. Perhaps Kenneth's father had dreams that this boy would become a lawyer or doctor. His mother, Catherine, who had been a teacher in suburban St. Louis before marrying, felt strongly that he would need a good education to succeed in whatever he undertook. Like most parents, they could only dream and hope. This son's accomplishments, however, would eclipse their most far-fetched dreams. He would grow up to make a significant civic mark on history over the next one hundred years—as a nine-term U.S. congressman, a World War II military historian, a trusted advisor to President Harry Truman, West Virginia's longtime secretary of state, and an environmental activist.

It is likely Clarence Mackay took note of this auspicious occasion, for he and Charles Hechler were as close as employers and employees can be. Yet as long as his prize Guernsey cattle were tended, and the rest of the sprawling estate functioned smoothly, Mackay gave only brief attention to what occurred in the homes of his other employees. Indeed, their children seldom saw this well-dressed man, who sported a large red mustache.[3]

The task of running the estate belonged to the proud new papa, hired as its superintendent in 1909 without having to even apply for the job.[4] Charles Hechler, a graduate of the University of Missouri, had such a far-reaching reputation in animal husbandry that Mackay had sent for him. When Hechler arrived on the estate for his interview, the construction of the mansion, sprawling gardens, cow barn and dairy, swimming pool, polo stables, greenhouse, indoor and outdoor tennis courts, and casino, as well as homes for the superintendent, tennis pro, dairyman, and other top level managers, had been completed. Rumors of the cost of building the estate, which was double the size of the principality of Monaco,[5] reached $6 million, when in reality it was a fraction of that. Nevertheless, the house alone cost $830,000 when completed in 1902. This was before Mackay amassed his extraordinary collection of art, tapestries, and medieval armor for display there. With a commanding view of Long Island Sound, the mansion resembled a somewhat smaller version of Asheville's Biltmore House, home of George Vanderbilt. Designed by famed architect Stanford White and erected on the highest point on Long Island, Mackay's three-story manor home, enormous for the times, was twice as large as the Parthenon in Athens, Greece.[6] Sadly, the estate no longer exists; only the ornate gates remain.

Behind those wrought iron gates, Ken Hechler spent a charmed but somewhat lonely childhood. His only playmates were the other children of estate workers, and according to Ken, there weren't enough boys to form a sandlot baseball team except at birthday parties. On those occasions, however, no one wanted to play for fear that sliding into base would dirty his good clothes.[7] Though

Ken preferred to play outside, reading and learning were at the top of his mother's list of acceptable pastimes for her children. She taught each of her boys to read when they were toddlers. Ken could recite poetry at age two and continued to love it for the rest of his life. Ken recalls that instead of reading fairy tales to him and his brothers at bedtime, his mother chose biographies of famous men and women throughout history, hoping to inspire her sons to achieve great things. She also paid the boys ten cents for each Bible verse they memorized. When he entered first grade, Ken already knew addition, subtraction, multiplication, and long division, and was familiar with the lives of many important historical figures. This educational head start meant he usually earned the best grades in his classes; in addition, it enabled him to skip third grade.[8]

Even though his mother often referred to him in public as her baby and kept him in bobbed hair long after he should have been allowed to sport a more manly style, Ken admired her and believes he's more like her than his father.[9] Freed from most household chores by two servants, Catherine Hechler delighted in growing prize-winning chrysanthemums and spent countless hours volunteering for the Red Cross and the Roslyn Garden Club when her boys were young. A lifelong Republican, she was active in local politics by the time Ken was in junior high school. Later, when Ken began leaning toward a more liberal position after becoming disillusioned with Herbert Hoover's handling of the Depression and its aftermath, his mother wrote to him at Swarthmore, saying, "You can become a damn Democrat if you like, but please do not argue about it at home. I do not like quarreling."[10] Apparently, her rule against using bad language, for which she once washed Ken's mouth out with soap, didn't apply to her. Still, her greatest wish for her sons was that they succeed. As Ken grew, his father encouraged him to become a businessman, but his mother simply challenged him to be the best he could be.

The Hechler family, l to r: George, Ken (on his mother's lap), Catherine, Charles Jr., and Charles Sr., circa 1915. (Photo by Underwood and Underwood Photography, Courtesy Ken Hechler)

Having two brothers relieved Ken's loneliness only when they were young, for they were not particularly close as they matured.

Indeed, the three were quite competitive, perhaps contributing to Ken's feelings of being alone. He maintains that each was always jealous of the others. Charles, the middle brother, was exceedingly handsome and popular with the girls, a source of jealousy for Ken. He recalls, "I asked Charles, 'How do you get such nice black eyebrows?' and Charles said 'I comb them every morning.' I resorted to combing my eyebrows to make them jet black."[11] Although George, the eldest son, was very bright, he envied Ken, whose grades were consistently better.

The Hechler home, supplied rent-free by Mr. Mackay, was a rambling, two-story, sixteen-room frame, with a covered porch that stretched its entire length. Since the estate had its own water and sewage system, the Hechlers, like the rest of the employees, had indoor plumbing. Since most villagers had outhouses, Ken recalls a steady stream of visitors who came not to visit but to use the bathrooms. He also remembers tricycle racing his brothers down the long front hall, hiding from his parents in the memorabilia-filled attic or the massive cellar to avoid punishment, and stealing forbidden strawberries from the strawberry patch. The only time he was able to avoid his father's razor strap—his weapon of choice, according to Ken[12]—was when, at age three, he said he'd eaten only the green ones, since his father had described strawberries as "those red berries." His parents laughed instead of punishing him. This is Ken's earliest memory.[13]

Ken also recalls with pride his father's civic accomplishments as well as his success in managing Mackay's some 180 employees and the affairs of the estate. In a move to reduce Mackay's property taxes, Charles Hechler supervised the 1931 organization of the Village of East Hills, where the rates were set below those that were imposed by the town of Roslyn at the time. His mother served as a village trustee, while his father was elected town clerk. For a time, the Hechler's living room served as the new village's town hall.[14] A loyal employee, Hechler did not believe in talking about either his own or Mackay's personal affairs, since his boss chose to give information only through his company. It was a lesson Hechler learned well and passed on to his sons. As an adult, Charles Jr. was upset when another employee's son, Stewart Donaldson, wrote and distributed a lengthy description of life at Harbor Hill.[15] Even though Ken has always been quick to publicize his accomplishments, to a large degree he, too, always kept his private life under wraps.

Like most boys, Ken ran afoul of his father on more than one occasion. Mr. Hechler's reaction was usually exacting. When Ken wanted a baseball glove during the Depression, he pleaded for money to add to that which he had earned in order to buy it. But his father considered sports foolish and, at the height of the argument, slapped Ken in the face.[16] More often than not, however, Mr. Hechler used the silent treatment on his boys, and Ken says it was very effective.[17] In the face of his dad's harsh temper, especially when he was drinking, Ken tried hard to please both his parents and, as he matured, wanted to emulate them. His respect for his parents stemmed from their positions in the community, their sense of ethics, and the moral compass he could sense in both of them.[18] According to Ken, as a boy he felt they were the greatest hero and heroine in Roslyn. He recalls everyone in the community calling them for interviews about their involvement in political and charitable organizations. He especially noticed the attention their activities gained them.[19] However, there was one time when this admiration backfired. His father smoked long black cigars, and Ken thought they were evidence of his high standing. Perceptively, his father recognized this and left them in plain sight one day as he announced he'd be leaving for a couple of hours. "He put two on the table with matches, knowing full well what I would do," Ken says. "I never got so sick in my life. That cured me forever of smoking."[20]

It wasn't always tense at the Hechler home, however. As superintendent of the estate, Ken's father had access to the mansion when the Mackay family was not in residence, which was often. On January 24, 1925, he took his own family to the topmost pavilion of the soaring country home to watch the total eclipse of the sun. Ken recalls, "It was so magnificent to see the shadow of the moon obliterating the sun into complete darkness down at the Atlantic Ocean and then to see that darkness spread from the Atlantic Ocean north across Long Island, which is about twenty miles wide, and then to go out across to Connecticut."[21]

Two years later, Ken and his father watched Charles Lindbergh take off down the dirt runway of Long Island's Roosevelt Field on his solo flight across the Atlantic. The following month, after Lindbergh's return, Ken hid in the shrubbery hoping to catch a glimpse of the famous aviator, who was the guest of honor at a spectacular party at Harbor Hill. For the occasion, Mackay had festooned the trees and shrubbery with seven thousand illuminated Japanese lanterns and installed spotlights that played over the entire estate.[22] No doubt Ken's father would have meted out a punishment if he'd known, but the guards all recognized Ken and said nothing.[23]

Ken's father also taught him the value of good customer relations, a lesson that no doubt colored the way he dealt with his electoral constituents later in life. As a magazine route salesman at age twelve, Ken attained senior rank among the junior salesmen ranks of the Curtis Publication Company. The newspaper article that accompanied this honor noted, "He sells sixty *Saturday Evening Post* and twenty-four *Country Gentlemen* magazines per week as well as thirty-five *Ladies Home Journals* per month."[24] But Ken recalls one Saturday when he didn't want to leave his cozy fireside seat on a fur rug to deliver his magazines in eight inches of snow. His father reminded him that his customers would be quite upset if they didn't have their magazines to read the next day. Angry with his father, he went nonetheless. His first customer was so overjoyed to see his magazine arrive that he invited Ken in for hot chocolate. As he sipped the warming beverage, he realized his father was a lot smarter than he was.[25]

Ken loved and admired his paternal grandfather, George, as well, and recalls sitting on his lap during visits to hear stories of his Civil War service. Eventually, Ken wrote the book *Soldier of the Union* about him. As he was writing it, he regretted not asking his grandfather more questions before he died in 1927.[26] Born near

Heidelberg, Germany, in 1840, George was the son of Gottfried Hechler, a farmer. Traditionally, the Hechlers were craftsmen—coopers, carpenters, and glaziers—or farmers. In 1850, Gottfried left Germany and settled in Marietta, Ohio; his son George was thirteen. Seven years later, when their father broke his leg, George and his younger brother, John, assumed all the farm duties.

The stories of how his grandfather enlisted in the Ohio Volunteer Infantry Regiment after the harvesting was completed captivated young Ken. From grandfather George, Ken learned how his great-uncle John, who had enlisted a month earlier, was captured at Chickamauga and died in Andersonville Prison three years later;[27] and how George fought valiantly throughout the war, was discharged at the end of it, and returned to Marietta for a short time. Ken heard how George then struck out for Missouri, where he later operated a 357-acre livestock and grain farm in Dalton, about seventy miles from Columbia. It was there, at the University of Missouri, that he afforded all three of his sons—Ken's father and his brothers, George and Roy—a college degree.[28] Following in the farming tradition, Charles earned his degree in animal husbandry, but he had greater hopes for his own sons.

Ken first wanted to become a forester, because he thought an outdoor life would be a healthy one, but by high school, writing had become his passion. Actually, he'd been writing since he was much younger. At age twelve he wrote the *Weekly Grunt*, a newspaper he gave away to his weekly *Saturday Evening Post* subscribers; other customers received only a monthly free copy. At age fifteen he kept a diary, in which he sounded quite mature in his early musings on politics but typically youthful in the listing of Christmas gifts he was thrilled to receive: "two pencils, a fountain pen, four books, three neckties, a pair of gloves, socks, a cap, Arctics, [boots] and a handball." When a local supervisor was reelected in his district, Ken vowed to become a Socialist because he didn't like the man's politics.[29] At about the same time, Ken began writing sports columns at ten cents a line for both the local newspaper and the *New York Times*, reporting on a local minor league baseball team, the Roslyn Red Sox.[30] As salutatorian of his 1931 high school graduating class, his speech, titled "Journalism as a Career," extolled the virtues of writing about great athletes.[31]

Outdoor activities and sports were important to him throughout his youth, and professional athletes, especially baseball stars, were his heroes. He wanted to follow in the footsteps of his track-star brother George, but Ken wore thick glasses and wasn't athletically gifted. Therefore, he settled for managing the school's various athletic teams instead. He did play tennis, however, and played it vigorously until a hip replacement at age ninety-three kept him from being able to charge the net successfully. It was the only competitive sport at which he excelled.

As a Boy Scout, Ken attained the status of Life Scout and attended Scout camp on Long Island every summer. His first summer camp included a humiliating initiation he remembered into adulthood. His chore was setting the table for dinner, and he thought he'd done it correctly until one of the boys asked where the toothpicks were. Told to go to the superintendent for them, he hiked there, only to be told to climb another hill to the doctor's office for them. When that also proved fruitless, he returned to find a chorus of boys yelling a childish taunt, and then giving him the "raspberries" sound. While this initiation was standard treatment for all the newbies, Ken was mortified.[32]

It wasn't the last time he'd be teased or shunned. To earn his Scouting badge in dairying, he rose at 5 a.m. to milk the cows and test the milk's butterfat content. Without a bath, he then headed for school. When he arrived, the lingering smell of souring milk and manure caused the girls to move to the other side of the classroom.[33] While most teenage boys realize that figuring out girls is difficult, for Ken it was a serious dilemma. "From the age of fourteen on my loving juices began to run and I tried to develop an amorous friendship with a number of young ladies, all of whom rejected me," he recalls. This included the captain of the girls' basketball team, who kissed his best friend, Bill Letson, instead. Finally, "a Polish girl named Jennie Longskie smiled at me," he says. "I used my writing power to develop a close relationship with her much to the disgust of my parents who considered Poles and Italians a cut below them socially. They felt they were mainly there to be laborers on the estates and Republican voters at the polls." In spite of this, Ken defied his parents and continued the relationship through high school and into his freshman year at Swarthmore. He labels it an intense but stormy relationship, conducted mostly through letters, which she asked him to return once she'd ended the relationship. In college, he misinterpreted the hints another Roslyn girl, Ruth Mary Lewis, tried to give him. When he didn't recognize or respond to her sexual advances, she began dating another boy.

This inability to attract girls readily, combined with his lack of athletic prowess and his jealousy of two brothers who were more successful in both areas, led to such a lack of confidence that Ken developed a serious inferiority complex, which today we would call low self-esteem. Afraid of disappointing his parents, he turned to his public speaking teacher for support. Leona Ruth Kimball became his confidante. Of her he says, "Miss Kimball was one of the few people I could talk to about my problems: mainly a terrible inferiority complex from which I suffered. She was a tireless, sympathetic person on whose shoulder I could cry (figuratively). She boarded with the Letson family about a quarter mile away from our house in Roslyn, and on vacation from Swarthmore I would go over to talk with her about my hopes and dreams."[34] He also admits that these feelings about his problems goaded him to work harder to succeed at everything he undertook.[35]

While he believes he favors his gentle mother rather than his strict and parsimonious father, Ken's legendary frugality must have sprung from his father's example. At age twelve Ken opened a savings account, in which he deposited the earnings from his magazine route. In high school, his sports-writing earnings went in as well. When he graduated from high school in 1931 at age seventeen, he had to use his savings to supplement his Swarthmore tuition. This was during the depths of the Great Depression, and while his father's salary was still considered too high for Ken to qualify for a scholarship, his family had suffered financially.

Charles Hechler's boss was devastated by the Depression. By 1927, Western Union had captured the lion's share of the telegraph business and Mackay's Postal Telegraph and Commercial Cable company had fallen behind in paying its debts. In 1928, he sought and secured a merger with Sosthenes Behn, owner of International Telephone and Telegraph. Unwisely, he accepted his nearly $300 million payment in stock in ITT. On Black Thursday, his fortune nearly evaporated in what was said to be one of the largest losses of the crash. Somehow, however, Mackay managed to keep Harbor Hill going. In 1931, following the death of his Catholic ex-wife Katherine—Mackay had forsworn remarriage while she lived, regardless of their divorce—he married Anna Case, and the two settled at the estate. Realizing the severity of their situation, the new bride apparently took matters into her own hands and fired most of the staff, including some who had been there since the mansion was built.[36]

Charles Hechler was tasked with the remaining firings. Mackay reduced Hechler's salary by two-thirds, as well. Because Mackay could no longer afford the coal to heat the mansion, he shuttered it and forced the Hechler family to move so his family could occupy their home. This created a residential ripple effect. The Hechlers took the tennis pro's home, the tennis pro took the chauffer's, and so on. Fortunately, according to Ken, because his father also had real estate and banking interests, he was able to feed his family and provide partial college tuition for his three sons: George at Cornell, Charles at Antioch College, and Ken at Swarthmore. His formative years over, Ken headed to college unsure of himself and his future plans. One thing he did know for certain was that life on the campus of Swarthmore—the co-ed college he'd chosen to be far enough away from his parents to be independent but close enough to return home on holidays[37]— would be markedly different from the sheltered existence he'd known for the past seventeen years.

2

BIG MAN ON CAMPUS

As the 2013 Swarthmore College alumni parade begins to assemble, a golf cart moves to the head of the procession. An enormous banner reading "Class of 1935," the year its passenger graduated, covers the front of the cart. Inside, smiling and waving to the crowd, is ninety-eight-year-old Ken Hechler, then the oldest living Swarthmore alumnus. No doubt traveling back to this Quaker institution outside Philadelphia was nostalgic for Hechler, who at age seventeen began his first four years away from home on its campus and who also received an honorary doctor of letters degree there in 2001. Memories of the bonfires, the blue-lit annual Christmas tree, the caroling seniors, and Tuesday gatherings at Collection Hall filled his mind. Riding past solemn-looking, limestone Parrish Hall also must have brought back fond memories of the coeds who lived there, especially those who captured his heart. As a senior, his aim was to date every freshman girl—and he succeeded. Perhaps he recalled long walks with some of them along Crum Creek, or studying with one as the sweet scent of wisteria filled the air.

The Depression showed no signs of abating when he enrolled in 1931, and although Hechler was ineligible for any scholarships, he was in line for a working scholarship the following year.[1] He entered Swarthmore as an economics major, but he struggled with the required courses—courses his father hoped would prepare him for a future in business. Adjusting to college life and competition from better-prepared students, he ended his first year with two Bs and eight Cs, hardly the distinguished record he was accustomed to in high school. The higher marks of the "brilliant students" in his classes added to his staggeringly low self-esteem.[2] Furthermore, because his parents couldn't spare extra spending money, Hechler *had* to work. His freshman budget and account book shows that his average expenditures totaled less than fifty dollars per month,[3] further foreshadowing the frugal lifestyle Hechler would later be kidded about.

With an old Essex automobile he purchased for fifty dollars and had the Mackay blacksmith retrofit with a rod across the back seat, he picked up and delivered laundry for Harris & Company, a Philadelphia dry cleaner. He continued his successful high school sales career, as well. Now selling subscriptions for the *New York Times*, his route included the entire campus. By convincing all the political science and economics professors to make the *Times* required reading for their students, he ensured his success.[4] He and the newspaper tangled, however. Apparently his entrepreneurial spirit ran counter to the paper's business model. Clearly, he was a master promoter, but the *Times* objected to his methods. A letter from *Times* executive Charles Muldaur, chastising Hechler for suggesting the paper drop its prices to get more subscribers, explains it. Muldaur wrote, "I have felt for some weeks that your attitude in your work is a strange mixture of justifiable pride and unjustifiable conceit. There comes a time when all of us have to take orders and I fail to see why you should make such an issue of taking yours." Hechler had also sent Christmas cards to his customers against his supervisor's orders to the contrary.[5]

Once again, he became engrossed in writing for the school newspaper, the *Phoenix*, and served on the school publicity committee. He quit the *Phoenix* at the end of his freshman year, however, because he was worried about his C average grades.[6] Even though he read extensively for his upcoming classes, his sophomore year didn't improve much until the second semester, when he met Dr. Robert C. Brooks. His course was Political Motives, and while the subject intrigued Hechler, he stumbled through his first paper. In fact, he wrote the professor an apology on the front page. When his paper came back, Brooks had written, "No, excellent paper, since you analyze each circumstance. You have done twice as much as I could reasonably expect, but that's the sort of thing I wish to encourage."[7] This was just what Hechler needed. Soon, Brooks had taken Hechler under his wing, invited him to his home, and taught him how to study more effectively. Hechler received his first A in that class, but it would not be his last.

In one class, Brooks posed an assignment: Pick an elected office, and outline how you would run for it and what you would do.[8] Hechler responded that the first thing he'd do would be to change his name from Kenneth to Ken because he thought it sounded less pretentious.[9] He also recalls thinking that "Kenneth sounded like your mother saying, 'Please clean up that ring around the bathtub that you left after your bath, Kenneth.'"[10]

Realizing Brooks's classes had piqued his interest in politics and government, Hechler used some of his obligatory daily time at the Friends Meetinghouse "to contemplate their belief that you owed back to society the things that society and your country had given you. We sat in silence trying to plan the most important priorities in our lives," he later recalled.[11] Perhaps it was there where he decided to forgo a future in business and devote his life to more lofty activities. Despite his parents' wishes, Hechler changed his major to political science and took an ethics class, a discipline his mother termed all "talkie, talkie."[12] In each course he had under Brooks, Hechler earned an A. By the time he graduated, he had the highest average in the political science department, and his self-confidence had been boosted considerably.[13]

The previously promised working scholarship kicked in during his sophomore year. It gave him a position serving meals in the dining room, and provided his food, as well.[14] School wasn't all work and study for the future big man on campus, however. When he discovered that Swarthmore had disbanded its marching band some years back, he sought to resurrect it. He sent postcards to all incoming freshman in an attempt to solicit new members and received some laughable responses from those who were not musically inclined.[15] In October 1933, the newly formed band, "resplendent in garnet capes and white trousers," performed at a football game against Dickinson College, another Pennsylvania school. And though Hechler played clarinet and would have normally been part of the event, he was absent, recovering from an appendectomy.[16]

In his junior year, he wrote his mother that he'd discovered dating and had taken thirty-two freshmen out so far. "It's fun," he wrote. "I'd never tried it before."[17] Still somewhat socially inept, he told his mother in 1933 that he "thought he ought to learn to dance next summer."[18] One grave disappointment marked his junior year, however. Hechler's desire to be inducted into the prestigious Book and Key Society—an elite group of only seven senior members who met in secret in their own building—was dashed on Tap Night. As the entire five-hundred-member student body assembled in front of Parrish Hall, Hechler waited in vain for the telling tap on the shoulder that would signal he had been chosen. He felt his accomplishments, including reestablishing the marching band, merited selection, but it was not to be. No doubt this exclusion galvanized his desire to succeed in other ways.

As a result, by his senior year, he may have been the busiest man on campus. As manager of the varsity baseball team, he was inducted into KWINK,[19] a private organization that voted on which candidates for the various team managers deserved to be included in its ranks, and eventually became its chief. As baseball manager, he was responsible for everything from oiling the gloves to scheduling the games.[20] Since Swarthmore had no staff handling the college's publicity, this task was entrusted to an all-student committee. He served on that committee during his first two years on campus and, at least according to Hechler, got more scoops than anyone else on staff, including an interview with Albert Einstein on a tip from Swarthmore president Frank Aydelotte. Sadly, Hechler admits, he understood very little of what Einstein said but was clearly in awe of the man.[21] Smarting over the previous chair's attempt to replace him on the publicity committee,[22] Hechler worked even harder—once he got the chair position—in his senior year. As chair, Hechler flooded ten metropolitan dailies with regular press releases and earned $22,000 for writing assignments from New York and Philadelphia newspapers. He changed the name of the committee to the Press Board and also broke the gender barrier, including coeds on the committee so that news of their activities would be reported as well.[23]

By graduation, both his activities and his smile were well known on campus. According to the 1935 *Halcyon*, Swarthmore's annual, the popularity of "the Major," as he was nicknamed, nearly forced the college to build a coliseum to house his friends and visitors following his 1934 appendix surgery.[24] Clearly, Hechler's self-confidence was restored by the time he left Swarthmore's idyllic campus.

Swarthmore challenged its students to "develop a thorough analysis of many, many different subjects, all the way from reviewing the autobiography of Lincoln Steffens to analyzing the relationship between eugenics and politics," he said in a 1985 interview.[25] His papers for Dr. Brooks bear this out: studies of Anna Howard Shaw, Emma Goldman, Brand Whitlock, Susan B.

Ken Hechler's Swarthmore College annual picture in the Halcyon (Photo by Carlton, Inc., Courtesy Ken Hechler)

Anthony, William Jennings Bryan, Woodrow Wilson, Teddy Roosevelt, Herbert Hoover, Gandhi, Mussolini, the two political parties, the Constitution, the Supreme Court, governmental reform, communism versus capitalism, and anti-Semitism.[26] "We had great emphasis on biography at Swarthmore, along the lines of the [Thomas Carlyle] Carlylian theory of history—that great men, through their intellect, skills, or charisma make events, rather than events developing men."[27] While he had believed this since his first grade teacher introduced him to a book about great men and women called *Builders of Our Country*, and seen it firsthand in his parents' lives, Hechler would continue to explore this theory both in his graduate studies and as a teacher.

Inspired by the way Professor Brooks took him under his wing, Hechler decided to use his knowledge of political science to educate other young men and women. Realizing he'd need advanced degrees to teach on the college level, he enrolled at Columbia University the summer following graduation to pursue a master's degree and thereafter a PhD. According to Hechler, transferring from the quiet Swarthmore campus beside Crum Creek to the jam-packed streets of Morningside Heights in New York City was terrifying. "I recall after rattling uptown to the 116th Street stop on the Broadway subway, I was overwhelmed by the pushing mob that dominated the university dining hall, causing me to beat a hasty retreat to nearby Amsterdam Avenue where I bought a box of Fig Newtons and a quart of milk for my dinner."[28]

Not long after he had adjusted to a school with four times the student population of Swarthmore, he saw an advertisement on campus for ushers at the Davis Cup and other matches at the West Side Tennis Club in nearby Forest Hills, New York. He applied and spent several summers ushering. Given a rag to clean damp seats, he soon learned to act as if the seat had something on it, for the harder he wiped, the bigger his tip.[29] The woman in charge of the Columbia Appointments Office, through which all students applied for work, took a liking to Hechler and alerted him whenever a new job was announced. Mary Wegener also helped him obtain a seasonal job selling men's pajamas at Bloomingdale's Department Store. This job taught him the wisdom of discretion. Told in orientation that the store carried four sizes—A, B, C, and D—he was instructed to size up the potential customers. When a little shrimp of a guy came in, Hechler directed him to the size A stack, but the man said, "No, I want a pair of Bs." Hechler tried again to convince him that they would be too big, but the man just looked at Hechler and said, "Buddy, when I buy a pair of pajamas, I want my wife to be able to get in them, too." Hechler never questioned a customer's decision after that.[30]

Although he received a scholarship and a fellowship that enabled him to move into a residence hall, Hechler still held several part-time jobs. He taught tennis, waited tables, became a weekend companion for an incorrigible and emotionally disturbed eleven-year-old boy in Scarsdale, and was the private secretary for Milton Hackes—the retired editor of *Jewelers' Weekly*. Each week Hechler rode the subway to Hackes's apartment to type letters, since the man suffered from Parkinson's disease. Hechler says he turned down actor Clifton Webb's request to drive him around New England while he performed in summer stock, because it would mean an end to his other part-time jobs.[31]

In spite of the time these jobs required, Hechler still received his master's degree in one year. As he prepared to write his thesis, Robert Brooks—his former Swarthmore professor, who wrote to him regularly during his Columbia days—advised him to narrow his subject, saying, "There's enough material [here] for three or four theses."[32] Hechler took his advice and chose the upcoming 1936 presidential election of Franklin D. Roosevelt as his topic. Submitted in May and titled "Will Roosevelt Be Re-elected: A Prognostic Analysis of Faces, Factors, and Figures in the 1936 Presidential Election," it covered Roosevelt's opponents, his economic and political philosophies, the campaign issues, the national convention, the media's part in influencing public opinion, and Hechler's predictions of the state box scores of votes. In his preface, Hechler admits that his subject was met with "universal disapproval," and therefore, he tried to provide a "firm basis of factual information to supplement pure prophecy." The last paragraph is typical Hechler: "Since a frankly journalistic approach has been attempted, apologies are made for errors of fact or hasty judgment. For flippant facetiousness, no apology is offered."[33] The entire thesis was over three hundred pages, but the last chapter—the conclusion—contained only one word: "Yes."[34]

Hechler's conclusion ran contrary to the infamous poll that had run in the *Literary Digest* earlier that year. Even if the magazine had correctly predicted the previous four elections, it was wrong in 1936. According to after-the-fact analyses—and Hechler—the problem was the polling sample. Because the editors used their own subscriber list, along with lists of automobile owners and telephone users, the results were skewed. Those lists, which had previously represented a cross-section of voters, were now primarily made up of relatively affluent Republicans who could still afford cars, telephones, and magazine subscriptions. This faulty prediction ultimately led to the demise of the magazine and came to be seen as the beginning of more scientific polling methods.[35]

Conversely, Hechler recognized before the election that most of the country was still struggling with the Depression, which many thought to be the fault of the previous Republican president. He used that insight not only in writing his thesis but to good personal advantage as well. Because the popular polls favored Alf Landon, Hechler placed a bet through his old friend Billy Letson, who was working on Wall Street at the time, taking 5–1 odds on Roosevelt. At the end of the day, he had received his master's degree and made $150. No doubt his Swarthmore classes and this research helped shape the way Hechler viewed the world and began to create the political animal he would become.

Hechler didn't change his party affiliation to Democrat for many more years, but his research had made him an outspoken advocate of Roosevelt and his New Deal—both on campus and in his classes—in opposition to a great many people, including his parents, who remained staunch Republicans. In his thesis, Hechler analyzed Roosevelt's personality with an insight even he probably didn't spot. His description of Roosevelt is a markedly prescient description of the author himself. "Here was a crusader, who pitched into his task with abounding zeal, making sure that all of his spectacular efforts were well-publicized. Is it any wonder that Roosevelt is rated as being more popular than his party?" Then he agrees with quotes from James P. Warburg's book *Hell Bent for Election*, saying, "Roosevelt's prime motivation is the desire to be liked by everybody with whom he comes in contact. In addition, the voluminous amount of correspondence he carries on helps him in maintaining these contacts."[36] Both statements accurately describe the future congressman, Ken Hechler.

By May 1937, he had been granted a two-year George William Curtis Fellowship, which enabled him to continue his graduate work pursuing a PhD at Columbia. The grand total of $750 was to cover both years. Eager to begin teaching, he sought out fellowships across the country for his upcoming second year. After several rejections, an offer arrived from the University of Nebraska. Hechler excitedly showed it to his department head, who countered with, "Why would you want to go to a god-forsaken state like Nebraska? We can give you a fellowship to teach at the Columbia University Extension Department."[37] Hechler jumped at the chance. Since most classes there were geared toward a working student body, this position would allow him to teach during the day and take classes at night. In the fall, with one day's notice, he took over his chair's course in Great American Political Personalities. This was Hechler's first chance to inspire students, as the book of his youth, *Builders of Our Country*, had inspired him. That book had taught him to respect what principled leadership had meant to the country, and he now hoped to impart that to his students.

Hechler dove in zealously, even though at twenty-three he wasn't much older than many in his class. In fact, he'd been playing softball with some of his students the previous week. It was a double challenge, he says, because at the extension college, other students were substantially older. "I noticed a lot of the students would ask me very challenging questions, which sometimes had a somewhat nasty twist to them, as though they were expecting I wouldn't be able to answer. So I started the practice of, two hours before every class, I would think of the dirtiest, nastiest, most acrimonious questions that would be asked and I'd figure out how I would answer them. By the time I got to class, those nasty sounding questions sounded pretty mild compared to the ones I'd dreamed up."[38] The students soon realized he actually knew the material, and that seemed to ease their concern that their teacher was much younger than some of them.

Perhaps too eager to impart what he'd been studying only semesters earlier, Hechler presented a daunting 104-page bibliography to the incoming students. They would study such political luminaries as John Calhoun, Alexander Hamilton, Andrew Jackson, Thomas Jefferson, John Marshall, Teddy Roosevelt, William Jennings Bryan, and Congressman "Uncle Joe" Cannon. The course description indicated it would "concern itself with the careers, ideas, and influence of statesmen in American political history."[39] He might have been overly ambitious in his expectations, but if so, none of the students complained.

A call from home in October 1937 abruptly interrupted Hechler's first teaching foray. His eldest brother, George—the one he always described as the overachiever—had died. An Eagle Scout, high-jump champion, and trumpet player, George had won a scholarship to Cornell, where he had wanted to be first in his class. Sadly, by Thanksgiving of his freshman year, he had had what was then described as a nervous breakdown and was institutionalized. He had told Ken at the time that he had tried to stay up all night and even neglected visits to the bathroom in his attempts to best the other students.[40] Eventually, George was diagnosed with dementia praecox,[41] an illness that today is called schizophrenia and can often be treated with medication. In the 1930s, however, the treatment was to lock such patients in what were called insane asylums.

At first, George had received special treatment from a private New York City organization that served people who were overworked or had suffered a nervous breakdown. Looking back, Ken doesn't remember exactly where it was located, but he does recall George's return from the city while Ken was still in high school. "When he came home he looked like a new person, and had put on weight. They apparently had some formula to fatten people that had this disability. Sadly, his strength gradually slipped away and he slipped back to having delusions," Hechler says. "One evening he told me a story about how people were chasing him and harassing him in the southern part of Long Island," he continues. "It persuaded my mother and father to drive out to see if they could track down these people, but it was all in his mind. The next day he had been left alone and he left the house. George wandered around the Mackay estate until one of the employees called up and said that he was completely disoriented and had wandered into their home. That is when my father decided to send him to Kings Park, which was almost like a jail."[42]

Kings Park asylum was a state institution, which has since been closed, near the Hechlers' home. According to all reports, patients were viewed as less than human. Because of its proximity, visits were easy for the family, but knowing how the patients were treated, Hechler never made the trip to see his brother. During one of his mother's visits, however, George became agitated and slugged one of the officials. They immediately overpowered George and beat him.[43]

According to Hechler, there were scant medical facilities at Kings Park, and no efforts to rehabilitate the inmates. They were treated like prisoners; their decaying teeth were pulled instead of treated. Hechler believes George died as a result of this mistreatment, which included repeated beatings and removal of all his teeth. The funeral director made an attempt to make Hechler's father feel better by saying that George's body, in contrast to others brought to the funeral home from Kings Park, was in good shape. Of course, Hechler says that because of his mistreatment, that statement could not have been true.[44] While his death was a blessed relief for Hechler and his parents,[45] watching their oldest son deteriorate from a star student and Eagle Scout to a tortured inmate hurt them so deeply that almost no mention was made of George after his death.

Following the funeral, Hechler resumed his teaching load and added a lighter note to his classes. Hechler says,

> I used to do a lot of crazy things in my classes at Columbia in order to make the classes more interesting. One of the students, named Michael Gelber, was very extroverted. He would help me a great deal on these hijinks that we would pull in class, such as illustrating the campaign of 1840. That was the year William Henry Harrison ran against Martin Van Buren on the slogan of "Tippecanoe and Tyler too," and used the log cabin and hard cider symbols. One day Gelber dressed up in a Daniel Boone outfit and rushed into the classroom swinging two jugs of cider and yelling "Tippecanoe and Tyler too." Then we proceeded to discuss the issues of the campaign of 1840.[46]

While incidents like this may have earned him the enmity of his department chair, Grayson Kirk,[47] they also gave his classes a note of popularity. Still, several students did add a note of criticism to their evaluations, which Hechler required at the end of the course. They said they had expected to learn more about the individuals' human traits and how those had factored into their adult lives. One girl also asked if he'd really remembered the students' names or just memorized them for the first day of class.[48]

Minor criticisms from students notwithstanding, Hechler quickly became highly regarded as a teacher with a "fresh and refreshing approach."[49] Still inspired by the attention Dr. Brooks had given him as an undergraduate, Hechler spent hours writing personal notes to his students, analyzing their work. He also played tennis and softball with them, hoping to humanize his approach to teaching. A diary of his classroom performances noted which jokes bombed, so he wouldn't use them again. According to Hechler, his dean commented that she was fortunate to have him on her staff.[50]

In the summer of 1938, eager to get his PhD, Hechler began considering subjects for his dissertation. Before he could begin, however, he had to sit for several oral exams, two of which were in languages. He chose French and German, learned them easily— his high school language studies had helped—and handily dispatched the exams. He also was quizzed in political science, his major, and American history, his minor. The first went well, but as he put it, he got "his come-uppance" in history. One of his examiners happened to be an outspoken critic of the author of one of the books Hechler admired and quoted in his answers. He failed the exam. "I was so shocked that I determined that I was going to write a dissertation that would knock their socks off in American history," he said. According to Hechler, that setback became a standard for his future actions. "Whenever there's a setback, I do something to show that you can overcome it," he says.[51]

He'd long been an admirer of Senator George Norris of Nebraska, calling him one of the most farsighted individuals he'd ever met. Norris was instrumental in pushing the idea of the Tennessee Valley Authority long before FDR was elected. Fascinated with Norris and his ideals, Hechler kept the senator's picture on his desk for many years. What Hechler admired was Norris's support for unicameral government, his success in convincing Nebraska to institute the only such governing body in the country, and his ability to push a bill through Nebraska's legislature that gave the state, rather than profit-seeking private companies, ownership of the electric utility. His success, according to Hechler, lay in his ability to work with legislators on the opposite side of the aisle. One of Norris's most famous quotes, "I'd rather be right than regular," resonated with Hechler, who would later adopt the same philosophy. Norris was also one of the so-called insurgents, a group of congressmen from both sides of the aisle who banded together in the early 1900s to take on issues in the public interest over those of their own party. This made Hechler wonder just how and why that had happened and became the subject of his dissertation.[52]

Titled "Insurgency: The Personalities and Politics of the Taft Era," his dissertation was lauded upon publication by two outstanding history professors at Columbia.[53] The extensive research it required also set the stage for Hechler's future career. It focused on

the revolt of the pre–Teddy Roosevelt progressive Republicans in the House of Representatives and the Senate, who fought against the policies of William Howard Taft [in the early 1900s], and who fought for progressive measures like postal savings and railroad rate reform. Additionally, they fought against the Payne-Aldrich Tariff,[54] and the dictatorship of Speaker "Uncle Joe" Cannon[55] in the House of Representatives. This group of primarily Midwestern Republicans had teamed up with Democrats in the House of Representatives and the Senate to form the type of coalition that carried forward Teddy Roosevelt's policies.[56]

Hechler had long admired Teddy Roosevelt for his stand against big business and his creation of the national parks. His Sagamore Hill home was only fourteen miles from Hechler's boyhood haunts, so it's no wonder the budding politician chose such a weighty subject. As a child, he'd even seen Roosevelt at a political rally. He remembered Roosevelt entering from the rear of the hall, shaking hands with the audience as he went. To the three-year-old Hechler, Roosevelt's much-caricatured grin made his teeth look as if they were moving from side to side. Later, Roosevelt's style and his stand on issues would also resonate with Hechler. He admired Roosevelt's support for the rights of the powerless in several speeches and his intervention in a coal strike that was settled in the miners' favor. It impressed Hechler that Roosevelt was the first president to invite a black person—Booker T. Washington—to dinner at the White House, that he inspired those who had been exploited by large corporations, and that he pushed through Congress a bill giving the Interstate Commerce Commission the power to regulate then-exploitative railroad rates. Hechler would later emulate the campaign style that won Roosevelt an overwhelming majority in 1904 as well. Roosevelt campaigned to the people, making over six hundred speeches and covering twenty-three thousand miles doing it.[57] Like his latter-day cousin, Franklin Delano, Teddy gained enormous popular support, as would Hechler with West Virginia voters fifty-some years later.

The following year, 1939, Hechler took on more teaching responsibilities: classes at Barnard—Columbia's sister institution—and Columbia. Teaching at Barnard at age twenty-five turned Hechler loose on a classroom of coeds only a few years younger. He laughingly claims he sometimes had trouble concentrating on the subject at hand.[58] One young woman, Jane Chippendale Stewart, captured his heart, and they developed a long-lasting romance.

His full fifteen-hour teaching load included three men's classes at Columbia and two for the women at Barnard. All focused on political life, American political personalities, political parties, American government, and the legislative process. In June 1939 he was invited to teach a class at Yale, but declined because he felt he would be stretched too thin with his teaching and dissertation preparation.[59] At this time, Hechler began inviting outside lecturers to his classes to provide firsthand experience about subjects his students were learning. He began with New York state officials, including New York City mayor Fiorello LaGuardia, but he was unavailable for the requested date. Unlike many professors, Hechler liked grading papers. It inspired him, and he felt it was a way to get closer to his students.[60] His files are full of letters offering encouragement and constructive criticism of their work.

During his 1939 summer break, having just lost Ruth Mary Lewis—his first real girlfriend from high school—to a Theta Sigma Pi fraternity brother from Swarthmore, and determined to avoid participating in their wedding, as she had requested, Hechler fled home and hitchhiked across the Midwest. His stated mission: to interview some of the now-aging liberal insurgent congressmen for his dissertation. Without modern recording devices or a working knowledge of shorthand, he recorded all his research notes in longhand. This pilgrimage proved to be a heady experience, for he succeeded in meeting many of those he admired who had served in the late 1900s.

He recalled finding a boardinghouse one night that offered a room—complete with an alarm clock—for thirty-five cents a night. In Virginia, he interviewed former congressman Miles Poindexter, but he had to climb to the loft of his barn to work through the congressman's many disorganized papers. Upon arriving in Emporia, Kansas, he knocked—uninvited—on the door of William Allen White, the editor of the *Emporia Gazette*. White initially thought Hechler was just another down-on-his-luck drifter, but the two ultimately became friends.

While interviewing White at his newspaper's office, White excused himself to tell his front-page composer, "If war breaks out, use those big, two-inch black letters in the headline." He then returned to the interview as if nothing unusual had happened.[61] Hechler wasn't surprised by the remark, because he had been working on FDR's papers and knew of the probability of war. Painfully aware of Hitler's march to take over countries in Europe, Hechler had initially believed that we had no business getting involved. Perhaps the influence of the Quaker philosophy of pacifism taught at Swarthmore had instilled in him that fighting was not the way to preserve the principles of our founding fathers. Yet by the time he met White, Hechler had changed his mind.[62]

Hechler found insurgent senator Joseph Bristow's papers in the basement of his son's bank in Salina, Kansas, and spent several weeks making notes from them. Thrilled with his discoveries, Hechler describes the papers as containing very revealing descriptions of the group of insurgents. Among the papers was this quote from Bristow, which Hechler says he subscribed to throughout his own political life: "And that is the reward after all, namely realizing in your own mind that you have done what you thought was right, and had made the best effort you could, and that the people whom you are trying to serve believe that you have done that, and are satisfied with your course."[63]

As Hechler's fall term began, Hitler invaded Poland on September 1, marking the official outbreak of World War II. Two days later, Great Britain and France declared war on Germany; two weeks later, the Soviet Union invaded Poland from the east. The so-called Winter War began on November 30, when the Soviet Union advanced on Finland to take back territory lost to it during the Russian Civil War of 1917–1922. The League of Nations declared the action illegal and expelled the Soviets from its body, but the conflict continued.[64] Keenly aware of what was happening, Hechler began inviting more outside lecturers to address his students. Among them were the heads of each major political party: James A. Farley (Democrat), John D. M. Hamilton (Republican), and Norman Thomas (Socialist). Since the Communist Party also fielded a candidate for president each year, Hechler felt he should invite Earl Browder, the party's general secretary and chief spokesperson. Of course, Hechler knew Browder had been banned from the campus of nearly every leading college and university, so he struggled with how to accomplish bringing him to Columbia. First, he enlisted the support of the student newspaper, and then he told his students what he planned to do. Next, he visited the Communist Party headquarters in New York, which he said reminded him of a speakeasy.[65] After a female secretary "furtively swung open a secret panel" and told Hechler that Browder wasn't in, he wrote Browder and invited him. Browder accepted but cautioned Hechler to keep the visit from the press.

Unfortunately, the story was leaked, and Hechler was called on the Barnard carpet with a strict admonishment forbidding Browder's appearance. With a straight face, Hechler calmly assured the dean, Virginia Gildersleeve, that Browder was not coming to Barnard. In fact, he was coming to Columbia on December 15 instead. After some subterfuge to hide the actual date of the visit, Hechler snuck Browder into the building, and the talk went off without a hitch. However, after the story hit the papers the following day, Hechler received flack from both sides. A Finnish worker, obviously upset by the Soviet Union's invasion of his country, wrote, "Why the hell you let Browder speak? People like you ought to go back where they came from . . . teach communism in the red schools but not in New York City." On the other hand, a party comrade who thought the Soviet Union's action was justified complained that the talk was only delivered to "a handful of bourgeois underlings" instead of being broadcast to the masses, and was upset that Browder was "allowed to be heckled . . . when he dared to reveal the truth about the Finnish situation."[66]

That fall semester brought more teaching innovations. In November 1939, because of the outbreak of World War II in Europe, Hechler decided to focus his Columbia senior seminar on governmental problems in wartime. His ten students asked about inviting Herbert Hoover to the class, so Hechler called him. Hoover indicated that his schedule was too tight for a visit, but he invited Hechler to his apartment in New York's Waldorf Astoria Hotel to get answers to the students' questions. During their conversation, Hechler impetuously asked Hoover if his students could come for the visit, since Hoover couldn't come to Columbia. Surprisingly, he agreed. In preparation for their November 4 visit, Hechler cautioned his students to stay away from politics and to stick to "broad and enduring principles of government."[67] According to Hechler, "We spent an hour and a half in his apartment and he really let his hair down completely. . . . He answered every question directly, without flinching, and we really laid his heart bare on every conceivable personal and political question; and only once, when making a crack about the Stalin regime, did he caution that 'everything was off the record.'"[68] Hechler was pleased with the visit and proud of his students. "The students were in top form," he wrote in a recap of the visit.[69]

As if the many visits from leading political figures weren't enough, Hechler often made it a point to mention the names of those in government who did the behind-the-scenes work. One he regularly referred to, former New York Supreme Court justice Samuel I. Rosenman, was one of Franklin Roosevelt's top speechwriters. In Hechler's view, even with his other fine qualities, Roosevelt was a bit of a scatterbrain, but Rosenman was highly organized. Hechler told his class how Rosenman kept a series of brown envelopes labeled with everything from agriculture to zebras, and whenever Roosevelt came to a town where he was to make a speech, he would ask Rosenman to find something to say about the town. Rosenman always came up with the right thing.[70] Not surprisingly, when Hechler performed the same role for Harry Truman, he adopted a similar system.

One day in early 1939, after he mentioned Rosenman in class, one of Hechler's students announced that he was serving as a tutor and companion for Rosenman's sons and asked if Hechler would like to meet the judge. He also said Rosenman was looking for a young professor interested in research for a project that he was too busy to handle on his own. Of course, Hechler jumped at the opportunity. Their initial conversation cemented a friendship that lasted throughout Rosenman's life and led to Hechler researching and helping to annotate all of Roosevelt's messages to Congress, requests for legislation, press conferences, and other documents of the administration. The project involved putting in Roosevelt's own words the circumstances, rationale, background, and results of certain actions taken or orders given during his administration. The volumes covering 1933 to 1941 were in Roosevelt's own words, but the rest were annotated after Roosevelt's death. In them, Hechler ghostwrote in Roosevelt's style and vernacular his many extemporaneous talks. In preparation, Hechler first obtained recordings of FDR so that he could capture the lilt and syntax of his statements. Hechler says, "I was a little scared at first getting into so many different subjects that I wasn't familiar with, but one thing Rosenman taught me was never to be afraid to tackle something new." Eventually, the project stretched to thirteen volumes, which were published by several prominent publishing houses: five by Random House, four by Macmillan and Company, and four by Harper and Row. The first volume covered Roosevelt's New York governorship, and the rest dealt with his presidency, one for each year of his four terms until his death.[71]

This project also enabled Hechler to meet Roosevelt on many occasions, but to his regret, he never had the good sense to ask for a picture with him.[72] Hechler recalls vividly his first—and totally unexpected—encounter with the man he so greatly admired:

> Judge Rosenman brought me into the Cabinet Room. I'll always remember Roosevelt coming into the room where Federal Security Administrator Paul McNutt was displaying a number of photographs and broadsides that were being used to help raise the morale of the civilian population. The first thing I saw was almost like a cartoon caricature: the end of a long cigarette, then the cigarette holder, and the prominent chin, and then the massive shoulders, and then the sudden shock you get from seeing Roosevelt in a wheelchair, which you immediately forget as he begins speaking and you experience the dynamic character of this great chief executive. After talking with Paul McNutt for a while, Judge Rosenman then introduced me to the president, who made some remark like, "I understand you're the only

person who's read every word of all of my speeches, press conferences and letters."[73]

By 1940, as Hechler was completing his dissertation, teaching, and working on Roosevelt's papers, he spent the summer working at the U.S. Census Bureau. "When I was teaching at Columbia I saw an advertisement on the bulletin board for the office of junior professional assistant, and it paid $1,440 a year. As a result of my score on the Civil Service Examination, I was told that I would be appointed to a federal office," he says. He loved the Census Bureau job and the challenge it gave him. As a clerk, he reviewed the reports of census enumerators, a task that required accuracy and attention to detail. "It was a hot summer with no air conditioning, but I thrived on my work. I got room and board for thirty dollars a month at 331 North Carolina Avenue and I was the most eager person there," he recalls. Within a month he was promoted to assistant section chief with a raise to $1,620 a year, and two or three months later he became section chief. His salary was a magnificent $1,800 a year. The work ended with the summer and he returned to his teaching position at Columbia for another academic year.[74] This minor taste of governmental involvement no doubt lingered with Hechler and heightened his interest in being in on the action.

Although his visiting lecturers had proven quite a hit with his classes, Hechler went a step further in the 1940–41 school year. Knowing that there would be high-ranking federal officials who could not come to New York, even if they wanted to, he had a phone line and an amplifying system installed in his classroom, so that he could call them to discuss specific points the class was studying. He got the idea from the autobiography of James Farley, who had used the same technique to line up delegate support for FDR during the 1932 Democratic National Convention. "When I read that, I thought to myself, what a wonderful idea for a class-room! So, in all my classes I would call U.S. Senators and Supreme Court Justices and others that could not possibly make a trip to class and give the students an opportunity to ask them questions," he recalls.[75]

Hechler's Politics and Legislative Process class of twenty students was treated to another firsthand learning event when Hechler arranged for them to travel to Washington for five days to attend a Senate hearing, meet with senators and Supreme Court justices, and attend a session of the court. In addition to visiting retired Supreme Court justice Louis Brandeis at his apartment,[76] they toured the White House, both chambers of Congress, several embassies, and the *New York Times* Washington Bureau office. The event was reported in the January 31, 1941, issue of the *Times*. The story closed with this observation: "They should be a terribly well-educated crowd of Columbia College boys when they get back."[77] That was Hechler's goal: to give his students a firsthand look at what was going on in Washington. But with the growing call for the United States to become involved in the war in Europe, Hechler began to feel he was merely on the sidelines. He wanted to get closer to the action, yet he had been classified by the military as 1-B because of his poor eyesight.[78] As a result, he was eligible only for limited military service.[79]

Additionally, while Hechler's classes received high student praise and favorable media attention, he knew that his department chair, Grayson Kirk—who would later serve as Columbia's president during the student protests and campus takeover of 1968—didn't like him and disapproved of his teaching methods, calling them "gimmicks."[80] Hechler felt that his position was precarious at best as long as Kirk remained his superior. Therefore, as America's involvement in World War II grew closer, Hechler resigned following the 1941 spring term, left the halls of learning, and aimed for the heady seat of government. While hoping to land a position in Washington, yet needing to retain some source of income during his quest, he proposed commuting back to Columbia each week to give a seminar on government. Kirk turned him down, however, saying it wouldn't be feasible. Nevertheless, the parting seems to have been amiable.[81] Hechler continued working on the Roosevelt papers with Justice Rosenman, along with noted English author Archibald MacLeish.

Armed with the biblical teachings from his childhood, his parents' example of community involvement, the value of independent thinking, and the Carlylian theory that great men create great events, an idealistic Hechler headed to Washington. If he saw himself in some leadership role, the only question in his mind must have been where to apply himself to fulfill the dream. Clearly he wanted to do his part for the war effort, but he also needed to supplement the income he was receiving for working on Roosevelt's papers.[82] When Rosenman learned that Hechler wanted to come to Washington, the judge wrote letters to William J. "Wild Bill" Donovan, who was head of the Office of Strategic Services (OSS)—the precursor of the CIA—suggesting he hire Hechler. He wanted that job but was never granted an interview. Instead, the OSS's personnel director suggested Hechler try the newly created Office for Emergency Management, which he did and was hired. Once Hechler got a taste of public service, his path was set.

3

OVER THERE!

As if watching an approaching storm as it blackens the distant sky, Americans listened to the ominous sounds of war on the radio with dread, as Hitler, Mussolini, Stalin, and Hirohito wreaked havoc on Europe and the Pacific Rim. Would the war eventually envelop the United States? While some advocated nonintervention, others preached a different approach. Hechler was originally among the former, until he began discussing the situation with Justice Rosenman while they read and edited Roosevelt's papers. Hechler became convinced that something would have to be done to stop Hitler and his kind. Still, Hechler did not enlist. If he was going to support the war effort, he preferred to be drafted, to begin at the bottom.[1] Instead, as the saber rattling grew louder, Hechler was busy recruiting personnel for defense agencies at the Office for Emergency Management (OEM), where he had gone to work after leaving Columbia in the summer of 1941. Housed in the Old Executive Office Building, the agency had been created to assist the president in collecting information on defense matters, creating coordination between the various defense agencies, and coordinating the national defense program,[2] but Hechler says he was no more than a glorified personnel officer.[3]

In truth, Hechler only took the job because he was running out of money. He'd wanted the position Rosenman had suggested in the Office of Strategic Services (OSS) under Donovan, but he'd probably damaged that possibility by asking if he could continue teaching at Columbia one day a week while working for the government. Since Columbia's Grayson Kirk had already turned down that idea, it's unclear why he thought he could convince OSS of the plan's merits. Not surprisingly, the folks at the OSS also thought that was a ridiculous idea and nixed it before he ever secured an interview. He was soon offered the OEM position, but he didn't readily accept in the hope that the OSS would rethink his earlier request. "That was one of the most frustrating periods of my life," he says. From September until November he played golf and tennis—and waited. Worst of all, Rosenman was disappointed in Hechler's approach to the OSS, and the two men didn't speak for a time.

During his tenure at the OEM, the Japanese attacked Pearl Harbor. That Sunday afternoon, December 7, 1941, Hechler was ice-skating with friends at a Washington rink. One of his fellow skaters asked if Hechler had heard the news, and his first reaction was, "This is it!" For Hechler, the attack validated his earlier fears for the country. He now believed the United States was in real danger, and that while teaching was an investment in people's future, he needed to do even more to help the war effort. He felt that his decision to come to Washington had been the right one. Convinced that he would eventually be drafted, he didn't rush off to enlist. Then, his inner politician surfaced, and his second thought was, "Wouldn't it be wonderful if I could just sit in the gallery [of Congress] and listen to what I know is going to be the greatest speech in American history?" He was referring to Roosevelt's speech to Congress to be given the following day.

He wanted to request a ticket to the gallery from the president's office, but since he'd been working on the Roosevelt papers, Hechler knew the White House operator would recognize his voice and that his position probably wouldn't merit one. Therefore, he decided to disguise his voice as Archibald MacLeish—the distinguished poet and librarian of Congress, who had also been working on Roosevelt's papers. Acting as MacLeish, he called, asking for Justice Rosenman. The operator fell for it, addressing Hechler as MacLeish, and said that Rosenman was in with the president but could call him back when he was available. Hechler stammered, "No, thank you. I'll call again later." Hechler never tried voice imitation again.[4] Disappointed, he was resigned to listening to it on the radio.

Now worried for the country and those who would fight, Hechler continued at the OEM. Even though he thought his job was boring, he stuck with it until, in his zeal for efficiency, he clashed with his office manager. One weekend, he rearranged the desks of the five-person staff into one office instead of three. The manager objected and reassigned Hechler. Told to write a manual for new personnel officers on how to do their job, Hechler realized it was the manager's way of trying to get rid of him. Ironically, the manual was so well written that it was later adopted.[5]

In March 1942, Hechler was asked to transfer to the Bureau of the Budget, where they were conducting interviews with new defense personnel to write the administrative history of World War II. According to Hechler, Roosevelt himself had ordered the effort, knowing that if the lessons learned during the war weren't recorded, they would be lost to history.[6] Hechler knew he'd eventually be called to military service, but when he was offered $1,200 more per year than his current job paid, he jumped at the chance and resigned from the OEM. He also felt that he would be making a more important contribution to the war at the bureau. As it turned out, he loved the job. From March until July, when he was drafted, Hechler interviewed cabinet members and the heads of all the new agencies created for war preparations. It was just his kind of assignment; he could work independently without direct supervision. It also helped further hone the interview skills he would use later in the war.

Following Pearl Harbor, Hechler's original 1-B military classification was eliminated, making him eligible to serve in any capacity. Apparently Hechler was so good at his Bureau of the Budget job that when the postcard arrived in June telling him his draft status had been upgraded to 1-A, the bureau director wrote Hechler's local draft board requesting an occupational deferment for him. This did not sit well with Hechler. He wrote a follow-up letter saying he not only had no knowledge of the request but didn't want the deferment.[7] The draft board either was unmoved by the director's letter or heeded Hechler's plea, for in July, Hechler got his chance to start at the bottom with all the other privates.

On July 9, 1942, only a few days after Anne Frank and her family went into hiding from the Nazis in an Amsterdam attic, Hechler was inducted into the United States army at Fort Myer, Virginia. In line for his eye examination, he couldn't have known of the Franks and their terror, of course, but he did have a sinking feeling of his own. With his poor eyesight, he knew he would fail the test. Now, Hechler admits that he knew that if he ever ran for political office, the only way he could get elected was to have served in the military.[8] With this nagging him, he suddenly recalled reading that Harry Truman—in his effort to serve in the military after his poor eyesight denied him admission to either of the service academies—had memorized an eye chart after listening to six or eight people read it correctly,[9] so Hechler did the same thing.[10] Fortunately, he passed and soon shipped out to Fort Croft, South Carolina, where he was assigned to the 36th Infantry Training Battalion for basic training under the command of Lt. Col. Maynard Harrison "Snuffy" Smith.[11]

From his admission that he may have had an ulterior motive for wanting military service, it is clear that the dream of elected office, first piqued by Dr. Brooks's test question at Swarthmore,[12] had remained in the back of Hechler's mind. And although it would be nearly two decades before he would act on it, he says that being drafted enabled him to identify with rank-and-file soldiers.[13] The man who grew up in the rarified air of a country estate knew this would eventually stand him in good political stead. In college, Hechler had been shrewd enough to believe that his carefully planned efforts to manage the baseball team, revive the marching band, and serve on the Press Board were potential stepping-stones to selection to the exclusive Book and Key Society. Similarly, his choice to serve as a drafted soldier was just as cleverly conceived.

Already a lover of the outdoors and a rugged tennis player, Hechler says basic training in mosquito-infested South Carolina's stifling heat made him realize "how important it was to absorb all of that mental and physical toughening." Upon reflection decades later, he reiterated that basic training also taught him "to get to like the challenge of getting to know and help fellow recruits from all walks of life. Getting along with [those who were] rich and poor, friendly and disagreeable, hyperactive and lazy . . . helped me when I campaigned and was elected to office."[14] Despite the tremendous change from classroom to barracks that required the formerly desk-bound teacher to march twenty-five miles with a full pack each day and run six miles before breakfast,[15] Hechler says military life was a breeze. He relished not having to prepare for class or scrape up money to meet his limited budget. He liked adhering to a schedule and to priorities set by others. "I found the whole experience sort of like a camping trip into the wilderness," he said.[16]

Toward the end of basic training, however, Hechler realized that fighting was not going to be like camping. He and his fellow recruits would soon become infantrymen—reputed to be the branch with the highest casualty rate and the worst place to spend the war—and he, no doubt, had second thoughts. Told that the way to avoid that fate was to apply to Officer Candidate School (OCS), he considered it. Yet in a letter written in December 1942 to his former boss at the Bureau of the Budget—noted political scientist Dr. Pendleton Herring—Hechler seems conflicted. On the one hand, he wants to serve alongside his fellow recruits, and doesn't want to spend the war pushing paper; on the other hand, he doesn't want to be on the front lines, where he's likely to be wounded or killed. In the letter, he says he's almost resigned himself "to putting intellect on the shelf in favor of combat"; yet he longs for a furlough, so he can get advice from Herring, whom he respected.[17] Eventually, he opted for using his brains instead of his brawn. He and many others applied for Coast Artillery OCS, thinking the Germans couldn't shoot across the Atlantic and they would be safe.

Still, Hechler was somewhat disappointed that he would miss the real fighting, and he expressed those feelings to his friend Jack Kelly. In his reply, Kelly sympathizes, saying, "I know how disappointing it must be to set down what we dramatically regard as the tools of war and go back to intellectual pursuits." Yet he tells Hechler, "[You] should be flattered at having your superior talent discovered and recognized." He continues, "I have no doubt this rather abrupt rearrangement of our ambitions and dreams may well be the most difficult thing you have to face."[18] Intellectual pursuits be damned. Ironically, Hechler and his fellow applicants were sent to OCS at Fort Knox, Kentucky, to become tank commanders.[19] It was February 1943, and though the Germans had recently surrendered at Stalingrad, there would be much more fighting ahead.

In one of the first "pep talks" the new second lieutenant heard after arriving at Fort Knox, a colonel announced that his task was to turn out murderous killers. He also told Hechler in a private interview that the trouble with the army was that it had too many educated guys: "You [educated guys] get into combat and you think the guy next to you deserves to die more than you do."[20] Although Hechler had originally decided he wanted to see combat, he quickly realized that he preferred "to serve in a more useful capacity" than as a murderous killer.

On furlough that summer, Hechler made his first trip to Huntington, West Virginia. Josephine Polan—a former Barnard student of his, whom he'd also known in Washington when she worked for a division of the OEM—invited him to come for a visit. He accepted and attended a dance at the Guyan Country Club, where the tall soldier in dress uniform probably stood out in the sea of smart tuxedos and fancy dresses. After ice cream in Ritter Park the following day, he called the bucolic, tree-lined park "one of the most beautiful he had ever seen."[21] No doubt, the visit was a welcome diversion from the grueling training he'd been undergoing. After returning to camp, he says he got used to the idea of driving a 35-ton Sherman tank, and that it somewhat appealed to him.[22]

Hechler's other talents were finally discovered and rewarded, however. During his last week of OCS, he was called out of ranks, told the big brass were coming in from the Pentagon, and instructed to write and choreograph a musical for their entertainment. Seems word had reached the commanders about Hechler's love of music and parody. He took the then-popular song "Praise the Lord and Pass the Ammunition" and rewrote it as "Praise the Lord and Pass Me My Commission." Fellow classmates acted and sang in what turned out to be a huge success, according to Hechler.[23] Following the performance, each member of the class was told to write an autobiography. Hechler decided to make his as colorful as possible and began with a noteworthy line of purple prose: "The smoke of Sarajevo had scarcely drifted away when a squalling, brawling infant burst upon an unsuspecting world."[24]

Upon reading Hechler's story, Brigadier General S. G. Henry, commander of the armored forces school at Fort Knox, called him into his office. Hechler and his buddies thought he was being called on the carpet, but Hechler was actually being commended, in a roundabout way. Hechler reports the conversation:

First he congratulated me on the musical production and on my autobiography. Then he made a very strange comment. He said, "The army would have no place for you as a tank commander because you don't have the killer instinct. Our objective here is to produce a bunch of killers." Then he read me a letter he'd written to Colonel Giles Carpenter at the army War College.[25] It stated, "this outstanding officer can serve our national war effort in a more advantageous manner than by assignment as a platoon commander in a tank company."[26] Hechler protested to Henry again, but Henry's response was that he felt "it is only fair to the army that you [Hechler] serve in a capacity which will exploit your very superior talent."[27]

Perhaps his protest was like that of Br'er Rabbit begging "Please don't throw me in the briar patch!" knowing it was his favorite hiding place, and if so, it worked. Hechler's plea fell on deaf ears. "The general said it was too late. I was being assigned to the European theater to act as a combat historian," he says. "When I asked what that entailed, Henry said, 'We'll give you a Jeep and you're to go up and down the front lines and get the in-depth account of the most critical actions along the front lines.'" The general made it clear, however, that this would not be an easy assignment. He told Hechler he'd still be under fire, carry a weapon (which he was to use), and be expected to capture prisoners. His primary task, however, would be to gather material that could be used at the service academies to teach the lessons learned in war with an eye toward making necessary changes.[28]

Before shipping out, he was assigned to the Public Relations Office of the Armored Force and told to write its history. Upon completion, he was sent to Washington to work with noted historians—including Bell Wiley, the author of several books on the Civil War—in order to drum up interest in collecting the war's history. Hechler called it a "dream assignment." Throughout the later months of 1943, now as a first lieutenant, he traveled to nearly every military installation in the country. His task was to convince the base commanders that history consisted not just of dates and actions but also of an analysis of the training offered, the mistakes made, and the lessons learned. This comprehensive approach became the model for how he would collect and analyze battle histories over the next few years. In six months, the task had been completed, and Hechler was eager to go overseas—to the European theater.

Even though his commander, Major Kent Roberts Greenfield, wanted to keep Hechler stateside, he relented, knowing that the army was developing a corps of combat historians that would be needed as soon as the planned invasion of Europe took place.[29] Reassigned to London headquarters, Hechler stayed in an apartment at One Upper Wimple Street. He found London fascinating. The political debates in Hyde Park especially attracted his off-duty attention. "There was a determined group of Irish that would defy the 11 p.m. curfew and would all be chanting, 'Up with de Valera' [the president of the Irish Executive Council] as the London Bobbies tried to break them up,"[30] he recalls.

Assigned to interview commanders of all the training units preparing to cross the English Channel, Hechler got a firsthand look at possible scenarios the troops might face upon landing. This tour of duty took him to Ireland and back to Atterbury, England,

Ken Hechler at work in the U.S. Army Public Relations Section, 1943 (Photo by Signal Section, U.S. Army HQ Armored Force)

where he was attached to the XV Corps reporting to the noted military historian Brigadier General S. L. A. "Slam" Marshall.[31] Although Hechler admired Marshall's historical thoroughness, he later ran afoul of the dynamic general. Apparently Hechler had questioned the rationale for one of his memos. In a letter to Hechler, Marshall said, "It is hardly becoming on your part to take the attitude that that which does not meet your personal approval is ipso facto a sign of administration going wrong."[32] This incident is another example of Hechler's willingness to challenge authority, be it the *New York Times* or the U.S. Army.

Following the invasion at Normandy, France, on D-day, June 6, 1944, Hechler's company of historians received their orders to ship out. Arriving a few weeks later, after the heavy fighting had ended, Hechler and his men landed in France in advance of their tents and other equipment. Hoping to avoid sleeping on the ground, he set out for a small town near the beachhead to see if he could procure any mattresses. He could speak textbook French, but he didn't know the word for *mattress*. Thinking it might be similar to the English, as are many French words, he asked the woman who answered the door at the first house, "*Vous avez un maitresse*," instead of *un matelas*. Shocked, she slammed the door in his face. Mistakenly, he'd asked for a mistress.[33]

Once on French soil, he went up and down the Normandy hedgerows, interviewing officers and enlisted men alike for details that would make the after-action reports more meaningful. Once the reports had been compiled, Hechler would supplement them with his own analysis:

> We'd try to catch these things while they were still hot in the minds of the people. We would start generally at the army level by getting the overall strategic plan, and then follow at the corps level on what was being done there, and then work our way down to the division, regiment, battalion, company, and platoon levels. We would frequently get a group of soldiers together that were involved in an action, and have a group interview, which was a particular history-gathering technique that Marshall previously had developed. It was very effective, because lots of times people would see things a little bit differently, and this enabled us to get a more accurate and more dramatic story.[34]

Hechler and Marshall clashed more than once, yet Marshall's interview techniques became Hechler's standard, and he used them effectively throughout the rest of the war.

He also clashed with more than one commander, it seems. While Hechler's company was still on the Normandy coast, General George S. Patton arrived in camp. In preparation for embarkation from England, the soldiers had been instructed to waterproof the Jeeps, the spark plugs, and all electrical connections with a waxy brown rust-preventive called Cosmoline. Hechler recalls Patton arrived wearing "three stars on his helmet, shining like diamonds in the sun." His Jeep carried signs saying, "General, General, General, and a big red flag with three stars proclaiming he was a Lieutenant General." Because the soldiers had also covered their helmet insignia with the sticky stuff so German snipers wouldn't single them out as officers, Patton was incensed. Unfortunately for Hechler, the captain's helmet insignia caught Patton's eye. "He saw me about twenty-five feet away with this stuff all over my insignia and he said, 'Come over here, damn it! Are you proud of your damn rank?' Of course I saluted weakly and stammered, 'Ye—ye—yes—si—si—sir,' with my knees shaking."[35] Patton stuck his chin in Hechler's face and proceeded to chew him out for what felt like thirty minutes, he says. "Patton concluded with, 'if you don't show you're proud of your rank by removing that stuff, I'll take your damn rank away from you right here and now!'" Hechler says he learned several new swear words that day, but he removed the Cosmoline, at least until after Patton left camp.[36]

In "How to Interview," a paper written for the army, he outlines the device he used: "Seek out your man as soon after the action as possible. Even if another big push is in the offing, he will probably like to talk about what he observed." Hechler's paper clearly shows he had a feel for how to bring out the best in his interview subjects, understood the psychology of military officers, and was an expert listener. He knew how to restate a question to get more details, calling it "down-stream" questioning, which went indirectly to the heart of a matter that someone might be reluctant to discuss. He also argued strongly against using a stenographer.[37]

At 163 pounds, this nearly six-foot-tall soldier moving through the trenches would have been called "Skinny." Neat and trim and wearing wire-rim glasses, his already receding hairline hidden under a steel-pot helmet, carrying his notebook and pen to the front lines to capture an accurate account of what had happened, he must have seemed quite an anomaly to the often dirty, always weary soldiers on the front lines. Although the main fighting was over by the time he got there, the man with no killer instincts, who'd been issued a .45-caliber pistol and twenty-one rounds of ammo, still had to contend with regular German artillery fire, snipers, and sporadic bombing. "There were lonely sorties by many German planes," he says. "One we used to call 'Bed-check Charlie' because he'd come along about eleven o'clock when we were trying to get to sleep."[38]

For the next two years, Hechler traveled across Europe in his Jeep, recording the account of each combat operation: in northern France, the liberation of Paris in August 1944; during the winter of 1944–45 in the dense Ardennes Forest in Belgium following the Battle of the Bulge; in Luxembourg, Holland, and the Rhineland; and at the Rhine River at Remagen after U.S. troops crossed that ill-fated bridge on March 7, 1945.[39] His proximity to the action was a matter of luck. According to Hechler, it was a leaden, dismal day when the phone rang with news of the Remagen battle. Stationed at the Third Corps' headquarters about ten miles from Remagen, he heard the call come in. "A little sergeant . . . threw down the phone and yelled, 'Hot damn! We got a bridge and we're crossing over,'" he recalls. As the commander of a four-man team of historians, Hechler knew they had a story to cover.

Regardless of Hitler's orders to destroy all bridges across the Rhine in the face of the advancing American troops, the Ludendorff railroad bridge still stood, albeit precariously. Earlier Allied bombing had taken its toll. American armored engineers disconnected all the German wiring set to detonate the bridge while the American troops were on it.[40] Once over the bridge, the U.S. military was able to establish a bridgehead on the eastern side of the Rhine. This hastened the end of German resistance and no doubt shortened the war. When the smoke cleared, Hechler went to Remagen and talked with thirty officers and men who had been involved in the defusing and crossing operation. In the preface to *The Bridge at Remagen*, the book he wrote in 1957, he says that the operation was not only "a moving human story, but a brilliant stroke of military daring."[41] Ten days later, the bridge finally collapsed into the river as a result of the earlier Allied attacks.

A month later, Hechler received a field promotion to major as well as another criticism from General Marshall after Hugh Cole, the deputy theater historian, complained about the promotion. Cole had been Hechler's superior officer in the Third Army, and the two frequently clashed. According to Hechler, Cole thought him incompetent. Additionally, Hechler and a Cole favorite, Roland Ruffenthal, had been promoted to captain at the same time and had come to the European Theater of Operations together, but Ruffenthal had yet to advance to the rank of major. This angered Cole, who wrote to Marshall. In response, the promoting officer, Major Richard Shappell, defended Hechler's promotion with a litany of Hechler's accomplishments, and the matter was dropped.[42]

While some who were wounded in combat may have seen Hechler as a Johnny-come-lately to the battles, he was nevertheless in danger each time. He still recalls the fear he felt while riding along a ridge with German artillery bursts close behind. "When one shell lands fifty feet to your right and the second fifty feet to your left, you better dive into a ditch because the next one is going to blow your vehicle apart," he says. "That's what was happening."[43] For his efforts, he was awarded five bronze battle stars, the American Campaign Medal, the Bronze Star Medal for meritorious service under fire from Normandy to the Elbe River, and the World War II Victory Medal.[44] Additionally, the citation read, "Major Hechler recorded historical data with great ability and diligence which contributed materially to the history of the war. At all times he played a leading part in solving many problems confronting field historians. . . . New sources of information developed during the campaigns were due to his ideas and experiences."[45] His old commander and onetime critic, Brigadier General Marshall, personally awarded Hechler the Bronze Star Medal in 1945.[46]

All was not gunfire, bombing, or interviewing, however. A September 1, 1944, letter to Jane Chippendale Stewart—the coed he'd become close to at Barnard and nicknamed "Penny"—describes his spare-time activities: "Paris is fabulous today. Several days ago, I got a thrill walking under the Arc de Triomphe and down the Champs d'Elysées. Saw the Louve, Notre Dame Cathedral, and spent a good deal of time in the gardens of The Tuileries," he wrote. Unfortunately, Jane may never have known this. The letter constituted a violation for revealing the location of his unit, and he was reprimanded for writing it.[47]

Actually, Hechler wrote many letters to Jane throughout the war. He wrote from Fort Knox, on trains and buses heading west as he gathered the histories of the armored force training facilities, and from overseas. Though he has repeatedly referred to her as his girlfriend, some of the letters contain detailed accounts of

Jane Chippendale Stewart, Barnard days (Courtesy Ken Hechler)

flirtatious encounters with other women, which a serious lover would resent. In a letter from a train he called one young woman "one of his little necking acquaintances," and tells how she invited him to ride with her to New York. He grabbed his coat and toothbrush and left. In one missive, he calls himself "a wolf"—the term of the day for a sexually aggressive man—and at thirty, he seems to relish the role. He also notes that traveling for the army offers a wonderful opportunity to meet the fairer sex, "for which, as you know, I have a *magnissimus* weakness."[48]

Earlier in 1944, Jane had become angry with him because he wouldn't kiss her and wrote him a blistering letter in which she says, "This is going to hurt. If it doesn't, let me know and I'll re-write it."[49] It seems she wanted more from the relationship than he was willing to give, and emphasizes his inability to form an intimate relationship. In response, he wrote that everything she said was right on target, but that it made him realize how much he loved her.[50] Perhaps Jane should have recalled Hechler's earlier self-admission. In explaining why he never signs his letters "with luff," he wrote,

> Failure to sign my letters "Luff" [love]—etc. etc., arises from the fact that [brother] Charley and I had a funny upbringing in some ways. Look at the family skeleton closet, and it reveals the following: great emphasis on finding a place in society *as a whole* (as contradistinguished from very close individual friendships); great emphasis upon the fundamental that he who works 1 1/2 times harder gets 3 times as much accomplished; unfair emphasis upon the stone-around-the-neck qualities of females in general. Result is that Charley and I both start with psychological handicaps in regard to some very wonderful people, for the simple reason that many of the latter happen to wear skirts.[51]

While Hechler isn't usually given to introspection, this self-termed "handicap" accurately describes a bias that continued to plague him throughout his life. Even though he had short-term relationships with many women, he treated them as objects rather than equal partners.

True to form, "wolf Hechler" also wrote to numerous young ladies he met overseas. Fortunately, his earlier foreign language studies saved the day, for most of the letters from the women to him are in French or German. Snapshots show them to be as curvaceous as he described them; one is even labeled "Luxembourg sexpot."[52] But by the end of the war, Hechler was eager to go home so he could ask Jane to marry him.

He'd seen a lot, including the concentration camp at Buchenwald. In order to record the atrocities there, he'd toured it on April 12, 1945, the day after American troops liberated the camp. Because Buchenwald, near Weimar, Germany, was not technically an extermination camp, many prisoners were still alive. Yet according to the SS records left behind, over 33,000 people were killed at Buchenwald. Other reports, however, raise that number to more than 56,000.[53] Corpses were stacked like cordwood, Hechler says, and the remaining prisoners were walking skeletons, which by their very appearance told what they'd experienced. Even though it took him a long time to rid himself of the memories of the place, Hechler remains impressed with the American generals who, under orders from General Patton, rounded up civilians from Weimar and brought them to witness the horror of Buchenwald. He wanted the citizens to see what they had ignored in their midst. Hechler recalls seeing the visitors vomiting when they saw the prisoners' physical condition and where they had been kept.[54]

Following the tour and back at headquarters, he received another shock. "I remember the major called us all together and said, 'We have just received the sad news of the death of our Commander in Chief, Franklin D. Roosevelt.' Then he said, 'The current information'—and he picked up a piece of paper as though he didn't know what he was going to say—and read: 'The current information is that a man named Harry Truman will succeed him; at least that's the latest report.' "[55] Apparently the name of

Roosevelt's latest running mate wasn't a headliner in the war zone. While there's little doubt that Hechler must have wondered what effect Roosevelt's death would have on his suspended task of editing the president's papers, he certainly could not have foreseen the significant impact Truman's succession would have on his life.

He spent the next two months traveling to American prisoner-of-war camps to interview German prisoners. According to Hechler, those held at one prison in Oberursel, a town northwest of Frankfurt, were treated very poorly. This made it difficult to interview the prisoners. Many had been well-respected professors before the war but were now being treated like hardened criminals. Hechler took pity on one, Percy Schramm, who had taught history at the University of Göttingen. Surly at first, the man admitted to Hechler that he was worried about his wife and family. After Hechler drove the man to Göttingen so that he could spend a day with his family, he was very cooperative. Hechler also visited the wives of other prisoners in an attempt to reassure them that their families were well.[56] By now, the war-weary Hechler was ready to wrap up his duties and head home, but the army wasn't through with him yet.

After Hitler and Eva Braun—his longtime companion whom he had married less than two days earlier—committed suicide on April 30 and Germany surrendered on May 8, the German officers began surrendering. Some, knowing that continued fighting was futile, did so in the days preceding the formal surrender. In mid-June 1945, Hechler was called back to Paris to help work on the first draft of the war history, compiling all the notes, maps, reports, and interviews he had gathered over the past two years.[57]

While there, he received one last assignment. One of his former European history professors at Swarthmore, Dr. Troyer Anderson, had recommended to his superior officer, Undersecretary of War Robert Patterson, that he send a group of historians to Europe to interrogate the former high-ranking Nazi officers, who were being assembled and detained at a small town in the duchy of Luxembourg. Prisoner of War Enclosure No. 32, code-named Ashcan, was the Palace Hotel—a former luxury resort—in Mondorf, Luxembourg.

The small spa town of Mondorf is a suburb of the country's capital city, which in the 1940s regularly attracted well-to-do members of the Nazi Party who wanted to escape the fighting. But in 1945, the imposing Palace Hotel became first a billet for U.S. troops, then the prisoner-of-war home for the senior German officers who were awaiting trial at Nuremberg. Two fifteen-foot-high electrified barbed-wire fences topped with concertina wire, guard towers with machine guns, and klieg lights quickly surrounded the four-story hotel and its grounds. Spartan cots and tables replaced the hotel's fine furniture. It is reported that security was so tight that the MPs guarding the place knew who was imprisoned but didn't know exactly what transpired inside.[58]

Anderson believed the Nazi officers could provide information (before they could gather to agree on a party line in hopes of avoiding inevitable prosecution) on what had transpired inside Hitler's headquarters as the war unfolded. Headed by the president of Hunter College, George Shuster, the unit included two university professors and two army officers, one of whom was a retired history professor. A fifth member was to be an officer with the rank of general, but none were willing to serve. General Marshall thought the whole thing a waste of time but suggested that perhaps Hechler could do it. However, certain people at the Pentagon thought Major Hechler wasn't at all qualified and were rankled because he was only a major.[59] Hechler says that got his adrenaline up and made him determined to prove otherwise.

Looking back, Hechler recalls being overcome with awe when he arrived in Mondorf on July 17, 1945. He felt he'd been given an assignment that other historians would have given their right arm to do. He was floored that so many others had passed up what he considered the opportunity of a lifetime.[60] Even though it was originally a one-week assignment, he spent the next two months interviewing the top German officers, not about war crimes but about military strategy and actions. Hechler realized that if he began to talk about what had happened in the concentration camps, he would encounter inordinate resistance and would no doubt be unable to complete his assigned task. "I wasn't the least bit interested [for the purposes of the upcoming interviews] in the Holocaust or any of the crimes against humanity that they had committed," he says. "I was primarily interested in collecting military information. That's one reason the material that I elicited was not used in Nuremberg."[61] As soon as the German officers understood Hechler's purpose, they opened up and were willing to answer his questions. This encouraged him to continue to bury his revulsion of the terrible crimes for which they would later be tried.[62]

The camp's commander, Colonel Burton G. Andrus, was, in Hechler's eyes, not particularly competent for the job. Hechler had encountered him before and believed he lacked judgment and was petty and naïve. Nonetheless, Andrus had assured the Shuster Commission he knew how to keep the "SOBs" in line. According to Hechler, Andrus put Goering on a diet; deprived von Ribbentrop of a belt, necktie, and shoelaces, then laughed at how funny he looked; and took away their pillows and mattresses if they wouldn't talk. Additionally, the prisoners were made to eat only with spoons and were forced to watch movies on Nazi atrocities. They were also told that if they got within two feet of the barbed-wire fence, they'd automatically be shot or electrocuted.[63]

Yet because the prisoners had yet to learn of the impending war-crimes trials, they were in a relatively good mood, considering their situation. Hechler says they were starved for news from outside the walls, and responded well when he and the other members of the Shuster Commission offered it. "By the end of the day . . . I became gripped anew with the consciousness that here was probably the most important work I was ever to do in my life," he says.[64]

Throughout July and August, Hechler came and went through the heavily guarded gates of Camp Ashcan, interviewing Hermann Goering, Walter Warlimont, Wilhelm Keitel, Alfred Jodl, Albert Kesselring, Heinrich Kittel, and a number of other German field marshals and generals. Goering was the highest ranking of the forty-some prisoners detained at the makeshift prison. He held the rank of field marshal, was commander in chief of the German Air Force, and was the second most powerful leader of Nazi Germany. He had also become a drug addict after receiving morphine to ease the pain from wounds incurred during the unsuccessful Munich Beer Hall Putsch of 1923. After failing to defeat the British at Dunkirk and embracing the disastrous war against Russia, by 1942 he had fallen out of favor with Hitler. Goering's attempt to succeed Hitler as the Soviets surrounded Berlin had been the final straw.[65] Hitler stripped him of his command, drummed him out of the Nazi Party, and ordered his arrest.[66] According to Hechler, Goering surrendered when he learned an execution squad was after him. He had decided he'd fare better in the hands of the Americans. "He sent a message to the American army [telling] where he was and how he would like to surrender," says Hechler. "For the first few weeks of his surrender to the 36th Infantry Division, they, of course, were so pleased that they were able to capture him, not realizing what the background [of his surrender] was. Goering always had the mistaken impression that he could convince General Eisenhower that he was able to help him in case there was trouble with the Russians. He was arrogant enough to believe that Eisenhower would listen to him, but Eisenhower sent a message to the 36th Division saying he should be treated as a criminal and not as a friend."[67]

Of course, Hechler and the other commissioners had to show a pass to enter the compound, but as the guards got used to seeing Hechler, they never inspected what he brought in. It was this lapse that allowed him to provide some creature comforts to one of the prisoners. According to Hechler, he'd become intrigued with General Walter Warlimont partly because he was highly Americanized, spoke perfect English, and was married to a member of the Anheuser-Busch beer family.[68] One day Hechler asked him if there was anything he needed, and Warlimont said yes. "So, I went to see his wife. She got a lot of clean underwear and other items he particularly needed and I put them in my briefcase," Hechler recalls. "They were not examined when I got into the camp. I could have brought him or Goering a cyanide capsule, which I'm sure somebody did."[69] (Goering did commit suicide by taking cyanide, but how he obtained it was never determined.)

Although Hechler was sympathetic to Warlimont, he says Goering depressed him. While Reichsmarschall Goering often tried to use the persuasive powers that had gotten him to his vaunted position, he was much more arrogant than Hechler had expected him to be. Goering seemed to regard the whole war as something of a joke.[70] He was completely unrepentant about what he'd done and never admitted to his differences with Hitler, which had been widely reported. Hechler was fully aware of the atrocities of the concentration camps, knew that Goering had created the Gestapo, and understood that he was also the director of the slave labor program, yet he carefully put all of that out of his mind and deftly avoided speaking of those matters in all their interviews. Though he sometimes had to pinch himself to avoid being taken in by Goering's hyperbole,[71] Hechler says he "had a pretty fixed mind-set. I could always shift gears."[72]

At Mondorf, Goering was generally treated with disdain. Each time Hechler arrived to interview him, the guards would call down, "Send Fat Stuff up to Major Hechler."[73] Hechler, however, always addressed him as Reichsmarschall Goering, which flattered him. At their first meeting, Goering got the jump on the interview and asked Hechler a question before he could ask his own. He wanted to know if Hechler knew General Eisenhower. Hechler fudged more than a little, saying, "*Ja.*" Before Hechler could respond further, Goering said, "You tell General Ike that I am the Commander of the Luftwaffe, and here in this enclosure is Admiral Doenitz, the head of the Kriegsmarine [the Navy,] and army Field Marshal Keitel and Lt. General Jodl. Tell him I will mobilize the German Army, Navy, and Air Force, and we'll team up with the Americans, and beat hell out of the Russians, and you won't have any problems in the world from then on." Hechler, of course, never delivered Goering's ridiculous demand.[74]

Following his service on the Shuster Commission, Hechler returned to Paris and subsequently to Saint Germain, about twenty miles outside Paris, to help compile the first draft of the history of the war. Manuscripts were brought to the publications office to be assembled into booklets. According to fellow soldier Ed Martz, who served in this section, around five o'clock each evening Hechler would knock on his door, and they would sing together for an hour or two. The two became good friends, but by December, the job was nearly finished and Hechler told his commander he was ready to get back to civilian life. He wanted to resume teaching, if possible. In January 1946, Hechler and Martz were asked to take the historical documents, which were still classified as top secret, back to the Pentagon. Weighing forty-four tons, the material was loaded into freight cars and onto the SS *Muhlenberg Victory*, where it was shipped from Le Havre, France, back to Washington.[75] Hechler was in charge; he was finally going home.

4

PRINCETON'S PROFESSOR
OF POLITICS

When Hechler landed back on American soil in March 1946, he was, like most soldiers, ready to be done with all things military and to get on with his life. In love with Jane Stewart, he planned to ask for her hand in marriage and return to teaching. However, the war followed him home, and Jane had other ideas. After an unsuccessful attempt to get a job with the army's Office of Military History, he went back to the Bureau of the Budget in April. According to federal law, he was given the same position—administrative analyst—he had held when he left, but with a substantial raise in pay. However, his assignments still smacked of wartime, and one in particular seemed to almost be a continuation of his military duties. He was tasked with overseeing the development of the war histories in every agency—war and nonwar, military and nonmilitary—and ensuring that they all had adequate financial support from the bureau for the job. His other duty was to help recruit the top personnel for agencies that had been war agencies for the last five years but were now returning to civilian status. Even if these weren't his dream assignments—and he blamed one of his old adversaries, Hugh Cole, for ruining his chances at the Office of Military History—he was ultimately glad that things turned out as they did. The bureau job kept him in touch with all the branches of government, which would eventually prove invaluable to his career.[1]

His interviews of the German high commanders at Mondorf followed him home as well, but not in a manner to his liking. About six months after he returned, a six-part series of stories—bylined by Lt. Gen. Walter Bedell "Beetle" Smith, Eisenhower's chief of staff—appeared in the *Saturday Evening Post*. Titled "Eisenhower's Six Great Decisions," Smith quoted, without attribution, from Hechler's interviews with Goering, Keitel, and Jodl, among others. According to Hechler, when he complained to his always-adversarial supervisor about what Hechler considered blatant plagiarism, Cole merely laughed. He told Hechler he'd simply been scooped by someone with a higher rank, and there was nothing he could do about it.[2] Initially, Hechler had hopes of writing his own account of those days, but after Smith's series appeared, he dropped the idea until many years later. Comparing Hechler's 2011 book, *Goering and His Gang*, to Smith's series does reveal exact quotes from those interviews. Yet Hechler had done them under orders. Who is to say they were proprietary?

As for his personal life, things didn't go his way there, either. While Hechler was overseas, Jane lived in Detroit, so Hechler headed there to propose. With his mother's engagement ring in hand, he popped the question. Jane responded, "You know, that's a very serious question. Can you give me a month to think about it?" This stunned and devastated Hechler. After returning home, he told his mother that if Jane had to think about it that long, she wasn't for him. At the end of the requested month, Jane wrote to say yes, but it was too late. As he later said, "By then, I'd washed that woman right out of my hair."[3] He didn't pursue her again. Perhaps he saw her refusal as an out and realized he could get on with his career without the encumbrance of a wife. Perhaps he was reacting like a child who, shunned from a game, says he didn't want to play anyway. Or, more likely, this second rejection was simply too hard to bear, and he was trying to put a good face on it for his mother, who, Hechler says, always expected silent suffering from her son. Given their stormy relationship throughout the war, however, Hechler shouldn't have been surprised that Jane didn't jump at the chance to marry a self-described "wolf" for whom forming close personal relationships was difficult, as he'd told her previously. For her, it was important that the man in her life be able to express himself emotionally as well as intellectually, and she wasn't sure Hechler could do so, based on what he'd told her of his background. She knew his whole goal was to get on with the action, whatever it was at the time. This didn't stop her from liking him, however, or from wanting to maintain their friendship.[4] He eventually recovered from her snub, and the two remained lifelong friends.

Instead of preparing for a wedding, Hechler dove into his work at the bureau, making friends with Patterson French of Yale and George A. Graham of Princeton, both of whom were doing double duty by working there. Graham's other position was chair of Princeton's Department of Politics. A specialist in public administration, Graham began talking with Hechler about becoming associated with the university. With the large influx of GI Bill–funded students flooding college campuses everywhere, Princeton badly needed more faculty members. Hechler's previous teaching experience made him a prime candidate. First, Graham secured a grant from Princeton and assigned Hechler the research task of developing a classroom textbook on legislation and legislative procedure. Although Hechler took on the assignment and eventually produced a four-hundred-page manuscript, it was never published. According to Hechler, the peer-review jealousy of someone with a competing text torpedoed the project. Nevertheless, Graham was sufficiently impressed with Hechler's research work that he offered him an assistant professorship to teach politics during the fall 1947 semester.[5] Hechler accepted and resigned from the bureau. Administrative work was never Hechler's favorite, and he knew that teaching would give him the opportunity to be in contact with higher governmental decision makers and lawmakers, and possibly lead to a job in the higher echelons of government.

Despite his great reluctance to see him leave, Hechler's bureau supervisor, Patterson French, filled his letter of recommendation to Graham with superlatives on Hechler's behalf. He wrote, "My only regret in recommending him for an academic position is that I feel the government will lose an unusually fine and competent person when Mr. Hechler carries out his intention of returning to academic life."[6]

Subsequently given a three-year contract with Princeton University at an annual salary of $4,000, Hechler would teach two courses each semester from July 1947 to June 1950: Politics 203 and an upper-level course on political parties.[7] One of his first questions when he arrived on campus was about the department's name. He recalls asking, "Why is it that every other college has a Department of Political Science, but at Princeton, it is termed the Department of Politics?" The answer came back loud and clear. A faculty member said, "Before running for governor of New Jersey in 1910, Woodrow Wilson was the president of Princeton. Wilson stated, 'There's no science in this; it's all politics.'"[8]

Hechler plunged into each course with the same intensity he'd previously shown at Columbia. The syllabus for his upper-level Political Parties 306 class carried extensive reading assignments of pending federal legislation, the *Congressional Record*, and political science textbooks. Admittedly, the reading assignments for Politics 203 weren't much lighter. They included texts from the *Congressional Record*, books, senate reports, and speeches.

Analysis was a key component in both courses, as was debate and rebuttal of the theories Hechler threw out during the small, required preceptorial discussions. Students were also expected to analyze the presidential campaign of 1948, as well as each outside speaker's remarks. The essay tests were grueling. Each question required critical commentary, such as comparing a bill's strength and weaknesses.[9]

His return to teaching meant a revival of the amplified lecture system he'd instituted at Columbia. At Princeton, he made greater use of it than ever before, and it cost him approximately $500 each year.[10] This time, his unorthodox teaching method attracted the attention of the media, including the *Saturday Evening Post* and *Time* magazine. The huge amplifier dwarfed the desk and the telephone beside it, but it enabled the class to talk directly to such modern political luminaries as Harold Stassen, Robert Taft, and Norman Thomas of the American Socialist Party. Class members also questioned industry leaders, such as Studebaker president Paul Hoffman and Roosevelt's former right-hand man, James Farley, who was then chairman of the board of Coca-Cola Export Corporation.[11] It was Farley from whom Hechler stole the amplification idea back in his days at Columbia. When Hechler woke his good friend Sam Rosenman for his interview, Rosenman quipped, "It's novel to be attending class in my pajamas."[12]

The list of those invited to speak to his classes in 1947–48 is long and includes senators, university presidents, congressmen, the secretaries of state and agriculture, New York governor Thomas Dewey, Harold Ickes, Henry Cabot Lodge Jr., Joseph McCarthy, Estes Kefauver, Sam Rayburn, Helen Gahagan Douglas, and Henry Wallace (FDR's vice president during his third term).[13] His days were filled with writing to those he wanted to invite to speak, preparing for his lectures, grading papers, and meeting with students. The mundane things of life took a back seat, especially meal

Professor Hechler demonstrates his amplified telephone system (Courtesy Ken Hechler)

preparation. Unschooled in the culinary arts, Hechler found a little diner with a menu to both his liking and his budget. The affable owner of Griggs Imperial Restaurant not only provided Hechler's every meal but also made sure Hechler wasn't late to class.[14]

While some may have considered it more theater than education, Hechler's amplification technique garnered praise from professor Arthur Schlesinger Jr., who said he wished they had something like it at Harvard.[15] Both the Laundry Board of Trade and Towson State Teachers College wrote Hechler, expressing a desire to employ a similar teaching method.[16] From his required evaluations, it's clear the system was a favorite among his students. One, who asked at least one question of every person called, said,

"You pick up things you'd never get out of an ordinary lecture . . . stuff—*good* stuff—that you can't find in any book in the world, or get in any lecture."[17] Despite some criticisms, Hechler's teaching methods were groundbreaking. At that time, professorial lectures were the accepted fare; outside speakers were rare, and class participation in a political campaign was revolutionary. Amplified telephone lectures were unheard of until Hechler introduced them at Columbia and continued to use them throughout his teaching career.

Between lectures, amplified interviews, and preceptorial discussions, Hechler took his students to Washington for visits with those in government who couldn't come to Princeton or weren't available for a phone interview. Since the school was on the Pennsylvania Railroad line, with regular service to Washington, D.C., Hechler and his students went frequently.[18] In preparation for one April 1948 trip, he briefed his students about those they would visit. Of Allen Ellender, Democrat from Louisiana, Hechler said he was "a graduate of the Huey Long school of tommy-gun politics." He referred to Senator Harley Staggers, Democrat from West Virginia, as looking like "Friar Tuck without his cowl." About Senator John F. Kennedy, he wrote, "30-year old; youngest Massachusetts congressman in half a century. . . . Looks like a cross between Van Johnson and Charles Lindbergh. . . . A strong battler for decent housing and liberal social legislation."[19] Each paragraph precisely summed up the subject's positions and gave the students suggestions as to what they might ask. He knew his senators and had done his homework.

Hechler employed one other teaching method that forced his students to think critically. To his Politics 203 students, he sent a weekly mimeographed sheet called "Tuesday at 8:40" (the time of the class) in which he made a challenging statement and offered five dollars to the student with the best rebuttal. One such statement charged, "The 1948 GOP candidates for Congress are pygmies compared to their Democratic opponents."[20] He had organized his course that term around the upcoming election, devoting each week to the political behavior of various voting groups—farmers, labor, businesspeople, political machines, and so on. In the final two weeks, the class analyzed both the political organization of Congress and the political process as the presidential office influenced it.[21]

Even though Hechler was already voting as a Democrat by then, he allowed those at Princeton, who were primarily Republicans, to believe he was still a Republican, which was true.[22] In fact, in one amplified conversation with Congressman John McCormack (D-MA), he admitted that he was a registered Republican but failed to mention his true politics.[23] Perhaps he was merely trying to get a rise out of the congressman in their discussion of Roosevelt's alleged attempts to shove legislation down the throat of Congress.

Nevertheless, one student, Peter Bunzel, wrote to Hechler at the course's conclusion, discussing his stiff critique of Politics 306. Apparently Bunzel hadn't fallen for Hechler's subterfuge, for he says, "Look here; you're not a good Republican at heart, any more than [Senator Wayne] Morse or [Congressman John Albert] Carroll are.[24] As I said on the test, I think they are your heroes." Although undated, his letter must have been written during Hechler's last term at Princeton following the November election, for he alludes to the rumor that Hechler will be leaving shortly. Bunzel presciently predicts that his former professor will run for elected office someday and hopes it will be in New York so he can vote for him.[25]

Whatever his legal political registration, Hechler thought Dwight Eisenhower would make a good candidate in the 1948 election, but he had refused to run. At this time, Hechler had not met

Truman but didn't think he had much of a chance to win, even with his tenure as president after Roosevelt's death. Hechler says that like most Americans, he believed the polls and felt that the pendulum had swung toward the Republican Party. Additionally, with the 1946 mid-term Republican wins and the split in the Democratic Party by Strom Thurmond's States' Rights Party and Henry Wallace's Progressive Party, both fielding third-party campaigns, Hechler was certain the Republicans would siphon off enough votes for Dewey to win handily. He would turn out to be as wrong in this prediction as he was right in choosing Roosevelt in 1936. Furthermore, when he directed his class to choose a party, participate in the campaign, and predict its outcome, not a single one of the nearly three hundred students predicted Truman would win. He now admits that having them read *Time, Newsweek,* and the leading newspapers was probably a mistake, for their pundits were wrong as well.

Truman went to bed the night of the election expecting to win, based on his advisors' poll of the Electoral College. His tally equaled a majority. Hechler, however, went to bed sure Dewey would win. In fact, even after the news reports said otherwise, he thought the decision would be so close it might have to be decided by the House of Representatives. Totally chagrined, he had to admit to his class that he'd been wrong—something he felt was inexcusable for a university professor. Although it seems an overreaction, Hechler began to consider resigning his post at the end of that semester, in light of his mistake.[26]

In an embarrassing faux pas, Hechler had already scheduled Allen Dulles, brother of John Foster Dulles (who would later become Eisenhower's secretary of state), for an in-class lecture the day after the election. Allen Dulles was a close associate of Thomas Dewey and had served as Dewey's foreign policy advisor during both of his unsuccessful runs for president. Because he'd scheduled Dulles thinking he'd come and talk about how Dewey had won, Hechler quickly gave him the opportunity to bow out. Dulles, however, whose son was in the class, said he would honor the commitment, regardless of the loss. As bewildered as everyone else, Dulles simply threw up his hands and said he'd assumed that because Dewey had such a commanding lead, he didn't need to respond to any of the negative charges Truman had been levying at him. While Hechler's students appreciated Dulles's candor, they were more eager to learn how Truman had won.

In response, Hechler scheduled George Elsey, one of Truman's assistants. The previous year, one of Hechler's students at Princeton had been Clifford Kurrus, the nephew of Clark Clifford, Truman's White House counsel. Because Hechler often referred to how things were run in the White House, Kurrus had offered to introduce Hechler to his uncle and namesake. During that meeting, also attended by a number of Hechler's other students, Hechler met George Elsey, then Clifford's assistant. Elsey, a Princeton alumnus, took a liking to Hechler, possibly because he was teaching at his alma mater, and asked him to come see him when he next visited Clifford.[27] The two soon became friends. Thus, Elsey readily agreed to speak to Hechler's class on January 11, 1949, just before Truman's inauguration.[28] The talk, in which Elsey explained that he knew Truman would win after counting the probable Electoral College votes, enhanced the friendship between the two and ultimately led to Hechler's next career change.

Sought after as a professor and an able administrator in political science arenas, Hechler had received an offer in December 1947 from Amherst to teach American politics but had turned it down, saying, "The kind of person you want is older and more stable; I am addicted to roaming around the country and the world and could not stay put for long in one place." He said he wanted to stay at Princeton for at least one more year.[29] Earlier that same year, he'd also been asked to serve as the secretary for a meeting of the American Political Science Association on "Representative Government and the Political Process."[30] Yet when he left Princeton, it was for neither of these institutions.

In January 1949, still smarting from his embarrassment over his election prediction and itching to get into the field he'd been teaching, Hechler tendered his resignation to Princeton a year before his contract expired. Writing to his friend and department chair, George Graham, he said, "As you appreciate, incurable restlessness and ambition are the underlying causes for this decision, which I hope are not to be interpreted as dissatisfaction for Princeton and the wonderful education it has given me in the past year."[31] His resignation was effective on February 1, 1949, at the end of the first semester. Before he left for Washington, his restaurant-owner friend, Mr. Griggs, gave him a going-away gift at his establishment—a porterhouse steak dinner. Fixed by the man whose ancestors were slaves,[32] it was a meal on which frugal Hechler would never have spent his hard-earned money.

When he resigned, Hechler returned home to Roslyn to finish the final four volumes of the Roosevelt papers. They were in the galley-proof stages, and the Harper publishers were eager to have them. Excited by the prospects of Truman's next term and by his overwhelming victory, Hechler also began to think about how he might become part of the administration. He began writing to George Elsey on a variety of subjects and seeking his advice on issues in the Roosevelt papers as a ploy to make himself seem valuable.[33]

The timing was perfect. During Hechler's years at Columbia, Judge Rosenman had often suggested that Hechler should be working at the White House. While their work on Roosevelt's papers often took Hechler there, the judge had been unable to persuade either Roosevelt or Truman to hire him. Now that Hechler and Elsey had become close, Hechler got his break. In September 1949, Rosenman wrote a glowing note to Clark Clifford about Hechler and his ability to assemble data in a hurry. Amusingly, he does not recommend Hechler as a writer, however, saying his English is fairly complicated. However, he does suggest that Hechler would be ideal to join the staff to work on Truman's public papers.[34]

Apparently, it worked. Elsey wrote asking when Hechler planned to be in Washington next. "I'm very anxious to talk with you about your work with Judge Rosenman and the FDR papers because there's been a proposal for a similar edition of President Truman's papers," he wrote. "Call me collect any time within the next few days."[35] Hechler, however, did not want to get involved in another presidential papers project. "I was anxious to get away from research and get into the hurly-burly of actual day-to-day constructive work that would help the ongoing operations at the White House," he says. "This is what I was basically interested in. So I threw cold water on George's idea that I participate in the public papers of President Truman."[36]

Still, letters continued to fly between Rosenman and Elsey, Rosenman and Clark Clifford, and Hechler and Elsey. A position with the National Security Resources Board opened and Hechler was considered for it, but he ducked all communication about it. Phone calls went unanswered, and when he checked out of the YMCA to return to Roslyn, he left no forwarding address. Finally, after receiving an offer from the State Department to go to Frankfurt, Germany, to work on pulling together materials for the work of the High Commission, Hechler wrote Elsey asking if anything else had turned up.[37] He was hoping for something that didn't smack of the historical work he'd done before.

Hechler recalls the serendipitous event that happened next:

Meanwhile, one of those wonderful breaks occurred that has really characterized almost everything I've done in life. It's just amazing; it just happened out of the blue. Somebody sent President Truman a copy of an article by Arthur Schlesinger Jr. in the *Reporter* magazine, which was one of the early liberal magazines, which has since gone out of existence. The Republicans had been attacking the Democrats for creating a welfare state, and Schlesinger's theme in this article was that the welfare state really started with Alexander Hamilton and his program of subsidies for business, banks and [indirect subsidies] through the protective tariff. The article said that so long as the subsidies went to big business nobody ever criticized them, but as soon as they started to go to education and health, like the Democrats were proposing, then all of a sudden it became a terrible thing called a "welfare state."[38]

Because it was December—time for preparation of the State of the Union address and the budget—no staff members had time to respond with facts to substantiate Schlesinger's claim, so Elsey got in touch with Hechler saying that "the Boss," meaning President Truman, wanted someone to do a study on corporate welfare. He wanted someone to put together all the examples of past land grants, subsidies, and tax breaks to businesses and to put a dollar figure on some of them to counterattack the Republican charges. Although he wanted to do something other than research, Hechler agreed. He pulled together a list of the points he planned to cover in only two weeks, but the entire report took longer to complete.[39] "I worked eighteen hours a day for over a month or two," Hechler recalls, "and produced what I think could qualify as a master's thesis on the subject. It showed that the federal expenditures for corporate welfare far exceeded the projected expenditures for education, housing, and [other programs] giving a better break to average people."[40] Clark Clifford loved it and sent a note to President Truman saying how useful it would be for presidential speeches.[41] As a special consultant, Hechler was paid twenty-five dollars a day while doing his research at the Library of Congress. He says he really earned it because of the extremely long hours. During those work-filled six weeks, he again lived at the YMCA. But he still wasn't on staff, which was where he wanted to be, and he still had not met the president.

After he finished the study, Hechler got a call from Elsey inviting him to the White House Christmas Party, saying that since Hechler was now a White House "insider," he was welcome. As Hechler made his way through the receiving line, President Truman mentioned the study and told Hechler how much he appreciated it.[42] Hechler was ecstatic. Still, no full-time job had developed. Between Christmas and New Year's he stewed but kept calling Elsey to see if there were anything else he could do. Finally, on January 30, Elsey told him they were looking for help with the speech for the Jefferson-Jackson Day Dinner.

He also asked Hechler to study all the doom-and-gloom predictions Republicans had leveled in the past and to prepare a collection of what Truman termed "scare words" and "calamity howlers." He was referring to GOP criticisms, which in hindsight sounded ludicrous, of great events in American history, such as the Louisiana Purchase and the Lewis and Clark Expedition. Again, Hechler headed for the Library of Congress and put together the list.

According to notes Hechler kept in lieu of the diary he'd been warned to forgo, he spent hours on February 3 working on a draft of the Jefferson-Jackson Day Dinner speech scheduled for two weeks later. He thought it had all the points they wanted covered and plenty of applause lines, and according to Elsey, it had been written in a style that sounded like Truman. However, on the following Tuesday, from the comments and looks of the other writers at the speech session, Hechler could tell he'd flunked his first effort at speechwriting. A new speech would be drafted.[43] As Judge Rosenman had previously commented, it seems Hechler's research skills still outshone those of speechwriting. Yet Truman used six of Hechler's zingers in his actual speech, which made Hechler feel as if his contributions were constructive.[44]

In March, with a raise to thirty-three dollars a day, Hechler was asked to do the local color on Truman's upcoming May 1950 train trip to the Northwest for the rededication of the Grand Coulee Dam. This was Hechler's transition to becoming a permanent member of Truman's staff. He was to write pieces of local color for each stop along the route, which Truman would then incorporate into his speeches. While working on these three projects—the collection of scare words, the Jefferson-Jackson Day Dinner speech, and the local color reports for the trip—he was termed a WAE (when actually employed) special consultant; but following the whistle-stop tour, he was named a full-time White House staff member, with the title of special assistant.[45] At last, he was where he wanted to be. In a letter to Judge Rosenman, he naively said, "This is so much fun, I am swimming in a purple haze."[46]

5

THE TRUMAN WHITE HOUSE

Once Hechler was a full-time member of the White House staff, he moved into a second floor office along the miles of black-and-white tiled corridors in the ornate Old Executive Office Building. He would share this double suite with his boss, George Elsey, for the next three years. Strategically located to provide quick access to the president, for Hechler, it was an easy thirty-second walk to the White House for speech sessions or to see the president, who lived in Blair House at that time. Due to the ongoing extensive renovations at the White House, Truman and his family had moved into Blair House in 1948, which was normally the presidential guesthouse. Blair House, with its distinctive white façade, is actually a series of four connecting town houses, yet each retains the look of an individual residence.[1] Next door to the Renwick Gallery, Blair House is directly across the street from the Pennsylvania Avenue entrance to the Old Executive Office Building, now called the Eisenhower Executive Office Building.

Although Hechler would be a frequent visitor, he had to pinch himself the first time he walked under the tunnel-like awning, knocked on the paneled door, and stepped into the drawing rooms of the federal-style residence. There, hanging as if they were photos of old family members, he saw the portraits of Abraham Lincoln, Robert E. Lee, Andrew Jackson, James Madison, and some of the country's other early founders. For Hechler, it was awe inspiring. As he recounts it, Truman often told those gathered at the morning staff meetings that he'd heard the floors of Blair House creaking the previous night, and that at one time or another, he'd seen the ghosts of every former president walking around the house.[2] Perhaps a bit of an exaggeration, however, for the former home didn't become the official presidential guesthouse until 1942, when FDR persuaded the government to purchase it. It had been, however, a political gathering place since 1837, when its namesake, Francis Preston Blair, and his wife moved in.[3]

Hechler didn't spend much time in his office. His task as a research assistant found him spending countless hours hunched over a table in the Library of Congress, looking for information to include in the position papers Elsey or Clark Clifford would then summarize for members of Congress. These summaries were designed to convey Truman's position on various subjects under scrutiny for legislation that was being drafted. The president wanted to be sure the Democrats in Congress knew exactly how he felt on each issue so that they would vote "the right way."

As spring and Truman's 1950 "nonpolitical" whistle-stop tour to rededicate the Grand Coulee Dam approached, Hechler continued to compile the research necessary for stump speeches in the cities and towns—some of which had a population of only five hundred—that would ensure Truman's image as a man of the people, one who knew about and understood their problems. Hechler pulled together tour brochures, news articles, information from local history files, the names and backgrounds of local officials, and the voting records of the local congresspeople. He studied the area's industries, economic outlook, employment data, and local politics, and from them prepared a two-page analysis for each town.[4] He even talked to cab drivers and beauty shop operators to see what the townspeople were talking about.[5]

However, when the presidential train, the *Ferdinand Magellan*, pulled out of Washington's Union Station on May 11, Hechler was not aboard. He was the only member of the speechwriting team left behind, but with good reason. The rest of the staff was relying on him to provide additional details or speech suggestions for the stops they would make en route. Although his research was extremely thorough, the staff still wanted someone left behind to provide additional details if they were needed.[6] He relished the work, and apparently his bosses applauded his efforts. Though an eight-man team had done this job two years earlier, Elsey said that Hechler outdid them all by himself.[7]

As the tour—covering sixteen states and 6,400 miles—wound down, Hechler arrived in Cumberland, Maryland, to listen to one of Truman's final stump speeches.[8] Truman's assistant special counsel, Charles Murphy, suggested that Hechler join the train and ride back into Washington with the president and the rest of the speechwriters. "Although I hated to desert the friends with whom I had driven to Cumberland, it didn't take much arm twisting to get me aboard for the leisurely trip into the nation's capital,"[9] he recalled. Even with the toll the long days had taken on the press, he found the mood on the train upbeat, even jovial. Truman had been well received, impressing audiences with the knowledge that Hechler had supplied. The president returned to Washington with a new sense of confidence that his domestic goals would be achieved.[10] According to Hechler, it may have been the high point of Truman's career.[11]

The buoyant mood didn't last, however. On June 25, 1950, North Korea crossed the 38th parallel and invaded South Korea, signaling the beginning of the Korean War. Unfortunately for Truman, the conflict soon consumed much of his attention, leaving him unable to push through his domestic programs. This lowered his popularity and ultimately set the stage for a Republican presidential win in 1952. On the other hand, it greatly increased Hechler's involvement in political matters. He was charged with helping Murphy and Elsey push for the establishment of a research division in the Democratic National Committee that would be a repository of complete facts and figures for their candidates and members of Congress. At one time, Elsey suggested that Hechler become the director of such a division, but Hechler, wanting to remain at the White House, bucked him. "I spent a tremendous amount of time in this period feeding information to our friends on Capitol Hill on various subjects, to help them prepare speeches, to provide background data, and to try to orient the activities of the Democratic National Committee a little more toward substantive research," he recalls. "The aim was to develop ammunition that would be useful both in the midterm election of 1950 and looking toward the election of 1952. In addition, whenever there was a research study that the president suggested or anybody else found necessary, they would always turn to me to do a whole series of what were essentially master's theses that were turned out in two or three months."[12] While this may sound like braggadocio, Hechler doesn't mean to inflate his importance. He is quick to point out that while he had a good rapport with members of both houses of Congress, he was, in fact, just a junior member of the staff, without the clout the more senior staffers had.[13]

The next challenge for Truman, and Hechler, was how to deal with the bombastic Republican senator, Joseph McCarthy, from Wisconsin. In early 1950, in self-aggrandizing fashion, McCarthy had begun his politically exploitive hysteria campaign to "rid the government of communists," which he claimed worked in the Democratically controlled federal government. On February 9, he'd made a speech in Wheeling, West Virginia, claiming to have "here in my hand a list of 205 . . . names that were made known to the secretary of state as being members of the Communist Party and who nevertheless are still working and shaping policy in the State Department." Two days later, he repeated the claim to President Truman, though the number was now said to be 57, since,

McCarthy said, Secretary of State Dean Acheson had already dismissed either 80 or 300, depending on which records he quoted. McCarthy demanded that Truman require Secretary Acheson to prepare a complete report of everyone placed in the department by accused Soviet spy Alger Hiss, and that he revoke his previous order that such information was forbidden to a congressional committee review.[14] In order to further enhance his own importance, McCarthy began holding congressional hearings to personally investigate his claims, rather than turning the list over to the FBI, which would have been the logical course of action.

Truman had expressed concern about this type of hysteria, which had produced demagogues long before McCarthy appeared on the scene. In 1949, Brigadier General Robert Landry had prepared, at Truman's request, a study of widespread obsessions, from the Salem witch trials to the present. After McCarthy made his demands and this new wave of panic began to build, Truman wanted to dust off the report, have it edited, and add new material. He turned to Hechler. After approximately one month, he'd rewritten the report using original research to expand the section on the Alien and Sedition Acts, which were passed by Congress in 1798 but had later expired.[15] Additionally, he'd edited out now-irrelevant material and included a section proving that strengthening the economy was a means of combating communism. He concluded that fortunately, periods of hysteria had generally been temporary, and that reason had eventually prevailed. He pointed to the Bill of Rights, our educational system, and our allowance of free discussion as bulwarks against such hysteria.[16] In Truman's ongoing attempts to counter McCarthy over the next few years, he used the text frequently in informal speeches.[17]

Nonetheless, McCarthy's investigations continued throughout the early 1950s and, after conflicting accusations between McCarthy and the army, culminated in nearly three months of nationally televised hearings in the spring and summer of 1954. Each day, television audiences and Capitol visitors watched as McCarthy's daily harangues echoed through the marble-columned Senate caucus room. Finally, on April 22, after McCarthy condescendingly accused one of army attorney Joseph Welch's colleagues of having communist ties, Welch, with controlled anger, uttered his famous statement. "Until this moment, I think I never fully gauged your cruelty or your recklessness," he said. "You have done enough. Have you no sense of decency, sir? At long last, have you left no sense of decency?"[18] With this exchange and the media attention of McCarthy's outrageous accusations, the senator's power finally began to wane. Soon, the Senate had had enough of McCarthy as well; the body voted to censure him on December 2, 1954.[19] Of course, by then, Truman was out of office.

McCarthy's accusations that Truman was soft on communism, the charges of corruption in the administration, and the war in Korea caused Truman's popularity to drop in late 1950—and, with it, the futures of the congressional Democrats.[20] Truman knew the midterm elections were critical, so he campaigned strenuously. As if that worry wasn't enough, a week before Election Day, two Puerto Rican nationalists attempted to assassinate the president. Upset that he had characterized a recent revolt as merely an incident between two Puerto Rican factions, they hoped to call attention to and advance the cause of their country's independence by killing Truman.[21] Believing Puerto Rico was still a victim of American colonialism, they approached Blair House on November 1, 1950, planning to overpower the Secret Service officers and gain entry to the house.

Hechler arrived on the scene as the incident unfolded. "I was just returning from a late lunch on an unseasonably warm day," he recalls. "Rounding the corner of Pennsylvania Avenue toward my office, I heard the rapid 'pop, pop, pop' sound, like Chinese firecrackers. A wild-eyed man ran past yelling, 'They've killed the president and seven Secret Service men!'" Of course, that was not true, but Hechler does recall, "Uniformed policemen and disheveled intruders were sprawled on the sidewalk in front of Blair House. . . . Still it seemed unreal, like a Hollywood film being produced. But the wail of sirens, the ambulances screeching to a halt, the police cars converging, and the inevitable crowds finally convinced me that an attempt had been made on President Truman's life."[22] "They had cordoned off Pennsylvania Avenue opposite Blair House, and I couldn't get in. I went up on the steps of the Executive Office Building, looking right across the street to see the confusion there."[23]

While several officers were wounded, only one died. Later Hechler would remark, "What really struck me was the determination and courage of the president to go out to a speech that afternoon. I thought this was remarkable, although he took very personally, very much to heart, the death of Leslie Coffelt, the White House policeman, who had been killed."[24]

The 1950 midterm elections were a disaster for the Democrats. They lost twenty-eight seats in the House of Representatives and five in the Senate.[25] One particular race caught Hechler's attention. In the California senatorial race, Richard M. Nixon defeated incumbent congresswoman Helen Gahagan Douglas, the wife of actor Melvyn Douglas. Name-calling marked the contest, with Nixon printing a document pointing out that Douglas's earlier voting record aligned perfectly with that of Vito Marcantonio from East Harlem. Marcantonio, citing Second Amendment rights, opposed restrictions on the Communist Party. Thus, Nixon implied that Douglas was also following the Communist line, regardless of what the vote was about. These tactics earned Nixon the lingering appellation of "Tricky Dick"—and Hechler's enduring enmity.[26]

Following the Democratic losses, Hechler's research quickly focused on a lengthy survey of the recent election, which he completed within a month. The survey brought high praise from George Elsey, who remarked, "Ken's report on why the Democrats lost the mid-term elections was perceptive and right on the mark."[27] Unlike his feelings toward some of his other bosses, Hechler was very fond of Elsey, but he was still Hechler's superior. He warned Hechler to tone down the "unfavorable descriptive terms of individuals. An example is the phrase 'lower level demagogue' applied to Senator-elect Nixon."[28] Hechler did as Elsey suggested, but his opinion of Nixon didn't change. This would later play a part in altering Hechler's career.

Hechler's report was so roundly applauded that one Truman advisor suggested sending him on a tour to explain the losses to big city party leaders. Hechler didn't want to be labeled as a political analyst, but moreover, he didn't want to leave Truman's side. "Working for President Truman was a political scientist's dream. I loved the people I was working for and with and savored the thrill of taking part in a great program whose ramifications were worldwide," he said.[29] Fortunately for Hechler, the idea was dropped, and throughout the rest of Truman's presidency, he continued doing research projects for "the Boss." While he didn't influence public policy, his grasp of it allowed him to suggest how it could best be presented.

One evening Matt Conley, Truman's appointment secretary, called Hechler, saying that while Truman's wife and daughter were home in Independence, the president didn't want to dine alone. He asked Hechler and some of the other speechwriters to come and eat with him. "After dinner, the president sat down at the piano and began to play some Chopin and Mozart," Hechler recalls. "He never liked anybody to think of him as anybody bigger than an ordinary human being, and as he looked over at me, he could tell

I was soaring up into the clouds as I contemplated the scene. I could sense that he was going to say something to bring me down to earth. His fingers were moving easily among the keys and he looked at me and he said, 'You know Ken, if I hadn't gotten into trouble by getting into politics, I would've made a hell of a good piano player in a whore house.'"[30]

The following year brought more trouble to the White House. Truman and the new Congress were butting heads on a variety of issues, and the army was suffering setbacks in Korea when another thorn poked Truman in the side. Again, he relied on Hechler to help remove it. This time he needed a publicly acceptable rationale to explain his dismissal of General Douglas MacArthur. Even though MacArthur enjoyed wildly popular support among civilians, if not the troops, several incidents had soured his relationship with President Truman. In March and April, Truman's closest advisors recommended that MacArthur be recalled for one insubordinate statement or another. The act that Truman says cinched his decision, however, was the message MacArthur sent on March 24, 1951, threatening to annihilate the Communist Chinese at the same time the White House was trying to negotiate a cease-fire.[31] Hechler felt it was more likely, however, that the general's statement dismissing the Communist threat in Europe was the final blow.

After a lengthy meeting with four of his top advisors—Averell Harriman, Dean Acheson, and generals Omar Bradley and George Marshall—Truman asked the secretary of the army, Frank Pace, to take the recall orders directly to MacArthur in Tokyo. Secretary Pace was in Korea at the front, however, and didn't get the message. When Truman told his staff of his decision, the press got wind of the impending recall and broke the story. The night of April 10, things got interesting. Fearing MacArthur might preempt Truman's action by resigning, the staff assembled to consider its options. Afraid of the public outcry the popular general's recall would no doubt elicit, the staff began preparing statements explaining Truman's decision and justifying the constitutionality of his action.

Hechler was front and center. Truman asked him to prepare a comparison of the current situation to the contentious relations between President Abraham Lincoln and his brilliant general, George McClellan, whom Lincoln had relieved of his duties at the height of the Civil War.[32] McClellan had repeatedly ignored Lincoln's orders, and his delays had allowed Lee's Confederate army to escape on many occasions. Lincoln, also worried about a mutiny in the ranks and the political repercussions, had finally replaced him with the more aggressive General Ambrose Burnside.[33]

"When I started this, I wasn't sure what it was being designed to prove," Hechler says. He spent the night in the Library of Congress stacks reading Carl Sandburg and other biographers of the two men. His memo was in the president's hands the next morning. "I discovered that the president had put his hands on a brilliant analogy," he says.[34] Hechler's analysis pointed out that while McClellan was not aggressive enough and MacArthur was too aggressive, both had either disobeyed or disregarded their commander in chief's orders, allowing each to invoke his presidential prerogative to change commanders.[35] The next day, Truman relieved MacArthur of his duties and brought him home, saying only that "'MacArthur did not agree with Washington's policy' and that his relief was essential so that 'there would be no doubt or confusion as to the real purpose and aim of our policy.'"[36] MacArthur's insubordination was never mentioned, for that could have initiated a court-martial. Later, Truman said, "I fired him because he wouldn't respect the authority of the president. I didn't fire him because he was a dumb son-of-a-bitch, although he was, but that's not against the law for generals. If it was, half to three quarters of them would be in jail."[37]

Even with the long hours Hechler spent digging into Library of Congress records or preparing reports for Elsey or the president, life in the Truman White House wasn't all work—even for Truman. During his presidency, Truman made eleven visits to Key West, Florida, where he spent a few weeks, usually in the winter.[38] There he resided at what had once been the home of the base commander of the Key West Naval Air Station. Although Truman wasn't the only president to stay there, he called it his "Little White House."[39] As you would expect, a retinue of staffers and the press went along. While he likes to exaggerate it, Hechler was invited only once,[40] but it's one of his fondest memories of his time with Truman.

When Truman arrived on November 9 for his 1951 visit to Key West, Hechler did not accompany the initial party as they flew into Boca Chica airport. He arrived ten days later with four other White House staffers to spend the Thanksgiving holiday with the president and those who had made the original trip.[41] He recalls clearly the drive to the compound. They drove to the base and, after showing identification to the guard on duty, through the gates of the annex, past rows of identical white houses, which had originally housed the naval officers, to the iron-fenced grounds of the white clapboard house on Front Street. Although the house is actually a modest, two-story, narrow building, Hechler found the setting a bit imposing. Perhaps it was the expansive, lush lawn or the towering live oaks and thick sago palms. In any case, Hechler was assigned to quarters in a building adjacent to the residence but took his meals with the presidential party.[42] He recalls it as a muggy evening, with swarms of mosquitos out in force. Huge sprayers were fogging everything in an attempt to rid the area of the pests.

Of course, the junior staffers had arrived in suits. It didn't take them long, however, to find wildly patterned and colorful sports shirts to match the style Truman favored while in the semitropics.

Even in this relaxed atmosphere, there was an air of tension among the senior staffers, Hechler says. He thought Truman's pending departure that day for Washington to give a speech to the Women's National Democratic Club was the reason. Little did Hechler know that Truman had recently told his senior advisors that he did not plan to run for reelection. Following dinner and a movie, Hechler and the staffers who remained gathered around the large cabinet radio that evening to listen to the boss's speech. They heard but may not have caught the hint the president gave, as he said he wasn't ready to make any announcements naming a possible candidate for his job.[43] The following afternoon, the president and his party returned to Key West accompanied by Chief Justice Fred Vinson, his wife, and Mrs. Truman. That night, fully relaxed, they all watched *The Lavender Hill Mob* on a movie screen brought into the living room.

On Thanksgiving Day, Hechler and a few others accompanied Truman on his daily walk to Truman's Beach, where they sunned and played volleyball. Hechler's team won two of the three matches. That evening, they enjoyed a traditional turkey dinner, beginning with shrimp cocktail and ending with several desserts. On Saturday, Hechler tried his hand at boating, but the records don't reflect his success—or lack thereof. Volleyball was his game, even though his team sometimes lost in what were described as "closely contested games."[44] Hechler recalls Truman's daughter, Margaret, who had arrived early Sunday morning, as a very poor volleyball player,[45] but her team beat Hechler's in three straight games that afternoon.

At one of the picnic lunches Truman often held on the shady lawn, Hechler found himself in line following the president,

Ken Hechler with President Truman at Truman's Beach, Key West, FL, 1951 (U.S. Navy photo)

Mrs. Truman, Margaret, and Clark Clifford. "There was a series of five or six round tables that had room for seating of about eight people," he says. "Margaret was sitting, having been second in line or third in line . . . she was sitting at one of these tables. I got my plate of food and was looking around. She was sitting all alone at a table and when she saw the look of apprehension on my face she began to sing a then-popular song, 'Come on to my house, my house, a-come on,' which of course melted my heart."[46] Hechler admits to having a crush on Margaret, but since he realized that life with her would be like living in a fishbowl, he never pursued his interest.[47]

One of Truman's favorite pastimes was poker, and even if Hechler never played, he loved to kibitz and listen to the conversation around the table. "I wish I'd had a tape recording of some of the wonderful stories that passed around. For example, one day they started a poker game in the morning and adjourned for lunch. When they came back somebody discovered that there were five aces in the pack. Chief Justice Vinson, who spoke in a slow and pragmatic voice, said, 'What would the people of the United States think if the President of the United States and the Chief Justice of the U.S. Supreme Court were playing poker with five aces?' Of course, everybody got a good laugh out of that. You could learn a lot about people's character and what their ideals were by just listening to the talk around the poker table."[48] Hechler did learn by listening. He readily admits that he learned the campaign style he would later use from Truman.[49]

Even though Truman had told his senior advisors in Key West that he wasn't planning to run again, he didn't make his decision public until much later. By then, he'd discussed the issue several more times, with many of his advisors agreeing that he should not run. In early March, he was shocked to discover he had lost the New Hampshire primary to Estes Kefauver, even though his name had been entered without his consent.[50] Additionally, earlier problems at the White House were deepening: the Korean War was at a stalemate; Truman's support within his own party was getting thinner in Congress; and the charges of corruption in the administration were growing louder. Furthermore, no clear standard-bearer had surfaced to run in his place. Some of the staff supported Averell Harriman, others Adlai Stevenson, with whom Truman had a cool relationship. Echoing his boss's antipathy, Hechler was initially in Harriman's camp, despite his concern that Harriman did not project a strong enough image of leadership. Truman's public announcement on March 29, at the Jefferson-Jackson Day Dinner, shocked the gathered Democrats.[51] In private handwritten notes from April 1 through April 4, 1952, Hechler writes, "Tears came to my eyes as I listened to the president describe what he planned to do after leaving the White House. He said he would continue to work for world peace and for the welfare of all the people."[52]

In July, the 1952 Democratic National Convention began without a clear nominee. Four strong candidates vied for the top job: Senator Estes Kefauver, Senator Richard Russell, Harriman, and Stevenson. At the beginning of the convention, Stevenson stated emphatically that he wasn't a candidate, but after some persuading, he informed Truman he would accept if nominated. Truman asked Harriman to release his delegates, and the race was over. Stevenson chose John Sparkman of Alabama as his running mate.[53] Truman's role now was to campaign for the ticket, hoping to keep a Democrat in the White House. Running on the Republican ticket were Dwight D. Eisenhower and Richard M. Nixon.

And campaign he did. In advance of the summer conventions, Hechler had prepared a fifteen-page list of questions that might be asked, with an eye toward embarrassing members of the opposition.[54] Throughout the fall, Truman repeatedly boarded the *Magellan* for another of his whistle-stop tours. And, once again, he called on Hechler to supply the support material. No doubt the embarrassing questions document was among the material he provided. Other documents included speeches by Thomas Dewey in his losing campaign against Truman, the opposition views on demobilization following the Korean War, and the usual in-depth study of each town on the tour. The day after Labor Day, the train departed for a one-day tour of Pennsylvania, Wisconsin, West Virginia, and Ohio. Three weeks later, it embarked on a grueling two-week Western tour that would reach clear to California, Washington, and Oregon.[55]

As soon as potential schedules were available, Hechler would begin gathering information on the towns Truman would visit.

Ken Hechler stumps for Adlai Stevenson with President Truman, September 1952 (Courtesy Ken Hechler)

His desk, piled high with newspapers, brochures, magazines, books, timetables, and working drafts, began to look like a trash heap. Stacks of paper also littered the windowsills, the sofa, and all the chairs. It's a look his office retained throughout his political career. Hechler's office was off-putting to Charlie Murphy, Truman's special counsel after Clark Clifford left, but Hechler knew at any given time where he'd put any particular piece of information.[56]

This time, however, Hechler's role was much larger; actually accompanying Truman on his tours. While drafts were usually done before the trip, Hechler actually wrote a number of the whistle-stop speeches on the train. It seemed he had a knack for finding well-turned metaphors for Truman to apply to certain situations. One stop at a small mountaintop town called Helper, Utah, evoked this bit of metaphorical humor. The town was so named because it required an extra engine to get a passenger or freight train to the top. This was called a helper engine. Hechler told Truman this, so he concluded his speech there by saying "it's going to take a heck of a lot more than one helper engine to get the Republican Party's ideas understood by the voters in this country."[57] While Truman sometimes used Hechler's writing verbatim, it wasn't often. According to Hechler, Truman's extemporaneous delivery and his personality shone at these stops, unlike in his major speeches, where he could sound a bit flat.[58]

Speechwriting on the move proved difficult, he says. "One of the first things I discovered on the campaign train was that I was cut off from my customary sources of information and intelligence. I couldn't switch on radio or television to find out what was happening in the world. If the president wanted a fact or figure checked out before using it, I couldn't pick up a telephone and go right to an accurate source." Once, when Hechler did jump off to double-check a fact, he nearly missed getting back on. He ran down the track, but the train was already moving. If not for a well-muscled Secret Service agent, Hechler might have spent the rest of the trip in whatever town they had just visited.[59]

While the president's train car was plush by 1950s standards, Hechler recalls the other twelve cars as rather sparse. He had to share a roomette with fellow speechwriter Dick Neustadt,[60] but Hechler did get the lower berth. He recalls eagerly awaiting visits to the larger cities, where the staff could get off and take a shower. However, most stops were in smaller towns, where Truman could connect with the common people. "I think one of the things that President Truman always wanted me to do was to go out among the crowd and listen to what people were saying," Hechler says. "I remember one day the crowd was very, very quiet and they weren't responding. So, on impulse, I just clapped my hands and yelled to the back platform, 'Give 'em Hell, Harry,' and everybody got a good laugh out of that."[61] Later Margaret Truman quipped that her dad's campaign train was the only one to carry its own heckler.[62]

By Truman's own count, he had made more than two hundred speeches and traveled seventeen thousand miles in the two months he was on the campaign trail for Stevenson.[63] Regardless of Truman's efforts and Hechler's "whip-up-the-crowd" speechwriting, Stevenson lost badly to Eisenhower, who carried thirty-nine of the forty-eight states.[64] Looking back, Hechler says Truman thought Stevenson didn't campaign aggressively enough.[65] But Hechler thought Stevenson's staff should have read the signs better. He believed they had underestimated Eisenhower's popularity and the respect accorded him by his leadership during World War II. Even Hechler got caught up in the campaigning, forgetting that he had supported the man himself in his "days of sin," as he called them, at Princeton.[66] Nevertheless, the Democrats had lost, and Truman's staff began casting about for jobs.

As Truman prepared for the transition, he gave Hechler and the rest of the staff one last task. In a handwritten memo, he requested a complete copy of every single public statement Eisenhower had ever made: his campaign speeches, his position on various policies, his statements about McCarthy, and so on. He also wanted an analysis of Nixon's attack on the president in which he had called Truman a traitor. The "Ikelopedia," as the mass of Eisenhower's statements was later dubbed, eventually ran over six hundred pages. Hechler used the bowling alley in the White House basement in which to assemble the document. When Truman left office, Hechler was still working on it; he eventually turned it over to the Democratic National Committee.[67]

In December, Truman held a dinner for the men who had served during his administration, those currently employed as well as some who had since left the White House. Among them was George Elsey, Hechler's former boss, whom Hechler deeply admired. When Elsey left that position, Hechler handwrote a note telling him that he'd never had a better boss.[68] The two had great mutual respect for each other. Elsey once praised Hechler for "helping make Harry S. Truman the president the nation now knows him to have been."[69] Hechler recalls the evening's cocktail party in the Blue Room and reception in the Red Room. But he was most impressed by the seating arrangement in the State Dining Room. Rather than the usual round tables for guests and a head table for Truman, one long rectangular table had been set with places designated for each guest. "We were all equals at one head table, with no special ranking," he said. He felt that was characteristic of the man who treated everyone as an equal.[70] It's a trait Hechler would emulate later in his own political career.

Even though Truman graciously vacated the White House for the Eisenhower administration, Hechler did not. He simply remained at his Old Executive Office Building suite while completing his work on the Ikelopedia. Hechler says it started as a joke. "Somebody asked me if I was going back to work the next day, and I said, "Sure, why not?" And then I decided that night that I would just try it to see what would happen." Each day he reported to work at the same office, and each day he went across to the White House mess, where he'd always eaten lunch. "Everybody was slapping everybody else on the back, including me, saying, 'Welcome aboard. Welcome aboard.' Pretty soon they began to ask me what I did there, and I always said I did research. They said, 'Great, you know research is important. We need good research.'"

Then the personnel director circulated a memo indicating that since the mess room was getting crowded, only certain members of the staff over Grade GS-12 were eligible to eat there. Surprisingly, Hechler's name was among them, so he continued eating with the rest of Eisenhower's staff. One day, when someone asked him whom he worked for, Hechler replied that he worked for the special counsel. From the end of the table came this remark: "I'm the special counsel; what do you do for me?" Even though he had been caught, the personnel director actually offered him a job paying half his former salary, and Hechler accepted it.

Hechler stayed until he took the position of associate director of the American Political Science Association (APSA) in March, but he didn't actually resign. "I was still kind of interested in what excuse they would utilize, because it is in the law that if you fire a veteran, even if he is in an exempted position, you have to give a reason; it can't be a political reason. So I got this letter saying, 'Your services are not required . . . because you have completed your assignment.'" Even though he'd been dismissed, Hechler was pleased. He believes it's the only time he was ever told he'd completed something.[71]

6

THE ROAD TO CONGRESS WINDS THROUGH WEST VIRGINIA

President Truman held one last staff meeting after he left office, and Hechler was invited, even though he hadn't regularly attended them when Truman occupied the White House. Held at the Mayflower Hotel during the summer of 1953, the meeting was chaired by Truman's former appointment secretary, Matt Connelly, and the former president. Seated at the head of the T-shaped table, Connelly opened the meeting by asking Hechler to talk about his experiences working in the Eisenhower White House. Hechler says the question embarrassed him, since he felt he might have violated "the boss's" wishes. "The reason I was embarrassed was that President Truman had emphasized so much that he wanted a smooth transition. I didn't want to go into all these details, but he started to laugh a little bit when I began. I got warmed up a little after that, but it did embarrass me a little bit at first."[1] It would not be the last reunion of all the Truman White House fellows. Whenever Truman returned to Washington, he held gatherings of one group or another. These would be bittersweet for Hechler, sitting on the sidelines at APSA.

Compared to life in the White House, the next few years must have seemed like an overlong intermission between acts in the political life Ken Hechler was trying to build. The year 1953 saw several dramatic shifts in world power: Stalin died in March, and Khrushchev was appointed the first secretary-general of the Communist Party in Russia; King George VI had died the year before, and his daughter, Queen Elizabeth II, was crowned in the first coronation ever televised. The news of the groundbreaking conquest of Mount Everest by Sir Edmund Hillary and his Sherpa guide, Tenzing Norgay, reached London on May 29, the day of her coronation. Finally, the long-hoped-for Korean armistice was declared in July,[2] but Hechler was no longer even a bit player on the stage of world events. Still in Washington, he could only read of these happenings in the *Washington Post* as he worked from his associate director's office at APSA, the position he had assumed on March 20, 1953. Now for the long-legged Hechler, his walk to work from his apartment at 1801 I Street was metaphorically and geographically in the opposite direction from his previous one in the Old Executive Office Building.

Although his $10,000 salary was much less than it had been at the White House,[3] Hechler did have the pleasure of again working with his old boss from the Bureau of the Budget, Pendleton Herring, who was now the president of the association.[4] Here, Hechler's main responsibilities were to contribute to the deliberations of the Fulbright Scholarship Awards Committee,[5] to recommend potential candidates for political science teaching positions at colleges and universities when asked, and to bring in national speakers for various association conferences. It was this duty that earned him the Sheraton Corporation's prestigious Green Line credit card, issued only to association executives who added greatly to the company's coffers.[6] It was an odd perquisite for the typically frugal Hechler.

His most notable contribution during his four-year stay, however, was the establishment of the Congressional Fellowship Program in 1953. Initially, this program brought young political scientists and journalists, chosen only after a lengthy application and interview process, to work for ten months as interns on congressional staffs. The goal was to give them practical experience that would ultimately benefit their work. Over the years, the program was expanded to include domestic and foreign policy experts from the federal government, health policy professionals, various academics, and scholars from the international community, as well.[7] One notable alumnus is former vice president Richard B. Cheney. Still functioning today, the program was immensely popular, as was Hechler. When the first group graduated, they penned a poem in his honor. Later, Frederick Clark, who was working to establish an alumni association of the former interns, referred to Hechler as the "virtual father of the Congressional Fellows Program."[8] According to former program director Jeffrey Biggs, "Over 2,600 alumni owe Hechler a real debt of gratitude."[9]

In early 1956, Hechler took a leave of absence from APSA to again join a presidential campaign—this time as Adlai Stevenson's research director. Back in the political fray, Hechler was in his element. His first assignment was to draft statements to be used by various delegates endorsing Stevenson at the Democratic National Convention. As the August date of the convention drew closer, Stevenson asked him to "prepare the strongest arguments for *and* against any person mentioned for Vice President."[10] Potentials included Al Gore Sr., Hubert Humphrey, Stuart Symington, Henry Jackson, Lyndon Johnson, Estes Kefauver, and John F. Kennedy, as well as some lesser-known governors and large city mayors. Because Stevenson planned to throw the choice of a running mate open to the convention delegates, Hechler analyzed in great detail each candidate's assets and detrimental stands or comments. They chose Estes Kefauver—whom Truman disliked and always called "Cow-Fever"[11]—and the campaign began.

Once again, Hechler prepared detailed notes about each city stop on the campaign trail. He also prepared criticisms of the Republican Party and Eisenhower's administration on civil rights, business, education, fiscal and budgetary policies, health, high-ways, housing, immigration, juvenile delinquency, labor, and the Bill of Rights. He also wrote position papers on a vast range of topics, including agriculture, civil liberties, the Catholic vote, African American voters, civil rights, education and hous-ing, Social Security, peace, the H-bomb tests, truth in govern-ment, Nixon, unemployment, and natural resources. Each section of the notebook contained quotes (ostensibly by Eisenhower or another Republican) that Stevenson could rebut, and then listed the candidate's positions and proposals on that issue.[12]

Hechler and Stevenson had a very close relationship during the campaign. Hechler was often invited to Stevenson's Illinois home, where he played tennis with Sargent Shriver and his wife, Eunice Kennedy Shriver.[13] Hechler was the only speechwriter who traveled with Stevenson in Florida, Minnesota, California, Oregon, and Pennsylvania, among other states. While Hechler referred to himself as a speechwriter, he merely suggested anecdotes, based on his research, to Stevenson, who then wrote his own platform remarks. Whether whistle-stopping by train, flying, or traveling by car, it was grueling, but Hechler loved it. Stevenson followed Truman's campaigning methods, but according to Hechler, he didn't have the popular appeal of either Truman or his own running mate, Estes Kefauver. Hechler says Stevenson's extem-poraneous campaign speeches were never quite as effective as Truman's, especially the ones given from the rear platform of a train. Stevenson spent much more time polishing his speeches, and thus the ones he prepared for formal speaking engagements were more effective.[14]

Hechler thought Kefauver was a typical politician whose power was exaggerated.[15] Yet Stevenson, unlike Kefauver, didn't have a down-to-earth, folksy way about him. At one stop in Minnesota, Hechler saw the contrast between the two clearly. "Kefauver had this little routine he would always pull with his staff," he says. "One of them would invariably come up to him, [interrupt,] and in a very loud voice say, 'Senator, you realize you're behind schedule and that we are going to have to leave.' Kefauver would turn angrily to his staff member and say, 'Now don't take me away from these good people. They're the most important people in this whole campaign and I intend to stay here as long as I want to and you're going to have to put that in your pipe and smoke it.' He'd do this time after time. Stevenson would never think of doing a thing like that; [he] would resent [Kefauver] putting on this kind of act as being insincere and hypocritical."[16]

As the campaign drew to a close in October, Hechler accompanied Stevenson to the West Virginia Forest Festival in Elkins. An unscheduled stop in nearby Belington caught Stevenson without a prepared speech. Hechler realized he would have to make some remarks and worried about how he would handle an impromptu speech. When Stevenson emerged to see a crowd of young students, one yelled, "We like Ike." A West Virginia politician quickly turned to Hechler and asked how Stevenson could keep from talking over the heads of the kids. The candidate rose to the occasion, however, asking, "How many school children here would like to be candidates for president someday?" The crowd of fifty all raised their hands. Then he asked, "How many candidates for president would like to be school children?" He stuck his own hand high in the air and gave a cheer. He won them over, and they listened attentively afterward.

Hechler greatly admired Stevenson, and calls Stevenson's prepared speeches "the most inspiring documents of the twentieth century." Of the man, he says, "I've never known a man who combined such high qualities of courage, principle, courtesy and human sensitivity." He also says Stevenson was ahead of his time in his calls to deal with the nation's poverty, to fight juvenile delinquency, to create job training programs, and to provide grants to cities to improve and repair their infrastructure—issues we still battle today. Hechler believes all those who campaigned with Stevenson were, like Hechler, inspired to do so as a patriotic obligation.[17]

Hechler later found himself driven by the same basic ideas Stevenson had inspired, especially his attempts to get young people involved in public affairs. Stevenson spurned the backstabbing, double-talking tactics of many politicians; he refused to engage in backroom deals or under-the-table maneuvers. Hechler would emulate Stevenson in this, as well as by adopting his deep belief in the people themselves.

The November 1956 loss was a bitter blow to both the candidate and his staff. Stevenson lost by an even greater margin than he had in 1952. Eisenhower's popularity was simply too strong to overcome. Hechler was in despair. "I wanted to get as far away as possible from politics. I felt impelled to go out and teach as far away from the Ivy League atmosphere as possible."[18] Instead, he returned to his position at APSA. He didn't stay long, however. After the rigors of the campaign, where sixteen-hour days weren't unusual, the slow pace at APSA was unsettling for Hechler. He called it a *mañana* attitude.[19] Furthermore, he was still smarting from Stevenson's loss and stewing in his hatred of the reelected vice president, Richard Nixon, and the kind of dirty campaigns he had waged. Hechler wanted desperately to get out of Washington.

One day a letter came from Marshall College (now Marshall University),[20] a small institution in West Virginia, seeking a professor of political science. Reading the letter, he recalled Justice Brandeis's recommendation when Hechler was teaching at Columbia in 1941 that he should be in the boondocks helping people at smaller colleges instead.[21] Impulsively, Hechler offered his own name to Marshall in place of the three names he normally sent.[22]

Following an interview, he received a letter from Conley H. Dillon, head of Marshall's political science department. Dillon wrote that the college "would be extremely fortunate if we could obtain a person with your outstanding training and experience" but warned that it would be for only one semester and that he would hold only an assistant professor's rank, due to budgetary restrictions.[23] Despite Dillon's assumption that he would not take the position, Hechler accepted without reservation. In December, he received a confirmation letter from the dean of the College of Arts and Sciences, Dr. Frank Bartlett, stating that his salary for that semester would be $2,082.20,[24] a far cry from his five-figure salary at the White House.

Hechler's trip to Huntington, where Marshall is located, wouldn't be his first. He'd visited there when he was stationed at Fort Knox during World War II, and again on a whistle-stop tour with Truman. He knew the city, having prepared research on the local color before Truman's visit, and thought it would be a great opportunity to get out in the grass roots, to teach, and to participate in local community activities, much as his parents had done in Roslyn.[25] Hechler boarded the C&O's *Fast Flying Virginian* on January 22, 1957; paid $31.57 for his one-way fare; and headed to Huntington.[26] While Hechler says he arrived that night more by a happy coincidence than by design, his fellow Marshall political science professor, Simon Perry, tells a different story. "I learned of Ken Hechler many years before I ever met him," he says.

I was working on my PhD at Michigan State University. I had a young professor named Ralph Goldman.

Dr. Goldman had been a fellow at the Brookings Institute, where he met Ken Hechler. In this seminar with Goldman, we were discussing the question of how ambitious political types start their political careers. He then told an amazing story about Ken Hechler, who [sic] I had never heard of. Hechler, he said, did a study of congressional districts in order to identify the ones where he would have a chance to win. As Goldman told the story, Ken looked at all kinds of factors: the liberalism and conservatism of the district, how the district had voted in previous elections, the district's tendency to be friendly toward newcomers, and, of course, the final factor, the age of the incumbent, and perhaps [the] vulnerabilities of the present office holder. So with this study completed, Ken picked Huntington, and the rest is history.[27]

Hechler says that's only part of the story. Admittedly, he had studied some of these factors as part of his research for Truman's whistle-stop tours, and knowing the expert researcher he was, it's not hard to believe Goldman's tale. Years earlier, he'd been challenged by Swarthmore professor Robert Brooks to state how he'd get elected to Congress, and Hechler had a ready answer. He also confessed that he was always intrigued by the congressional power held by those he'd gotten to know through his amplified classroom interviews, while working for Truman, and through the Congressional Fellowship Program at APSA.[28] Additionally, he clearly recalled thinking, when he worked for Stevenson, how wonderful it must be to be able to get up in the morning and decide exactly what issues you want to confront, and then to be involved in bringing them to the forefront instead of being on the sidelines, where he'd been for so long.[29] Now, when asked if he came to Marshall with an idea of running for office, he says, "[It] was not my aim to use that as a launching pad, but it was certainly a subsidiary. That has always been in the back of my mind."[30]

In any case, accepting the job got him out of Washington. He was ready to settle in to his new life. When he alighted from the train in Huntington the following morning, Hechler headed straight for the home of Carl Leiden, the man he was replacing for the semester. Leiden had offered his home to Hechler for the duration. Earlier, Leiden, who was on sabbatical to study at the University of California, Berkeley, had written a very welcoming letter to Hechler in which he had suggested that the two of them coauthor a book dealing with contemporary political party issues. He offered to let Hechler be the senior writer discussing the Democratic Party, while he'd take the Republican Party issues.[31] Regrettably, the book never materialized.

Upon his arrival, Hechler began his usual thorough job of researching the matter at hand. In this case, Marshall and the community. Even though he had prepared an analysis of the city for Truman and had visited previously, he knew little about the college, so he dug further. He visited the tree-studded campus and read the student handbook, the college's catalog of courses, the faculty directory, and the latest report on Marshall compiled by its accrediting body, the North Central Association of Colleges and Secondary Schools. He also obtained an industrial survey of Huntington produced the previous August by the local Chamber of Commerce.[32] Before he left Washington, he had contacted Congressman William E. Neal, representing West Virginia's 4th Congressional District, and asked what community and political leaders in Huntington he ought to call on, since he wanted to do more than simply teach. Neal gave him a list of those Hechler called the "movers and shakers" in both parties, saying that if Hechler got to know them, he'd soon know everyone.[33] It didn't take long. According to his new neighbor, Ann Dexter, Hechler cut quite a figure in his newly purchased red-and-white Chevrolet convertible, thus immediately impressing the young people in town. Dexter had two teenagers, and they were fascinated when he came to dinner—which was often, since he never learned to cook.[34]

Though he'd been told he'd be merely an assistant professor, when classes began a week later, he found he'd been promoted. Associate Professor Hechler was ready and determined to be the best teacher on campus, and he says he was. Almost immediately, he asked for and received permission from Dean Bartlett to install his now-famous amplification system in Room 203 of the Old Main building.[35] He would be teaching several courses there, including Political Science 101, required at the time for liberal arts students. Stories of that first day in class are now legendary. His student assistant, Mike Perry (no relation to Simon Perry), worked with several of the professors in the department, but he was particularly impressed with this unique individual. "In many respects," Perry says, "he was a breath of fresh air." Perry recalls,

The most distinctive thing that you remember [about] the first class you have with Hechler was generally at eight o'clock on a Monday morning there would be thirty-five to forty freshmen students from everywhere. . . . After they would take their seats, he would announce that he wanted them to tell him their name, where they're from, and how they'd like their coffee, black or with cream and sugar. He proceeded to walk up and down the rows in that Political Science 101 class and each one would tell him those three pieces of information. Then on Wednesday morning [when the class next met] at eight o'clock, he would have me go over to Wiggins [restaurant] across the street and get large containers of coffee and cream and sugar. As the students arrived he would ask them all to take their seats, but to feel free to move around wherever you want. Then he would proceed to go up, call each student by name, tell them where they were from, and then pour them a cup of coffee, either black, with cream or with sugar. There were at least a minimum of 120 possibilities that he would have to memorize, assuming a class of about forty, and that's not even counting the variations of cream and sugar. He did this for all of his classes.

Perry says he never saw him miss more than once or twice, and it was never the student's name.[36] Hechler admits it was one of the tricks he mastered to make the students talk about his classes. He wanted them to say, "Do you know what happened in Ken Hechler's class today?"[37] Additionally, Hechler could remember each student outside class, calling the student by name and asking how things were in whatever hometown he or she was from. It made the students love him. Perry, who became a highly respected Huntington attorney and banker, says that in all his years of dealing with politicians and businesspeople, he's never met anyone who could match Hechler's memory for names.[38]

The trick gave him pause only once. As he called the roll to get each student's first name, the first one happened to be Atkins. Hechler asked his first name, and the boy replied, "G. M." Hechler said, "Don't you have a first name? You have only initials?" The student answered, "That is my first name: Jim." Hechler says it took him some time to understand the young man's Mingo County dialect, which had made the one-syllable name into two.[39]

When class began in earnest, Hechler's teaching techniques were just as popular as they had been when he introduced them at Columbia almost twenty-five years earlier. Although he assigned a textbook, his tales of working with Truman, other elected officials, and well-known governmental staffers made political science come alive. Equally exciting were his amplified calls to the senators, representatives, and Supreme Court justices he knew in Washington, including Estes Kefauver and Jimmy Roosevelt, Franklin Roosevelt's son. Everybody wanted to be in Hechler's class, according to another of his students. And they rarely cut, for they never knew what they might miss.[40] Hechler once engaged a drama student to portray Alexander Hamilton for the class. He rented a costume complete with buckled shoes, long white stockings, and a tri-cornered hat, and asked the student to burst into the classroom while Hechler was discussing Hamilton and Thomas Jefferson. The two debated, much to the surprise of the students, with Hechler taking Jefferson's positions.[41]

In his upper-level class, American National Government, he had the students go outside the classroom. For their first assignment, Hechler had them write an assessment as to whether or not Huntington should adopt a council-manager form of government. At the time a strong mayor headed the local government, but there was a burgeoning move to make the change. The students were to work in the precincts, polling at least fifty voters each, in order to draw their conclusion.[42] Another assignment had the students studying their home county political organizations to discover the name and background of the party chair, and the structure of the party. They were also tasked with listing their respective local election results for the presidential, gubernatorial, senatorial, and congressional races in 1952 and 1956.[43] In retrospect, those reports no doubt became valuable information for Hechler when he later decided to run for Congress.

In a less well-known move, when his students were reading about political life in another country, they discussed how it would feel to always carry a gun. At the next class meeting, he brought unloaded rifles and gave them to the students, telling them to wear them on campus to see how it felt. After a few days, they reported that the other students were used to seeing the rifles and did not ask questions.[44]

To educate them about the voting process, Hechler had an actual voting machine delivered to his classroom at his own expense, even though with the voting age then set at twenty-one, most of his students were still too young to vote. However, he regularly admonished them to vote when the time came. "The theme of my classes at Marshall was that every student had an obligation to be a part of the political process," he says. "I'd tell them, if you sit on the sidelines you're really contributing toward mismanagement, corruption, and the election of candidates that don't truly represent the people."[45]

In the spring, Hechler organized a trip to Washington for his upper-level course but made participation a competition. Each student who wished to go had to write a paper telling why. Those students whose papers were deemed good enough were chosen, but they had to pay their own expenses. They boarded a Trailways bus on April 25, 1957, bound for the capital. Because the five-day visit unfortunately coincided with the congressional Easter recess, many senators and representatives had left the city. He was able to schedule student meetings with John F. Kennedy, the ambassador from India, Everett Dirksen, and Estes Kefauver, however. According to the student reports required upon their return, the trip was a huge success. Hechler had wisely scheduled two fun nights in addition to the dozens of meetings; one evening was spent cruising down the Potomac on the SS *Mount Vernon*.[46] Touring the Russian embassy during the Cold War made a vivid impression as well.[47]

All of these unusual teaching methods made Hechler so popular that many people have the impression that he taught much longer than one semester. Leiden returned shortly before the

Ken Hechler's Marshall College class heads to Washington, D.C., 1957
(Photo by the *Parthenon*, Marshall College)

semester ended, and he and Hechler engaged in a debate in one
of Hechler's classes. They argued the differences between the
two political parties—the suggested topic of the book they never
wrote.[48] As he had done at Columbia and Princeton, Hechler asked
the students for evaluations following their final exams. One
noted that Hechler's decision to largely eschew the textbook was
a good one. Another confessed that he came to the class with a
bad attitude, but Hechler changed it with his revolutionary teaching methods.[49] A year after Hechler left the campus he held a class
reunion, which most of his students attended, attesting again to
his enormous popularity.

Hechler was a popular figure outside the classroom as well.
He and Spanish professor Jim Stais became good friends and, as

bachelors of a certain age, were often invited to campus dances, dinners, and other social functions. It's a wonder he had time to prepare for class. He was especially popular with the Sigma Sigma Sigma sorority, acting as both a frequent chaperone and a much envied dance partner. According to one member, he knew how to work the room even then. He'd walk up to a table of girls with their dates and begin asking their names, what their major was, and what they were interested in. Then after several dances, he'd return with his current dance partner and introduce her to the entire table without missing a beat.[50]

While Hechler was a hit in Marshall's classrooms, another man held the students' attention on the basketball floor. Hal Greer, a black athlete born in Huntington, had been admitted on a scholarship in 1955, thus becoming the first African American to play for a major college team. The talented guard was named Mid-American Conference (MAC) All-Conference player in 1957 and 1958, and an All-American in 1958.[51] Greer had also caught the eye of the NBA, but there was a hitch. He was enrolled, like most of the male students, in the ROTC, the Reserve Officers' Training Corps. This meant that he was required to attend periodic weekend drills and a two-week summer camp at one of the army's training facilities, and was subject to being called to active duty. Al Cervi, head coach of the Syracuse Nationals, wanted Greer if he decided to become a professional player, but Cervi knew the army stood in his way. Although he was no longer teaching at the time, Hechler was still a force on campus. He tells the story this way:

> They did not communicate it directly, but they let it be known that they would not recruit Hal Greer unless somehow he could get out of the army two weeks early. They wouldn't recruit him if he stayed in the army. I talked

to my usual contact at the Pentagon, and he laughed and said, "You want this guy to get out of the army to play basketball? You gotta be crazy." The way he said it insulted me so I went to his boss, a Brigadier General, and said, "Look, this guy can't learn anything in two weeks and this is his life. Five years from now you're going to see his name in the headlines," which of course occurred.[52]

After being chosen as a 1958 second-round draft pick, Greer went on to become one of the Philadelphia 76er's greatest players and is the only African American from West Virginia in the Naismith Memorial Basketball Hall of Fame.[53] Even though it's a little-known story, among those who did know of Hechler's part in it, he became even more popular.

Following his single-semester teaching stint, Hechler returned briefly to Washington but maintained a home in Huntington, to which he planned to return. He'd been asked by Senator John Carroll of Colorado to come help him during a big civil rights fight raging in Congress in the summer of 1957. Lyndon Johnson had introduced a civil rights bill, but it stipulated that jury trials were necessary for violators of the act. Carroll and Hechler knew that no southern jury would ever convict civil rights violators, so they were trying to get that excised from the bill. The two men had met when Hechler was teaching at Princeton and Carroll was serving as a member of the House of Representatives. They'd become close, so Hechler agreed to go for the summer, regardless of his misgivings. "I've always been interested in civil rights, but I was reluctant to come to Washington because I was already planning to run for Congress in 1958. I had no business to go to Washington when I should have been out mending my fences for the 1958 election," he says.[54] Nevertheless, they fought from July to September but eventually lost the battle to Johnson, with Hechler correctly predicting the vote count. Jury trials remained in the legislation.

While Hechler was with Carroll, he also researched and wrote background material for Carroll's Senate speeches, and attended all the sessions of the Kefauver Subcommittee on Antitrust and Monopoly. Here he helped feed questions to Kefauver to use in quizzing the executives of the country's major industries then under scrutiny for possible violations of the legislation currently on the books.[55] Such activities no doubt heightened his desire to be in Congress in his own seat. When he returned home, he regretted his absence from the state, fearing he'd lost ground with his supporters. He says his popularity with the students and the release of his book, *The Bridge at Remagen*, in November quickly repaired his support, however.

Since World War II had ended just twelve years earlier, the topic of his book—the Allied capture of the German bridge over the Rhine River—was still fresh in the minds of many. As an army historian, he'd arrived there only hours after the capture and had interviewed both officers and foot soldiers. In preparation for writing about his experiences, he'd returned to Germany in 1954 and interviewed the German commandant at the bridge, the residents, and some old soldiers still living in the town.[56] He wanted to be certain the book not only was historically accurate but also told both sides of the story. Although many veterans disagreed with his political position, they were very excited about the book. Hechler believes it became the cornerstone of his reputation in Huntington. He sent free copies to people around the state and got rave reviews. The newspapers covered it—and him—broadly.

Upon his return to Huntington, Hechler first tried to persuade Marshall's president, Stewart Smith, to let him set up a program on campus to encourage more people to become active in community service. He was requesting foundation support, but according to Hechler, President Smith perceptively smelled a rat. He realized this was something to build up Hechler's political capital rather than an intellectual or academic activity. He turned Hechler down. Without a job, Hechler began casting around for other opportunities. He first considered opening a bookstore, but the initial investment proved too daunting. He then approached one of the local television stations suggesting a local version of *Point/Counterpoint* featuring the Democratic and Republican points of view on public affairs. WHTN, the ABC affiliate, found the idea worth pursuing.

With its innocuous name, his show, *Comment*, aired in the fall of 1957 on Sunday afternoons and featured Hechler—who earned $13.40 for each segment[57]—on the Democratic side and the professor he briefly replaced, Carl Leiden, on the Republican side. The partnership didn't last, however, for Hechler wanted the show to be newsworthy, and Leiden wanted to keep it on a very academic plane. Leiden eventually resigned, and Hechler replaced him with a local Republican lawyer, Richard Tyson.[58] That matchup worked much better. Hechler recalls the two of them getting together to decide which points they would agree on and which points would make them appear to attack each other's jugular vein.[59] While they seemed to be bitter enemies, they actually became good friends. Tyson recalls an evening when the two were meeting at his home to prepare for their upcoming show. Tyson left the room to go to the bathroom and returned to find Hechler standing on his head with his feet against the wall to the delight of Tyson's young daughter.[60]

At the same time, demand for Hechler as a public speaker was growing. Having someone who had been part of President Truman's staff in the community made quite a stir. His book and his experiences as a war historian also made him a popular guest at both local and regional Rotary and Kiwanis meetings. He often used the occasions to ingratiate himself to the community and into the minds of future voters. He recalls, "If we had a small group of less than twenty-five, when everybody else was eating I would be asking the chairman to put out the names of each of the people in the audience and what they did for a living. During my speech I would use a technique that Robert Byrd was always very good at. [I would] interrupt the speech by saying, 'Now isn't that right, Jim,' pointing to one of the members of the audience."[61]

According to those who heard it, a speech he gave to Marshall's Young Democrats on January 10, 1958, was the first indication that the course of his life was about to change. Despite the fact that he's always encouraged the story that his student supporters goaded him into running for Congress in 1958, he admits it's an exaggeration: "I'd pretty well made that decision myself, although I never would have if my students had been opposed to it, because they were really the core of my support."[62] Nevertheless, several audience members recall the exchange with the students that followed. Bobby Nelson, who would serve as Hechler's administrative assistant for ten years, was majoring in journalism at the time. His assignment that day was to cover the meeting because Hechler was the speaker.

Nelson, a young ex-Marine who admits he knew nothing about politics back then, says that while Hechler's speech was quite interesting, his manner of dealing with the students was extremely engaging and inspiring. "His personality came across because he made it like a conversation, not a speech," Nelson says. "He was talking not about his career, but that one of the great things anyone in life can do is to give public service, to give back to their country or their community." At this point, the story goes that one of the students challenged Hechler, essentially saying that if he thought this was so important, why didn't he run for office? Nelson says,

"Ken responded, 'I just might do that.' Then he said, 'and if I do, I'll ask all of you to volunteer and be in the campaign.'"[63]

Nelson was excited to think he'd just heard a bit of news in the making. He approached Hechler afterward and asked if he was serious. Hechler demurred but replied that the students inspired him. Then he told Nelson, "I'll tell you what, if I decide to run for Congress, and that is what I'd run for . . . I will give you a scoop. I'll let you know first and you can get the scoop. You can scoop the [Charleston, WV,] *Gazette*, and the *Washington Post*."[64] Nelson says he thought no more of it until a few weeks later, when Hechler called the journalism department and asked Nelson to come to his office. When he arrived, Hechler handed him the press release announcing his bid for Congress from the 4th Congressional District. The release said the campaign would be run solely by volunteers and characterized it as one for "the young at heart." Excited at his treasure, Nelson ran back to the journalism department to share the news with his professor, Mrs. Virginia Lee. She took one look at the release and told him to put it in the trash, saying, "We don't do political stuff. You are here to learn to be a journalist and we're not going to get involved."[65] The student newspaper, the *Parthenon*, had missed its chance at history.

7

ROGUE CAMPAIGN

When Hechler finally decided to jump into the political fray, the Democratic "state-house machine," which had dominated state government since 1940,[1] dictated party politics in West Virginia. It decided whom to anoint for office, whom to support, and whom should be ignored. Those so anointed would cozy up to the members of the executive committee, visit the courthouses, and get put on the ticket. Furthermore, as a Democrat, if organized labor didn't support your candidacy, you were defeated before you even began. Hechler did none of this; therefore, he had the support of neither the party nor labor. To win, he would have to do things differently—and he did.

While the popular incumbent, Republican Dr. Will Neal, was expected to defend his post in the 4th Congressional District, the former Democratic nominee for the seat, Maurice "Bernie" Burnside, had decided not to run, leaving the field wide open. He'd held the seat from January 3, 1955, to January 3, 1957, but Neal had defeated him in the 1956 election and served the next two years. Burnside had then found himself in a bit of political trouble for using non-union workers when he built a tobacco warehouse and thus was moving out of state. Hechler saw his chance and took the plunge, announcing his candidacy on March 28, 1958—five months after the Soviets launched Sputnik II, which carried a little dog, Laika.

Undeterred by the existing political system, the renegade Hechler announced:

I hope to give this congressional district the leadership it deserves in the great industrial development of the Ohio River Valley on which rests our future progress. And I'll raise my voice on behalf of the laborer, the small business-man, and the small farmers who are suffering from the recession. Schools and roads are state and local questions, but in the absence of leadership on these issues I plan to speak out on what West Virginia can do to revitalize our educational system and our highways. And I'll have a lot to say about taxes, state and federal.

Yes, this is going to be an exciting campaign. It's a campaign for the young in spirit. Right now I'm definitely the underdog. But having cut my political eyeteeth with a great fighter, Harry Truman, in the 1948 campaign, I love an uphill fight. I'm going to put on a clean, hard campaign in every city, town, village, and out on the farms up and down this district and I won't quit until the people have won the fight. To all the other candidates, I say, "Come on in, the water's fine."[2]

With this declaration, Hechler not only outlined his unique campaigning style but also declared his unwavering commitment to serving the people of West Virginia, rather than kowtowing to the established political machine. It marked his entire political life. He never ran a negative campaign, never took part in the election shenanigans that had marked politics-as-usual in the state, and never changed his position on an issue to please the party regulars.

Hechler loved a good debate, and he meant what he said about hoping others would run—and they did. Well-respected Hunting-ton attorney Tom Harvey filed, as did two Parkersburg native sons: attorney William Jacobs and magistrate Dorr Casto. Harvey was the son of a Huntington scion, William "Coin" Harvey, so named for his support of William Jennings Bryan's desire to use cheaper silver instead of gold as backing for United States currency. With political clout in the district's two largest cities, all three had more statewide credentials than did Hechler. But Hechler had Washington experience, and he intended to capitalize on it. Even if in his announcement he had fudged a bit about which campaign he had "cut his political eyeteeth with Truman" on—he didn't work for him until 1950—he had been on Truman's staff, and he felt that would carry substantial weight.

Hechler filed first. On a drizzly spring afternoon, at a student rally he'd organized near Marshall's campus, he invited those gathered to accompany him to the secretary of state's office in Charleston. Helen Holt, who had recently been appointed to the office by Republican governor Cecil Underwood, recalled April 29, 1958, vividly: "All of a sudden one afternoon in came to my office a marching band. Then pretty soon a group of singers came and they were singing a song to Ken Hechler."[3] It was a parody of "Sugar in the Morning" called "Hechler in the Morning," which Hechler had composed and printed on his invitations.[4] He'd even gone to the trouble to have the words copyrighted.[5] "He was filing to run for Congress," Holt says. "I was sort of new and I wondered if that was the way they did it every time."[6]

Although the Democratic Executive Committee had used Hechler to lead a weekend seminar earlier that year at the Daniel Boone Hotel in Charleston to teach state precinct leaders how to train poll workers,[7] it now dismissed his candidacy as a joke. When Dorr Casto died in a June drowning accident, the Democratic Party bosses threw their support to the two attorneys: Harvey and Jacobs. Either man, they probably reasoned, would have a better chance than newcomer Hechler.

Hechler didn't waste a day, however, according to Bobby Nelson, who was now actively supporting him.[8] Nelson had

CANDIDATE HECHLER WITH GROUP OF MARSHALL COLLEGE SUPPORTERS THAT AIDED IN CAMPAIGN

Ken Hechler campaigning for Congress in 1958 with Marshall's Young Democrat Club, Bobby Nelson at far right (Photo by the *Huntington Advertiser*)

willingly signed on to help Hechler's campaign, as had dozens of other students. Hechler had also recruited a quartet of Marshall coeds, billed as the Quartertones, that he'd heard sing. Two of the members, Sandra and Alison Roush, were from Mason County, where Hechler would be looking for votes. The quartet became his live commercial, accompanying him on campaign stops to sing parodies he had written to promote his candidacy.

Each day he revved up the Chevy convertible, which he later traded for a red Jeep; threw several boxes of his book, *The Bridge at Remagen*, in the back; and took off across the ten counties that made up the district, with Nelson riding shotgun. Nelson remembers one day especially:

He [Hechler] wanted to go to Ravenswood. Jackson County was in the district at that time, and Kaiser Aluminum was a big plant there. It went over to the river and had a couple thousand employees and a lot of them were veterans. He got there and got out these books—boxes of books. Every person that came out or went in, whether it was management or employee, he gave them a copy of his book. If they wanted him to autograph it, he autographed it right on the spot.[9]

When Hechler's editor at Ballantine Books learned he was running for Congress, he published a campaign edition of *The Bridge at Remagen*, with Hechler's platform included. Hechler bought thirteen thousand copies for ten cents each and gave them out at industrial plants throughout the district. He believes that won him the rank-and-file vote.[10] The workers, many of whom were veterans, had never experienced such personal campaigning. In return, they broke with their union bosses and voted for Hechler.

Since Hechler had heard Tom Harvey's wife boast that if her husband could get all those who had historically voted in previous elections to vote for Tom, he would win hands down, Hechler concentrated on the nonhistorical voters. "I began to recruit all the garbage workers, truck drivers, and people who were unhistoric voters to tell them how important their influence could be if they would support me.[11] Mrs. Harvey also mentioned that they weren't going to pay attention to the smaller counties. This made me sure that these small counties were given first class attention. That's where the expression arose that 'I had shaken every hand and milked every cow.'"[12]

Nelson says the man never stopped. Campaigning from early morning until late at night, they'd visit small towns and rural farms in the district. "If there was someone walking along the highway, he would stop, get out, shake hands, give them a book

Ken Hechler catches a train engineer during his 1958 campaign (Courtesy Ken Hechler)

or talk to them. I remember once there was a dairy farmer out in the field with his cows. Ken goes way out in the field and talks to this guy. There'd be a train going up the railroad and he'd hop on the car and go in and talk to the conductor."[13] Nelson shakes his head incredulously at the memory.

Hechler inspired students and friends to work for his campaign in the same way. Each student volunteer was given a copy of his platform, his background information, and instructions on how to campaign. He knew from campaigning with Harry Truman that he had a better chance of getting a person to vote for him if he talked to him one on one. He even stressed this in his instructions to his volunteers.[14] Hechler left no stone unturned in his search for those nonhistorical voters. His former neighbor, Ann Dexter, held neighborhood coffees, talked with her neighbors, and distributed his campaign materials.[15] He attended dinners, civic club picnics, teas, and any place he could talk to potential voters and distribute his card.

At night, he wrote letters home to solicit support from those he'd known as a young man. One, to his parents, didn't elicit the response he wanted, however. In answer to Hechler's request to announce his candidacy in the Roslyn newspapers, his father wrote, "Both your mother and I say 'thumbs down' on *Roslyn News* publicity at this stage, or any petitions. Always remember you have been away from here for nearly twenty-five years."[16] Still, other support letters did arrive: one from his old friend Billy Letson; one from his old commander, S.L.A. Marshall, who offered to come campaign for him;[17] and one from Hubert Humphrey, which stressed the importance of Hechler's knowledge of Congress and its inner workings.[18]

But Humphrey's letter backfired, and may have been one of the first weapons used to try to discredit Hechler. Hechler used it to show his high-profile support, but that elicited refutations from his opponents, who claimed that Humphrey wrote it as a personal note and did not mean to be supporting Hechler over the other two Democratic candidates. They claimed that Humphrey had written to them as well, saying as much, and charged Hechler with playing dirty politics.[19]

He was also attacked for having previously registered as a Republican and called a "Trojan horse."[20] People had apparently learned that he had registered as a Republican on Long Island— though he had done so strictly to honor his mother's wishes. In response, he pointed out that he had never voted Republican. Furthermore, he said he'd changed his registration to Democrat when he went to work for Truman.[21] As these protests fell on deaf ears, he solicited support letters to help counter the claims, including one by Clark Clifford, who wrote, "If Ken's Democratic faith was good enough for FDR and Truman, I'm sure it's good enough for the Democrats of West Virginia."[22]

Shortly after filing, Hechler had received a letter from Mr. and Mrs. Homer Peyton, a Huntington couple, claiming that Hechler was not only a "carpetbagger" but unfit for the office because he'd never actually worked for FDR or Truman. In his response, Hechler wrote, "I didn't have a choice where I was born, nor into what kind of political family I would be born. But I did choose after I grew up to become a Democrat by conviction and a West Virginian by choice and conviction."[23]

Nonetheless, the charges continued. Hechler never attacked his opponents, whom he preferred to call "competitors." Instead, with the August 5 primary looming, he took out a full-page ad in the *Parkersburg News* on July 20, 1958, to refute the charges. It included a personalized picture of him with President Truman on the campaign trail, along with letters from Truman, Clark Clifford, the Democratic National Executive Committee, David Lloyd (Truman's former administrative assistant), and Brigadier General Marshall attesting to his loyalty to the Democratic Party and extolling his service during World War II. It also included evidence Hechler had recently acquired proving that his grandfather had fought in the Civil War for the Union with the Ohio Volunteer Infantry and had shed blood in West Virginia. He hoped this would put all the accusations to rest and end the mudslinging as well.[24]

In his short ten-second television commercials; in his letters to leading Democrats, fellow teachers, and Marshall students;[25] and in his personal appearances throughout the four-month campaign, Hechler stressed that he was a Roosevelt-Truman Democrat, that he'd be the people's representative, that his door would always be open to them, and that they'd get action no matter the issue. He instructed his teams of volunteers to stress the same things and to promote both his opposition to reducing income taxes for the rich and to lowering corporate taxes, and his intention to work and vote for lowering the Social Security eligibility age, raising minimum wages, and increasing the unemployment compensation benefit period. He summed it up in the words of Thomas Jefferson: "Equal rights for all; special privileges for none."[26]

On the day before the primary, he made a speech on the radio in which he said, "I have traveled over 14,000 miles, worn out three pairs of shoes, and had the wonderful opportunity to make thousands of friends throughout this great area. . . . If you send me to Congress, you can be sure that my door will always be open and you won't have to sit around and wait or go through a lot of red tape to see me. . . . You can write to me, telephone me, and you'll get action. . . . Every cent of my campaign fund came out of my own pocket from money I earned myself—so nobody can put his feet on my desk and tell me what to do, except you the people of the 4th Congressional District."[27]

The following day told the tale. Despite all the obstacles and predictions that he and Harvey would split the vote so Jacobs would win, Hechler came out on top. He needed only a plurality, but he won every county in the district except rural Lincoln County, which went for Harvey, and Wood, which went for native-son Jacobs. The following day, Hechler published a letter in the *Huntington Advertiser* thanking the voters.[28] According to Hechler, he also went to Lincoln County with a big "Thank You Voters" sign, which drew the laughter of the local politicians. "One of the machine leaders told me that Harvey and Jacobs had argued until three in the morning the night before the election as to who was going to put up the most money for the machine," Hechler recalls. "Harvey finally won the argument by agreeing to put up $2,500. They said to me, 'We did not invite you to this bargaining meeting because we knew darn well that you were not going to contribute a red cent.' "[29] Hechler spent only $4,981.52 on his entire campaign and received no contributions.[30]

In the end, it was the rank-and-file voters who gave Hechler his victory, as Bobby Nelson says. "When he first filed for Congress, he probably knew fifty or sixty people outside the campus. By the time the primary came around, he probably knew more than 95 percent of the people who lived in the 4th Congressional District. And he made it a point to learn about the district, know the people, know the issues, and he went everywhere."[31] That personal connection—a favorite Truman tactic—worked wonders.

His win was such a surprise that Sam Mallison, a former West Virginian who had been active in Republican politics for twenty years, wrote to Hechler praising his public relations work. He said, "In my opinion, you rate so far ahead of the Madison Avenue boys that any comparison would be ridiculous."[32] Hechler's former student Michael Perry says that the campaign taught him a valuable lesson, in that "Hechler took a negative—that he wasn't born here—and quickly turned it into a positive by saying he'd *chosen* to live here; that he'd picked us to represent."[33]

Now he had to hope his campaign tactics would carry him to victory in the general election on November 2. With only three months to combat his Republican opponent, incumbent Dr. Will Neal, Hechler hit the ground running the very next day. Dr. Neal, ironically the man who had given Hechler the names of Huntington's movers and shakers when he'd first come to town, was a highly respected physician in Huntington, who had been delivering area babies for over fifty years. One of his campaign slogans ran, "I delivered you when you were born; now you deliver for me at the polls."[34] Hechler knew he had an uphill battle ahead. First, the 4th Congressional District had traditionally been a GOP stronghold in the Democratic state; second, Neal was a popular incumbent; and finally, labor hadn't supported Hechler in the primary.

Once he was the candidate, however, labor reluctantly swung behind him. Support from the WV Labor Federation came via a letter, but only after Hechler had answered a lengthy questionnaire and was interviewed by the federation's president, Miles Stanley.[35] The other labor organizations followed suit. To further dampen Hechler's natural enthusiasm, the party regulars barely endorsed him. Indeed, they didn't quite know what to make of his victory, according to Nelson. "They accepted him, but they didn't embrace him as much because they said, 'Well, he's going to be mincemeat for Neal,' "[36] he recalls.

Neal, however, who wasn't much of a public speaker, wasn't the real threat. His spokesperson, Mrs. E. Wyatt Payne, was. She, as Neal's mouthpiece, began harping on the carpetbagger moniker again. At a Republican rally on October 10, 1958, where Vice President Nixon was the keynote speaker,[37] Payne distributed mimeographed copies of a song she'd parodied to the tune of "Ruben, Ruben" and invited the audience to sing:

Hechler, Hechler
We've been thinking
What a fine state this would be
If all the New York office seekers
Came to save us
Just like thee.

Each verse contained another slam at Hechler, but many Republicans who knew of Hechler's popularity at Marshall were skeptical that he could be as bad as she was depicting him. Without retaliating, Hechler began using some unexpected praise another conservative speaker had thrown him. On April 8, 1957, a conservative coalition, including Mrs. Payne, had invited Raymond Moley to speak at Marshall while Hechler was teaching there.[38] Moley, a conservative who had originally been a member of FDR's brain trust but had broken with him in 1936, was answering questions after his speech when Hechler stood to address him with one of his own. Hechler had previously known Moley well and had replaced him as a Barnard professor. Hechler recalls that before he responded, "Moley said, 'That young man that just asked me the question is one of the best teachers in the business.' He went on to praise my teaching at Barnard to the horror of Mrs. Payne who had invited him to show the other side of politics."

Although Mrs. Payne constantly nettled Hechler, his relationship with his opponent was better termed a friendship. At one campaign tour in Roane County, the two were in the same convertible during the Black Walnut Festival Parade. Hechler noticed that the congressman was ignoring a large crowd that was waving and cheering wildly from a nearby hill. As Hechler waved back, he asked Dr. Neal why he wasn't waving. Neal responded, "You can have all their votes. That's the insane asylum."[39] The friendship didn't include getting into a debate, however. Hechler proposed one, but Neal refused. "His advisors told him that that was the wrong thing to do because it would show up the difference in our ages. I was forty-four and he was in his eighties and it would be so obvious that I was the younger, more vigorous candidate no matter what we would talk about," Hechler recalls.[40] Much later in Hechler's career, forgetting this advice would come back to haunt him when he participated in a joint campaign appearance with a much younger Betty Ireland, his Republican opponent in 2004.[41]

Hechler again wrote letters—lots of them: to Marshall students, factory workers, and Democratic Party leaders. In one, he tells the Cabell County Democratic Executive Committee he plans to work for and with them, and says he'll welcome reminders if he doesn't appear to be acting as a "team player."[42] While there's no indication he got either overwhelming support or outright rejection from Democratic superstars, at least one turned down Hechler's request to campaign together. In response to a letter to then congressman Robert C. Byrd, he got this terse reply: "My experience has convinced me that two persons can see more people and cover more ground in a shorter time by traveling separately than by going together."[43] Byrd had rebuffed Hechler's overtures before, claiming a scheduling conflict or that he was unable to make it, but now, the answer was clearly no. Perhaps he felt he had nothing to gain by teaming up with a candidate everyone thought would lose.

Even his Republican mother joined the letter-writing campaign. Hechler persuaded her to write to fellow Republicans in the district. She sent a handwritten letter, which looked like an original when reproduced. It said, "I have never asked anyone to vote for a Democrat and I don't intend to, but let me tell you about my son and his interest in education." Hechler says, "It went on to a very soft sell and the very last line was, 'I repeat, I am not asking you to vote for him, I'm simply asking you to be fair and to listen to him.' I had so many Republicans who came up to me after the election saying I disagree with every damn thing you stand for, but when I got that touching letter from your mother I just had to vote for you. With the young people it was, 'my parents didn't want to vote for you but I insisted that they do it.' "[44]

Hechler fought tirelessly for every vote. He continued his relentless pace, meeting people in every county, giving speeches, studying, and discussing the issues. He took strong stands on national issues: lowering the Social Security eligibility age to sixty, extending unemployment benefits, working for a medical care plan for retired people that would be linked to Social Security, extending minimum wage laws, and fighting the Nixon proposal to cut income taxes for the very rich. Clearly, he was casting himself in the Roosevelt-Truman mold. He also spoke out against right-to-work provisions, inflation, and the GOP attitudes on senior citizens. But he often stated publicly that his main concern, if elected, would be serving the people of the 4th Congressional District.[45]

In his research, Hechler gathered material showing that Congressman Neal had voted against a $10 million increase of the Veterans Administration's funding to support hospital administration and housing services, and had voted to cut $186,000 from the VA's Reemployment Rights fund housed in the Labor Department's budget.[46] In true Hechler fashion, he never used this information in attack ads or remarks against Neal. He also instructed his volunteer staff to never mention Neal's age. As a Marshall professor, he had asked why his students had such a negative attitude toward participating in elections. When they said that there was so much mudslinging that it turned them off, he proposed that a campaign could be successful without resorting to that. He was holding fast to the belief that a candidate should simply state his or her positions and let the voters decide.[47] It's the way he conducted every campaign throughout his career.

At one point, a postcard survey taken to determine potential voter turnout for the looming election showed that if the Democrats could get out 62 percent of the vote and they remained party loyal, the GOP couldn't possibly win. Moreover, even if there were an even turnout of voters in both parties, the Democrats would win because they had the higher registration. But if the GOP turned out 75 percent and the Democrats got only 65 percent, the win would be harder to assure.[48] With this knowledge, it's no wonder Hechler went after the nonhistorical voters. They could swing the election his way.

When it began to look as if Hechler might have a fighting chance at the seat, the Democratic National Committee sent in some nationally known speakers to support the campaign. President Truman arrived in Charleston on Hechler's forty-fourth birthday, September 20, 1958. Although he had originally planned to continue on to Huntington, rain and fog had caused his plane to circle for two hours, wearing out the seventy-four-year-old man. Hechler was in Charleston to meet him and could see that he was exhausted. Truman admitted that he just couldn't make the drive, but his speech at the Charleston airport quickly dispelled the rumors that Hechler had been merely a mail sorter in the basement of one of the federal buildings. Unfortunately, the large crowd that had gathered in Huntington to hear the former president was sorely disappointed, as was Hechler. Later, Tennessee senator Al Gore Sr. came in and made several speeches, as did Texas senator Ralph Yarborough, whom Hechler paraded downtown, asking shoppers if they'd like to meet a real live U.S. senator. A number of congressmen came as well, and according to Hechler, all these appearances helped swing votes his way.[49]

With Hechler's camp making waves, the Republicans dropped a bombshell on Hechler in the closing days of the campaign. On October 31—three days before the election—a story broke in the *Point Pleasant Register* accusing Hechler of putting his book in public assistance food packages in Putnam County and then asking for a fifty-cent donation.[50] The truth was that a friend of Hechler's, Homer Harrison, who was the chief distributor for surplus commodities, had been putting a copy of *The Bridge at Remagen*, which he had purchased, in each bag distributed in the town of Hurricane. Hechler knew nothing of this, and says he would have objected if he had.

The Republicans decided they could gain traction with this revelation. Republican governor Cecil Underwood immediately called a press conference and denounced Hechler's alleged actions as "the most despicable act of political chicanery that a person, like the candidate for Congress, should try to play on the fact that poor people would be forced to pay fifty-cents for a copy of the book. I don't think this candidate is worthy of citizenship. He hasn't been in West Virginia very long."

Naturally, the press wanted a rebuttal from Hechler, but all they got was this quote: "Governor Underwood is a fine gentleman, but he has some nasty speech writers who have put those terrible words into his mouth, and they do not really represent what Governor Underwood thinks of me." At this point, Hechler produced a photograph he had received when he presented the governor with one of the first copies of *The Bridge at Remagen*, which he had signed. The press had covered the ceremony because Hechler had taken with him a veteran of Remagen. Governor Underwood had inscribed his personal photograph, "To Dr. Ken Hechler, who is providing intellectual leadership in West Virginia." Underwood's remarks and the whole incident blew back on the Republicans and gained even more support for Hechler.[51]

November 2 dawned cool and foggy. Hechler made the rounds of the polling places, hoping to get a feel for how the election would swing. He'd worked from "can to can't," as the old-timers say, and he was tired but excited. As the early returns began to come in, it looked as if he would lose. But when the smaller communities began to report in, he managed to forge ahead. When all the votes were counted, the Republicans were in shock. Hechler had won by 3,503 votes and carried five counties, including the two most populous: Cabell and Wood. He also carried Putnam, Wayne, and rural Lincoln County,[52] where he'd earlier refused to put money into the party kitty. As one GOP wag said later, "Our trouble was we didn't take this guy, Hechler, seriously enough, soon enough."[53]

Hechler says he didn't get much sleep that night. Aside from staying up late to monitor the returns, he got up at five the next morning to go to the International Nickel Plant in Huntington to thank the voters for having helped him.[54] Congratulatory letters poured in from his Washington colleagues and bosses. Adlai Stevenson wrote, "If all congressmen were as worthy and intelligent as you we would not have any difficulty in getting our affairs in order."[55] David Lloyd, fellow Truman White House staffer, commented that Hechler was "a political wizard of the first rank; I have never heard of anything like it. We are all standing around here in Washington in awe and admiration."[56] Even President Truman said, "Your victory was one of the finest in the country and one that made me as happy as any that took place."[57]

In retrospect, Hechler had no choice but to mount a renegade campaign. First, that kind of person-to-person campaigning was all he knew. Second, it was the only way he could have gained attention. As many people said, "Everyone was against him but the people." Nelson believes Hechler had just introduced a new way of campaigning, at least in West Virginia. "He overcame so many obstacles that were thrown in his path, simply because he came across as a very caring, considerate, committed public servant."[58] Furthermore, the young people believed in him. Hechler knew they'd be future voters, even if they couldn't vote for him this time. He also firmly believed it was critical to get the youth energized about politics and public service. In this, he foreshadowed John F. Kennedy's inauguration plea to "ask what you can do for your country" two years later.

It had taken more than twenty-five years, but the prediction of Hechler's beloved professor, Dr. Robert Brooks, had finally come true. The Honorable Ken Hechler was headed to Washington.

8

YOUR SERVANT IN CONGRESS

Shortly before the 86th Congress convened in January 1959, *Washington Post* society columnist Dorothy McCardle assessed the eligible bachelors among the incoming congressional class for their ability to enhance the upcoming social season. Headlining them was Ken Hechler, about whom the columnist wrote the following:

> Democratic bachelors incoming here include forty-four year-old Kenneth Hechler of Huntington, West Virginia, who has been here before as a speechwriter for Presidents Roosevelt and Truman. During those years, he neatly sidestepped the attentions of most Washington hostesses, concentrat[ing] upon a love game on local tennis courts rather than upon the social scene. Born in Roslyn, New York, and with a Ph.D. from Columbia University, he would add brains to any dinner table chit-chat here.[1]

But once again Hechler would disappoint district hostesses and datable women alike. He had no intention of spending his evenings making idle dinner-table chatter. The task-oriented man undoubtedly saw such gatherings as a frivolous waste of his time. Actually, as Judy Roach Deegans, who ran his Huntington office from 1971 to 1977, says, "He had very, very poor social skills. He didn't know how to chit chat and make small talk, and do the social circuit."[2] By his own admission, he had never learned those skills as a young man, and it seemed he had no desire to do so now. Besides, any romancing Hechler did was conducted strictly behind the scenes.[3]

Hechler's excitement that January stemmed from his impending opportunity to influence government. At last he was in his element. He felt a spine-tingling thrill as he climbed the Capitol steps on his way to the January 7 group swearing-in ceremony. Though he'd been in the halls of Congress many times, that day marked the culmination of a long-held dream. "I felt I'd come to the end of a long trail and I still could not believe that I had made it there,"[4] he says. As he entered the House chamber, its august trappings must have awed him: the gigantic American flag behind the Speaker's seat; the bronze fasces on either side of the dais, symbolizing the strength of the republic; the oversized paintings of Washington and Lafayette; and the massive eagle skylight in the ceiling, positioned as if spreading its wings protectively over that governing body. As he drew his eyes from these icons, he looked up to the gallery on his right and spotted his mentor, former president Harry Truman, seated in the presidential box. Truman leaned over the rail and waved at Hechler. Hechler smiled, returned the greeting, and then took his seat along with his fellow Democrats.[5]

Once he was sworn in, the freshman representative began organizing his office, located in the basement of the Cannon House Office Building. He had lured Virginia Skeen, a former Ripley, West Virginia, bank teller, to be his receptionist. His early letterhead lists Skeen, Nancy Book, and Bobby Nelson, "plus any volunteer help we can get,"[6] as his assistants. By governmental regulation, Hechler's staff was initially quite small, as was his spartan office. But for him, its advantage was that, located near the exit facing D Street, it was only a two- or three-minute walk to his second-floor apartment in a rooming house on the same street.[7] Hechler's pack-rat tendencies surfaced quickly, so it didn't take long for the few rooms in the office suite to look like the aftermath of a cyclone. According to the descriptions of those who worked for him, this look followed Hechler to each of his offices, regardless of their size or increasingly prestigious location.

Ned Helme, who worked as Hechler's legislative director in his Washington office from 1972 to 1975, recalls that when reporters began writing articles about the messy office, it infuriated Hechler. "He got very mad so he changed his office," Helme says. Hechler put a row of bookcases in the sitting room of his congressional suite to separate it into two spaces. He moved his desk behind this row of bookcases, which the staff called Hechler's "inner sanctum." Soon, it was just as messy as the main room had previously been, according to Helme. "The papers were like six or eight feet high. I'd go and say, 'Congressman can you give me a copy of this or this?' I'd sort of watch around the corner of the bookcase. He'd go in there and he'd carefully reach down two feet and pull out [what I'd requested.]" Helme says that Hechler had no filing system, but he knew where everything was. He allowed no one, particularly reporters, to go into the inner sanctum. "The space to get between the end of the bookcase and back to his desk was like eighteen inches," Helme says. "He was thin and he would squeeze by them and go back to his office. If he didn't want to meet with somebody, they wouldn't know he was there because he's back behind the pile. Once, he tore his pants on the bookcase. It was a plaid suit and he got it sewed back together but, of course, they did such a bad job the pattern didn't match." He wore it anyway.[8]

One of the first projects Hechler undertook grew out of a free trip to Washington for some of his supporters to thank them for putting him in office. The idea engendered a program that soon became an invaluable educational tool for West Virginia students. Called the Week in Washington program, it was partially modeled on the Congressional Fellowship Program he'd created while working for the American Political Science Association. Hechler funded the trip for many of the early groups, but later solicited financial support from various corporations or foundations.[9] While the APSA program had brought young political scientists and journalists to work as interns on congressional staffs to give them practical experience for future jobs, the Week in Washington program was more of an observational experience for high schoolers. To participate, high school juniors had to enter a competitive program in which they wrote an essay on why they'd like to work in their congressperson's office. Judged by an independent group from the League of Women Voters, the winners got to see the workings of the federal government.[10] Runners-up were awarded a day in Washington at the end of the summer. Hechler recalls, "I always encouraged those students when they got back to school to talk about their experiences."[11] Of course, by so doing, he knew he would gain future voters—and perhaps even campaigners as well.

In 1960, Hechler chose his new chief of staff, Bobby Nelson, to run the program. Each year Hechler would hire a couple from his district to bring the group on the bus to Washington for a week in June and to chaperone them while they were there. Interestingly, according to Judy Deegans, he did not pay for the chaperones' meals while they were there. He reasoned they would have had to eat anyway.[12] One week, six or seven boys would come, and the following week, the same number of girls.

Before their arrival, Nelson would have arranged their transportation and housing, and scheduled their meetings with dignitaries. With Hechler's knack for making contacts, getting people like John Glenn, the Speaker of the House, the majority leader of the Senate, and others to meet with them was relatively easy. When Hechler was serving on the space committee, he took them to hear a demonstration of the astronauts talking from space.[13] "The students arrived on Saturday, and the first thing we'd do on Sunday

Ken Hechler's Week in Washington students listen to President Kennedy, 1963 (White House photo, Courtesy Bob Withers)

was take them to Washington National Cathedral. They'd go to church there and [they'd see] the Blenko glass all throughout the cathedral," Nelson recalls. "On Sunday nights we'd go to the Tidal Basin near the Lincoln Memorial for the big concert." The schedule always included a lunch in the Senate dining room and a stop at Andrews Air Force Base when President Kennedy would be returning there from Hyannis Port.[14] Thanks to Hechler's connections, the students were allowed to go out on the tarmac, where they could see Kennedy and wave to him. Sometimes the president would come over and say hello to the students.

Hechler used these occasions to teach them how to get an interview with the president. "I said, 'If you get within thirty feet of the President of the United States, join arms, face the president and yell, "Mr. President," and he will always come over and talk with you.' Every Monday morning he would land at Andrews Air Force Base and walk one hundred yards to the helicopter, and we would always intercept him halfway. He was always very gracious because West Virginia had given him the victory."[15] According to Nelson, one week a schedule change caught Kennedy off guard. "Alan Shepherd, I believe, was going to be down at [a] NASA [event] and so on an early Monday morning we took the students over there to try and see these astronauts instead of going out to the airport. After we did that we came back to the office to go to a committee hearing and Dr. Hechler was there. He said, 'Where you guys been?' I said, 'Well, we went down to NASA.' He said, 'President Kennedy called; he didn't see you all at the airport.'"[16]

Over the eighteen years of Hechler's tenure in Congress, hundreds of students participated in the Week in Washington program, and he rarely forgot a single one. One was Pulitzer Prize–winning journalist Julia Keller. Another, Raamie Barker, who later became senior advisor to West Virginia's 35th governor, Earl Ray Tomblin, says, "I've never met anybody that [Hechler] took under his wing for just a short period of time, or even a long period of time, that wasn't profoundly affected by his philosophy, his example, and his experiences. He's like [Sir] Thomas More; he's a man for all seasons."[17] Throughout Hechler's career, teaching was a high priority, and this program was just one more effort—like taking his Columbia students to meet former president Herbert Hoover—to teach young people the importance of becoming involved in the political system.

Hechler's district offices had the same disheveled look as his office in Washington, despite the impression they might give his constituents. Of the Huntington office, located on the second floor of the Federal Office Building, Deegans says that when she went to work there, she had a space of about twelve square inches in which to work. "Any flat space was occupied with stuff piled up," she says. It took her years to make enough headway to clear off the desk and file the papers that had accumulated there. A second office within the Huntington complex served as Hechler's inner sanctum when he was in town. Large and well furnished, with leather couches and an elegant desk, it, too, was piled with papers, books, articles, and magazines.

It was here where he would hide if someone he didn't want to see was looking for him. Deegans says they had a telephone line between the two offices with which she could signal the all clear when the person had given up on seeing the congressman. Usually, she says, they were young ladies he had met. "He would go maybe to Mingo County, or Logan County, or wherever, and be in a meeting and some young lady would strike his fancy, and he would part with her on the note of, 'Well, if you're ever in Huntington, stop by and see me.' Sometimes, the next day they were in Huntington and they would come in and identify themselves and say they would like to speak with the congressman. If he were at his apartment, I could call to warn him, and he could come and go into that other office and nobody would ever know. Sometimes, however, they would almost wait him out."[18]

Hechler found these follow-up social visits unnecessary. But he was adamant about dealing well with those who truly needed his services. Letters had to be acknowledged the day they arrived, even if it was just to say the congressman was working on the request. According to Deegans, there was no office manual, but the staff knew what he wanted. One of the things he insisted on, something he had no doubt learned from Truman, was to write letters the way people talk. That meant no stilted language and no five-dollar words. Research was his bailiwick, and he did it himself until the workload required that he add assistants to help. Nelson says the staff had no office hours; they simply toiled "until the work was done, and the work was never done."[19] Hechler came back to West Virginia nearly every weekend. His constituents were his primary focus, and everyone in the office knew it.

Hechler even held office hours on his weekends home, albeit unconventional ones. He recalls it vividly. "I would get a dozen folding chairs and I'd stop near city hall, or the post office, or some central point in town and I'd set up a small table and put these folding chairs out," he says. "I had a big sign that said, 'Ken Hechler, Open Air Office Hours.'"

While it was a great gimmick that drew attention to Hechler, he says it was also a good way to shorten conversations. "Ordinarily, if a person wanted to visit me in the office, they would take an extraordinarily long time to talk at great length on a lot of different subjects; but outdoors if a person was taking a good deal of time, there'd be a lot of clearing of throats [from others waiting to see Hechler,] and that caused the visitor to shorten the conversation. Additionally, people would drive by and honk and wave without even stopping and they'd spread the news that Ken Hechler was out with his open-air office hours." Another of his gimmicks was to announce that on a certain day, he rather than his secretary would be answering the phone and handling everything.[20] Of course, this made him even more popular with his constituents, who saw him as being deeply concerned about their personal problems.

Unlike many congresspeople, Hechler focused on specific issues, usually ones that would have importance for West Virginia or his own district. In this, he was upholding his campaign pledge to be an ombudsman for the people of his district. Of course, he didn't hesitate to submit press releases stating his stand on national issues, such as the Vietnam War, civil rights, and Nixon's impeachment; but for the most part, his legislative work concentrated on environmental issues, coal mine safety, strip mining, and personal

Ken Hechler conducts outside office hours (Courtesy Ken Hechler)

issues brought to him by his constituents.[21] In his first year alone, he introduced twenty bills, several of which dealt with coal mine safety, increasing benefits under the Railroad Retirement Act, giving more money for food commodities, and establishing a basic fuels policy for the entire country. One, however, would have given eighteen-year-olds the right to vote. Happily, Hechler saw his idea come to fruition when the 26th Amendment passed in 1971,[22] while he was still in Congress.

According to Nelson, Hechler soon gained a reputation for being a dogged and determined fighter for any information that would help a constituent. If an agency stalled or responded with the usual, "So and so is in a meeting," Hechler would march to the office and sit there waiting until he got what he wanted. Staffers soon learned to give it to him as soon as he asked.[23] Senator Robert Dole, who became Hechler's close friend, says, "Hechler reminded me of a windmill. He was everywhere. He was always in the front row, the back row, always buttonholing somebody, and always talking about something for West Virginia or his constituents."[24] In at least one instance, he drove a long-awaited Social Security check back home to Logan and personally delivered it to the family that had been waiting for it.[25] Senator George McGovern echoed that same sentiment many years after Hechler had left Congress: "I can't think of anybody in public life who has so systematically committed himself to be of service to people. I think it's on his mind all the time: 'What can I do to be more useful to these people in West Virginia?'"[26]

Hechler's reputation with his constituents bears out Senator McGovern's sense of him. In talking with dozens of people who met Hechler, asked for his help, or encountered him in the halls of the Capitol, the response was the same. No visitor left without a grand tour of the building, with Hechler leading the way at a rapid clip, giving a detailed history, and greeting everyone he met by first name, including the elevator operators and janitors.[27] If the visitor was a Huntingtonian, he loved to go to the Speaker of the House's desk and ask the visitor to look under it. There he'd placed a Marshall College sticker when he'd first joined Congress.[28] Once, he even held a visitor's baby so she could visit the House gallery and watch Congress in session. And this is a man who likely had no experience with babies.[29] Each constituent felt as if Hechler were working personally on his or her issue. And each had a story to tell—like the young economics graduate student who went to Washington seeking funds for his dissertation research: "I stopped by Congressman Hechler's office to see if he could be of assistance, although I didn't know him or have any connections to him. Not only did he agree to see me, after sitting down in his office with me, he decided he would personally take me to the agency with which I was dealing. He opened doors that might otherwise have remained closed."[30] Or the veteran on assignment in the jungles of Vietnam: "I was Airborne Infantry. We'd been there four or five months in the jungle and no one knew where we were. My mom passed away, but they couldn't locate me to tell me. My aunt contacted Ken Hechler and he put pressure on the army. They found me and notified me. If he hadn't done that, I would have missed the funeral."[31] And the West Virginia sailor who discovered that the mess hall at the naval station in Charleston, South Carolina, was missing one flag—that of his home state. "A call to my distinguished congressman, Ken Hechler, remedied that problem very quickly," he says. "I seem to recall that approximately two weeks later a box arrived at my duty station. In it were two large West Virginia flags, one for the 'mess' and one for me, along with three desk sets with the United States and West Virginia flags attached, and a note that no West Virginian should ever be so far away from home that they didn't have a flag to fly to remember our home."[32]

One other constituent's story is legendary. A Huntington woman went to the main post office and mailed a request to Hechler's office, which was in the same building, for a cookbook Hechler was distributing. A postal worker who was sorting the mail saw her letter, processed it, and simply took it to Hechler's office rather than putting it out for delivery. Hechler arrived a bit later, got the letter, and personally delivered the cookbook to the woman only minutes after she had arrived home.[33]

He also never forgot to read into the *Congressional Record* remarks or kudos to honor his district constituents. In the case of West Virginia native Colonel Charles E. "Chuck" Yeager, he lobbied to have a special medal struck and awarded to the aviator. He worked diligently from 1973 until December 23, 1975, when the bill was passed, to obtain this unique honor for the man who broke the sound barrier on October 14, 1967. In letters asking his colleagues to join him in sponsoring their own private bills for the cause, he noted, "A young Air Force Captain, Chuck Yeager, squeezed himself into a tiny Bell-X1 test plane and achieved a great and historic first in aviation."[34] Ultimately the bill passed, and Hechler then asked President Ford to present it to Yeager at the National Air and Space Museum,[35] but Ford chose the White House as the location instead.[36]

Hechler felt as much pride in his well-earned reputation of being "your servant in Congress" as he did in his nearly 100 percent voting attendance record, which he also unabashedly trumpeted during his subsequent campaigns.

During his eighteen-year congressional career, he missed only forty-two of 4,942 roll call votes. Through 1972, his record was perfect.[37] He recalls the first vote he missed. "I was very interested in the Watergate trials. One evening, I remember right after dinner, they announced that they were going to have a review of the hearings that day. I was living in an apartment close to the

Speaker of the House Carl Albert congratulates Ken Hechler on his 2,500th vote (Courtesy Ken Hechler)

Capitol, but it didn't have direct contact with the Capitol. There was no phone service back and forth, so when I went home to watch those hearings late in the evening, they had a vote; and that's when I missed."[38] There was no telephone service only because Hechler didn't install one. In his words, he didn't because he was "just a cheapskate."[39] If Hechler was needed in Congress, a staffer would have to go knock on his apartment door to summon him, but on this night, all the staff had gone home.

Hechler's reputation as a cheapskate was legendary. Even later in life, when it was suggested that he bought his clothes at Goodwill, staffers replied, "No, he's had those clothes since the Truman administration."[40] More politely, Deegans said he wanted to be known for running a thrifty office, not spending the taxpayers' money unnecessarily.[41] Even if Hechler did receive some campaign donations, he refused to actively solicit campaign funding for any of his nine congressional races, preferring to use his own savings instead. Throughout each of those races, he kept up the grueling door-to-door style of campaigning that had marked his first race. His trademark red Jeep would be seen everywhere, and he won by increasingly large margins.

9

CONGRESSIONAL CAMPAIGNING, HECHLER STYLE

Since congressional terms are only two years, campaigning is an ongoing task for most officeholders. With Hechler it was no different, except that he had no political organization whatsoever. But since little often distinguishes one campaign from another—except perhaps for the opposition—I've combined all Hechler's congressional reelection battles here to demonstrate the strength of his support and the unique style of campaigning he introduced. To begin, he tapped Bobby Nelson to manage his first reelection campaign, which coincided with the 1960 presidential campaign and John F. Kennedy's historic West Virginia victory. But Hechler did not organize "get-out-the-vote" efforts, didn't hold political rallies, didn't waste money on gimmicky handouts, and used only volunteers to help his reelection efforts. He figured that if the public knew him and his reputation after his first term and wanted to vote for him, they would.[1] And he made sure they knew him by continuing the door-to-door, farm-to-farm, factory-to-factory campaigning he'd done in his little red Jeep in 1958.

He also wasn't above what some referred to as corny campaigning, as it attracted attention—and that's exactly what he wanted. He continued to write parodies and to enlist coeds to join him on the campaign trail to sing them. Often their songs became part of his radio or television advertising. One story is legendary, although the date of the race to which it is tied has been lost to memory. Two anchors at WSAZ-TV, the leading television station in the state, tell it best. In his book of political anecdotes, Bob Brunner says the incident occurred in 1968.[2] News anchor Bos Johnson doesn't recall the year but says that like most politicians, Hechler had a video statement ready to use if he won reelection. He'd sent it to all the stations, but when WSAZ got it, they didn't view it ahead of time. During a commercial break, the Associated Press declared Hechler the winner, as was expected. Bos remembers telling the control room, " 'When we come back, let me intro the Ken Hechler victory tape.' They told me it was ready, and I said, 'We have this victory statement from Congressman Ken Hechler.' "[3] The tape rolled, showing a set reflecting what some art director thought an 1800s western church should look like, and a whole string of Hechler's staff, with their arms linked, danced into view, singing, "Thank you for voting for Ken Hechler" to the tune of "Get Me to the Church on Time." Then Hechler danced into view and sang, "Thank you for voting for meeee." According to Bos, the entire newsroom collapsed into laughter. When the camera returned to him, all he could say was, "I can't believe I ran the whole thing."[4]

Hechler's relationship with the press wasn't always so pleasant, however. Just before the 1970 primary, in which he was running for reelection, Hechler dropped into the *Charleston Gazette* pressroom unannounced, as he was prone to do. Apparently he'd brought something he wanted them to run. Possibly because of his interruption, he was cussed at and treated badly. Hechler complained in a letter to publisher Ned Chilton that only one man, Harry Hoffman, spoke nicely to him. "I want to thank you for the courteous treatment I received in your office on Friday," he began sarcastically before launching into his complaint. It wasn't their first clash. In March, Chilton had sent Hechler a letter, stating, "If we printed every telegram you send to the president, we'd never get out a daily paper. Honestly, fella, you've got to allow our news editors the right to decide what is and isn't news."[5]

In his first reelection campaign, his primary opponent, Nye King, was a Huntington attorney who had just opened a new office. After Hechler attended a reception there, which drew mostly a handful of local lawyers, he concluded that King was running merely to promote his new practice.[6] For his GOP spot on the general election ballot, coal executive Clyde Pinson had defeated Hechler's old nemesis, Mrs. E. Wyatt Payne, in their primary. Even though Hechler called on Pinson, whose nickname was "Froggy," to join him in signing the state's Code of Fair Campaign Practices, Pinson refused. Hechler's slogan, "One good term . . . deserves another," was then fodder for Pinson's jibes. He accused Hechler of having done nothing during his first term in Congress and of being obsessed with reelection. Although Hechler refused to run a negative campaign vilifying his opponent in public, he wrote to Pinson refuting each of the points he had made.[7] In case his charges didn't have the desired effect, Pinson also distributed fuchsia-colored flyers depicting an old-fashioned carpetbag and headlined "Carpetbagger Go Home."[8] Of course, Pinson never admitted the flyers were his handiwork. When Hechler defeated him by 9,845 votes,[9] Pinson blamed his loss on an Eisenhower veto of a bill to help the depressed areas of the state.[10] Actually, John F. Kennedy's presidential sweep of the state would probably have doomed *any* GOP hopeful in 1960.

After the 1960 census figures were compiled, West Virginians saw in black and white that the state's population loss had cost them a congressional seat. Subsequently, political controversy ensued over how to redraw the state's six districts into five. In his analysis of the eventual legislative decision on the matter, Department of Defense systems analyst Victor Heyman observed that since the state legislature was dominated by Democrats, a Democratic governor, and a congressional delegation weighted five to one Democratic, the obvious redistricting by the party in power would mean that Republican Arch Moore Jr. would be subjected to what political scientists called the "elimination gerrymander" and lose his seat.[11] The question then became how Democrats could get rid of Moore, and who could defeat him after they readjusted the district lines. One potential realignment of counties would have pitted Moore against Hechler—a battle some would have relished—but that option was rejected. Furthermore, eliminating elder congressman Cleveland Benedict's district was deemed unseemly due to his age and seniority in Congress. Ultimately, it was John Slack whose 6th district was divided. Hechler's new oddly shaped 4th Congressional District stretched along the Ohio border and gained four counties, along with the possibility of even larger margins of victory based on the number of Democratic voters in it.[12]

This set Hechler up for another battle with Republican Clyde Pinson in 1962, but not before he found himself in political hot water on several fronts. On September 7, 1961, he wrote to former governor Cecil Underwood, who had lost a senatorial race to incumbent Jennings Randolph in 1960, urging him to run for Congress in 1962. Hechler suggested that the popular Republican would be a strong opponent to battle. As a *Washington Post* editorial pointed out, this was a clever campaign tactic. It would have forced Underwood, if inclined, to declare his candidacy; if he was not willing to run, Hechler could accuse the GOP of fielding less-than-stellar candidates.[13]

Two weeks later, one of his primary opponents, Daniel Dahill from Logan, wrote to Hechler, chastising him for the letter to Underwood and suggesting that perhaps he was still a closet Republican. Apparently before writing to Hechler, he had also released the story to the Logan papers, because Hechler replied to Dahill that he'd received phone calls on the matter before Dahill's letter had even arrived. Nevertheless, Hechler responded without animosity, welcomed Dahill to the race, and added a humorous note: "What a funny world this is! I write a letter to Governor Underwood. He doesn't answer, but you write instead. Now if you would just write a letter to Mrs. E. Wyatt Payne, then maybe I would hear from Governor Underwood."[14]

The second political dustup of that campaign wasn't as benign. In fact, it became a firestorm that left a bitter taste in Hechler's mouth long after the election was over. One of Hechler's former employees, George McClung, decided to oppose Hechler in the primary contest. McClung had been a student of Hechler's at Marshall College in 1957, and Hechler had hired him in 1959 to work in his congressional office. After working there for three years, McClung had left Hechler's employ in January 1962 for a higher-paying job with the Air Force, which Hechler had helped him secure. After he left, Hechler had spoken with McClung, who gave no indication he was disgruntled with either Hechler or his current position. Yet less than a month later, on February 3, McClung quit his job and filed against Hechler for the newly expanded 4th Congressional District seat. He then leveled allegations regarding how Hechler had operated his congressional office. In a March 25, 1962, letter to Attorney General Robert Kennedy,[15] McClung charged that Hechler had demanded kickbacks or salary set-asides from his employees, had put employees of his own business—a series of coin-operated laundries—on his congressional payroll, and, instead of tending to his congressional duties, had spent governmental time writing a book from which he would profit personally.[16]

Although McClung had sworn to run a clean campaign in the manner of his former employer, he hadn't hesitated to distribute, at least in Sistersville, West Virginia, what a friend termed a "rat sheet" listing these charges against Hechler.[17] This came as a shock to Hechler, because McClung had earlier refused to use some materials potentially damaging to Hechler that had been offered to him by Clyde Pinson.[18] However, Hechler says, "Unknown to me he was very ambitious. After he left the staff, I remember one evening—I always did a lot of work in the evenings—I came back to my office and he was in my office looking through the files."[19]

To bolster his charges, McClung took and passed a polygraph test and then distributed and released the examiner's report to the press and to the AFL-CIO, presumably in the vain hope that the union would transfer its financial support from Hechler to him.[20] Not only did Hechler publicly refute the charges point by point, but a Justice Department investigation into McClung's allegations turned up no evidence of any violation of federal criminal statutes. The matter seemed to lose steam after a *Charleston Gazette* editorial opined that the Justice Department's report should put an end to it, and cleverly noted that McClung had not levied his charges until he filed for the office himself.[21] While the matter did die down in political circles, Hechler resented his former employee's betrayal, and spoke of it only reluctantly in his latter years. "His aim was to get so many voters to believe that I was a corrupt congressman and then they would turn to him and he would get nominated instead of me," Hechler said.[22]

Primary election day came and went. The following morning, McClung found himself on the losing end. Hechler had won with 37,832 votes and had beaten both his rivals handily. Dahill had garnered 10,335, while McClung had nabbed only 2,085 votes with his destructive campaign.[23] The victory was bittersweet, however. On the same day the results were announced, Hechler learned that his father had died. Charles Hechler Sr. had been suffering from circulatory issues, which finally took his life at age eighty. Hechler, who felt some comfort in knowing his father had known of the victory,[24] traveled back to Roslyn, New York, for his father's funeral on Friday, May 11, and then returned to the campaign trail.[25] The fall election resulted in a similar outcome to that of the primary. Again, Hechler had defeated Pinson, this time by nearly thirteen thousand votes.

While Hechler ran unopposed in the 1964 primary, the fall general election wasn't without a few hiccups. His GOP opponent, Jack Miller of Parkersburg, had also dashed toward the fall election without a fight, but he seemed to want one with Hechler before November 3. Hechler's Parkersburg office manager, George Lantz, got wind of a local radio announcer praising Miller without announcing that the message was a paid political one.[26] He alerted Hechler, and the ads stopped. Then, a Huntington GOP spokesman named Robert Fletcher erroneously reported that Hechler had voted against university status for Marshall College. This riled Hechler, who produced the *Congressional Record* of June 3, 1959, in which he had urged the legislature to make the change. Fletcher's charges brought a rapid response in the form of a rare extra edition from the now university newspaper, the *Parthenon*, stating that Hechler had consistently supported university status for the college, which had given him his political liftoff.[27]

Early in the 1964 race, *Charleston Gazette* political columnist Thomas Stafford alleged that Hechler was "worried" because his 4th Congressional District was considered a swing district that had often voted Republican. He claimed Hechler was worried about his GOP opponent, Jack Miller, whom Stafford called young, vigorous, and articulate.[28] It was as though Stafford was rooting for Miller. Next, Stafford claimed in his column that Hechler had made his fellow representatives "hopping mad" for a remark he supposedly made when stating why he was opposed to congressional pay raises. Stafford claimed Hechler said that many of his colleagues didn't earn their current $22,500 salaries. Hechler was livid and responded that the column had totally misrepresented his views. He further said that while his colleagues weren't angry before, they were furious after reading the column. His actual reason for opposing the bill was that it would have set congressional salaries above the ceiling imposed on salaries in the executive branch, which he thought should be raised simultaneously.[29]

Not long after Hechler put those charges to bed, Miller began campaigning in earnest. He sent Hechler a telegram on October 13, challenging him to a televised debate a week later, using the format followed in the Kennedy-Nixon debates. Hechler refused, thereby giving Miller fuel for blasting him. Conversely, Hechler stated that his congressional votes were a matter of public record and that the public knew where he stood on any issue.[30] Instead of debating, he traveled the state in his iconic red Jeep, speaking at schools, political gatherings, and civic dinners. It worked. When the results were published, Hechler had won by a 40,034-vote margin. He was also elected as a delegate at large to the 1964 Democratic National Convention,[31] where he intended to support Hubert Humphrey.

This victory signaled a sea change in West Virginia politics. On November 10, 1964, an article appeared in the *Huntington Advertiser* stating that Hechler's overwhelming victory signaled a "political revolution in the 4th District. For the past half century the 4th District had been basically the Ohio River group of counties that extend from south of Huntington to a point about fifty miles north of Parkersburg." In twenty-one congressional elections from 1916 through 1956, the GOP had won twelve times, while the Democrats had won only nine times. And only three times had the winner's majority exceeded ten thousand. Hechler carried Cabell County by only 373 votes the first time he ran in 1958, by

2,765 the second time, by 7,204 the third time, and by a record 11,701 in the 1964 election. Similar margins were recorded in Wood County, where his opponent lived. There, Hechler registered the largest majority scored by any candidate in history, Republican or Democrat. The same could be seen in Jackson, Wayne, and Putnam Counties. Hechler gave credit to President Johnson, saying his coattails were long and helped all the Democratic candidates, but agreed that "the silent revolution which has taken place in the 4th District appears to be a very deep-rooted one."[32]

In 1966, Hechler once again attracted some primary opposition. One was his old challenger, Bill Jacobs from Parkersburg, whom Hechler had defeated in his initial 1958 campaign. Again, Hechler, who had become the fourth-ranking member of the thirty-man congressional Science and Astronautics Committee,[33] defeated Jacobs as well as W. G. "Woody" Jefferson—a small loan company owner and insurance agent from Huntington. Even with a low voter turnout—only 37 percent—Hechler received about 69 percent of the vote, winning 37,236 to Jefferson's 13,936 and Jacobs's 2,496.[34] In the general election, he trumped Harry D. "Pinkie" Humphreys, a Huntington pharmacist, by more than 23,000 votes, prompting Hechler's mother to write an open thank-you letter to voters for being so kind to her son.[35]

Hechler's political star continued to rise with the 1968 election. Again, he had no primary opposition and garnered 44,089 votes. On the GOP roster, country-and-western singer Ralph Shannon—nicknamed "the Wayne County Whippoorwill"—bested Hechler's previous opponent, Pinkie Humphreys. When the general election came around, Hechler made light of Shannon's nickname, pointing out that whippoorwills are known for singing in the dark and fleeing in the light of day.[36] Again, Hechler carried the election, beating Shannon with a 41,871-vote margin and earning more than half the votes cast.[37] His win also set a record for the most consecutive terms a Democrat had been elected from the 4th Congressional District.[38]

The upcoming 1968 presidential election enticed Hechler to run again for an at-large delegate's seat at the Democratic National Convention in Chicago, scheduled for August. To assure himself a seat, he campaigned on the statewide slogan, "Throughout West Virginia You Can Vote for Ken Hechler." Again, his volunteers were Marshall University students, some of whom were required to take an active part in the upcoming election by their political science professor, Dr. J. Melvin Miller, who borrowed that teaching method from Hechler.[39] Dozens volunteered to work for Hechler, canvassing likely voters in their hometowns—especially those outside of Hechler's district.[40] The tactic worked, and Hechler went to the convention uncommitted. While he admitted that he was impressed with Eugene McCarthy,[41] his heart was with the old warrior, Hubert Humphrey, whom he'd actually favored over Kennedy in 1960.[42]

In June 1970, President Richard Nixon signed an extension to the Voting Rights Act of 1965, which required lowering the voting age to eighteen. While the movement still required a constitutional amendment to be ratified, the youth had won a great victory. By July 1, 1971, eighteen-year-olds were full voting citizens.[43] This was a boon to Ken Hechler, who had always appealed to young people and used them extensively as campaign volunteers. Adding to his popularity, the movie *The Bridge at Remagen*, based on Hechler's book, had premiered in Huntington the previous summer, serving to remind voters of his earlier accomplishments and endearing him to veterans.

In spite of Hechler's growing opposition among coal companies, the United Mine Workers, business users of third-class mail (which Hechler had been battling), and groups upset with his liberal and anti–Vietnam War votes,[44] both elections were nearly

Ken Hechler signs the sidewalk in front of Huntington's Keith Albee Theater for *The Bridge at Remagen* movie premier (Photo by Lee Bernard, Huntington Publishing Company)

formalities. Hechler beat his primary opponent, James R. Burton, 32,033 to 7,778, and again beat Ralph Shannon in the general election 62,531 to 30,255.[45] Hechler's press release boasted: "It was the highest popular vote and largest majority among the West Virginia representatives. His victory statement was also the shortest: 'I'm speechless.'"[46] Hubert Humphrey sent his personal congratulations.[47]

That election cycle wasn't without controversy, but it wasn't to be found in Hechler's campaign. His old chief of staff, Bobby Nelson, was running for a seat in the West Virginia Senate, and Hechler was supporting him, albeit quietly. Nelson's opposition was nationally famous golfer and insurance executive William C. "Billy" Campbell. Since Campbell had been a longtime friend of Hechler's, the match put Hechler in a bit of a pickle. In the past, he'd written nice things about Campbell and had entered them into the *Congressional Record* to mark his golfing accomplishments. But Nelson had been Hechler's right-hand man in the early days of Hechler's congressional career. Hechler even credited him with his first win. Yet Nelson says he never saw Hechler attending any of his rallies.[48]

However, just because he didn't support Nelson visibly didn't mean he wasn't operating behind the scenes. When Hechler learned that a radio ad supporting Campbell was using a voice that sounded like his own, Hechler demanded its removal. Campbell offered to substitute another voice, but Hechler was adamant. The ad had used Hechler's *Congressional Record* remarks about Campbell, thus giving the further impression that Hechler supported him. After he protested to the Fair Campaign Practices Committee by telegram, Campbell accused Hechler of submitting contribution reports before the deadline to hide late contributions to his own congressional campaign. In the same personal and confidential letter, he also said that Hechler was submitting post-election reports four days late to make them look better than they actually were. Hechler shot back, "It was interesting that you do not take kindly to the idea of having your integrity questioned and then proceed to question the integrity of others."[49]

Interestingly, Hechler thought Campbell would beat Nelson, since Nelson was running against a man Hechler called a "legend." He had even prepared a concession speech for his old staffer. "I thought it was a hopeless race, but Bobby simply outclassed him on the things it takes to win an election," Hechler recalls.[50]

By 1972, West Virginia had been redistricted once more. Another congressional seat had been lost due to the continuing decline of the state's population. And once again, the legislature went after Hechler. It was the entrenched politicos' way of trying to eliminate Hechler, who was a firm opponent of the Democratic Party machine. His 4th Congressional District was merged with James Kee's 5th district, which put 65 percent of Kee's district into Hechler's territory and forced a primary face-off between the two. Hechler admits he always loved a challenge, perhaps because he felt his lopsided victories had become too easy. Nevertheless, despite the new challenge the redistricting presented, Hechler launched into not one but two races.

Although advised against it, Hechler also filed for Randolph's senatorial seat, as he told Randolph, "primarily to assist in bringing out issues of concern both to you and to all the people of West Virginia." Even the *Charleston Gazette*, which sometimes took issue with Hechler, editorialized that Hechler could best serve by ending the Kee dynasty.[51] He assured Randolph, however, that he would not campaign outside his district, and that he would concentrate his efforts on the congressional race to retain his 4th district seat.[52] He did ask the senator to debate ten issues, but Randolph demurred, saying that there were many other important issues and that Hechler's format wouldn't allow for discussion on all of them.[53] By March 10, Hechler had officially withdrawn from the Senate race.[54]

This sort of maverick move drove the politicians crazy. As Bobby Nelson had said more than once, "The politicians always hated Ken, but the people loved him."[55] An editorial in the *Beckley Post Herald* suggested that the problem was that Hechler usually voted his conscience and favored the people. "This makes it uncomfortable for the other West Virginia congressmen, who go down the line with their own special interests. . . . Hechler's performance shames them and they are naturally not too fond of him. So they brought their influence to bear in the gerrymandering that put Hechler against Kee in a district that was largely Kee's in the past."[56] One other name appeared on the primary ballot: Dr. Hawley Wells. According to a *Bluefield Daily Telegraph* editorial, he had been encouraged to run by the same political leaders who were itching to be rid of Hechler.

However, the better-known Kee—a Bluefield man who had succeeded his mother, Elizabeth Kee, in the 5th Congressional District when she decided to leave her seat in 1964—was also known as an absentee representative, a fact lampooned by political cartoonist Jim Dent in the *Charleston Gazette*. It showed a man standing in front of Representative Kee's desk holding a newspaper with the headline "Kee absent on 42% of House votes." Kee's cartoon rejoinder was, "A fella works hard, he's entitled to a few days off now an' then."[57]

Furthermore, Kee had stirred the ire of environmentalists by testifying as a member of the House Interior Committee that he favored strip mining because "it let the sun shine in the forests." Naturally, the League of Conservation Voters applauded Hechler as the first Appalachian member of Congress who ever dared to lead a crusade against that destructive practice.[58] His other opponent, Dr. Wells, ran afoul of the tax department shortly before the primary, when the West Virginia Tax Department charged him with not paying his income taxes.[59]

Meanwhile, Hechler, who was well known for his athletic prowess, challenged Kee to a "Decathlon Duel" because Kee had pointed out the three-year difference in their ages. Hechler suggested they engage in ten events ranging from a twenty-minute one-on-one basketball game to a twenty-five-mile walk. He also challenged Kee to a series of six televised debates,[60] but no response from Kee to either is recorded.

Hechler's victory was resounding. He received 42,397 votes; Kee managed 14,831, and Wells ran a bit shorter with 12,182. Hechler then went on to win the general election by 61 percent against Republican insurance broker Joe Neal, son of his first congressional opponent, Dr. Will Neal. In a year when the Republicans gained twelve seats in the House as part of Richard Nixon's landslide victory, Hechler's win attested to his overwhelming popularity with the voters.

By 1974, Hechler was beginning to cast around for a change. The political climate surrounding Washington had soured him. Watching the object of his long-held enmity, Richard Nixon, play fast and loose with the law nearly made him lose all hope in politics. Personal jibes had also taken their toll. In his December 1973 *Newsletter*, the headline screamed: GOODBYE FOR AWHILE. He went on to say,

Whatever the future holds, this will be my last *Newsletter* for an extended period. I'm not a very good politician because to be successful as a politician you need the hide of a rhinoceros. . . . A thin skin is a handicap when it worries you about cynical and distorted attempts to taint, tear down, and destroy a great educational program like the "Week in Washington."

I'd really like to go back to teaching and writing, where
I can get away from the cesspool of corruption, cynicism
and compromise, which has infected the nation's capital.
There is only one sustaining argument which deters me
from carrying through on my overwhelming desire to
change jobs: I can already hear the jeers and cheers from
certain sources which would greet such a move a mite bit
too triumphantly. It's almost enough to give you a tough
skin overnight!! Your servant in Congress, Ken Hechler.[61]

He further outlined his determination to leave Washington
in an undated press release, stating, "There is a poisonous atmosphere in Washington which has pervaded all phases of public
life. I hope by returning to West Virginia to breathe the fresh air
of truth, justice, and confidence."[62]

His announcement caused waves of protest from ordinary
citizens, as well as from state and local officials. Even though
Hechler wanted out, these pleas found fertile ground; he recon-
sidered and announced on January 11, 1974, that he would again
defend his seat.[63] Again, the mail deluge was overwhelming, and
now was congratulatory. One man even asked Hechler to help
fire Nixon.

Once Hechler announced, he realized that all political hopefuls, Democrat and Republican alike, had given up fighting to
unseat him. He ran unopposed in both the primary and the general election and received 66,420 votes in the general election,
according to a proclamation from then governor Arch Moore.[64]
Perhaps Hechler felt it was a hollow victory, since he later confessed, "Yes, I did get restless, because in '74 I had no opposition
at all in either the primary or the general election. I got very bored.
I love campaigns and I wanted to debate the issues, and nobody
would argue with me."[65]

Perhaps it was this feeling of boredom that led Hechler to make what was arguably the biggest political mistake in his life. When it came time to file for reelection, Hechler again placed his name in two slots: his 4th Congressional District seat and that of governor. Although it now seems an unnecessary afterthought, he then sent a questionnaire around to friends asking their opinion on his action. An overwhelming number said they thought it was a bad move but believed he'd drop out of the governor's race.[66] Instead, he did the opposite. Two days later, on March 12, 1976, he issued a statement that began, "I have asked the secretary of state to include my name on the primary ballot for only one office—Governor of West Virginia."[67]

Although he had put out a few feelers on the matter, the announcement came as a shock to most of his friends—and all his supporters. According to Nelson, that was typical of Hechler. He liked surprises, and never hinted at what he was planning to do; he just did it. In fact, he didn't even tell Nelson, who was his close friend. By the time he learned Hechler was in the race, Nelson had already committed to support Hechler's opponent, the labor candidate Jim Sprouse. Furthermore, as Hechler's protégé, he would have had a good shot at winning Hechler's congressional seat himself.[68] But Hechler made the decision alone and apparently never felt it necessary to give Nelson that chance.

Hechler's announcement soured his relationship with at least one supportive member of the press as well. Stratton Douthat was a Huntington correspondent for the Associated Press, who had done numerous features and positive stories about Hechler and his fights for labor and the average person. When he learned that Hechler was considering the governor's race, he called often, asking if he'd made a decision; but Hechler kept demurring on his decision. The day before the filing deadline, Douthat made one last call, asking Hechler point blank about his decision and receiving the same answer. Within minutes, Douthat called the Charleston AP desk only to learn that Hechler had made the announcement twenty minutes earlier from his Washington office. From then on, he wrote fewer stories about Hechler.[69]

In true Hechler form, he had made the public announcement from a guard hut on the grounds of the governor's mansion,[70] declaring that he would not live there if elected and would sell all the limousines, traveling in his ubiquitous red Jeep instead. It would be the end of the imperial governorship.[71]

According to those who helped run the campaign, Hechler chose to run for governor for several reasons. Deegans, acting as his campaign manager in Huntington, says he wanted to broaden the discussion to include the issues he was passionate about,[72] like strip mining, which neither Sprouse nor Rockefeller were discussing. Hechler's admission that he didn't care about winning bolsters this point. Second, he wanted to prove he could fight without spending all the money Rockefeller was spending. Yet some believed he thought Sprouse and Rockefeller would split the vote and he'd come up through the middle as the candidate for the people, as he had in the past.[73] Unfortunately, it didn't turn out that way. Hechler came in third, with less than half the votes of Sprouse, who was second, and only one-fourth of Rockefeller's 202,732 votes.[74]

Although Deegans was nominally his campaign chief, she says Hechler ran the campaign. He had no schedulers or advance people, and he rarely, if ever, sought advice.[75] Neither did he take polls. In hindsight, Hechler admits he should have listened to his friends and informal advisors. "I wanted to defeat a person who was buying the election. It was the stupidest political mistake I ever made . . . because it was very obvious from the beginning that his multimillions would drown out my little red Jeep against [his] Mercedes Benz."[76]

Next, he made the second worst mistake of his political life. As an independent, Hechler attempted a write-in vote for his old 4th Congressional District seat, which newcomer Nick Joe Rahall had won in a ten-person Democratic primary field when Hechler left the race. At the time, twenty-eight-year-old Rahall had never run for a political office except as a delegate to the Democratic National Convention. He had worked for Senator Byrd but had been planning to run for the West Virginia House of Delegates when Hechler withdrew from the congressional race. Rahall had seen his opportunity and jumped into the void. Now he faced GOP candidate Steve Goodman from Huntington, who had been the president of Marshall's student body and was the director of the Tri-State Transit Authority. Since both Rahall and Goodman were quite young and very inexperienced, the *Herald-Dispatch* endorsed Hechler's write-in campaign.[77]

Hechler's decision to attempt a write-in campaign wasn't without thought, however. On this, he met with labor leaders, sought advice regarding the legality of the move, and solicited opinions on what roadblocks the move might encounter. Regardless of indications that the hierarchy of the AFL-CIO would not support him as they had in the past, and with a clear understanding of how difficult the write-in vote might be, he jumped into the race.[78] To be legal, Hechler's name had to be spelled correctly and be preceded by an X. To assure this was done, he printed up stickers that could go over Rahall's name in counties where voting machines were used, and bought rubber stamps for use in those that still used paper ballots.[79]

In the long run, many saw his attempt to regain the seat he'd willingly abandoned as arrogant. Although staffers reported incidents of poll workers warning voters that the stickers might jam the machine or invalidate their entire ballot, it may have been this perception of being a poor loser that worked most against Hechler this time. He lost by more than fourteen thousand votes. Still, at the time, he got the most votes anyone running for Congress as a write-in candidate had ever received. That's no surprise, for despite his mistakes and some negative opinions regarding the race, he was still a very popular man. The people hadn't forgotten the hundreds, if not thousands, of personal requests he'd responded to over the past eighteen years. At that time, only 10 percent of the public could name their congressperson; in the 4th Congressional District, Hechler had 86 percent name recognition.[80] Despite his loss, Hechler was still a formidable political figure.

10

SPACE . . . WHERE HECHLER DIDN'T EXPECT TO GO

When Hechler campaigned in 1958 for his first term in Congress, he intended, and promised, to do great things for his constituents, his district, and his state. And eventually he *was* able to ensure black lung benefits for miners, to usher in legislation making the mines safer, and to have Congress declare part of the state off limits to industrial development, to name just a few of his accomplishments. He also worked diligently to prevent or stop strip mining, yet the bill that passed fell short of his expectations. But when given his first congressional assignment, he could see no connection to the things he hoped to accomplish, and he didn't hesitate to register his disappointment.

In a draft letter accepting his assignment to the Committee on Science and Astronautics Hechler wrote, "I am frank to say that I requested membership on the Committee on Banking and Currency, which handles distressed areas, housing, and other legislation of interest to my state." While he accepted "humbly and with constant need of the guiding hand of our Creator," he reiterated that he wanted to "serve notice, however, that my primary interest in Congress will be to further the passage of legislation which will restore prosperity in West Virginia and enable my state to move forward." Despite his reluctance to serve in this capacity, he did admit that being placed on that "space" committee defied his imagination.[1]

The prospect of space exploration had defied all our imaginations until the October 5, 1957, headlines across the country announced in extra bold type, "REDS LAUNCH 'MOON' INTO SPACE."[2] The Russians had named their instrument-filled satellite Sputnik I, and launched it on October 4. Newspaper sidebar stories flatly stated that with the Russians' first step into the cosmos, the United States had lost the space race. Less than a month later, on November 3, front pages again carried startling news: "DOG HURTLING THROUGH SPACE." Sputnik II had been launched with a mixed-breed dog named Laika aboard, causing some to dub the capsule "Muttnik." Some reporters predicted a launch to the moon within a week.[3] With this, America's fear of Russian domination escalated, and the Cold War moved to new heights—literally. No longer would it be enough to best the Soviet Union on earth; now the competition included mastery of outer space as well.

While President Eisenhower claimed the Russian's feat did not constitute a "race" and had come as "no surprise," others in government were not so sure.[4] As the *Washington Post* opined, "not since the fall and winter of 1950 has a single event so shaken the established thinking in both parties." The columnist was referring to the way reversals in the Korean War had shattered public confidence in Truman's administration. He suggested the same could happen to the Republicans, who were then in power, if they didn't respond to the implications of the Russian launches.[5] In *Toward the Endless Frontier*—Hechler's history of the space race, which he wrote after he left Congress in 1979—he echoed a feeling held by many: "How could those ignorant Bolshevik peasants surpass good old American technological know-how? How could they manage to orbit a 184-pound payload, and then follow with the smooth orbiting of a 1,120-pound payload? How did the Russian scientists and engineers overtake us? These questions were on the lips of congressmen, officials in charge of our missile and satellite programs, and other national leaders."[6] While public officials pondered these questions, the public wanted action.

According to Hechler, the House and Senate leadership were more in tune with the calls for action than was the executive branch.[7] The public outcry prompted Congress to create, almost overnight, a new committee to deal with issues that might arise from these two events. During the 85th Congress, House majority leader John McCormack proposed that the United States form the Science and Astronautics Committee to "establish plans for the peaceful exploration of outer space." The National Aeronautics and Space Act of 1958 passed unanimously.[8] On January 3, 1959, as Hechler was being sworn in, the House Committee on Science and Astronautics also came into being,[9] and he was placed on it. Suddenly the freshman congressman was at the forefront of an exciting new age. He recalled the feeling of the committee, as well as his own, as it met for the first time on January 19, 1959. "There was a sense of destiny, a tingle of realization that every member was embarking on a voyage of discovery, to learn about the unknown, to point powerful telescopes toward the cosmos, and unlock secrets of the universe, and to take part in a great experiment. To be a charter member of a new committee was exciting enough, but to take part in those deliberations, which held such a great promise for the benefit of all mankind, was a challenge, which stirred the blood of all the members."[10] For now, pressing concerns of his district would have to take a back seat.

It didn't take long for Hechler to assert himself on the committee. Like others in Congress, he was concerned that our international prestige had been damaged by the launch of the Russian satellites. The following year found him bluntly exhorting the president to take the space race more seriously. In remarks on the floor of the House on February 18, 1960, he cited instances over the past three years when Eisenhower had continued to deny we were in a space race and had downplayed the importance of the Russians' successful launches. He nearly begged President Eisenhower to show more leadership.[11]

While space was certainly not his area of expertise, he dug in and learned quickly. Fortunately, he says, they had scientific advisors as consultants.[12] Through meetings with those consultants, including Wernher von Braun, whom he admired despite his Nazi background,[13] he became knowledgeable about the issues at hand and was soon prodding NASA to think ahead, asking what it was going to do next. According to Bobby Nelson, Hechler quickly became a staunch supporter of the space program, but he always approached it from the position of what it could teach us.[14]

Because Hechler was a charter member of the new committee, he didn't have to work his way up the ladder to gain a leadership position. The seniority necessary to be a subcommittee chair simply arrived on a silver platter in his second term, he says.[15] As the chair of the subcommittee on Advanced Research and Technology (the name it was given in 1963),[16] Hechler now gained some influence over issues that he felt would make a difference to his state. True to form, Hechler immediately did things his way. When he discovered that a number of the Republican members of his subcommittee didn't bother to attend meetings they thought were not very important, he violated the rules and began asking them to preside over some of the hearings. While the Democrats didn't like that, the Republican members loved it. They didn't realize it was Hechler's way of ensuring they would study the issues in advance and thus become effective participants in the hearings.[17] He never bragged about this position of power, however; he knew it came about because he was in the right place at the right time, rather than in recognition of his abilities or seniority.

Before the hubbub over space exploration, the government had already recognized the importance of radio communication and observation and, in 1956, had founded the National Radio Astronomy Observatory in Green Bank, West Virginia. The Pocahontas County area was chosen because of its sheltered valley location and its distance from large population centers. It also sits, protected from radio interference, in the center of a 13,000-square-mile National Radio Quiet Zone, created by federal regulations in 1958.[18]

In 1962, his subcommittee gained oversight of this observatory, as well as several others. Throughout routine hearings in August and September, he touted the value of radio astronomy and its weather-predicting capabilities. To Deputy Assistant Secretary of State Richard Gardner, Hechler termed weather satellites "tremendous weapons of freedom [which could] fire the imagination of the people throughout the world." He also pushed for greater efforts to make the findings from the TIROS (Television Infrared Observation Satellite) program available to everyone.[19] These reports were NASA's first attempt to apply information from weather satellites to indicate appropriate actions for those in harm's way.[20]

The 1972 name change of Hechler's committee to the Subcommittee on Aeronautics and Space Technology reflected his insistence from the beginning that aeronautics was a field that deserved increased emphasis. He wanted it on the same footing as manned space flight. When he began agitating for that view in 1967, NASA's allocation for the field was only 10 percent of its total budget. Hechler pushed for an increase from $2 million to $20 million. While the move failed, he led the committee toward its commitment to increasing funding for research on aircraft noise abatement, hypersonic flight, and vertical and short takeoffs and landings.[21]

Despite the far-reaching impact these more mundane issues would have in the future, all eyes were on the space race. Once the Eisenhower administration's position that ventures such as Sputnik were like an "outer space basketball game"[22] had been rendered irrelevant by the election of President John Kennedy, things heated up. Even in his 1961 inaugural address, Kennedy had implored Congress to "seek to invoke the wonders of science instead of its terrors. Together let us explore the stars," he said.[23]

But as Hechler points out, the real work actually began five months later. By then, Russian cosmonaut Yuri Gagarin and American Alan Shepard had successfully returned from nonorbiting space missions. Hechler recalls NASA's apprehension about Shepard's flight. James Webb, the head of NASA, had two statements prepared: one if the mission were successful, and one if it failed.[24] Fortunately, he was able to deliver the word that Shepard had succeeded in his fifteen-minute flight.

Americans collectively cheered, and then waited to see what would come next. They wouldn't have long to wait. Hechler vividly recalled the challenge that galvanized the United States' next space goal. "The members of the Committee on Science and Astronautics were easy to spot, even though they were scattered throughout the crowded chamber of the House of Representatives early on the afternoon of May 25, 1961," he says. "They applauded long and loudly when President Kennedy suddenly announced to a joint session of Congress the bold commitment 'to achieving the goal, before this decade is out, of landing a man on the Moon and returning him safely to Earth.'"[25]

For those who watched the subsequent televised missions—John Glenn's 1961 flight on Mercury 6, Gus Grissom's second flight into space in 1965, Ed White's first walk in space a month later, and the landing on the moon of Surveyor 1 a year later—they seemed miraculous. Yet few realized the number of endless meetings necessary to keep the missions afloat. Hechler was not a member of the subcommittee directly responsible for the oversight of space exploration, yet he faithfully attended the broader committee meetings, witnessed nearly every space launch after that of Alan Shepard's,[26] and was intimately familiar with what was afoot. Six weeks after the first two suborbital achievements, Congress received an appropriations request of $1.37 billion to forward space exploration. It was $142 million more than Kennedy's budget had requested[27] and underscored just how serious the committee was to win the race.

However, the Apollo mission to land a man on the moon did not always have unanimous congressional support. In the meeting rooms and halls of Congress, hundreds of hearings, budgetary compromises, and scientific advisory meetings were conducted by the larger committee to ensure the space race still strove for the goal outlined by Kennedy. As part of that effort, Hechler and other members of the committee toured NASA's relatively new Marshall Space Flight Center in Huntsville, Alabama, several times to gather firsthand information about the upcoming missions.

Throughout Hechler's congressional career, his interest in the space committee focused more on the technological advances that could be adapted for use by other industries, and the challenge it provided to young people, than on exploration for exploration's sake. This isn't to say he wasn't vitally interested in actual space exploration, for he was, but he always saw the broader implications, according to then congressman Tom Harkin, who served on the committee with him. He says Hechler was "always prodding and pushing about what were the new frontiers." But his prodding wasn't mean spirited. "He always had a great way of eliciting a laugh from us on the committee," Harkin says. He holds dear the memory of Hechler sitting with his head in his hands, probing and leading a witness toward a point he wanted to make.

It usually brought a chuckle from Hechler when a witness finally made Hechler's point.[28]

On the other hand, in typical Ken Hechler style, if he didn't agree with something, he never hesitated to say so. When Gus Grissom, Ed White, and Roger Chaffee died on January 27, 1967, in the flash fire that swept through the Apollo 1 command module during a launch rehearsal, Hechler was quick to say he thought the tragedy was avoidable. "We asked . . . how could this possibly happen when so many safety-conscious engineers were laboring to achieve zero defects?" He said that the committee grilled the contractor who built the capsule and NASA officials alike, scrutinized every piece of evidence, and viewed carefully the charred capsule.

Although both NASA and the major contractor, North American Aviation, denied it existed, the committee obtained a copy of a report, commissioned by NASA, which was highly critical of management deficiencies by North American Aviation. As a result of the committee's work, major safety improvements were undertaken straightaway.[29]

When the Saturn V rocket roared skyward from the Kennedy Space Center on July 16, 1969, carrying the Apollo 11 command module, with astronauts Neil Armstrong, Buzz Aldrin, and Michael Collins aboard, Hechler and five thousand other distinguished guests watched from the VIP viewing site. He'd gone down the day before to attend a prelaunch ceremony. In a speech three days later he described his reaction: "It lifts slowly and agonizingly . . . off the pad [amid] spurts of flame and a great cloud of smoke . . . as it gains speed. Suddenly, across the beaches and the grass, the roar hits you! It tingles your viscera, and it runs up and down your backbone like a xylophone." While he was thrilled with the spectacle and the mission's success, he then questioned whether or not we might have been better off having spent the

Ken Hechler inspects capsule at the Kennedy Space Center while astronaut Frank Borman briefs members of the House of Representatives subcommittee on the space capsule fire, 1967 (NASA photo)

resources necessary for the moon launch to solving problems on earth.[30] It was a predictable comment from one whose eye was always on bettering the lives of his constituents and humanity in general.[31]

Any misgivings Hechler might have had about the value of the mission notwithstanding, as a member of the committee ultimately responsible for the entire space program, his name was included on a small silicon disc that was left on the surface of the moon, along with an American flag and a plaque inscribed, "Here men from the planet Earth first set foot upon the Moon July 1969 A.D. We came in peace for all mankind."[32]

Once Armstrong and company returned to earth with enough booty to keep the scientists busy for decades, each state was given one of the 270 moon rocks, while the others were distributed among 135 territories and foreign countries.[33] As a member of the committee, Hechler received some of the first to be distributed for display. One of his staff members, William Hutchinson, commonly called "Hutch," was instructed to pick them up and deliver them without letting them out of his sight or telling anyone he had them. "They were in this big locked box," Hutch recalled. "I was driving them back to West Virginia and stopped in this diner to eat. I was never supposed to let them out of my sight, so I set them on the table next to me. The box was so obvious that it was so important or something. . . . It has these locks and NASA insignia on it." When a couple asked what was inside, he told them. "I did what I wasn't supposed to do. I figured they belonged to the American people and people should get to see them, so I opened the box up and showed them to the waitress and a couple of people sitting there next to me. Then I just finished my lunch and put them back in my car and drove to West Virginia." Because Hutch knew it was the sort of thing Hechler would consider a firing offense, he didn't tell Hechler that story for over twenty years. By then, Hechler found it humorous.[34]

Once Kennedy's goal had been achieved, congressional support for more manned space exploration waned. Hechler characterized the 1970s as the worst of times for the space program. Debates over the shuttle programs held sway, with some arguing for continuation and others, including Hechler and ultimately Tom Harkin, questioning exactly what it would accomplish.[35] Hechler thought NASA was spending too much money on manned flight. He believed the agency should stick with unmanned missions instead.[36] This is not to say the committee lacked for issues to work on, but issues like converting to the metric system, investigating reports of unidentified flying objects (UFOs), fighting for funding of the National Science Foundation, or arguing about whether or not the federal government should have oversight of textbook material paled by comparison to the thrill of manned space exploration.

When the committee took up fossil fuels research, it was clearly more to Hechler's liking. The committee also had jurisdiction over nuclear research and was tasked with trying to determine an energy policy for the country. In a budgetary committee hearing after Apollo 11, he urged the House to adopt an amendment to increase by $3.9 million the space-related technology transfer from the NASA budget to improve methods of extracting coal in order to increase mine safety, and provide a more efficient way to combust coal. "If the space program is going to mean anything, it must consist of more than picking up rocks on the moon," he admonished. "The billions we have spent and are spending can, with a slight twist of the wrist, be effectively applied toward the solution of the energy problems which grip our nation."[37] He pointed to one program, which teamed NASA with the Bureau of Mines to research ways of adapting techniques and equipment that had been used in space to combat mine safety problems,[38] as the sort of thing that should be continued. Of course, Hechler fought the notion of replacing fossil fuels with nuclear energy, but upon reflection years later, he wondered if that had been a wise decision.[39]

In whatever setting Hechler found himself—committee hearing, social setting, or confronted by a crowd of hecklers—he didn't hesitate to champion the broader benefits of the space program. One August night, as he and fellow congressman James Symington were leaving the Century Plaza Hotel in Los Angeles, where Nixon had held a lavish reception honoring the astronauts, they were confronted by a mob of protesters. "We were dressed in tuxedoes and they were saying that all this money being spent on space should be spent on needs of the people and not in support of the space program,"[40] he recalled. Symington suggested they stop and reason with the protesters. They listened intently as Hechler agreed that Congress needed to deal with problems on earth but then went on to explain that a lot of the money spent on space was actually being used for improvements in the country's radar system and improvements in medicine, like the adaptation of technology miniaturization for medical uses. The protesters were grateful, saying no one had ever told them that. Symington described the incident as "a Hechler kind of thing to do." He called it "one of the best moments of my life."[41]

It is interesting to note, however, that as important to the country and the world as this committee was, Hechler usually minimizes his accomplishments on it. Even though he served on it throughout his entire congressional career, he chooses instead to boast of the accomplishments that benefited his state and region. When he does speak about it, he usually points to the educational value of the space race and the benefits of its scientific discoveries—from the grooving of highways to prevent hydroplaning accidents to using lasers for eye surgery—just as he did that hot August night in Los Angeles.

It's also a point of interest, but probably no surprise, that Hechler's assignment ten years later to write the history of the Science and Technology Committee (its name had changed in 1974) caught much flack in his home state. A *Charleston Daily Mail* editorial accused Hechler of being hired to write a history of little interest to anyone save those on the committee themselves. The criticism focused on the size of the committee staff, which was growing at a time when the committee's existence was being phased out. Bob Kittle, author of the *Charleston Daily Mail* column Dateline Washington, wrote, "Perhaps his [Hechler's] fruitless attempt to regain his seat after losing it in a 1978 gubernatorial bid [The bid was in 1976; this is the reporter's error] has left him so embittered that he has decided the only wise course is to climb aboard the bandwagon he decried for eighteen years as a House maverick."[42]

Hechler responded to a similar editorial in the *Charleston Gazette* by saying he didn't ask for the job but was implored by the then-committee chair, Representative Olin Teague, to undertake it. Teague believed Hechler's years of service and experience as a researcher and historian made him eminently qualified. Hechler then says, "Three courses of action were open to me. I had offers to become a lobbyist at a far better salary, but unlike many of those who leave Congress, I had no stomach for that kind of job. Second, I could have simply loafed and drawn my pension retirement, which . . . would have been tax-free for the years I paid into the system. As a loafer, my take-home pay would have exceeded the amount [$46,000] for the exacting job you label as a 'boondoggle.' I decided to go to work, as a third choice."[43] Years later, when asked why he didn't explain this to the reporters who dogged him for an answer, he merely replied, "I wanted to get the job done for Teague, and I knew their nitpicking would delay completion of the task."[44]

11

WIN SOME, LOSE SOME

Although Hechler's first committee assignment wasn't initially to his liking, participating on the House Committee on Science and Astronautics didn't stop him from taking on battles he considered more important to his constituents as well. After all, he'd been elected on the sole platform of becoming their "servant in Congress." Therefore, Hechler's breadth of legislative interests was eclectic, to say the least. Letters from his constituents on multiple issues regularly filled his congressional mailbox. He answered all of them, promising to look into each issue, regardless of whether or not his stand would put him in opposition to his fellow representatives. And it often did. Folders containing news clippings, letters, and reports on gun control, health care, highways, housing, rural medical care, mental health, sales tax, orphan or secondary roads, junk mail, senior citizens, pay raises for state employees, the treatment of state police, financial aid for college students, taxes, teacher pay, unions for public employees, welfare, utilities, the state budget, the impact of western coal on West Virginia, and women's rights fill his congressional papers.[1] Of course, his position on most issues leaned liberal, as it had since his days at Swarthmore College. It's there, he says, that he came away with a "social conscience and a certain perverse independence in the face of frequently-accepted mass opinions."[2]

In many instances he was ahead of his time. He introduced bills that would have provided Braille designations on paper money to indicate the denomination. He wanted to require Congress to use recycled paper in the printing of the *Congressional Record* and to prohibit travel at government expense by members of Congress who had resigned, retired, or been defeated. He argued for prohibiting smoking on certain aircraft, wanted those serving in the Women's Army Corps to be considered on active duty in the Armed Forces,[3] and he consistently voted for raising the minimum wage.[4] With West Virginia's Hershel "Woody" Williams in mind, he also favored raising the monthly pension for Congressional Medal of Honor holders from ten to one hundred dollars and having payments start at any age, rather than sixty-five.[5] That same year he came out in favor of amending the IRS code, stated he was in favor of changing Social Security and retirement benefits to keep up with inflation, and argued over who increased the size of the national debt—Eisenhower or Truman. Of course, Hechler had the facts proving that his old boss, Truman, had reduced rather than increased it.

Hechler held the former president in high esteem all his life and tried to push for a number of the issues Truman had been unsuccessful in seeing come to fruition. Among those was national health care. In 1957, a bill had been introduced in the House by Representative A. J. Forand of Rhode Island as an amendment to the Social Security Act to provide hospital benefits for the aged.[6] When Hechler ran for his initial congressional post in 1958, he had stumped in favor of even broader coverage: national health care for everyone.[7] But in 1960, when the Forand Bill, named for its author, was reintroduced as H.R. 4700, Hechler couldn't support it wholeheartedly. Not surprisingly, the American Medical Association, doctors, and medical societies within Hechler's district wrote him in opposition to the bill. They felt it would eventually undermine the current voluntary health insurance system. Hechler also received letters from the labor unions, which supported the measure.

Although he had preached the virtues of national health care only two years earlier, he had concerns about this particular proposal. His consistent response to those who wrote him was, "I have been deeply disturbed by the rising costs of health care, particularly for older people who find they cannot afford the cost of surgery and hospitalization. However, some aspects of the governmental control involved in the Forand Bill disturb me, and I will probably vote against [it] this year. What concerns me even more, however, is the failure of the medical profession to come up with any constructive suggestions in this field."[8]

The measure failed that year and for several more years. What we now know as Medicare did not become law until 1965, under President Lyndon Johnson. He held the signing ceremony at the Truman Library in honor of the former president's leadership on the matter. Of course, Hechler favored the bill, voted for it each time it came up to a committee vote, and voted yea during the final House vote on April 8, 1965. He even attended the signing ceremony on July 30 and watched President Johnson enroll President Truman as the first Medicare beneficiary.[9]

If Hechler was not fully knowledgeable about a constituent's concerns, he looked into it. To a food broker from Huntington who wrote of his opposition to a bill prohibiting additives to whole foods on the basis they caused cancer, and to another constituent about giving tax deductions for legislative and lobbying efforts, he said he'd have to look closely at the legislation before voting. While his initial responses may sound like standard politician-speak, Hechler did as he promised. His files contain all the "pinks," as he called the carbon copies of his responses, to every letter sent to his office. He told a Huntington man that while he had voted for the civil rights legislation that passed in 1960, he didn't think it was a very strong bill. He wanted efforts to make school desegregation more effective.[10] And to a Parkersburg man, he railed, "I have yelled, hollered, spoke softly, written articles, pleaded with other representatives, and done everything I could think of to try and get something done for the distressed areas of our state."[11]

In one instance, however, he bowed out of the debate. In 1974, Kanawha County, West Virginia, which was not in Hechler's district, became embroiled in a highly charged debate regarding the content of school textbooks. To those who wanted him to get involved in selecting new ones, he wrote, "When I first came to Congress in 1959, we considered for the first time legislation to provide Federal Aid to Education. At that time many people feared that federal aid would mean federal dictation of school policies. I made it a firm policy not to become involved in local school disputes since I feel these can best be decided by the local people involved. You should get together with others who feel as you do on this issue, for the best and most permanent solution will be one which is arrived at locally without federal interference."[12] When Hechler received a 1975 letter from a Huntington student, Matt Wolfe, complaining about how outdated his history textbooks were, Hechler referred the letter back to the state level as well, sending it to Daniel Taylor, the superintendent of schools.[13] Though these responses probably didn't please the letter writers, he knew what fights were worth tackling.

In the 1960s, which proved to be the last decade of the Post Office Department's existence, Congress began debating two issues regarding postal rates: the cost coverage of the various classes of mail, and the acceptability of so-called junk or third-class mail. Although he had received constituent mail on the subject of postal rates for several years, it's unclear how Hechler got embroiled in this controversy. It's likely that his "waste not, want not" nature drew the matter to his attention. For instance, in February 1967, when proposed legislation to end congressional franking privileges was under debate,[14] Hechler had favored the bill, even though all his future mailings would have been at his expense. He had also joined a lawsuit to stop the Post Office Department from arbitrarily closing rural post offices. On May 1, he issued a statement that a bill he introduced (H.R. 99) would have allowed recipients of unwanted junk mail to return it to the sender at the sender's cost. He also wanted to raise junk mail rates by 50 percent; neither idea gained any traction, however.

That July, President Johnson called for a 10 percent income tax surcharge, which would have undermined a House proposal to raise third-class postal rates and would have increased the cost of a first-class letter to nine cents. At the time, a first-class letter cost only five cents. Hechler opposed the measure, saying that first-class rates already paid 103 percent of their delivery costs, so the increase would only further subsidize the cost for delivering junk mail. He believed second- and third-class rates should be raised first. At the same time, he strongly supported Postmaster General Lawrence O'Brien's proposal that the Post Office Department be removed from the ranks of politics and placed in a governmental nonprofit corporation.[15] The following year, 1970, his idea became law, and the department became the U.S. Postal Service.[16]

Largely, Hechler's constituents agreed with his position on junk mail. However, it raised the ire of many businesspeople who relied on direct mail, which carries third-class rates, to market their services. He was the target of a one-million-piece letter-writing campaign, sponsored by third-class mailers who opposed him. In response, Hechler had a flyer produced that reprinted an editorial in the April 3, 1967, edition of the *Washington Daily News* that supported his position.[17] One man from Manhasset, New York, said since he couldn't vote against Hechler, he'd do the next best thing and send a substantial donation to Hechler's next opponent. Hechler replied that he'd gladly supply him with the name when one surfaced. He wrote, "One of the great things about this country is the freedom of choice at the ballot box. The voters have a right to pick a candidate who is willing to let the taxpayers continue to subsidize the lucrative direct mail advertising industry, or to elect a man who will stand up and fight to get this profit-making industry to pay its fair share of the cost of operating our postal system."[18]

That summer, he threatened to "fight to the finish on the House floor this brazen attempt to saddle millions of taxpayers with six-cent first class and ten-cent airmail rates, at the same time as the taxpayers have to shell out for subsidies to the junk mailers." And fight he did. In August, he brought a rural mail carrier from West Virginia to Washington to testify about his support for a raise in the third-class rates and his opposition to pay raises for postal employees. Nevertheless, on December 16, the bill Hechler opposed became law. It raised first-class rates from five to six cents, postcards from four to six cents, and airmail from eight to ten cents, while imposing very small increases, phased in over three years, on second- and third-class mail. The effect was that junk mail was still being subsidized by first-class mail.[19] The business interests had won, and in Hechler's mind, the people had lost.

Though he was on the losing side of that battle, some fights he won. On the subject of gun control, one letter so impressed Hechler that he agreed that a bill on firearms control under consideration would place unfair restrictions on West Virginia hunters.[20] However, a few years later he was being urged to support strict gun-control laws. In reaction to the assassinations of Martin Luther King and Bobby Kennedy in 1968, Hechler changed his stand and introduced an administration-backed bill banning the mail-order sale of firearms, and restrictions on the interstate shipment of guns and ammunition except by licensed dealers. His position, of course, resulted in plenty of opposition from West

Virginia hunters and sportsmen. Some suggested that the government enforce the laws already on the books. Even in the face of this outcry from his constituents, Hechler voted for the bill,[21] which passed the House on July 24 and the Senate on September 18. President Johnson signed it into law on October 22, 1968.[22]

The following month, Richard Nixon was elected president, much to Hechler's dismay. He had disliked Nixon—and even admitted to hating him—from the time Nixon had served in Congress years earlier. Sentiment against the Vietnam War had been building, in spite of the January Tet Offensive, in which Viet Cong forces pulled a devastating surprise attack on U.S. troops. And though Hechler had once supported the Vietnam War, by now he had changed his position and had spoken out against it. Ironically, in June 1969, he found himself supporting Nixon in his promise to withdraw twenty-five thousand American soldiers from the country.[23] No doubt it galled him to support Nixon on any issue. Yet in a report that grew out of a Hechler-sponsored conference, Hechler joined fifty-five other representatives and senators urging an immediate start of the withdrawal of American troops from Vietnam.[24] On the other hand, he supported the 1971 publication of the Pentagon Papers by the *New York Times*, regardless of the fact that Daniel Ellsberg had stolen them. Surprisingly, Hechler says, in the long run, his opposition to the war did him no damage. Even though West Virginia has a consistently high percentage of citizens who either are or were in the military, his support on that position came from student protesters and university professors who were of the same mind as Hechler.[25]

Perhaps his fellow Marshall professors and its alumni supported him because of his stand on the proposed Marshall Medical School as well. In 1971, he discovered federal money that would assist in its establishment. The following year he urged community support of the move because of the help it would provide in serving the medical needs of southwestern West Virginia's residents. Throughout 1973, the project stalled due to delays and President Nixon's apparent opposition. The Veterans Administration had to approve the funding and the sites, but Nixon was trying to cut its budget. Although Hechler felt that a bill had been crafted that would be veto-proof, Nixon vetoed the funding bill because a tacked-on amendment cut off funds for the bombing of Cambodia. Despite the veto, the VA began reviewing applications for medical school sites and authorized five new schools—including Marshall's. Hechler had such faith in the ultimate creation of then Marshall president Robert B. Hayes's dream, he made a statement on June 22, 1974—reported in the *Bluefield Daily Telegraph*—that he expected MU would admit its first medical school class in 1977.[26] He was almost right; the first class entered in 1978.

In 1985, Hechler wrote of his contribution to the formation of the medical school in an essay for university communications director C. T. Mitchell, titled, "An Unwritten Chapter in the History of the Marshall University Medical School." He prefaced the chapter with these words: "Politicians are notorious for the twin traits of ego and pride. I possess no more and no less of these traits than the average politician." He goes on to speak of his pride in helping the process along, and says his only complaint is the omission of the role of the U.S. House of Representatives in it. Self-effacingly, he continues, "This is not done in the spirit of injured dignity, but rather to share my great enthusiasm for having played a role in one of the most significant achievements in the history of Marshall University."[27] Though Hechler protests that he didn't write the chapter for C. T. Mitchell's document out of pride, he would have been within his rights to do so. After the medical school graduated its first doctor, much credit was given to Governor Moore; the state's two senators, Byrd and Randolph; President Hayes; and local doctor Dr. Albert Esposito.[28] Dr. Hayes's

2006 book on the subject, *$7,000 in the Bank . . . the Remarkable Story of Marshall University's Joan C. Edwards School of Medicine, 1972–2005*, calls his compatriots, plus MU Board of Regents member Ed Greene and the school's first dean, Robert W. Coon, the school's "linchpins." He failed to include Hechler.[29]

One disappointing battle he lost was the fight to build an airport in Putnam County, midway between the state's two largest cities, Huntington and Charleston. In the 1960s, the two cities were slowly growing toward each other into the relatively flat open land along I-64 in Putnam County. Both Huntington's Tri-State Airport and Charleston's Yeager Airport were perched on top of hills and were considered by most pilots to be among the most dangerous airports in the country. Studies had shown that expansion at either would be difficult and expensive. A new, larger airport between the two would have meant potential new service by larger airplanes and increased opportunities for business growth.

Following a study commissioned by civic leaders from Charleston, a site called Guthrie near Sissonville was recommended, and potential funding seemed secure. However, many residents west of Charleston suggested it might be better to consider that a total of 500,000 people lived in these two metropolitan areas. To them, building an airport at a more central location that would serve the entire market more conveniently made better sense. Throughout 1966, the debate between these two factions raged. In July, the Kanawha County Court applied to the Federal Aviation Authority (FAA) for funding, to be supplemented with other resources, to build an airport at the Guthrie location. But the FAA still favored the Midway site, pointing out that building there would be more economical than at the Sissonville site. Naturally, residents and business leaders in Huntington and the surrounding Cabell County area supported the FAA's position, as it would have benefited them, whereas the Sissonville site would have been farther away.[30]

In reality, Hechler had little direct impact on the matter, since it was an issue the counties involved had to resolve, rather than a congressional concern. Nevertheless, he didn't hesitate to push his fellow representatives to take a stand on it, to state his own position on the matter, and to work toward it. He offered his support to his former administrative assistant, Bobby Nelson, who was in the West Virginia legislature at the time and had cosponsored the legislation creating the authority to construct the proposed Midway Jetport.[31]

In 1967, editorials in both Huntington's *Herald Dispatch* and Charleston's *Gazette* supported the points that building a Midway Airport would cost less than improvements to both the other airports and would help both cities grow.[32] Throughout 1966 and 1967, Hechler spoke on the House floor, and wrote many letters to the FAA and to Ohio and Kentucky representatives, soliciting—and winning—their support.[33] Hechler argued for the Midway site, saying it would mean more flights and better facilities for both cities, thereby resulting in a significant increase in air cargo to and from the state. He saw it as a win for both communities.

But according to Nelson, Hechler took off on his own, publicly pushing the Midway cause instead of quietly getting the congressional delegation to join in. This angered both Senator Randolph and Hechler's fellow congressman, John Slack, because it forced them to take a stand. Knowing that it was a divisive issue in Kanawha County, both men were initially reluctant to state a public position. But Hechler wouldn't let up. Spending much of his own money, he passionately promoted the Midway location.[34] While an internal memo to Hechler dated October 10, 1966, states that Randolph had proposed a Midway Regional Airport between

Huntington and Charleston twenty years earlier,[35] he now opposed the project and predicted it wouldn't be needed in the future because vertical takeoff and landing capabilities would be common for airliners, thus eliminating the need for long runways.[36]

By the end of the year, because the two cities were still fighting, the FAA announced it would conduct its own study. On May 15, 1967, Hechler and the other West Virginia congressional delegation heard the FAA representative say, "Weighing all factors, the FAA has come to the conclusion to support the Midway site as a regional airport for Southern West Virginia." Not only did the FAA make a public statement in favor of that site, but it made promises to commit funds to it—a first in the annals of the agency's history. But even with the FAA's pronouncement, in some quarters both Randolph and Slack alluded to the fact that funding might not be available from future congressional allocations even if the airport were to be built. Although Randolph later denied it, one 1968 letter to R. O. Robertson, then president of the Southwestern Airport Authority, clearly supported the rumors.[37]

Predictably, the Kanawha County Court was unhappy with the FAA's announcement. Knowing that both Cabell and Putnam counties had a bad record of passing bond issues, the court threw down the gauntlet, saying that if those counties wanted a Midway Airport so badly, they should put up or shut up. To the court's surprise, in the fall of 1967 both counties passed their bonds by huge majorities. Cabell County approved $2.5 million, while Putnam voted a $500,000 bond. On October 24, Kanawha County voters went to the polls to approve their $2.5 million airport bond issue. However, the voters found themselves facing a multi-issue bond instead. It had been back-loaded with another $9 million school bond issue, as well as $15.5 million for a new courthouse and other county improvements. Needless to say, the voters revolted and voted it down.[38]

Sadly, Hechler's stand resulted in a personal struggle with Slack as well. In 1967, before the matter was settled, Slack had made derogatory remarks on the House floor and in the media, claiming that Hechler had violated an ethics clause in his fight for the Midway site. After the election was over, Hechler wrote Slack two letters blowing off steam and demanding to know exactly what he'd done wrong, but he never mailed them.[39] By then, the rift between the two was complete. According to Hechler, the two remained bitter enemies.[40]

After the vote dashed the hopes for a Midway Airport, Captain Hugh M. Wilson of United Airlines wrote a prescient letter that supported Hechler's position. In it he cites Kanawha Airport's abrupt drop-off on approach, as well as the strong winds that create a downdraft just off the end. Saying that although a seven-hundred-foot extension would help, he still believes "this airport [Charleston] will never be other than a one runway, one direction, fair weather airport." Predictably, on March 12, 2015, following a major landslide off the end of one of Yeager Airport's runways,[41] in which an emergency overrun area collapsed, arguments again surfaced that echoed Hechler's efforts over fifty years earlier. Speculations that this couldn't have happened if Kanawha County had voted for the Midway site were rampant. Still fuming at the age of one hundred, Hechler remarked a few months later, "This never would have happened if they'd put it at Midway."[42]

12

MARCHING TO SELMA

Considering that his formative years were spent in the rarified air of a millionaire's estate on Long Island, New York, Ken Hechler's long-standing fight for civil rights may seem surprising. But it was precisely this upbringing that formed his egalitarian beliefs, diametrically opposed to those of his parents. Even as a youngster, while he admired their community-minded spirit and longed for the attention their involvement brought them, he acknowledged his parents' prejudiced attitudes toward anyone who wasn't like them. Nevertheless, inspired more by the civil rights crusaders and champions of women's rights he'd read about, Ken became convinced his parents were wrong.

When Ken tried to date a young Polish girl, his parents objected and told him to stay away from her, so he saw her in secret. Prejudiced against Jews as well, his father always referred to New York University (NYU) as "NY Jew." Later, fueled by his hatred of his father's beliefs, Ken wrote a paper on the contributions of American Jews to education, arts, and science. When it was published in the local *Roslyn News*, the article only further inflamed his parents.

While attending Columbia University in New York City, he attended, on alternating Sundays, one of two black churches in the nearby neighborhood of Morningside Heights, eschewing the formality of his Episcopalian roots. He loved their passionate choirs and fiery preachers, and the unbridled enthusiasm of the congregations. And he felt at home in the Cotton Club in Harlem, listening to Cab Callaway or watching tap dancer Bojangles

Robinson.[1] At Fort Knox, Kentucky, where Hechler was in basic training, he was assigned for a time to the public relations office. There he drew the anger of his commander by writing an article about how the army should improve the welfare of its black soldiers.[2]

Hechler's revered mentor, President Harry Truman, was a strong advocate for civil rights. In the typed draft of an upcoming speech, Hechler outlined some of Truman's actions in that area: setting up a Committee on Civil Rights in 1946, desegregating the armed forces, sponsoring antilynching legislation, reviving the Fair Campaign Practices Committee, and putting a strong civil rights platform in his 1948 campaign.[3] These remarks leave no doubt that Truman's beliefs were another influence on Hechler's unyielding position on the issue.

Hechler's first brush with congressional legislation on civil rights came even before he was elected to the House of Representatives, when in the summer of 1957 he went to Washington to help Colorado senator John Carroll. Torn between staying in West Virginia to curry favor with the voters he hoped would elect him to Congress the following year and going to Washington to help influence such important legislation, he chose the latter.[4] He and Carroll worked on the bill all summer, but the amendment they had hoped to defeat remained, and President Johnson's bill survived.[5] Jury trials in civil rights cases became the law of the land.

Once in Congress, he was invited to serve on an unofficial committee sometimes referred to as the Committee of Ten. This group of representatives, who also called themselves "the Mustangs," included Eugene McCarthy, Stewart Udall, George McGovern, and Hechler. According to McGovern, they were a group of compassionate men who felt the government needed to work harder on the pressing issues of poverty, racism, increasing militarism, and labor reform, to name a few.[6] It was right up Hechler's alley, for he'd already seen that many of the members of Congress were more interested in getting reelected than in being public servants.[7] Though it wasn't a formal committee, McGovern believes they were able to make progress in pushing these concerns, as well as laying the groundwork for the later antipoverty movement of President Johnson's administration, and accelerating the move toward civil rights legislation a few years later.[8] Hechler's inclusion on this committee also marked the beginning of a long friendship between him and McGovern.

As a congressman, Hechler had the privilege of appointing people to the summer post of Capitol police officer. In 1962, one of his appointees was a black basketball player from Marshall University named Phil Carter. During busy periods, Carter also worked in Hechler's office and got to know him quite well. Carter, now a professor at his alma mater, believes he got the post because his coach asked Hechler for a favor. Carter had been demonstrating for civil rights in Huntington, and Coach Jules Rivlin wanted him out of the city so he wouldn't get in trouble and ruin his last year of basketball eligibility. While the ploy worked in the short term, it didn't in the long term.

While in Washington, Carter met Frank Cleckley, who later became the first African American member of the West Virginia Supreme Court of Appeals, and the two began plotting about ways to bring about change for blacks. When Carter returned to Huntington, he demonstrated at one of the local movie theaters. Shortly thereafter, the theater began admitting blacks on the same basis as whites.[9] No more segregated seating. From there, he and others began trying to integrate lunch counters and restaurants.

This drew Hechler's attention. Two restaurants—White Pantry and Bailey's Cafeteria, which was one of Hechler's favorites when he was in Huntington—had historically refused to serve blacks. In 1963, Carter and many others began demonstrating at both.

Hechler followed the progress of the demonstrations, especially at the White Pantry, where the owner often sprayed bug spray nearby as the blacks sat at the counter, asking to be served. They were also gassed, cattle-prodded, beaten, and stabbed, but they continued to demonstrate and respond peacefully. In their midst, supporting them and often trying to reason with the owner, was Ken Hechler. According to Carter, Hechler was the only official—local, state, or federal—who did so. "We would watch him; and he would look with disgust and anger, and greet us friendly. He was sending a message to the people who were discriminating and shutting us out," Carter recalled. "He didn't have to say much. He was a United States Congressman and he was there. His presence was comforting."[10]

That September, when the White Pantry's owner sued for an injunction to stop the protests, Hechler attended the hearings.[11] Although the owner lost the case and both the restaurants were ordered to integrate, Carter and a white protester, Rick Deal, agreed not to eat there ever again.[12] Nonetheless, Hechler was pleased with the verdict.

Thus it should have come as no surprise that on March 20, 1965, when Hechler read of the events in Selma, Alabama, two weeks earlier, on what became known as "Bloody Sunday," in which police had clubbed, cattle-prodded, and, on horseback, ridden down the peaceful demonstrators, it reminded him of the events he'd witnessed in Huntington. And although he'd originally felt that the proposed 1963 March on Washington was a "dangerous move, which [would] hurt rather than help the cause for civil rights,"[13] it also rekindled the feelings he'd had as he listened to Martin Luther King's speech at the Lincoln Memorial during that march. Despite his initial concern that the average congressperson would resent the pressure King was bringing and his own call to the National Association for the Advancement of Colored

People (NAACP) to call off the march,[14] Hechler had attended the historic rally. Along with a quarter million or so others, he heard King start his speech by referring to the Constitution and the Declaration of Independence. He'd said that both were a promissory note that Americans had defaulted on, that America had given the Negro a bad check.[15] When this beginning drew few cheers, King switched to his now famous "I have a dream" analogy, which touched Hechler. He never forgot it.

Now, slated to travel to Cape Canaveral that Saturday to witness another space flight with his colleagues, he decided he needed to take part in the civil rights movement once again. He scrubbed himself from the flight to Florida, saying he had more urgent plans, and booked a flight to Birmingham without the knowledge of any of his staff. He stayed over Saturday night, and the next morning he rented a car and drove to Selma to walk part of the fifty-four-mile march in support of Dr. Martin Luther King and the movement.

On nearly twenty pages of handwritten notes—some on yellow legal paper, which Hechler must have jotted down on the flight home in preparation for later speeches—he writes firsthand of his experiences on that historic day, March 21, 1965. He describes Selma as "perched on a bluff beside the muddy Alabama River."[16] There was a palpable air of tension, he says. Not wanting to be recognized, he had gone incognito, wearing an old sweater, sloppy green pants, and an overcoat. He left the car close enough to walk to Brown Chapel AME Church, where Dr. King was to speak before the march began.[17] On Alabama Avenue, a Coca-Cola sign read, "Selma; Progressive & Friendly."[18] Hechler almost arrived late because he followed wrong directions purposefully given to him by several contemptuous white residents who were hell-bent on explaining how the Yankees had nearly destroyed the town during the Civil War. As he got closer, Hechler tagged along behind small groups of blacks that appeared to be heading to the church. The morning was brisk—only thirty-four degrees. By the time the marchers had assembled at the church, temperatures had warmed about ten degrees, but there was still a biting wind.[19]

He arrived at the chapel just in time to hear King say, "You will be the people that will type a new chapter in the history books, and more. Those of us who are Negroes don't have much. We have known the long night of poverty. Because of the system, we don't have much education and some of us don't know how to make our nouns and verbs agree. But thank God we have our bodies, our feet, and our souls. Walk together children, don't you get weary, and it will lead to the Promised Land. And Alabama will be a new Alabama and America will be a new America."[20] At the end of his twenty-minute speech, King called on the crowd to join in singing "We Shall Overcome." Hechler says he never belted out a song so loudly, and it gave him renewed courage, although he knew from reports on the radio of his rental car that President Johnson had federalized the Alabama National Guard and had sent federal troops to protect the marchers. "I did not know this when I started out for Alabama, but it certainly made me feel better to realize that Sheriff [Jim] Clark with his cattle prods, bullwhips, and fire hoses was not going to be there opposite me when I started the march."[21] Hechler joined the marchers eight abreast, taking a spot beside Charles Evers, the brother of Medgar Evers, who had been murdered two years earlier by a member of the Ku Klux Klan. They were several rows behind Dr. King, Ralph Abernathy, Hosea Williams, John Lewis, Andrew Young, Dr. Ralph Bunche, and other movement leaders as they started marching back through the portion of Selma known as "Colored Town."[22] Many of those on the front lines wore leis—gifts from a Hawaiian delegation, brought to show their state's solidarity.

The crowd walked on potholed streets through the black section, past dilapidated houses and a crumbling school, but as they turned into the white section on Sylvan Street, trees lined the smooth sidewalks. At the intersection with Water Street, a parked car's speakers blared "Dixie" and a man yelled, "Fifty miles? You won't make it fifty feet." An elderly marcher replied, "That man standing on the curb gives me the inspiration I need." Hechler had chosen a spot near the edge of his row in hopes of hearing the taunts. He got his wish. As they marched through the white section toward Broad Street and the Edmund Pettus Bridge, jeers spewed from the sidewalks. Three gray-haired women shouted, "There goes a priest. He's a disgrace to the Roman Catholics." Shouts of "Martin Luther Coon," "Go back to Africa and take those white niggers with you!" "Communist Goons," and "Outside clergy, go home!" assaulted his ears.

In response, some protesters strummed guitars; others waved banners and sang anthems. Next to Hechler, seventy-three-year-old Mrs. Mary Jane Johnson waved her hand overhead, saying, "I have never voted in my life. I don't think I'd know how, but I'd have to try it."[23] Another woman pointed out the Selma City Hall, where she'd been held for three days for contempt of court for trying to register to vote. A young black woman explained to Hechler what she hoped to accomplish by marching. "School for mah kids. Ah has four children. Ah want them to get schoolin'. Ah want them to go to the regular school."

At the Edmund Pettus Bridge, Dr. King held up the crowd, asking them to pray before they attempted to cross. As the entire entourage knelt, Hechler joined them. Years later, recalling the drama of that moment brought tears to his eyes.[24] As they rose and started across the arched-back bridge, a woman in slacks and a pink blouse ran into the roadway and spat on some nuns, then yelled, "Walking with nigger trash. Nuns walking with nigger trash," and spat again. Someone in the crowd yelled, "Lock arms or grab hands." Hechler took the hand of the black man next to him as a white man in blue denim spat at him and sneered, "Hold on to his hand, Reverend, 'cause he's going to need it."[25] When they reached the topmost point of the bridge, Hechler says the broad, open vista through which the four-lane Jefferson Davis Highway stretched truly looked to him like the Promised Land. His vision was destroyed, however, when a black car sporting a Confederate flag on the antenna and "MERIDIAN, MISSISSIPPI HATES ALL NIGGERS" painted in white block letters on the side cruised by.[26] Fortunately, National Guard troopers lined the highway, and helicopters buzzed overhead.

After a short rest stop, Hechler found himself beside an elderly black woman struggling with a huge pack. He hoisted it easily and carried it the rest of the day. Passing a typical Southern plantation along the way, they saw placard-carrying children pushed to the fence line by their elders. The sign read, "White trash go home." A Negro female marcher looked at the sign for a moment, took Hechler's hand, and drew him to the side of the road. She pointed back at them and said, "White trash *is* home."[27]

At dusk, the air turned chilly again, and Dr. King called a halt for the day. In a cornfield off the highway, where volunteers had pitched four large circus-style tents for the night, King approached Hechler. While he had tried to remain unrecognized, a *Baltimore Sun* reporter had seen Hechler and told King he was there. Hechler told King how much he appreciated his actions and apologized that he couldn't stay for the rest of the march because he had to return to Washington for an important vote the next day. King asked how he planned to get back to his car, and Hechler said he could always hitchhike back. King refused to let him, saying the road would be very dangerous and that the local rednecks would be ready to exact a toll on stray marchers while the troopers were still with the remaining group. He insisted that his four body-guards drive Hechler back to his car, but told him to lie down on the floorboards so no one could see he was riding with blacks. Among Hechler's lasting memories are King's parting words: "Always remember during your life that you've been a part of history. You will understand by the events of the next few days why this was so important to the whole civil rights movement." Hechler left, but the march continued for four more days, until it reached the steps of the Montgomery Courthouse, where King gave a victory speech to the weary marchers.[28]

A few days later, Hechler vividly recalled King's parting words from that day when President Johnson announced that he would immediately ask for a civil rights bill and ended with the words, "We shall overcome."[29] The euphoria of Hechler's experience faded quickly, however, as a deluge of hate mail began to flood his mailbox. The *Charleston Gazette* had published an account of his experiences in Selma. Shame replaced his earlier exhilaration as he lamented that his detractors failed to understand the ultimate goal and to realize what a powerful leader Dr. King was. One farmer from Putnam County suggested he should just say he got drunk and wound up down there.[30] In several letters he was accused of either being a Communist or belonging to a Communist-based organization. The general opinion, however, was that his job was to represent West Virginia and his constituents, not the black people of Selma. They made it clear they believed West Virginia didn't have a Negro problem and that he shouldn't have been bothering with Alabama's. Although many letters were signed "A former supporter," most were simply unsigned.

Hechler responded to each one who was brave enough to add his signature, stating, "I'm sorry we disagree on this, but I was glad to get your expression of opinion. Needless to say, I have received many critical letters, but when a matter of moral principle is concerned, an individual must listen to his conscience and not simply bow to the cries of the multitude." He also wrote to several constituents, explaining that their threats would not change his moral principles. He stated to friends, "It is difficult for me to describe to these people that matters of moral principle should not be decided by weighing the political effects."[31] No doubt in this he was channeling Harry S. Truman's oft-quoted sentiment that he didn't have to take a poll to decide right or wrong. The former president had famously once asked, "What would Jesus Christ have preached if he'd taken a poll in Israel?"[32] Hechler felt the same way and stuck to his guns.

Fortunately, Hechler *did* have supporters for his position and his actions. They, too, wrote—and in some cases even trumpeted their support in the newspapers.[33] Hechler was right; he was reelected in subsequent elections by even larger margins than before his participation in the march. And even though he didn't know it at the time, Hechler was the only member of Congress to attend or participate in the march.

By May 26, a voting rights bill had passed the Senate, but it took the House another month to debate it. Finally, when the Voting Rights Act of 1965 came up for a vote on July 9,[34] Hechler excitedly cast his yea vote in the House of Representatives. On August 6, 1965, President Johnson signed the act, which outlawed literacy tests and provided a method to investigate the use of poll taxes to prevent blacks from voting. Hechler proudly stood by as President Johnson signed the bill that provided some of the rights he had marched to secure. It was a satisfying day for the self-avowed fighter.

For his efforts to further the cause of civil rights, Hechler was awarded the twentieth Martin Luther King Jr. Achievement Award in 2010. This award is given annually at the Martin Luther King Jr. Unity Breakfast at West Virginia University to the West Virginia resident who best exemplifies King's legacy and commitment to the cause of civil rights. Speaking to the crowd gathered that day, the ninety-five-year-old former congressman said, "We still need to stand in times of challenge and controversy, but deep in my heart, I do believe, we shall overcome someday. Amen."[35]

13

FIGHTING FOR MINERS' LIVES

At dawn, on a damp, bone-chilling Wednesday morning, smoke, flames, and debris suddenly filled the sky over Farmington, West Virginia. In Consolidated Coal Company's No. 9 mine, between Farmington and Mannington—about six miles from Fairmont—a catastrophic explosion had killed and would eventually entomb seventy-eight men. News of the November 20, 1968, tragedy galvanized Ken Hechler into a frenzy of activity he'd never before undertaken in his ten years in Congress. Until then, he'd served diligently on the Science and Astronautics Committee, railed against junk mail, battled for and lost the fight for a new West Virginia airport, and marched at Selma. While he was aware of the state's long history of dependence on coal, with its attendant mine wars and strikes, as well as Mother Jones's battles there for unionization of the miners, his district—the 4th Congressional District—contained no coal mining communities when he was first elected in 1958.

Therefore, it wasn't until after the 1961 congressional redistricting that coal-rich Logan County came under his purview. Even then, he naively thought John L. Lewis and the United Mine Workers of America (UMWA) were doing everything they could to protect miners and make their workplaces as safe as possible. Rumblings of unsafe mining conditions and coal dust causing black lung disease were largely considered to be rumors, and were mentioned in only a few letters that reached his office.

But by 1968, the rumblings had grown louder; more letters were reaching Hechler about mine safety and the health of the miners. When Democrat James Sprouse mentioned the issues in one of his 1968 gubernatorial position papers as well, Hechler says he perked up. He suddenly realized the UMWA was *not* doing all it could, so he set out to see what he could do to change that. On September 11, 1968, President Johnson sent a mine safety bill to Congress, designed to strengthen enforcement of the laws then on the books. Hechler read the bill and immediately signed on. The next day, he drafted his own version supporting Johnson's and dropped it in the congressional hopper.[1] Little could he foresee what he'd gotten himself into.

As he wrote his support letter, he recalled his days with Truman in 1952, when mine health and safety legislation reached the president's desk. Hechler remembered Truman's ambivalence about signing what he considered a weak bill.[2] Even though that bill did become law, mine operators had since found loopholes large enough to drive a coal truck through, and as Hechler had discovered, enforcement of what *was* in it was lax. Furthermore, nothing had been done since to strengthen the law.[3] He was happy to support a bill that would now do so.

Two months later, when he heard about the Farmington explosion, Hechler drove there, expecting only to lend moral support to the widows, family members, and other miners. As he moved from family to family at the Champion Company Store where they were gathered, he heard talk about the need to improve enforcement of the safety laws. Miners and family members soon besieged him, saying, "You're a congressman. Why don't you do something about the safety conditions? Why don't you do something about all this coal dust?"[4] When Governor Hulett Smith told the gathered families, "We must remember that this is a hazardous business and what has occurred here today is one of the hazards of mining,"[5] Hechler became outraged. From his constituents' letters, he knew miners were being disabled from exposure to coal dust. He knew mine owners were often warned of impending inspections. He knew miners rarely had toilet facilities or even washrooms. And he knew there was much more the industry could do to protect its miners.

Deeply moved by the pleas of the families and infuriated at the callous attitude of Governor Smith, Hechler quickly said he'd take up the cause if they would help him. Several agreed, including Mrs. Sara Kaznoski, one of the new widows. Within days he had paid the expenses for a small Farmington contingent to come to Washington. They met with senators and representatives from non–coal mining states to make clear the depth and breadth of the problems.[6] The day after the explosion, UMWA president W. A. "Tony" Boyle made another insensitive statement that added fuel to Hechler's resolve. "As long as we mine coal, there is always this inherent danger," he said, adding that Consolidated Coal was "one of the best companies to work with as far as cooperation and safety are concerned."[7] Two days after the tragedy, Hechler outlined what he planned to include in the bill he would introduce early in the 1969 session.[8] Quick-study Hechler had been doing his homework.

Although he had supported Johnson's earlier bill, which had died without a single hearing,[9] he now criticized parts of it. He felt the limit of coal dust it allowed was too high; it left the administration of the bill with the Department of the Interior instead of moving it to Labor, where he thought it belonged; and it contained no language emphasizing safety over production.[10] On November 25, he called a news conference in the House press gallery, saying, "Coal miners don't have to die. In a civilized society it is nothing short of criminal to allow the present conditions to continue in the mines." Additionally, he took a few pot shots at the UMWA leadership, saying they hadn't been fighting hard enough for the miners they were supposed to represent. He charged that mine foremen knew when inspectors would arrive, that enforcement was weak, and that miners' families were being forced to take a fatalistic approach to their way of life.[11] It marked the first but not the last salvo Hechler would fire at Boyle.

As early as February 1968, consumer safety advocate Ralph Nader had been pointing out some of the facts that Hechler now trumpeted. Nader's prodding had been partially responsible for getting Johnson to draft the mine safety bill that had died.[12] In March, Nader made a report on the subject to Secretary of the Interior Stewart Udall and then began to speak out more publicly.[13] In response to Nader's charges, the UMWA brought Dr. Lorin E. Kerr, an assistant to the medical director of the union's Welfare and Retirement Fund to the podium during its September national convention. Asked to speak on pneumoconiosis—or "black lung," as it is more commonly known, Kerr may have given the UMWA members more than Boyle expected. Kerr outlined the disease's medical history, which dated back more than a century; described the differences between black lung and silicosis, which most coal operators *did* realize was deadly; and explained the efforts England had made since 1942 to combat black lung, pointing out that the UMWA had done nothing of the sort. His plain talk woke up the audience, which called for an intensive lobbying effort and the drafting of a model law regarding black lung prevention and compensation.[14]

Now the UMWA was forced to wrestle with criticism from within its ranks as well as outside. Three doctors were also railing against pneumoconiosis—a disease they had seen all too often among their miner patients. Drs. I. E. Buff, Donald Rasmussen, and Hawley A. "Sonny" Wells had been disheartened by what they'd seen in their practices as a cardiologist, a pulmonary specialist, and a pathologist. Buff, a flamboyant orator given to bringing dissected, diseased lungs to show his audiences, had been traveling the coalfields for months addressing miners with the dire warning that they would all die of black lung.[15] The insidious disease, pneumoconiosis, is caused by long exposure to coal dust. Called "black lung" for the appearance of severely affected lungs, it is incurable. Over time, the lungs fill with the dust, and unable to rid themselves of it, they eventually harden, causing the victim to die. Wells and Rasmussen, who still insists he never wanted to be a crusader,[16] were less colorful but no less insistent about the breadth of the problem and the necessity to address it. The trio met Hechler at one of their meetings. While they may have felt, until then, that they'd been merely preaching to the victims, now they had found an activist ally. And, no doubt, Hechler was glad to have them on his side, too.

Throughout December and January Hechler appeared on network television, addressed miners' rallies, and issued press releases to educate the public about the lack of safety in the mines and the inherent risk of coal dust to miners' health. Hechler wanted the law to limit coal dust in the mines to three milligrams per cubic meter or less, and to provide compensation for black lung sufferers.[17] Nader continued to speak out as well. By mid-January, as the crusading doctors' speaking engagements reached more people and pressure mounted, two West Virginia medical societies—one in Hechler's home county—issued rebuttals of the trio's claims, saying pneumoconiosis in its simplest form was "a condition compatible with reasonable health." The Cabell County Medical Society's president further asserted that there was no epidemic of this "man-made" plague among coal miners.[18] Hechler was infuriated, in no small part because the doctor who authored the opinion was his friend and former campaign backer, Dr. Rowland Burns of Huntington.

Two weeks later, Hechler retaliated. On January 26, he addressed a massive miners' rally at the Charleston Civic Center.

Ken Hechler waves a hunk of bologna at a black lung rally (Photo courtesy of the *Charleston Daily Mail*)

The same day, the Council of the West Virginia Medical Association was meeting elsewhere in Charleston. On the dais with Buff and Rasmussen, Hechler facetiously told the crowd of miners he'd received a secret message from the medical association. He held up a sign that said, "BLACK LUNG IS GOOD FOR YOU." They roared. After the reaction died down, he then held up a twelve-pound roll of bologna he'd bought for the occasion, saying, "This is what I think of the opinion of the coal company doctors and the medical societies."

The crowd erupted again. When the laughter subsided, he delivered a message from Ralph Nader, whom he'd met only two days earlier. It included charges of corruption in the UMWA that Nader had uncovered and shared with Hechler. Nader felt that rank-and-file members would accept his charges better if a West Virginian brought them to their attention. In their meeting, Nader had told Hechler he thought Hechler should come down harder on Boyle.[19]

Needled by the adverse publicity and the unrest in the rank and file, the UMWA got two separate bills introduced through industry-friendly congressmen.[20] However, Hechler and Nader had advocated a single bill dealing with both issues: health and safety. While the voters loved Hechler, he had few friends or supporters among the West Virginia congressional delegation. He'd locked horns with fellow congressman John Slack in a losing battle over the proposed airport between Huntington and Charleston; he'd served on a reform committee when most of his colleagues didn't want reform; and from the beginning, his maverick ways had assured he wasn't part of the political "good old boys" club.[21] Although he had criticized Jennings Randolph for introducing a bill written by the coal operators and fought with Slack,[22] Hechler said the lack of support from his fellow West Virginia congressmen amazed him. In his book *The Fight for Coal Mine Health and Safety*, he says they and other powerful members of Congress attempted to isolate him by criticizing his tactics, his legislation, and his analysis of what was wrong with the UMWA leadership.[23]

Furthermore, because he'd historically supported the coal industry—before he learned the real story following the Farmington explosion—his new stance sounded like treason to the UMWA. To knock him off his self-assumed pedestal, an article in the *United Mine Workers Journal* parodied Hechler's "How to Get Elected to Congress," which had been published as a 1959 *Pageant* magazine article. Hechler vehemently objected on the *Congressional Record* and nearly sued the union for slander.[24] He had clearly angered the union hierarchy and Boyle, who called him a "fink."

Because he felt having more allies would help force passage, Hechler didn't want to wage war with the union. Nevertheless, he resolved to continue speaking out. Once the *Louisville*

Courier-Journal's editorial board printed a strong endorsement of Hechler's position, he felt better. Energized, he persuaded House Speaker John McCormack to scrap the other two bills and then introduced H.R. 6504 on February 6, 1969, which called for the planks he'd long advocated for and went far beyond what the UMWA had originally proposed.[25]

With the three crusading doctors covering the coalfields with their message of doom, Hechler stepped up his letter-writing campaign to members of Congress. Speaking on the House floor whenever he could, he urged passage of his bill.[26] When the coal industry pushed the White House to replace the Bureau of Mines director, John O'Leary, with someone friendlier to the industry's position, Hechler again called on Sara Kaznoski. He urged her and the other widows to send telegrams to Nixon to object and invited them to come to Washington to meet with Secretary of the Interior Walter Hickel. She agreed, and Hechler again paid their travel expenses.[27] First he called the secretary's office to be sure Hickel's schedule was clear, then he ghost-wrote the telegrams and released them and the date of the February 24 meeting to the media. "This was part of a charade to make the visit of the miners and the miners' widows credible so he could not use the excuse that he would be out of town that day," he says. "This was all a put up job. I would write the script for her to make sure that it was so persuasive that no person in Washington could possibly deny them an appointment. I knew that and played on that sympathy."[28] It worked, and Nixon put the firing on hold.

Back in West Virginia, around the same time Hechler's bill hit the congressional hopper, the newly formed Black Lung Association (BLA)—a group of local UMWA leaders—introduced West Virginia state legislation calling for the presumption that after working in the mines for a few years, any miner with certain symptoms could be presumed to have black lung. Of course, the mine operators dug in their heels and called Dr. Rowland Burns, who had previously scoffed at Buff, Rasmussen, and Wells over the very existence of the disease, to testify. But under Wyoming County legislator Warren McGraw's questioning, Burns was forced to admit he had been paid by the coal association to testify. Still, the legislators refused to consider a bill.[29]

Impatient with both the lack of congressional action and the state government's refusal to act, the miners became restless. On February 18, a wildcat strike of nearly four hundred men in a mine near Beckley, West Virginia, broke out,[30] partially through the urging of some Volunteers in Service to America (VISTA) workers, who had persuaded the miners that only through organization and agitation could they make a difference.[31] Sympathy for the strikers spread wildly. Within one week, mines all across the southern West Virginia coalfields were closed, and the strike was moving north.[32] Hechler initially opposed the strike, believing it would make matters worse, but at a February 26 rally in Charleston, he apologized to the miners and donated $1,000 to the BLA. Hechler says Sonny Wells, whom he later suspected of wanting his congressional seat, had suggested he state his opposition.[33] It was bad advice; fortunately, the miners forgave him.

The widespread strike, which ultimately idled some forty thousand men, finally forced the West Virginia legislature to act. Governor Arch Moore had initially refused to sign an adequate black lung compensation bill without further discussion in the legislature. The miners called his bluff, saying they would continue the strike if he did not sign;[34] in March, he capitulated, and the miners returned to work. Mindful of the value of good timing and the publicity potential the signing afforded, Hechler took the opportunity to redouble his efforts for a comprehensive federal bill. Congressional subcommittee hearings had begun while the miners were still on strike. Now Hechler took every opportunity offered him to address the committees. On March 19 and 20 he again paid for Mrs. Kaznoski, two other Farmington widows, and four miners to travel to Washington, this time to bolster his own testimony. In addition to their statements, which he called "well received," Hechler used some of his time to outline his agreements and disagreements with the bill Nixon had proposed to Congress earlier that month.[35] In true Hechler showmanship fashion, he asked one of the miners suffering from black lung to bounce on his toes in order to demonstrate the effects of the disease. The fifty-one-year-old did so thirty-five times, and then collapsed in a chair wheezing. It took fifteen minutes for his pulse to return to normal.[36]

As Hechler was doing his research into the UMWA's actions regarding the health and safety of the miners, he began to see what he thought was more blatant corruption. Prior knowledge of visits by the mine inspectors was a badly kept secret among the miners. Forewarned, they were expected to tidy up and correct obvious irregularities. According to Bobby Nelson, whose mother ran a boardinghouse in Whitesville, West Virginia, she had special rooms for the inspectors. When word came, she made sure those rooms were spiffed up for the inspectors.[37]

In early April, when a methane gas explosion in a Mexican coal mine killed or trapped over 150 miners, Hechler traveled to Barroterán, Mexico, at his own expense. With an eye to strengthening his argument for the bill he had introduced, he wanted to see if lack of safety regulations there had allowed that tragedy.[38] "I'll always remember . . . when I asked how many inspectors they had in the mine that blew up," he recalled. "One miner said, 'Thirty, if you count the mules.'"[39] Knowing that inspections at Farmington had also been lax, he warned that the same thing could happen again in this country if his bill wasn't passed. Industry spokespersons lashed back, saying the "proposed health and safety standards might cost too much money . . . for it [the union] to absorb."

After receiving countless letters from widows and miners complaining that their pensions or health and medical cards had been cut off with no explanation, Hechler began wondering how the UMWA Welfare and Retirement Fund was being administered. On April 7, 1969, he asked Congress for a full investigation of the fund. And then he started digging himself. He questioned the fund's accounting methods, its oversight, its investments, and whether or not it was adequately serving its members.[40] He uncovered and then revealed a secret, well-endowed private pension fund for Boyle and his top union assistants. He complained about the more than comfortable salaries paid to thirty-seven employees of the fund and the $10,000 salaries of another 145 employees. He charged Boyle with nepotism in hiring his daughter and brother for jobs at which they rarely appeared. These allegations put Hechler squarely in Boyle's crosshairs.[41] All this, while miners that had been receiving a mere $100 per month retirement were suddenly being denied benefits because of new requirements so stringent that most didn't even qualify. At the same time, Boyle was drawing a $50,000 salary plus an unlimited expense account.[42]

Boyle wasn't the only person Hechler rankled. In his zeal to get a comprehensive bill passed, Hechler spoke passionately wherever he was invited. On the occasion of West Virginia University's April 9, 1969, Festival of Ideas, he joined Dr. Rasmussen on the program. In his remarks, Hechler called all mine conditions medieval, questioned how West Virginians could tolerate the way miners were treated, and suggested that the mining engineering school at WVU was part of the problem. "I regret to report that there has been little change in the School of Mines in the last forty years," he said. "What is being turned out are mining engineers who are primarily production experts rather than graduates who passionately believe that the first and foremost principle in coal mining is how you protect the health and safety of the men who mine the coal." While his criticism, suggesting that the school was complicit in tragedies like Farmington, was roundly denounced as irresponsible by the university and the press, it lit a fire under others who urged a probe of the school's curriculum.[43]

As versions of the mine health and safety bill were making their laborious way through various subcommittees, Senator Jennings Randolph continued to support the industry position. He was known to be squarely in that camp and believed the issue was a touchy one. Needing industry votes, he couldn't afford to ruffle the rank and file, so he introduced a bill on May 12 that he called "a workable compromise." It wasn't. Hechler knew it, and so did Ralph Nader. He begged Randolph to reconsider his position, saying his bill was a capitulation to the coal industry. This gave Hechler yet another chance to urge his strong position. While details were argued and Hechler continued his campaign against the union, things were heating up in the coalfields.[44]

In addition to hammering Randolph's bill, Nader persuaded a very reluctant Joseph "Jock" Yablonski to run against Tony Boyle for the presidency of the UMWA. Although Yablonski had once been a union troubleshooter and was deeply concerned about black lung,[45] he knew of Boyle's power. Boyle hadn't been challenged seriously since 1963, when he assumed office upon the death of the former president, Thomas Kennedy. The fifty-nine-year-old Yablonski, a former child laborer in the mines, had been active in the UMWA leadership since 1943. At his May 29 announcement, Yablonski listed the vast divide between the miners and the union leadership, the hierarchy's refusal to fight for the health and safety of the miners, and the way it had turned its back on the issue of black lung among his reasons for running.[46] Additionally, his son

Joseph A. "Chip" Yablonski Jr., a labor lawyer who often accompanied his dad on the campaign trail, says his father was incensed when Boyle castigated Hechler and the three doctors and ridiculed them as "black tongue people."[47]

Hechler supported Yablonski from the beginning, declaring his allegiance in the halls of Congress. He inserted Yablonski's platform into the *Congressional Record* on June 9 and called it a "veritable Magna Carta for the coal miners of America."[48] Hechler had met Yablonski at the Mine Safety Symposium in Morgantown when he crossed the room to thank Hechler for what he was trying to do for the miners. At that time, Hechler had been pleased to hear Yablonski support the lower coal dust standards Hechler had been insisting on. Now Hechler endorsed his entire platform.[49]

As Hechler stumped for Yablonski's campaign, he realized that Boyle could rightly criticize him for not knowing what he was talking about since he'd never seen the inside of a coal mine. To prevent the possibility, Hechler asked the president of Island Creek Coal Company to arrange for him to tour its Buffalo Creek mine in Logan County. After several hours underground, a coal-blackened Hechler emerged with his escort, confident he'd solved that potential charge from Boyle.[50]

That seems to have been his biggest worry, for he appeared with Yablonski at nearly every one of his West Virginia rallies, seemingly unfazed that he might be damaging his own career with his involvement in UMWA politics.[51] He knew he'd already become Tony Boyle's bitter enemy.[52] At a meeting of the Association of Disabled Miners and Widows in Beckley, Hechler verbally attacked Boyle, who was in the audience. He pulled no punches about the secret retirement fund and urged the miners to demand hearings whenever they were denied benefits. That evening, they found themselves on the same airplane leaving Charleston, West

Ken Hechler tours Wyoming County, WV, coal mine (Courtesy Ken Hechler)

Virginia. Hechler extended his sweaty hand to Boyle, but the ever-fastidious Boyle grunted and refused to acknowledge him.[53]

Although Hechler didn't know until much later just how much danger he faced personally, he admits he was often afraid as he traveled with Yablonski. Since he was never actually threatened, the fear didn't stop him, but the thugs who surrounded Boyle at every step and often attended Yablonski's rallies did intimidate him.[54] According to Chip, Boyle's thugs were there, recording speeches and photographing those in attendance.[55]

After the Senate unanimously passed its version of the bill on October 2,[56] Hechler spoke repeatedly to the House, urging passage of the bill. Sometimes he dealt with specific concerns, but more often he rose to object to either something being left out or damaging amendments others were trying to sneak in.[57] He was relentless, especially on the need to eliminate the UMWA's Board of Review, which was well known to be industry friendly.

As the Senate bill was being debated in the House, Hechler rose to offer amendments that were merely reiterations of the points he had consistently insisted be included. On October 23, 1969, as he was about to leave for the House to give a one-minute speech at noon to mark the removal of the body of the first miner to die at Farmington, fifty to sixty miners rushed into his inner office demanding to know why he wasn't supporting the union's mine safety bills. He tried to explain that his bill was stronger, but they wouldn't listen. One burly miner shoved him in the chest. With time running out, Hechler slipped out, leaving the miners to yell "chicken" after him. His mood lightened after one miner outside the office told him not to worry, as the UMWA had fed a line of bull to those inside. As Hechler reached the outer door, he spotted Tony Boyle in the hall. He appeared to Hechler to have been orchestrating the whole demonstration. Again, Hechler tried to shake his hand, but Boyle demurred, muttering, "Why, I wouldn't shake hands with you."[58] In early December, Boyle beat Yablonski for the presidency in a clearly rigged election. While the Labor Department refused to investigate, it did make public its findings of an audit of the UMWA's books. It confirmed many of the allegations Hechler, Nader, and Yablonski had been making.[59]

Finally a strong bill passed the House on October 29 by a vote of 389 to 4. All that remained was for the conference committee to iron out the differences. Now confident of a final bill, Hechler asked Nixon to invite the Farmington widows to come to Washington for the expected signing ceremony.[60] Hechler's dream bill, which both houses had agreed to by December 18, was about to become the law of the land. It had been little more than a year—an unusually short gestation period for legislation[61]—since the Farmington disaster, and he felt triumphant. But as rumors circulated that Nixon would veto the bill, Hechler began fuming instead of rejoicing.

He sprang into action, again calling on the Farmington widows to return to Washington. Because no commercial flights were available at such short notice, Hechler chartered two private planes to return them to the capital for the third time. Before they left home, the widows had persuaded some miners to stay home from work at midnight on December 28, in case Nixon did deliver his veto. And Hechler had also alluded to a walkout as he spoke in the House on December 23, suggesting that a nationwide strike would occur if Nixon carried out his veto threat. Hechler had no real evidence, but he felt certain it would happen.[62] "I didn't know what the hell I was talking about then, but it was effective," he recalls.[63]

The seven widows, including Mrs. Kaznoski, appeared in the late morning of December 29. They telephoned the White House and were told to arrive at the Northwest Gate at 12:15 P.M., which they did. Seven pens rested on President Nixon's desk, ready for presentation to the widows after the ceremonial signing. Soon, a Nixon staffer sent word that the president would not see them after all. They were to go to the Old Executive Office Building to meet instead with Richard Burress, Nixon's deputy counsel. Even though Hechler had accompanied the women, he was told that they alone were welcome to meet with Burress. Shunned, Hechler was left standing outside the gates. While Burress carefully outlined Nixon's objections to the bill, the telephone rang. It was the White House calling to say that Nixon had changed his mind. Bluff or not, widows pleas or not, Nixon would sign the bill. Given a consolation private tour of the White House, the Farmington widows were presented the signing pens, even though no ceremony would actually take place. Nixon signed the bill on December 30, boarded a plane, and departed without fanfare for the Christmas holidays at his home in San Clemente, California.[64]

In a terrible twist of irony, UMWA presidential hopeful Jock Yablonski; his wife, Margaret; and their daughter, Charlotte, were murdered the day after Nixon signed the bill. It took a week before the heinous crime was discovered, but when it was, Boyle and his henchmen were suspected of being behind it. It didn't surprise Hechler. "I saw these characters at every rally. I'd try to go over and shake their hands and they'd snarl at me and throw beer cans at me," he recalled. "There were rumors about violence all the time."[65]

Turns out Hechler had every right to be wary. At a post-election Yablonski gathering, Hechler arrived late and saw some men in a parked car. He went over, shook their hands, and invited them to come in, then entered the hall himself. "But those were the Yablonski assassins sitting in that car," says Donald Rasmussen. "They had followed Yablonski. They had even followed Hechler on several occasions because he was on the hit list along with Yablonski."[66]

The three Yablonski family murderers—Aubran "Buddy" Martin, Paul E. Gilly, and Claude Vealey—were convicted in 1972,[67] along with Boyle, who spent the rest of his life in prison for

Ken Hechler confers with Jock Yablonski on a black lung bill amendment
(Photo by World Wide Photos)

ordering the murder of Yablonski. Later, Vealey wrote Hechler
that they meant to kill him as well. Vealey admitted that as
Hechler was leaving a Logan area rally with Yablonski, the killers
had followed them, hoping for an opportunity to kill Yablonski,
but "since I was in the car, they didn't care if I got hit as well."[68]
"They meant to shoot both of us. Apparently the roads were
so winding they couldn't get a bead on us. That's why I'm here
today," Hechler said on the twenty-fifth anniversary of Yablonski's
murder.[69]

As Chip Yablonski looks back on those years, he says of
Hechler, "In this era of justified cynicism that our Congress is
bought and paid for by corporate money, it is refreshing to recall
a time when one Congressman took on the most powerful interest

in his state, pushed aside any worry about his personal safety, and willingly jeopardized his political career by standing up for the coal miners in his district and coal miners throughout the entire nation."[70] Hechler is widely considered to be the force that finally got a comprehensive mine health and safety bill passed by Congress. And it is widely considered to be the crowning achievement of his eighteen years there.[71] Rasmussen credits Hechler with single-handedly shepherding the bill through Congress: "He consulted all kinds of scientists, and experts. He didn't do any back-door deals or smoke-filled room stuff. He just did it straight up. He absolutely never rested and just became totally involved with it."[72]

While Hechler proudly points to this bill as one of his major accomplishments, he also gives kudos to the widows, who stirred public sentiment and helped spur the members of Congress to act. "Despite their grief and this greatest of all losses . . . the widows of Farmington . . . resolved that from this disaster must come the determination of this nation that coal miners and their families deserve to live and work in dignity," he said shortly before the bill's passage in a statement honoring them.[73]

Hechler only briefly savored his victory, however. Next, he would begin to tackle the destructive coal extraction practices of strip mining and later, mountaintop removal, while holding the Department of Labor's feet to the fire when he learned that the newly passed law wasn't being fully enforced. For years he borrowed a Mother Jones quote as he led these fights: "I was a fighter; now I'm a hell-raiser."

14

—

HECHLER VS. BIG
COAL—ROUND TWO

—

Hechler barely waited for the ink to dry on Nixon's signature bringing the Federal Mine Health and Safety Act of 1969 to life before renewing his battle against the UMWA and "Big Coal." As Nixon signed the bill on December 31, Hechler's congressional mailbox continued to fill with letters from miners and their family members needing advice on their lawsuits against various mining companies. Some had been fired without cause. Others implored Hechler to help them resolve disputes with both the union and the coal companies. One writer referred to an alleged secret agreement between the union and several coal companies concerning termination of employees or refusal to reemploy them if they had more than a 15 percent disability from silicosis. Still others told of a work stoppage undertaken because the mine owners had not corrected safety concerns and the union had not taken any action. In each case, Hechler agreed to look into the situation.[1] In response to one particular strike in April 1970, he wrote, "Not only has the UMWA failed the miners, the federal and state governments have not required adequate health and safety laws, and when laws are enacted, they aren't enforced. Who can blame the coal miner for walking out? I have gone to court in an effort to force federal mining officials to enforce the Federal Coal Mine Health and Safety Act that I fought so hard for in 1969."[2]

Some of the letters also called on Hechler to push for an immediate investigation into Yablonski's killing and applauded his efforts in battling Boyle's corruption and that of the UMWA.[3] Of course, the police were already on the murder case, so Hechler turned his attention to the current activities of the UMWA. Very little escaped his attention. He learned that the union was appointing doctors to the Welfare and Retirement Fund's board of directors who would be sympathetic to the coal companies, and that it was working to stop funding for Donald Rasmussen's black lung research lab at the Appalachian Regional Hospital in Beckley, West Virginia. With his discoveries, Hechler wrote to Senator Harrison Williams, the chairman of the Senate Subcommittee on Labor, outlining his concerns.[4]

He also complained to Secretary of the Interior Walter Hickel that the thirty-one top positions in the Bureau of Mines were being filled with officials serving only in an acting capacity. Also concerned that Dr. J. Richard Lucas might not be well qualified to serve as the bureau's director, Hechler questioned his nomination. He asked whether Lucas's former position as the head of the Mining Engineering Department at Virginia Polytechnic Institute had created overly strong ties between him and the industry.[5]

Hechler further fumed that the new bill's regulations seemed to be slow in coming together, saying, "It almost seems as if there were an attempt to sabotage the new law."[6] He had reason to feel that way. A government report indicated that through November 16, 1970, a year after the Farmington mine explosion, there had been 406 mine fatalities, whereas in the previous two years there had been 309, including the Farmington men.[7] Although Mine Safety and Health Administration statistics differ—203 fatalities in 1969, and 260 in 1970[8]—the less-than-dramatic reduction in deaths he had hoped for caused Hechler's frustration.

While the Department of Labor investigated possible fraud in Boyle's election, a number of rank-and-file miners issued a February 1970 statement claiming he was still illegally appointing union officials instead of allowing them to be elected by union members. Hechler kept up pressure on this issue for over a year, without resolution. Again, in February 1971, the miners returned to Washington, D.C., complaining that democratic elections were still being denied them.

Then, on March 2, Boyle was finally indicted on thirteen counts of corruption, embezzlement, conspiracy, and illegal use of union money. The following week, Hechler received word from the U.S. assistant attorney general that he was trying to pin down a trial date to resolve the issue of district union elections.[9] But it wasn't until June 1972 that the results of Boyle's election were finally thrown out, and the appointment system he had used to rule the UMWA was declared illegal.[10] A new election was held, and Arnold Miller became the union's president.[11]

Feeling confident that things would now change, Hechler congratulated Miller on his election and looked forward to the reforms he hoped the Miners for Democracy candidate would put in place. While other issues became more pressing once Miller was elected, Hechler never stopped working to get the miners their benefits. His papers on black lung issues following passage of the 1969 act occupy seventy-five cubic yards in the Hechler Collection at Marshall University. The fifty boxes of letters alone represent at least ten thousand unique individual constituent petitions or pieces of resulting correspondence.[12] In most cases, he was able to make a difference, but in some, petitioners fell outside the boundaries of the legislation and he had to advise them so.

Shortly after Miller's election, he wrote Hechler a letter that strengthened the congressman's renewed optimism. "As you have done so many times in the past, your energy and dedication to the welfare of coal miners, their widows and dependents is boundless," Miller wrote. "I can only say again, thank you for your constant endeavors on our behalf and I look forward to the strong personal working relationship we enjoy. I believe your presence and remarks on [sic] yesterday will be significant in persuading Congress to continue the Black Lung Benefits Program under federal control with claims being paid by the coal industry."[13] In a later letter, Hechler called Arnold Miller's victory "the greatest Christmas present—with the exception of peace in Vietnam—in the world." He also said, "[It] shows the world what a guy with guts, drive, and belief in his ideals, can do."[14]

Until Miller's election, Hechler had regularly pressured both the UMWA and the government on issues he felt were being ignored. In February 1971, he had demanded the resignation of Undersecretary of the Interior Fred J. Russell for appointing "unqualified hacks to a coal mine safety research panel." Claiming these appointments violated the new law, he called Russell a "true troglodyte . . . who believed in the divine right of well-heeled business contributors to run the country for their own benefit."[15]

A few months later, when Hechler learned the Department of the Interior was about to launch a publicity campaign aimed mostly at coal miners, he reacted vehemently. The purpose of the campaign was to remind the miners that they were mostly responsible for their own safety. Hechler was furious that the bureau would try blaming the victims. He said, "Why doesn't the Bureau of Mines get on with the job of enforcing the health and safety law, instead of trying to give the miners a snow job?" In response, he submitted an amendment to the newly enacted law that forbade use of any funds appropriated by the act to pay any public relations firms for promotional campaigns aimed at coal miners. It passed the House with a unanimous voice vote on June 29, 1971.[16]

In July, he charged that in the six months following enactment of the Mine Health and Safety Act of 1969, only a handful of fines had been levied, and clandestine meetings were still being held

Ken Hechler plans strategy with West Virginia coal miners before a Senate hearing, 1971 (Photo by Jeanne Rasmussen, Courtesy ETSU Archives of Appalachia)

between coal operators and Bureau of Mines officials. He further argued that the bureau should be transferred to the Department of Labor. He again quoted the number of deaths since the Farmington disaster, which by then had increased to 578.[17] Accusing the bureau of "pussyfooting," he said, "They act as though they feel a ton of coal is more valuable than the life of a coal miner."[18] Despite the continued violations, the situation did eventually improve for miners, no doubt as a result of Hechler's dogged insistence on strict enforcement of the 1969 act and his pursuit of their safety. Cecil Roberts, who became UMWA president in 1995, gives credit to Hechler for the resulting decline in mine deaths. According to him, in the twenty-five years before 1969, twelve thousand coal miners had been killed in U.S. mines. In the twenty-five years since its passage, there had been less than three thousand.[19]

Meanwhile, one constituent letter to Hechler in late 1970 alerted him to a new threat to his beloved state. As he was fighting to clean up the union with one hand and trying to hold governmental enforcement feet to the fire with the other, he learned that Island Creek Coal Company had its eye on strip mining in the protected area of Otter Creek, near Cranberry Glades, West Virginia. The company was trying to build a road into the area to test for coal it could strip-mine. In strip mining, giant machines are used to remove the topsoil and vegetation covering seams of coal relatively close to the surface. Unlike deep mining, in which a mine shaft is dug deep into a mountain, strip mining, or surface mining, creates large open pits so the coal can be easily excavated. Knowing this, Hechler was upset, to say the least, and responded immediately that he'd already introduced a bill to make this area a wilderness area, along with Cranberry Glades and Dolly Sods.[20]

With this new threat at hand, he began reading studies from other states that had dealt with this destructive mining practice, which Harry Caudill had warned about in his book *Night Comes to the Cumberlands*. On one study he jotted this reminder, "$200 per acre to reclaim strip-mined areas."[21] With the book by Caudill and Rachel Carson's *Silent Spring* in the back of his mind, in February Hechler introduced H.R. 4556—the Mined Area Protection Act of 1971—to stop the practice. Following on the heels of Nixon's newly created Environmental Protection Agency (EPA) and the designation of Earth Day the year before, he didn't think it would take long for Congress to act. Sadly, he was wrong. Several bills on the issue were introduced during that first session of the 92nd Congress, but none were as strict as Hechler's. The administration's bill gave states two years to submit plans for reducing or halting strip mining. Hechler called the bill "toothless."[22]

At about the same time, back home in West Virginia, a bill to abolish strip mining had been introduced in the state legislature, which would have dramatically strengthened the existing Surface Mine Reclamation Act of 1967. The bill's authors hoped to correct the flaws in the old bill, which they called a woeful failure. Coincidentally, it was introduced at about the same time Hechler's bill hit the congressional hopper. Then secretary of state Jay Rockefeller supported it, saying, "Because West Virginia is 98 percent hilly territory, reclamation of land torn up by surface mining is physically impossible. If strip mining companies work at the rate they are now—doubling their acreage—then a major portion of West Virginia will become unlivable and in the long term our economic development will be severely restricted."[23] Although he would later retreat from this position to win his second race for governor, Rockefeller even financed an organization called Citizens for the Abolition of Strip Mining, which combined the efforts of most of the abolition movements in the state. Later, when the group's funding dried up, Hechler hired its former director, Reverend Richard Austin, whose home in Boone County, West Virginia, was within sight of a large strip mine.[24]

When Hechler introduced his bill in early 1971, calling for the complete abolition of strip mining within six months of passage, he admitted the phaseout would mean 25,000 to 30,000 men would have to find other jobs. However, he believed the "damage to the ecology [was] a much greater consideration."[25] In this, thirty congressional cosponsors, plus environmental groups from the Sierra Club to the Environmental Policy Center, supported him. The bill never made it out of committee, but that didn't stop Hechler. He reintroduced his bill on the first day of spring, March 22, 1971, with even more cosponsors.[26]

New congressional staffer Ned Helme arrived in Hechler's office in the summer of 1971 just in time to help. A schoolteacher, Helme had been involved in anti-strip-mining activities, so he had volunteered to work on that issue for Hechler during his summer break. Hechler assigned him the task of gathering much of the research,[27] including amassing the letters that had poured in telling Hechler of the carnage the mining practice was wreaking on the state. Research on the equipment used in strip mining also introduced him to the $11 million wheel excavator that its German developer said could dig 235,000 tons of virgin soil per day. In the accompanying story, he read, "At that pace it could probably eat much of West Virginia by Christmas."[28]

Hechler, his cosponsors, abolition advocates across the country, and national environmental groups urged Congress at every turn to hold hearings, which they finally did beginning in September 1971. When the Mines and Mining Subcommittee of the House Committee on Interior and Insular Affairs opened its hearings, the first testimony came from industry supporters who had agreed to support a mild regulatory bill to quiet the public outcries Hechler had stirred up. Hechler was next.[29] "I had to use loose leaf binders with pages and pages of questions and answers," Helme recalls. "Hechler said 'You've got to think of every nastiest [sic] question you can think they'd ever ask us and have a good answer.' I put all this stuff together and I briefed him."[30]

During the hearings, testimony from one constituent described the destruction caused by the monster mining machines—the "GEM of Egypt," with its 170-foot-long boom, and "Big Muskie," the 13,000-ton machine that stood twenty-two stories tall.[31] Senator Howard Baker from Tennessee, whose state was equally affected by strip mining, warned, "I feel the situation . . . is an emergency and in two years will be a complete disaster." In order to back up his case, Hechler took three experts with him: UMWA president Arnold Miller, who shared Hechler's abolitionist views; West Virginia University economics professor William Miernyk; and West Virginia University wildlife management professor Robert Smith. Though Hechler had received permission to invite the three, the committee chair suddenly ruled they would not be allowed to testify because he had already turned down other requests.

Regardless of feeling he was ready, Hechler remembers the grilling he got. "For over three hours, I was subjected to the most hostile and vindictive questions and procedural rulings I had ever experienced in the nearly fourteen years of my service as a Congressman. Most of the three hours were taken up by humiliating questions as virtually every committee member tried to get me to change my support of abolition."[32] His bill eventually gained almost one hundred cosponsors, including Ohio congressman John Sieberling, who amended the bill to include cash payments and retraining funds for those who would lose their jobs. The amendment also moved to place the bill's administration with the fledgling EPA.[33] Although more than two dozen other bills on the issue were introduced in 1971,[34] and hearings were held, no other action ensued until early 1972, when the Committee on Interior and Insular Affairs voted to kill his bill.[35]

Hechler's bill might have remained buried deep in the congressional archives but for another mining-related tragedy in West Virginia. Early on February 26, 1972, three Pittston Coal Company impoundment dams, which held 132 million gallons of black sludge and wastewater from the company's cleaning plants, collapsed, and the water rushed into tiny hollows on Buffalo Creek—population five thousand—in Logan County. The disaster killed 125 people, injured over 1,000 others, and left 4,000 homeless in a matter of minutes.[36]

The night before, Hechler was in nearby Williamson giving out awards at a junior high school basketball tournament. It had been raining steadily for several days—typical for that time of year—and it had stormed again that night. Afterward, as he tried to drive back to Huntington on old Route 52, he encountered trouble. "As I came around a corner, my Jeep ran into a wall of water. A little creek named Mossy Fork had overflowed and caused a flash flood," he recalls. Determined to ferry the water, he gunned the motor and pressed on, flooding the engine with water. Abandoning the Jeep, he knocked on a nearby door seeking shelter, which the owners provided. The next morning, the airwaves were bursting with the news of Buffalo Creek, but he was stuck, unable to see if he could provide assistance to his constituents. After a friend rescued him and he returned to Huntington, he sprang into action. First, he hopped a helicopter with the Corps of Engineers to view the damage. Second, he called his old friend from the Truman White House days, George Elsey, who was then president of the American Red Cross, to make sure they would mobilize quickly to assist the survivors.[37]

From the air, what he saw was chilling, but it merely confirmed the magnitude of a problem he'd been railing against since 1967. In his fight to stop strip mining, he had learned how apprehensive the Buffalo Creek residents were each time heavy rainfall occurred. They feared massive, potentially life-threatening flooding if a dam broke. With their pleas for help and a report on the subject by Secretary of the Interior Stewart Udall, he had warned against the kind of sludge ponds in West Virginia that were a by-product of strip mining—and which eventually collapsed in Buffalo Creek.[38] Both the *Logan Banner* and the *Charleston Gazette* had reported on a July 1967 on-site tour Hechler had organized to show officials firsthand the damage done by a small slide. It consisted of masses of wet slate, or "gob," released in another Logan County community after water had saturated the slate piles left from strip mining. In one of the articles, Hechler was quoted as saying, "Some precautionary means must be taken immediately to insure that this threat is lifted for the well-being of the residents,"[39] but no one had listened.

Although he was proud he had blown the whistle early, now that his prediction had come true, he regretted that he could only offer assistance after the fact. As soon as he could he went to the scene, where he almost immediately began denouncing the recovery efforts. "One of the first things they tried to do," he said, "was to rebuild the rail lines, so the coal company could start shipping coal out again, instead of trying to help the victims."[40] Although Hechler realized that Pittston had been in violation of the laws in allowing that dam to threaten the valley, he knew little could be done on a federal level without the support of the Corps of Engineers and state officials. Ultimately, one 1974 lawsuit against Pittston forced the company to settle out of court for $13,000 to each of the six hundred survivors and family members of the victims.[41] Another suit later that year awarded an additional $4.8 million to 348 child survivors.[42]

A sidebar to the tragedy, however, was a renewed interest in legislation to curb or more strictly regulate strip mining. Hechler swung back into action by rehiring his summer volunteer, Ned Helme, who returned to work full time for Hechler in September 1972, becoming what the congressman called his "environmental conscience." For three years Helme acted as his legislative assistant, dealing with protection of the New River Gorge, Dolly Sods, Otter Creek, and other wilderness areas, but he spent most of his time on the strip-mining legislative battles. He obtained a series of images taken on 1971 field trips into the coal fields and created a slide show,[43] which Hechler used to persuade his colleagues to join him in the fight. "Part of my job was to put together . . . all these pictures of strip mines everywhere," Helme said. "He put the music on it. It was hilarious. He used the country song, 'I Never Promised You a Rose Garden,' and there'd be a big picture of a completely destroyed hillside."[44] Hechler added his gift for parody to the show, which he dubbed "Reclamation, or Putting Lipstick on a Corpse." Even with its comedic approach, the hard-hitting presentation created a groundswell of support around West Virginia, in other Appalachian coal-rich states, and in the west.

According to Helme, Hechler's appearance on *The Today Show* and being quoted in the *Washington Post* and the *New York Times* made a big impact. Even though Hechler wasn't in a House leadership position on this matter, Representatives Patsy Mink and Morris Udall, the leaders of the subcommittee, and Senator Henry M. "Scoop" Jackson used Hechler's arguments very effectively. Because he had stirred up the citizenry to demand abolition, his stringent stance helped them get a much stronger regulatory bill. "We offered fifty amendments during the floor debate and we got a lot of amendments [included] that strengthened the bill," Helme recalled. "It was a regulatory bill; it wasn't an abolition bill, but we fought for the strongest position.[45] In October 1972, the House voted to establish a federal program charged with regulating the environmental effects of surface mining, but it died in the Senate.[46] Hechler wrote to one supporter that he planned to reintroduce his own version in the next session.[47]

Throughout 1973, Hechler kept up the pressure both in the halls of Congress and in the media. Several versions of a strip-mine bill were introduced, but none were as strong as Hechler's. Again, Helme worked to draft amendments and follow the bill through the various committees. Hechler battled vigorously, and it was an up-and-down fight. Amendments were added, then stripped out in later committee markups. April saw a win for the coal operators when controls initially included were eased. In June, Hechler reported that the House had approved his amendment to ban strip mining in the wild and scenic river system, national wilderness areas, national parks, and wildlife refugees.[48]

In late 1973, Hechler issued a succinct statement on the whole situation. "While the great debate over strip-mining rages, Congress has fiddled around with strip-mining regulation bills for nearly three years without final action. The House . . . passed a bill on Oct 11, 1972, and the Senate passed a weak bill on Oct 9, 1973. Now it is the turn of the House to delay in order to please the strip-mining industry and their friends in the electric utility lobby. On Nov 12, 1973, a strip mining regulation bill cleared two House Interior subcommittees, and for some unexplained reason the full House Interior committee decided to take no further action until late January of next year."[49] Frustration set in, but Hechler continued to battle.

In October 1973, the Arab oil embargo began and continued until March 1974, sending oil prices spiraling out of sight and creating an energy crisis and long lines at gasoline pumps across the country. This caused Congress to reconsider America's dependence on foreign oil. Despite the situation, various strip-mining bills were introduced and debated when the 93rd Congress convened in January 1974. They represented three positions: abolition, regulation, and a strong bill with only a few amendments that Hechler could support.[50] When new amendments were offered to appease the coal industry, Hechler fired back with one that forbade strip mining on slopes steeper than 20 percent. It was rejected, however, because, according to Hechler, "there just happened to be more Congressmen subservient to the coal industry than there were genuine environmentalists."[51] He continued inviting colleagues to watch his slide show, hoping to swing them to his abolitionist position, but the number of his cosponsors decreased to sixty-six. That summer, he called on all churches to designate July 14 as "Save the Land and the People Sunday" in anticipation of an upcoming House debate.

The final blow came during the July 22 deliberations, when a Wyoming congressman introduced an amendment to allow mining companies to create so-called plateaus so that no "high walls" would remain on the stripped hills. Evidence had shown that strip-mining exceedingly steep hills would cause erosion, so this amendment was the recommended fix. But it doomed Hechler's provision to completely stop mining on those slopes. Hechler immediately saw it as the beginning of mountaintop removal mining and delivered a fiery rebuttal. "Mountaintop removal is the most devastating form of mining on steep slopes," he said. "Once we scalp off a mountain and the spoil runs down the mountainside, and the acid runs into the water supply, there is no way to check it. This is not only esthetically bad, as anyone can tell who flies over the State of West Virginia or any place where the mountaintops are scraped off, but also it is devastating to those people who live below the mountain."[52] The less restrictive amendment passed regardless of Hechler's vehement and prescient protests.

When the House and the Senate finally offered their conference report in December, Hechler voted against it, saying, "I regret that this conference report will only raise false hopes among people who think they will be protected, and will wake up to discover that those who are charged with protecting the public interest are officially sanctioning more destruction and exploitation."[53]

Hechler wasn't the only person who opposed the final bill. So did President Gerald Ford, but for a vastly different reason. By the time it reached Ford's desk, it had been watered down as Congress yielded to the demands of the industry. The coal operators then asked him to veto it, which he did just before Congress adjourned for the year. In so doing, he stated that passage of the bill would have meant higher unemployment, higher costs for electricity, and a reduced supply of coal during the nation's current energy crisis.[54] While it may have looked as if Hechler and the coal operators were on the same side, they weren't. He had opposed the bill because of its weakened stance on strip mining; Ford had capitulated to the coal companies because of the energy crisis.

Nevertheless, shortly after Congress reconvened in 1975, Hechler was at it again. In March, he issued a statement calling the latest and virtually identical bill "weak, wishy-washy, and watered down," and sent a special request to all the members of the House "strongly and urgently" asking them to vote against the House bill. He trotted out his slide show once again and urged them to come see it and to hear several West Virginia miners tell of the "human impact of strip mining in the mountains."[55] He also offered a laundry list of changes necessary for him to vote for it. Later that month, both houses passed a version of the strip-mining bill, and it was sent to a joint committee to iron out the differences.

Hechler's pleas were of no use. The weakened bill passed and was sent to President Ford, who promptly vetoed it again, citing the same reasons he had used in 1974.[56] This time, the margins by which Congress had passed the bill seemed strong enough to override the veto; but after a combined lobbying effort by the administration, the coal industry, and utility companies, that margin slipped. A switch of three votes would have changed the outcome.[57] Surprisingly, Hechler was one of those who refused to override Ford's veto. He issued a statement explaining his reasons: "I am tired of voting for Congressional Band-Aids, and weak, papered-over compromises, which do not begin to solve some of the serious problems the nation confronts," he said. "Although an abolitionist, I would have settled for a bill, which included some hope for the people in the mountains. . . . I did not go out to campaign in favor of sustaining the president's veto, because I respected the position of those who felt the bill was better than I did. If you will examine the roll call, you will find no environmentalists who were swayed by my vote because I made it a point to tell every member of the House that they should go ahead and vote to override if they felt it was the best bill obtainable."[58] Congressman Andrew Young, who had been one of Hechler's staunchest abolition supporters, felt betrayed and begged Hechler, unsuccessfully, to change his mind.[59] His fellow representatives weren't the only ones surprised. Ned Helme recalls the argument about Hechler's decision. "The biggest showdown was when Hechler voted not to override the veto," Helme said. "We had a big argument about that and the staff, all of us, were mad at him, but he was adamant."[60] Even as he let his vote stand, Hechler now says he was sure the regulation would never work.[61]

In fact, he told President Jimmy Carter as much at the White House Rose Garden signing ceremony on August 3, 1977, after the Surface Mine Control and Reclamation Act of 1977 finally passed. Although Hechler had left Congress by then to run against Jay Rockefeller for governor, he was invited to the ceremony, since it had been his early call to action that had led to the bill. Hechler recalls, "I told President Carter to his face, 'This law is not going to work unless it is very vigorously enforced,' and his response was, 'I've got a Secretary of the Interior, Cecil Anderson; I'll tell him that.'"[62]

Sadly, Hechler was right in his prediction. Looking back, he says the new staff tried very hard for the first few years to enforce the bill they were tasked with administering. But the difficulty arose when those aggressive staffers began resigning in frustration with the coal operators, and they were replaced with a more passive group that didn't want to fight.[63] In his later years, Hechler mounted the fight again, this time railing specifically against mountaintop removal coal mining. It was the very practice the final bill had made legal. Now, Hechler calls strip mining "the god-father of mountaintop removal."[64] The fight to stop this practice continues, with Hechler's name invoked as the canary in the coal mine that predicted the destruction that environmentalists now fight.

Although Hechler left office frustrated by this defeat, his place in history will long be marked by what he accomplished and by what else he tried to bring about for West Virginia's working class, especially the miners and their families. His ongoing fight to protect the state's land and its environment endeared him to some but made him a pariah to others. Still, his battles were always fought with an eye out for the little guy. Looking back at his childhood, his parents, and the influences of that privileged life, it's amazing he evolved into such a champion of the people. While they did work to make life in their community better, much of what the elder Hechlers did in forming the town of Roslyn Heights, or as town committee members, was done to enhance Clarence Mackay's position. No doubt Hechler's parents were proud of his achievements, but fighting on behalf of the little guy ran counter to their politics. Being a rebel hell-raiser suited Hechler better.

15

SAVING THE NEW RIVER

In the West Virginia mountains, there is a scenic river. Some say it is the nation's oldest, yet it is called the New River because it was unknown to the earliest explorers. It rushes northward from North Carolina near the Tennessee border about 350 miles across the Blue Ridge Mountains into Virginia, then into West Virginia. There it joins the Gauley River to form the Kanawha River, before flowing into the mighty Ohio and becoming part of the Mississippi on its way to the Gulf of Mexico. It's rimmed with steep cliffs and monumental rocky outcroppings, especially in its West Virginia gorge. Its breathtaking overlooks afford tourists spectacular views, and the third-longest single-arch bridge in the world crosses it at Fayetteville, West Virginia. Whitewater rafters call it heaven—and hell. Botanists marvel at its unusual plant life. Endangered fish species swim in its fast-flowing clear water. BASE (building, antenna, span, and earth) jumpers tempt it each October as they jump from the gorge bridge.

In 1974, Appalachian Electric Power (AEP) and its subsidiary, Appalachian Power, announced plans to build a pump storage dam near Galax, Virginia. To do this, they required approval from the U.S. Department of the Interior. Hechler, and later other members of Congress, set out to stop them. He had rafted the New River, knew its tourism value, and realized the building of the dam would ruin the state's budding whitewater-rafting industry. The proposed hydroelectric project would have been used only to provide peak load power for transmission to other parts of the United States. Moreover, it was slated for abandonment after fifty years.

AEP argued that the project was necessary because it would save an estimated six million tons of coal during its lifetime. It also warned that it was necessary to avert a projected energy crisis the company felt was looming on the horizon. Yet in the building process, it would flood some forty thousand acres of farmland, which produced $13.5 million in agricultural income in North Carolina; replace lush riverbanks with mud flats; jeopardize the bass fishing industry; and destroy a river that had flowed for a hundred million years.[1] When Hechler learned of the project, which AEP had been planning since 1962, he hired Darrell McGraw, who served on the West Virginia Supreme Court for twelve years and later became the state's attorney general, to research ways to prevent this tragedy.[2] In addition, he began agitating to get people involved and public sentiment on his side. For him, it was all about the environment. "We had great difficulty in the Congress at first, until I began to see the people of North Carolina were so interested in this, and [I] began to form a coalition with [them]," he said later as he reminisced about the battle.[3]

He'd heard rumors of the proposed dam two years earlier and had been working "to suspend further action on the proposed Blue Ridge Power Project on the New River until Congress has a chance to consider legislation."[4] Initially, he wanted the New River named as a National Park, but he was told the area did not fit the criteria necessary for such designation.[5] Then, in 1974, he and North Carolina representative Wilmer Mizell revived the bill and introduced it on June 3. Hechler had the support of environmentalists and most of his constituents as he argued for a two-year impact study before bulldozers moved in. The environmental group, Izaak Walton League, mounted a telegram campaign to Congress in support of the bill in the U.S. Senate. The group supported Hechler's proposal to include parts of the New River in the Interior Department's designated Scenic River System as a means of stopping the project.[6] In his remarks before the subcommittee, Hechler noted that even the Secretary of the Interior, Rogers C. B. Morton, who had formerly supported the Blue Ridge Project, now favored his proposal instead.[7]

Once again, Hechler was the lone West Virginia congressional voice supporting the measure. Though his old friend, United Mine Workers president Arnold Miller, urged Congress to "save the oldest free-flowing river in the world,"[8] Hechler met with strong opposition from others within his state. The building and construction trade unions, which could see only the prospect of jobs, were fiercely supportive of the proposed project. Governor Arch Moore strongly supported AEP as well, largely viewing the economic impact promised by the dam's construction. Despite this opposition, the House Committee on Interior and Insular Affairs favorably reported the bill to the full House to study conferring wild and scenic river status to the New River. However, intense lobbying by these groups and by AEP caused the House Rules Committee on December 11 to table the bill indefinitely, although the Senate had already passed it, 49–19, on May 28.[9] When Hechler learned that West Virginia governor Arch Moore had a hand in tabling the bill, he exploded. "I deeply regret that Gov. Moore, by his action, has stabbed in the back those many West Virginians who want to keep the rugged New River as a free-flowing stream," he said. Hechler felt the governor was as much a foe as AEP, since Moore had sent a letter to the committee stating his opposition shortly before the vote.[10]

Hechler then moved to suspend the rules to bring the bill to the full House. Under suspension of the rules, a two-thirds majority was needed, along with Speaker Carl Albert's approval, to place it on the calendar. In the meantime, the House Rules Committee's action had cleared the way to issue AEP a license to begin its project. In light of the perceived defeat, on December 15, 1974, a large crowd of New River supporters gathered under dull skies on the banks of the river near Thurmond in Fayette County, braving high winds and cold rain to hold a ceremonial funeral for the ancient river. Hechler spoke to the gathering, saying, "The New River may seem dead this afternoon, and God is weeping for the New River; but the New River will rise again." He then gave the listeners Speaker Albert's telephone number and urged them to call him asking to put the bill on the calendar before Congress adjourned for Christmas.[11] In spite of his efforts, the bill failed to get the necessary two-thirds vote, but it did garner a simple majority, 196–181.[12] This gave Hechler the encouragement to try again.

Just before January 2, 1975—the effective date of AEP's approval to begin construction—the state of North Carolina successfully challenged the license, saying that AEP hadn't properly considered the environmental consequences of the dam, nor had it considered archaeological evidence uncovered by two studies from the 1960s. Hechler knew North Carolina's governor, James F. Holshouser, and the North Carolina congressional delegation were unanimous in their desire to save the New River as well, so he aligned himself with them. Hechler spoke at a large meeting in Raleigh, urging others to join the fight. "I am confident that we can stop these mammoth dams either by action of the North Carolina General Assembly in conjunction with Secretary of the Interior Rogers Morton, or through the courts, or by action of the Congress itself," he said in his keynote address. He also complained again about the West Virginia governor's opposition. "I wish that Governor Moore would fight as hard to protect one of West Virginia's greatest natural resources, which is advertised in all our state travel brochures, and is now threatened with early destruction."[13] Hechler was leaving no avenue unexplored in his battle to save this pristine river.

In further efforts to educate members of Congress about the New River and its beauty, Hechler began inviting them to go on white-water rafting trips with him. Meanwhile, he and the North Carolina delegation, including conservative Republican Senator Jesse Helms, who usually opposed environmentalists, continued to educate the public about the river's scenic beauty and its tourism value. Public hearings were held while the study Hechler had fought for was underway. At the same time, the North Carolina General Assembly designated twenty-six and a half miles of the New River's South Fork as a state scenic river. This action placed it under state management. Following the study's conclusion in April 1976, the U.S. Department of the Interior extended the state designation to federal status as well.[14]

Now it was up to Congress to pass final legislation that would prevent this or any future power project on the entire river. This time, North Carolina's representative, Stephen Neal, and Senator Jesse Helms introduced companion bills in their respective chambers.[15] Although his colleagues were leading the charge, Hechler signed on—now with the support of fellow West Virginia representative Harley Staggers[16]—and introduced his own version, H.R. 13227, on April 13, 1976.[17] Support was mounting, and presidential candidate Jimmy Carter and West Virginia gubernatorial candidate Jay Rockefeller both publicly endorsed saving the New River.[18]

That spring, the upcoming presidential primaries were also in full swing. President Ford had earlier recognized the importance of saving the river. In the North Carolina primary, Ford's opponent, Ronald Reagan, also sided with Hechler and the environmentalists.[19] This was good news, for it assured that no matter who won in November, the new president would be on their side.

Again, public hearings were conducted. On May 20, Hechler addressed the Senate Interior and Insular Affairs Committee, warning that if the action he hoped for was not forthcoming, "the American Electric Power Company [would be] eager to move those bull-dozers in to begin ripping up the turf."[20] The following day, in his opening statements, AEP vice president John Vaughan admitted that all the charges about the destruction the proposed dam would cause were valid. But in so doing, he tried to mitigate them by offering land to North Carolina for parks and recreation, announcing the compensation the company was willing to pay the affected farmers, and stating that only 8 percent of the acreage to be flooded was under current cultivation.[21] Joseph Dowd, vice president and general counsel for AEP, followed, attacking Senator Stephen Neal's broadly distributed brochure, *Neal Seeking Support to Save New River,* as misleading because the five photographs it contained pictured West Virginia sections of the New River that would not be affected by the dam. He further argued that because the New River was not initially included in the list of 650 rivers named in the Wild and Scenic Rivers Act of 1968, it shouldn't be now. The arguments fell on deaf ears, and Senator Lee Metcalf of Montana dismissed each as ludicrous.[22]

Metcalf then pointed out that AEP and its four subsidiaries had managed to amass $17.4 million in recent tax credits and had paid no federal taxes despite an 18 percent return on revenue of $425,350,313. He said, "While I do not want to minimize the strong competition which that company has from other utilities, AEP's ability to milk the Treasure [*sic*] and bilk the (state) regulators establishes it as the number one seed in the 'Tax-keeper of the Year Open.'"[23] It was a quote worthy of Hechler. Metcalf's continued line of rebuttals had the effect of shooting a helium balloon from the sky. AEP appeared to have lost the fight.

According to then retired senator Sam J. Ervin Jr., by July, this was one of the most heavily lobbied bills of the 95th Congress. Virginia native Earl Hamner, of *The Waltons* fame, wrote to each

President Ford signs the New River bill and inadvertently hands the first pen to Ken Hechler (Photo by UPI)

member of the Rules Committee urging approval; farmers whose land would be flooded by the dam swarmed the halls of Congress to lobby their congresspersons; and NPR's *All Things Considered* did a piece about the controversy on June 24.[24] Senator Ervin also stated that if the bill didn't pass, "it would be gone forever and even the good Lord . . . couldn't replace it."[25] Congress couldn't ignore what had become a national issue. After another close fight among the House Rules Committee members, the House passed the bill, 311–73, on August 10, and the Senate followed suit on August 30, passing the bill 69–16.[26] The protracted four-year fight was over. The Blue Ridge Project was dead. Now the New River would attract canoe enthusiasts and daredevils from across the country instead of rich people running speedboats on a placid lake, as Hechler had feared would be its fate if the dam had been built.[27]

Later, Hechler characterized this issue as one of his most difficult struggles because, as he said, "I got no help whatsoever from my colleagues or the governor of West Virginia because they were in the pockets of the construction industry that would get so much out of the jobs, where I was interested in preserving the white-water rafting and the natural effects of the New River as a recreational area."[28]

President Ford signed the bill on September 11, 1976, in the White House Rose Garden, and Hechler was there. "President Ford had this long table where he had a number of pens that he was going to sign the bill with. He couldn't see who was standing behind him. The Republican governor of North Carolina was there. And a number of Republican members were right behind him. So, when he signed with the first pen, he reached the pen back, not realizing I was right back there to grab it. And right at that strategic moment, the *New York Times* photographer took a very dramatic picture that showed me with glee on my face, grabbing the first pen," Hechler recalls with a chuckle.[29] Once again, the quintessential David felt as if he'd slain Goliath.

16

HECKLING CONGRESS

The late senator George McGovern drew a distinction between politicians and public servants. He believed, "In the popular sense, politics is thought of as a game of winning elections at whatever cost, whereas, public service is dedicating one's life to the greater good of one's fellow citizens. It's what ought to guide us—the desire to make life better for the people we represent in public service."[1] While Hechler certainly won his fair share of elections, this ideal of being a true public servant is what drove him. Girded by his Swarthmore education and the model of his old boss, Harry Truman, Hechler preached the importance of public service in every classroom he graced. In his PhD dissertation, "Insurgency," he chronicled those progressive Taft-era congresspersons who had rebelled against the heavy-handedness of Speaker of the House Joe Cannon. Recalling their success, Hechler had no fear of speaking his own mind.

From his first term in Congress in 1959, Hechler had set himself apart as a rebel. When he aligned himself with the ten members of the House of Representatives who called themselves "the Mustangs," he stamped himself as different from most of the others in that Congress. Unlike many of his colleagues, Hechler, along with the others, was less interested in his own reelection than in being a public servant. The rampant "reelection first" mentality vexed the group, especially Hechler.[2]

As a freshman representative, he minced no words when complaining about the defense budget. Quoting statistics showing that

West Virginia had ranked at the top of the percentage of its population serving in the Korean War, he noted that it also ranked dead last in Pentagon spending. He perceived that as "a shameful discrimination" against his adopted Mountain State. "It is a national disgrace for West Virginia to be first in war, first in peace, and last in the hearts of the Pentagon," he said, putting his own twist on Henry Lee's eulogy for George Washington.[3]

In another parody to the tune of "Music, Music, Music," he sang:

Put another million in
Campaigns need more dough to win
They can't limit what we spend
So, spend it, spend it, spend it!

Whether it was on the issue of campaign finance reform or his challenge to Americans to participate in the political process— sung to the French national anthem—Hechler skewered the pretentious and his political opponents.[4] According to Iowa senator Tom Harkin, Hechler could always elicit a laugh from his fellow committee members as well. He says of serving on the Science and Technology Committee with Hechler, "He would be probing and all of a sudden, you would realize he was getting to a point he wanted to make that was kind of funny. The guy has a great sense of humor."[5]

Of course, he didn't always use humor to get his point across; sometimes he borrowed, or altered, quotes from others. In 1965, while arguing for the adoption of a bill he cosponsored to create the National Council on the Arts, he heard others say the United States couldn't afford to assist the arts and humanities. So he paraphrased a famous 1796 quote by founding father and ambassador Charles Pinckney, in which he said, "Millions for defense, but not one cent for tribute." Hechler's version: "Billions for defense, but not one cent to contribute to the arts and humanities."[6]

While Hechler was more than eager to vote yea on funding bills he felt would help ordinary citizens or the nation as a whole, like the bill to create the arts council, he consistently railed against congressional pay raises. It was an ongoing battle. Only five years after entering Congress, Hechler had denounced a congressional pay raise. In 1964, *Charleston Gazette* staff writer Thomas Stafford claimed that Hechler had said most members of Congress weren't earning the $22,500 salary they were currently being paid. Stafford then charged that the remark had put Hechler squarely at odds with his colleagues and had ended whatever honeymoon previously existed between them.[7] Hechler refuted Stafford's claim and also denied making his colleagues angry. In fact, he said Senator Robert Byrd told him he didn't even know Hechler's position on the pay raise bill.[8]

Whether you believe Stafford or Hechler, Hechler never pulled any punches on that issue. By 1965, congressional salaries had risen to $30,000, yet four years later, they were about to be increased again.[9] In 1969, the *Parkersburg News* published a valentine addressed to "All Congressmen," congratulating them on giving themselves a 41 percent pay raise by passing a procedural vote the previous year that made all such pay raises law within thirty days after they were recommended by the president. They didn't even have to vote on the specific raise. Signed, "A Taxpayer," the "valentine" gift was worth $12,500 for each member.[10] Now the salary was $42,000, nearly double what it was when Hechler took office in 1959. While he didn't initiate the valentine, he certainly approved of it. Several copies are in his files. He'd stated his position on this subject each time it had come up.

By 1973, Hechler had softened a bit on the issue, saying he could see the strength of arguments to raise congressional salaries along with those of federal judges and cabinet members, but he still opposed the measure in light of other recent moves to cut federal expenditures to stimulate the economy. For him, it was the wrong time to discuss the increase; thus, once again, he voted nay.[11]

Four years later, pay increases again surfaced, with Hechler making even stronger objections. Because an increase had been granted again in 1975, a group of citizens calling themselves We the People began protesting the proposed 1977 increase in congressional office expenses. Hechler, of course, approved of the protesters' efforts, saying they were simply trying to take control of their own government. In solidarity, he presented a protest petition carrying one thousand signatures to Congress. At the same time, he wrote a letter to newspaper editors charging that the proposal would allow a 250 percent increase in official expense allowances as well as another 29 percent pay increase. He believed congressional pay raises should be tied inversely to the Cost of Living Index; he thought this would make members of Congress pay attention to fighting inflation.[12] On February 10, 1977, he wrote a letter to the *Herald Dispatch* editors spelling out his reaction to the proposal. "Congress is not and should not be a career service, so you don't need the high financial incentives to attract good candidates. . . . This situation so shocked me that I returned to the U.S. Treasurer $175 per month of my salary, plus the $10,000 for newsletters which I didn't send out, plus $1,000 of the stationery account, and refused to accept goodies like the plants, flowers, and a refrigerator."[13] Actually, he was always the model of frugality, sometimes to the point of being penurious with allowed salary amounts. At the time of this proposed raise, Hechler still paid top staffer and public relations guru Dick Leonard almost $10,000 less than the maximum amount allowed.[14]

He also sent a tough message to Speaker of the House Thomas "Tip" O'Neill, denouncing the "devious and deceitful manner in which Congress is rushing through a salary increase without scheduling a recorded vote." He pointed out the benefits they currently had: "free round trips to Washington, four free offices fully furnished, $10,000 for newsletters, $6,500 for stationery, $2,000 for rubber bands and paper clips, free refrigerators, free junkets to all parts of the globe, and a standard of luxury living benefitting the oil sheikhs of the Middle East rather than the servants of the people."[15] This didn't sit well with Mr. Speaker. An undated report characterized their debate as a "toe-to-toe slugfest." O'Neill was unmoved. He let the measure pass without a vote. Hechler retorted, "Congressmen will all wake up next Sunday morning $13,000 per year richer, but I hope the American taxpayers will never let them forget the hypocritical charade they went through trying to convince the voters they were publically against a pay raise but secretly hoped it would sneak through un-noticed."[16] To a Marshall University Student Government Association meeting, he called the pay raise "the most scandalous exhibition of greed and gluttony since the Grant administration a century ago." He likened attempts by other members of Congress to make the public believe they had nothing to do with the increase, since they hadn't had to vote on it, to a car wreck. "To tell the truth, Congress has just run over the American people in a ruthlessly brutal hit and run 'accident' with every member of Congress loudly protesting that he fought valiantly against that pay raise and he just can't figure out where that big dent and blood on his fender came from."[17]

Salaries weren't the only area in which Hechler had a disagreement about the way Congress operated. In 1965, he was appointed to the Joint Committee on the Organization of Congress. Tasked with studying the operation and organization of Congress, the committee's work would be the first attempt to do so since 1945. The twelve members from both houses studied the relationship between the two houses, congressional pay rates, the system of committees, and chairpersonships. This effort partially grew out of a 1959 Democratic Study Group (DSG), of which Hechler was also a member. The DSG had criticized what the more liberal members perceived as long-held institutional roadblocks to progressive measures. When the Democrats won a majority in 1964, the group attacked again, seeking a change in the way minority members might thwart progressive presidential programs with which they disagreed. In so doing, the DSG forced the formation of the Joint Committee.[18]

While it took five years, reform was finally enacted in 1970. One of the most sweeping changes granted more power to minority members on a committee by ensuring that the chair, regardless of party affiliation, could not override the desires of a majority of the committee.[19] This weakened the seniority system, but despite the changes, which Hechler takes some small credit in bringing about, he still would have preferred the abolition of the seniority system entirely.[20] On at least one occasion, while still in Congress, Hechler returned to a Marshall University political science classroom to discuss Congress and its workings. In Dr. Simon Perry's class, he stressed the types of obstruction that often defeated legislation that he felt was vital to the country. But the subject he emphasized more than any other was what he called the "dreadful seniority system."

In a similar vein, Hechler said he thought Congress was actually a gerontocracy, based on the average age of its chairpeople. At that time, in the House it was sixty-eight, and in the Senate, sixty-eight and a half. Hechler felt this needed to change, saying some of the "mossbacks" needed to go.[21] Later this remark came back to haunt him. In March 2007, Hechler was being honored at Marshall, and Dr. Perry was invited to speak. By then Hechler had continued to run for political office at seventy, seventy-five, eighty, and eighty-five, and had run for West Virginia secretary of state only three years earlier. As Dr. Perry approached the dais, he warned the then ninety-three-year-old Hechler that he would not enjoy his remarks. "I said to Hechler, 'Ken, are you not ashamed to still be running for office at your age? After all, in the House and Senate, we had a gerontocracy, you said, at the age of sixty-eight,'" Perry said.[22] The audience laughed, as did Hechler, but he also responded the next day in a letter to Perry. "It is true that my attack [on the seniority system] did result in change, yet it is also true that when I got to be ninety years old I had to eat my earlier words. Adlai Stevenson once said, 'Man does not live by words alone, but he frequently has to eat them.' . . . There are many people who are senile at age thirty, and history is filled with examples of vigorous intellects among nonagenarians."[23] Of course, Hechler counted himself among the latter. And Perry had to agree. On that 2007 occasion, Perry says he was "amazed at the man's memory" and saw "absolutely no evidence that age had impaired his mind in any way."[24]

In one instance, however, Hechler used more than words to needle his colleagues. Before Congress adjourned for the summer of 1975, Hechler was again pushing congressional reform. Instead of staying on to address what Hechler felt were pressing issues, his colleagues voted themselves a pay raise and a monthlong recess, then left, with Hechler's vehement statement that their action was inappropriate hanging in the air. He felt they were shirking their duty, so he announced that while they were off on their junkets, he was going to work for no salary for anyone who wanted to hire him.[25] Although some detractors called his plan nothing more than a publicity stunt, he was determined to both show up his colleagues and actually work as a servant of the people.

As the sweltering days of August settled over West Virginia, Hechler rose at 4 a.m. for the first day of his "junket" to work the breakfast shift at the Lock, Stock and Barrel Restaurant in Williamson, in the heart of the mountains. From August 6 to September 1, he did manual labor his father would have required the uneducated hands on Clarence Mackay's estate to perform. Performing maintenance work at a Williamson high-rise for the elderly; collecting garbage in Iaeger; sweeping streets in Logan and Oceana; bundling and delivering newspapers in Lincoln, Logan, and Mingo counties; bathing, shaving, and changing the clothes of incontinent elderly mental patients at the Huntington State Hospital; washing windows and picking up trash at an employment office that had been without janitorial services since June; pumping gas; digging ditches; directing traffic; mowing grass; and bagging groceries were tasks for which Hechler had never trained, let alone done. Yet those and more occupied his days that month.

Once awakened by Henry, the family rooster, at a Raleigh County farm, he helped get breakfast—likely the only cooking he did in his life—before he went to slop hogs, collect firewood, put out salt licks for the cattle, run a brush hog, and drive a tractor.[26] He recalls those as fulfilling days. "Baling hay was my favorite occupation because it gave me a tremendous sense of power to drive a tractor," he says. "They said I had to do everything that a farmer did. One of my jobs was to castrate pigs, which I found the most difficult thing when you hear their pitiful squeals. On this farm, they grew a lot of cane and blading the cane was very difficult on your hands. It was very sharp and you had to wear gloves. Another difficult thing was what they called worming sheep. They would catch one of the sheep and hold it by the throat while you squirted this liquid down their throats."[27]

The following month he reflected on what the experience had meant to him, aside from making a point with his colleagues. He told one reporter that he'd learned never to pick up garbage at a doctor's office from the bottom because of the needles. He called

Ken Hechler mows grass at Stella Fuller Settlement Playground, Huntington, WV, 1975 (Photo courtesy of Huntington Publishing Company)

Ken Hechler collects garbage in Iaeger, WV, 1975 (Courtesy Ken Hechler)

tragic the sight of one ward at the Huntington State Hospital where only three people attended to the entire ward.[28] But, most importantly, he said, "I wanted to learn from the inside what working people and their families are up against in trying to make both ends meet," he said. "A lot of people talked to me about the unfairnesses [sic] in the economic system, and the failure of public officials to correct them." He heard ordinary citizens complain that the tax system continued to place a greater burden on them, while corporations and the wealthy were able to exploit tax shelters and loopholes. "I came away convinced that a revival of the work ethic is essential for the nation's progress," he said. "I hope my exciting and invigorating experience will inspire others to perform volunteer and community service work."[29]

Of course, while he got rave reviews for his summer work from most of his constituents, some felt it was little more than political grandstanding. The publisher of the *Welch Daily News* commented, tongue in cheek, that he would have "paid Hechler what he is worth, but there are federal minimum wage laws to consider." Nevertheless, he insisted on paying Hechler for the work he did selling ads. The check was for $12.36 and was the only pay Hechler accepted for outside work the entire month.[30] In September, he returned to Congress for another round of battles.

While Hechler's constant attempts to reform Congress were aimed at improving the body he served for most of his political career, his bill to impeach president Richard Nixon would have removed a man he had long believed was dangerous.[31] Because of his career-long distaste for Nixon, Hechler had been especially interested in the June 17, 1972, Watergate break-in. He had attended many of Senator Sam Ervin's committee hearings in the summer of 1973. In August, he cosponsored a resolution calling for the Judiciary Committee to be the depository of all Watergate materials.[32] Even before the October Saturday Night Massacre, when Nixon ordered Special Prosecutor Archibald Cox fired, Hechler's office door and an outside window proudly displayed the sign "IMPEACH NIXON–I love my Country." He challenged anyone to find another member of Congress with such a sign, offering $5 as a reward.[33] On October 23, 1973, Hechler introduced the first Resolution of Impeachment. In so doing, he said, "The president is clearly obstructing justice. Entirely too much emphasis has been placed on 'the tapes,' when the fundamental issue is whether the president is obstructing justice, placing himself above the law, and refusing to insure the laws be 'faithfully executed.'"[34]

As usual, Hechler stepped out in front of the issue while his fellow West Virginia congressmen, Slack, Staggers, and Mollohan, decided to wait to see how the wind blew before stating their position. Despite Hechler's enmity of Nixon and his strong conviction that justice had to be done, he hated the idea of what impeachment would do to the country. In a September 1973 poll by the *Charleston Gazette* of the entire West Virginia delegation, Hechler said, "If a vote were taken in the House today, I doubt there would be many votes for impeachment. Likewise, in my soundings in West Virginia, I have found little support for impeachment." Yet he continued. "I am so shocked by the corruption of the well-springs of democracy and justice that my strong inclination is to vote for impeachment."[35] In a survey conducted by United Press International, Hechler was asked if he would vote for impeachment or would like to see Nixon resign. "If he insists on a vote and trial, he's entitled under the Constitution to have one. I prefer impeachment over resignation," he said. He was in the minority. Most members of Congress were undecided, but there were those who still preferred to see him resign.[36]

In his reply to each of the letters received regarding the issue, he repeated this sentiment. Responding to one of his constituents, who wrote of her support for his impeachment resolution, Hechler wrote, "Much of my mail favoring this step is coming from many good West Virginia Republicans, including doctors, lawyers, investment bankers who said they not only voted for Mr. Nixon, but contributed to his campaign."[37]

As history proved, Hechler's moral compass was again pointing in the right direction. When Nixon was forced to resign, Hechler must have felt some measure of satisfaction in knowing he'd helped bring him down. Yet when President Ford later pardoned Nixon, Hechler was outraged anew. "The pardon creates a worse nightmare than Watergate, since it sanctions a double standard of political morality," he railed.[38] To a reporter, he said, "The quality of mercy is getting very strained. . . . It messeth up those that give and those that take."[39] In the end, he regarded the whole Watergate affair as "the most shameful episode in American history."[40]

Certainly, in Hechler's eyes, Nixon fell far short of the ideal public servant. In continuing to be the burr under the congressional saddle, Hechler was trying to get his fellow members to strive for the high standards he felt a congressperson ought to uphold. According to several of Hechler's colleagues, however, he was the epitome of that ideal. Senator Tom Harkin said Hechler exemplified something that he considered an important aspect of public service: leaving the ladder of opportunity down for others.[41] Bob Dole said that even with his willingness to confront his colleagues, Hechler knew everyone by their first name and was everybody's friend,[42] while McGovern called him a true public servant. "I can't think of anybody in public life who has so systematically committed himself to be of service to people," he said. "I think it's on his mind all the time."[43] Hechler once offered McGovern a biblical quote for use during some upcoming remarks, which typifies the way Hechler felt he, and all public servants, should act: "They will soar on wings as eagles; they will run and not grow weary; they will walk and not be faint."[44]

17

THE INTERREGNUM

On March 12, 1976, Ken Hechler made an announcement that would take him off the national stage for the rest of his life. That's the day he filed and announced from the guardhouse on the grounds of the West Virginia Governor's Mansion that he was throwing his hat in the ring to become the state's next governor, instead of running again to be one of its U.S. congressmen, the position he'd held for eighteen years. He'd considered leaving Congress a few years earlier, citing the poisonous nature politics had gained under Richard Nixon, but was persuaded to again defend his seat in the 1974 election.[1] That year, he had no opponents in either the primary or the general election, and it had bothered him.

He was sixty-two, the age at which many are contemplating retirement, but Hechler was bored and ready for a change. Even though he had never aspired to be governor, Hechler didn't like the idea that multi-millionaire Jay Rockefeller was likely to gain the state's highest office through the sheer force of his money. "I did it because I have a very strong belief that people should not buy elections," he said. "I wanted to defeat a person who was buying the election." Looking back, he says it was "the stupidest political mistake" of his career,[2] and it resulted in the first election he ever lost. And he knew early on that he'd made a fatal mistake. He'd gone to a campaign rally in Mason County, where he'd always run strongly. Hechler recalled, "When I walked in the door where some of my strongest supporters had previously given me overwhelming majorities, they were talking among themselves. The first thing I heard was: 'Of course we gave him

[Rockefeller] a standing ovation.' All [Jay] had to do was appear because they knew he was going to win and they wanted to attach to his coattails. I was almost completely ignored at that meeting where my strongest supporters immediately switched to Rockefeller. So that was a no-win contest and he rolled over me like an army tank."[3]

First, Hechler refused to take monetary contributions, saying the "People's Campaign," as he dubbed it, would accept only the work volunteers could provide. He suggested they use old shirt cardboards, cereal boxes, and paper bags to make signs to get his campaign message across.[4] He also distributed an endorsement letter signed by six of his former congressional colleagues, who said they wish he'd never left Congress.[5] Second, he opened no campaign offices around the state, as that would have cost money. Instead, he declared his red Jeep his campaign headquarters and festooned it with crepe paper streamers at each stop.[6]

Although his campaign approach was unorthodox, his platform should have appealed to ordinary citizens. In his announcement for the office, he stated, "I am running an affirmative campaign to provide the leadership independent of Big Business, Big Labor, Big Politics, or Big Money." He pledged to raise taxes to improve the state's secondary roads, but said those taxes would fall on Big Coal, big trucks, and the usual "sin-taxes" on liquor and cigarettes. He planned to shake up the tax system and repeal the burdensome business and occupation tax, replacing it with a progressive corporate income tax. He also promised to fight for the environment.[7] Calling politics as usual "political pollution," he pledged to establish small district offices around the state to bring state government closer to the people.[8] And, of course, he planned to forgo all the trappings of the office: he would not live in the mansion, would sell all the limos, and drive his red Jeep himself.

Unfortunately, his approach didn't work. Jay's money was used to flood the airwaves with television ads. They captured the voters, and Hechler lost badly in the multicandidate spring primary. The loss was a double whammy that month. His mother, Catherine, had died at ninety-six just a few days before the primary. He had soldiered on, however, hoping his name recognition, his immense popularity, and his folksy, personal campaigning style would again carry the day. But those days of succeeding by riding the roads in his red Jeep to shake the voters' hands were no match for the Rockefeller millions. Afterward, he admitted to a friend that mistakes had been made in his campaign, and he took full responsibility for them. In the same letter, he asked for advice on his next move: a potential write-in campaign for his old congressional seat.[9]

In so doing, Hechler faced Nick J. Rahall, who had stepped in and won the primary against a bevy of other political hopefuls when Hechler announced he was dropping out of the race after nine terms in Congress. Now Hechler was ready to fight him in the fall general election to get it back. A *Beckley Post-Herald* editorial applauded the move. "We have been concerned that we might lose adequate congressional representation, since Rep. Ken Hechler decided he would not seek re-nomination, but would seek the office of governor instead. However, since Hechler has decided to conduct a write-in campaign to retain his seat, we feel there is less about [which] to fret."[10] That sentiment wasn't universal, however. Some thought he should simply accept the consequences of his actions. Others suggested he wait until 1978 and run for Jennings Randolph's senatorial seat.

But Hechler was undeterred. He accepted monetary contributions this time, and used them to print stickers and buy rubber stamps to distribute to each precinct for voters who wanted to select him. Despite a ruling by West Virginia secretary of state James McCartney allowing the use of both, the state's attorney general, Chauncey Browning, issued an opinion that their use would not be allowed. In hindsight, the move probably created confusion and deterred voters. In fact, one editor suggested that as an avowed Rahall supporter, such was Browning's aim.[11] Evidently it worked. Hechler lost by almost fourteen thousand votes. In an ironic twist of fate, the untested Rahall's win echoed Hechler's newcomer win over the older Will Neal nearly twenty years earlier.

Suddenly, Hechler was at loose ends and out of a job for the first time in almost three decades. He says he could have become a lobbyist—there were several offers—or he simply could have retired at sixty-three, drawn his pension, and done nothing. Neither suited him, however, so he accepted an assignment to write the history of the Science and Technology Committee, on which he had served throughout his tenure in Congress. His book, *Toward the Endless Frontier*, was published in 1980 and remains the most comprehensive telling of the early days of the space race.[12]

But his disastrous decision to leave Congress still rankled. In fact, when Hechler lost in 1976, he announced he would seek a later rematch.[13] Things had changed in Washington, and he still wanted to get back on the national stage. Nixon had long since returned to California in disgrace. Ford had lost the presidency to Jimmy Carter in 1977, and the Democrats once again held sway. Sadly, though, Hechler's old friend Hubert Humphrey had died in January 1978.

That same month, Hechler filed to again run against Rahall in the upcoming spring primary. This time he hired Robert F. Miller & Associates to act as his campaign advisors. Miller organized media events, designed and bought billboards, and set up campaign headquarters across the state.[14] It was a dramatic departure from Hechler's previous campaigns and perhaps shows his determination to win back his old seat. With his announcement, the *Charleston Gazette* predicted Hechler would win by fifteen thousand votes,[15] but it didn't happen. On November 6, Rahall retained his seat, and Hechler announced, perhaps in a fit of pique, that he would never run for office again.[16] The day following the election, Hechler received a letter from Nick Rahall Sr. saying, "I just wanted to take a moment to write you this letter to assure you that I, as well as the entire Rahall family, remain as kind and friendly toward you today as we ever did. . . . I further respect you for the clean campaign you had with my son, Nick. I have never seen a cleaner campaign in my life and you know for a fact that we would have continued to support you had you stayed in the House and not tried to buck the Rockefeller millions."[17] Perhaps the letter was meant to patch the relationship between the two candidates, but they maintained some distance, and it wouldn't be the last political skirmish between them.

While Hechler had lost his congressional bully pulpit, he didn't stray far from the political scene. Even though he had taken an apartment in Charleston after he returned to West Virginia from Washington, he continued to maintain one in Huntington as well and to be concerned with his adopted city's affairs. There he organized a series of luncheons to examine the city's criminal justice system. At the time, in 1980, Huntington's chief of police, Ottie Adkins, had reported that illegal political contributions, jury tampering, and possible illegal procedures by bail bondsmen were preventing certain political figures from being brought to justice. Although an ordinary citizen at the time, Hechler didn't hesitate to speak out. On August 7, during a talk at a local hotel, he said, "Whenever forces of favoritism, or political protection, or outside pressures [occur], I believe that we as citizens ought to be concerned."[18] Following Ken's speech the county prosecutor launched an investigation that Ken hoped would change the way bail bondsmen could operate.[19]

Once Hechler finished writing *Toward the Endless Frontier,* he turned to producing a memoir of his years at the Truman White House. He spent months studying Truman's post-presidential papers at the Truman Library in Missouri; interviewing reporters and old colleagues; reviewing his own notes, papers, and diaries; and reading the papers of others who served under Truman.[20] It's remarkable that he could assemble such a detailed account of those days in the two years it took him to write the book.

By February 1982, Hechler had signed a publishing contract with G.P. Putnam's Sons to publish *Working with Truman: A Personal Memoir of the White House Years.* The book arrived in the stores in November and was widely acclaimed as an insightful and personal look at the former president.

The *New York Times Book Review* commented, "Politics and history buffs will find Mr. Hechler's version warm and welcome"; and Margaret Truman said, "It brought back wonderful memories."[21] Hechler received many letters praising the book and thanking him for their purchased autographed copies, but one man who had provided Hechler with some research help thought he should have gotten his copy for free.[22] By March 1984, however, the book was out of print, and Putnam had no plans to reprint it. Although the original retail price was $16.95, Putnam offered Hechler the books it had left for a paltry $1.75 each.[23]

Later, in 1995, the University of Missouri Press approached Hechler, asking to include his book in their paperback series Give 'Em Hell Harry, and he agreed. The new edition hit the shelves in 1996 with a promotional blitz to twenty-five thousand potential buyers.[24]

Meanwhile, in 1981, Hechler returned to the classroom and his first love: teaching. In preparation for a course at West Virginia's University of Charleston, he had contacted other political science professors asking for copies of their syllabi, so he could decide how

Ken Hechler poses with *Working with Truman* (Photo by Lee Bernard, *Herald Dispatch*)

he wanted to construct his course on congressional politics.[25] He told one reporter that he was looking forward to getting his students involved in politics and government.[26] It was the same sentiment he had voiced in 1957. The course was called How Congress Works.

Fresh from the halls of that body, there could scarcely have been a better instructor on the subject than Hechler. The syllabus designated no textbook but encouraged students to scour the newspaper and watch television every day for activities in Congress. He planned to emphasize the power structure of Congress and its committee system, and to talk about ethics and compromises. One assignment had students assuming the roles of members of Congress. They were to discuss, in class, what strategies they should use to get bills they introduced acted on favorably.[27]

During the spring 1982 semester, he taught Great American Political Personalities, a course similar to one he had taken at Swarthmore. The class examined the political lives of Thomas Jefferson, John Marshall, and others. His syllabus must have brought a chuckle to students who were used to stiff-necked professors. In it, he stated, "Although I'm rarely home, I don't mind being called between 10 p.m. and 8 a.m." Telling them he wanted to save them some money, he again assigned no textbook.[28]

His tenure at the University of Charleston was short lived, however. In the face of the institution's invitation to return the following year, Hechler declined, saying,

I want you to know how thoroughly I enjoyed offering the course in "How Congress Works," during the fall term last year. . . . You recall we talked about offering a course last spring, and I demurred because there was some thought I might re-enter the political lists. . . . We talked about the possibility of giving a course in "Congress" or on "Political

Parties" this fall . . . but Marshall University has just contacted me and asked me to give a course on "Harry S. Truman and the American Political System." This intrigues me because I have just finished a book called *Working with Truman*, which G. P. Putnam is publishing this fall.[29]

He accepted Marshall's offer and returned to his old campus digs in time for the fall 1982 semester.

It was a return to where it all began. In an interview with Marshall's *Parthenon* staff, Hechler said, "I do enjoy my freedom since I left Congress because I have more time to write, but I am very excited about returning to teach at Marshall."[30] His salary of $1,050 for the semester-long course paled by comparison to that of a congressman,[31] but he was thrilled to be back behind a Marshall lectern. Politics of the Truman Era was a senior- and graduate-level course. According to Hechler's syllabus, he required each student to write an autobiography answering twelve specific questions, some of which could have been viewed as an attempt to gather valuable demographic information that Hechler could use if he decided to reenter politics at some future date. The students' grades were based primarily on class discussions of such historically weighty topics as the Potsdam Conference, the firing of MacArthur during the Korean War, and the relationship between FDR and Truman. He had the class debate whether or not President Truman should have sanctioned the bombing of Hiroshima and Nagasaki.[32] The following year, the course content was similar, but that debate was not included.

Marshall added a freshman-level course to Hechler's part-time assignment in 1983. No doubt campus newcomers were surprised to read the American National Government syllabus, which invited them to drop by his office and "shoot the breeze anytime." He also announced a deal with the campus bookstore in which they could buy used copies of his required textbooks, thus saving his students 30 percent. He added that if they preferred, they could also share a book with a friend to save even more. Regarding the seating chart, Hechler declared that once set, it was frozen in place, unless someone wanted to "sue for divorce and do a switch."[33]

He taught the same course, now called American National Government and Politics, during the spring semester of 1984. As class opened, he read the introduction of the syllabus:

Well, Mr. Orwell, here we are in the year 1984, about which you wrote such a terrifying book. This is a great year to be studying politics because the entire subject will be swirling around you as we nominate and elect a president, a United States Senator, a governor, all the members of the U.S. House of Representatives, and countless other state and local officials. As students of this process, you will be keeping up with current developments, as well as examining how and why we got where we are politically, constitutionally, and otherwise.

For one assignment, students were to assume they were staff assistants to a member of Congress who had been overseas with his entire committee for an extended time. They were to write a paper explaining what had happened in Congress, indicating who had made speeches, and detailing what kind of analysis the member would need to understand all the issues at hand.[34] Hechler rarely just lectured. While he provided study guides for each test, he made his students work and think. And although he localized his political focus on occasion by inviting candidates for Huntington offices to speak, he required his students to make oral reports on the scope of presidential power, the potential reform of the Electoral College, and how we choose our presidential candidates. One midterm test question had students imagine they were hosting visitors from Australia to whom they needed to explain American politics. Their answers had to be nonpartisan in nature.[35]

Once again, students had to write an autobiography, then refer to it in the final exam by revealing whether or not their aims and goals in life had changed, and if so why. Hechler also explained that while he had refrained, in class, from taking sides in the ongoing campaigns, he would "take the gloves off" after May 14, the date of the upcoming primary. He also said, "If any member of this class has the urge to participate in a campaign which uses a little red Jeep, please do not resist that urge, but get in touch with me or anyone who answers my phone at . . ."[36] All this talk of politics had gotten to the professor, if not the students. His remark was tantamount to an announcement, for Hechler had filed for office once again. This time, when current officeholder A. James Manchin announced he was running for state treasurer instead, Hechler set his sights on becoming West Virginia's next secretary of state.

In his public announcement on March 21, 1984, the nearly seventy-year-old said, "I can never measure up to the charismatic flamboyancy of A. James Manchin, the present occupant of that office, but I intend to carry on the Manchin tradition of making this office the true servant of the people."[37] An undated flippant ad in the Marshall University *Parthenon*, urging student voters to elect Hechler, listed several bullet points: "Professor Hechler requires long term papers, makes students deliver oral reports, gives a lot of outside reading, flunks lots of students. Out of fifty-nine [students] registered this term, twenty-one have dropped out because Hechler is too tough and demanding. PROTECT YOUR GRADE POINT AVERAGE; SEND HECHLER TO CHARLESTON."[38]

While he easily earned the endorsement of folks like Donald Rasmussen, his fellow black-lung fighter,[39] he was verbally attacked by Chris Sowards, campaign manager of one of his opponents, Homer Heck. Sowards claimed Hechler was too old and out of touch after his long absence from politics. Hechler told him to keep up the negative campaigning and they would test the results in June. Chuck Smith, another candidate, told Hechler he should park his red Jeep and approach the state's problems with ideas and innovations. Hechler responded that while he didn't mind being criticized personally, his Jeep—like FDR's dog, Fala—*did* resent it.[40]

Apparently, the clever ads and his long-standing popularity worked this time. His resounding primary victory over five token opponents ended his eight-year absence from the political scene. As usual, he had taken off across the state in his Jeep, which also became the subject of that campaign's theme song, "A Red Jeep in the Mountains." Once again, he overcame his reluctance to accept campaign contributions, but solicited donations only for advertising and gas for the Jeep.[41] It was a bare-bones campaign. He shunned roadside campaign signs and, as he had done successfully in the past, spent his hours meeting the voters personally. He logged over fourteen thousand miles during the primary campaign alone and spent only $61,966, but $10,000 of that was his own money.[42]

While campaigning for the fall general election, where he would face Republican Michele Golden, Hechler had a run-in with Mingo County Democratic party leader, Johnie Owens. It wouldn't be their last encounter. At a Democratic rally for the party's gubernatorial candidate, Clyde See, Owens called Hechler out for remarks he had made previously. Hechler had promised, if elected secretary of state, to uphold the laws of the state and to see that the voter registration lists were correct. Now, Owens took exception to the implication that something was currently wrong with them. Hechler was recalling that three thousand ineligible names had been purged from the rolls three years earlier. Owens bristled. "We don't appreciate you getting up in other parts of the state and talking about Southern West Virginia like you do," he said. It didn't stop there. Following the public speeches, the two could be seen behind the podium exchanging heated words, but the conversation's content went unreported.[43]

Apparently neither the exchange, nor the reports of it, made much impact. Hechler won the November election with nearly 64 percent of the vote. Afterward, he repeated the sentiment he had voiced in his dust-up with Johnie Owens, saying he had run because he wanted to reduce election fraud. In response to another criticism about his long history of switching between teaching and running for office, he said, "You'll be a better teacher if you've had practical experience as a public servant, and you can be a better public servant if you stand off for a while and weigh the pros and cons of what you are doing."[44] It wasn't the first time he'd voiced this sentiment, which reflects his belief that the two professions are inexorably linked. And it wouldn't be the last time he'd give up one for the other.

18

THE PEOPLE'S OFFICE— THE FIRST TERM

West Virginia has a long and sordid history of election fraud. For generations, the Democratic political machine controlled all elected offices. Historically, a vote sold for a pint of booze. Voting the dead was a time-honored tradition.[1] Such blatant fraud became the topic of a book by Allen H. Loughry II in 2006. Its title, *Don't Buy Another Vote, I Won't Pay for a Landslide*, refers to a remark credited to Joseph Kennedy when his son, John F. Kennedy, ran for president in 1960. In Hechler's bid for Congress the same year, he lost votes in one county because he refused to provide funds to pay voters.

During his 1984 bid to become West Virginia's next secretary of state, he spoke often and vehemently about the need to get rid of election fraud. In 1967, disturbed by the Department of Justice's decision not to prosecute a vote fraud charge in Kanawha County, he had written an impassioned letter to U.S. assistant attorney general Fred M. Vinson Jr. asking, "If the laws aren't strong enough, how can they be strengthened?" Even though Hechler knew that this particular case had been dropped by the Department of Justice because Kanawha County had assumed jurisdiction, he used the incident as an opportunity to rail against the election fraud he knew was rampant elsewhere. He added, "I don't see how we can effectively teach the principles of democracy in our schools and colleges, and then turn around and practice corruption at the polls. Respect for the laws should start with respect for the election process." He also lamented the resigna-tion of voters to the situation. "Over the years," he wrote, "voting frauds have become so thoroughly a part of 'the system' in some West Virginia counties that helpless citizens have resigned them-selves to the inevitability of corruption."[2]

After the 1984 vote count verified his win, but before his inau-guration, Hechler began to plan ways to carry out his campaign promises and change the state's admittedly well-deserved repu-tation for accepting voter fraud as the norm. On November 20, 1984, he wrote to each county commission asking for a list of problems they had noticed with the current election laws. In addition, he wanted their recommendations on how to solve them.[3] Perhaps his eagerness to tackle this particular issue above all others caused Hechler to raise his arms in jubilation, yell "Hurray," and then come bounding down the Capitol steps after his inau-guration on a cold but sunny January 14, 1985.[4] According to staff deputy Barbara Myers, who was in attendance, Hechler then walked straight into the governor's conference room, at the end of the secretary of state's office, and held his first meeting with the initial staff.[5]

Hechler immediately organized his office much differently than had previous secretaries of state. First of all, he placed his desk near the entrance to the office suite instead of behind closed doors past a gatekeeping secretary. This openness and accessibil-ity amazed Paul Nyden, a reporter with the *Charleston Gazette.* "I guess anyone could walk into the office and immediately approach him, say something nice, ask him a question, or say they didn't like him," he says.[6] But dealing directly with constituents was Hechler's bailiwick, as it had been in Washington. Visitors quickly recognized the often sweater-clad man seated behind the precariously towering stack of papers on his desk. One employee recalls Hechler moving to another desk when the first one began

Ken Hechler's inauguration as West Virginia's secretary of state (Photo by Wriston Photography)

overflowing with papers. Yet just as when he was a congressman, he could still find a document in the stack whenever it was needed.[7] As usual, Hechler didn't waste taxpayer money on fancy furniture or furnishings. Therefore, the office was never what you'd call a classy place, according to Mary Ratliff, his deputy secretary of state from 1986 to 2001.[8]

Although Ratliff recalls having thirty-five full-time employees in the office, his letterhead—dubbed the "un-stuffiest letterhead they'd seen" by readers of the *Charleston Gazette*[9]—listed Hechler, seven deputies, directors, his special assistant Virginia Skeen, and "All the Volunteers We Can Get." Perhaps the large stuffed bears out front added to the impression of casualness as well. The first bear flanking Hechler's office suite took his place there in January 1986,[10] after it was killed by the Department of Natural Resources because it had begun scaring residents of Clay

County. Hechler bought the bear, which weighed about three hundred pounds and stood five feet tall, and then paid for its taxidermy and delivery. Hechler later added another bear to the tableau, and visiting schoolchildren began posing with them for pictures. At Christmastime, the bears wore Santa Claus hats.[11] Even though the state has more registered hunters per capita than any other state, Hechler is an avowed gun-control advocate. To level a dig at the National Rifle Association and perhaps in homage to the official state animal, he once put a sign around one bear's neck that read, "We support the right to arm bears."[12] It was typical of his wry sense of humor.

As he had done as a congressman, Hechler insisted on a high level of customer service and often rose from his desk as the first to greet constituents who dropped by. He didn't require anyone to have an appointment, but he didn't like to keep anyone waiting, either. He even insisted that calls be answered in the least pretentious manner possible. Instead of "How may I be of help?" he wanted the two staffers who took calls to say, "How can I help?"[13] He also had the uncanny knack of being able to greet international visitors in their native language, even though he couldn't get much further in the conversation.[14]

Another carryover from his days as a congressman was the creation of a Week in State Government competition, modeled on his popular Week in Washington program. He sent letters to all the state's high schools, 4-H organizations, and the media to announce the selection process. Each summer, a panel of donors and educators chose twelve to eighteen juniors, four from each congressional district, to spend a week in Charleston to meet with state leaders and officials, discuss local issues, and attend city events. Again, he solicited private donors to support the program.[15] As wildly popular as his earlier program, many students from across the state recall it as a seminal event in their lives. One, Phil

Hancock, a young black man from Bluefield, credits this program and Hechler himself as the reasons he became interested in politics. He says Hechler's political mantra, "Equal rights for all; special privileges for none," inspired him. In 2004, Hancock campaigned vigorously for Hechler when he tried to return to his position as secretary of state. Hechler thanked him by allowing Hancock to attend the Democratic National Convention in his place. There, Hancock met Senator Barack Obama before the historic speech that catapulted Obama into the national spotlight.[16]

A mere six months after his 1984 inauguration, Hechler had his first political corruption case handed to him. In July, forty sanitation and street employees in Charleston charged they had been told to change their party affiliation to that of newly elected Republican mayor Mike Roark or quit.[17] Hechler took the matter to the Kanawha County prosecutor, asking him to investigate the charges, but the prosecutor, saying he didn't have enough staff to take on the job, handed it back to Hechler's office. Hechler called on Roark to join him at a news conference to denounce the political coercion, but he declined and stated that the complaints were from only one or two disgruntled employees.[18]

Yet in January, one of Hechler's investigators took the sworn testimonies of all but two of the forty accusers. One man stated he'd been fired two weeks after refusing to switch. Another said the deputy mayor, E. D. Leonard, had brought in a list of candidates and told the employees which ones to vote for.[19] Hechler then accused Roark of coercing the employees through Leonard to "play the game from [President] Reagan on down or hit Rt. 60."[20]

After months of inaction and changes in prosecutors, the case came before a Kanawha County grand jury on October 22, 1986. Hechler asked to testify personally, along with those who had submitted sworn statements to him. Over one hundred city employees

initially filled the steamy hallway of the Kanawha County Courthouse, but when a yellow pad appeared and an investigator asked
those who wanted to testify to sign, only a handful did so. The
rest left, saying they didn't want to sign in their supervisors' sight.
Presumably, supervisors would then be forced to conclude that
their employees were there merely out of curiosity. Hechler says
he testified for about forty-five minutes, but from the slanted
questions they asked, it was clear to him the jurors had made up
their minds before he was asked a single question.[21] Two days
later, when the grand jury cleared Roark, Hechler was noticeably
disgruntled, since the evidence had shown that 81 percent of the
Public Works Department had switched to the Republican Party
after Roark was elected.[22] Roark couldn't stay out of legal trouble,
however. In 1989, while still mayor, he was convicted of cocaine
possession, was sentenced to nearly two hundred days in prison,
and resigned his position. His law license was suspended for
three years, a sentence he argued vehemently against, saying the
crime was unrelated to moral turpitude.[23]

Hechler's first actual voting fraud case opened a can of worms
that, in the opinion of some,[24] ultimately led to the 1990 conviction
of West Virginia governor Arch Moore on charges of extortion,
mail fraud, obstruction of justice, and filing false income-tax
returns.[25] The path was circuitous, but damning. It had started
five years earlier, following the May 7, 1985, primary election in
the small Mingo County town of Gilbert, when the town council
asked Hechler's office for help in the ensuing vote canvass. In
response, he impounded the voting boxes and learned that of the
350 votes cast, 105 had been challenged ballots. When it appeared
those voters either were not registered or lived out of town, Hechler
launched an investigation.

He interviewed over fifty witnesses, including election officials, campaign organizers, eligible and challenged voters, and

those who drove voters to the polls.[26] On July 20, he announced, "We have uncovered many apparent violations which range from petty items to more serious ones."[27] As a result, he brought a lawsuit to set aside the entire election and remove everyone from office who had been elected.[28] The Supreme Court of Appeals also granted his petition to remove from the case Elliott Maynard, the sitting Mingo County Circuit Court judge,[29] whom Hechler felt would have a conflict of interest should the charges come to trial. The court replaced Maynard with nearby Cabell County's Dan O'Hanlon.

According to Judge O'Hanlon, when the chief justice of the state supreme court called, O'Hanlon asked why he'd been chosen. The chief justice said, "You're the only judge in West Virginia that isn't from West Virginia so we know you can't be related to somebody or didn't date somebody's sister in college." O'Hanlon set aside the election and put the city in receivership. The receiver— Don Wilkes, from Hechler's office—was charged with running the city until a free and fair election could be held.[30]

Once a special prosecutor was appointed and state and federal officials were prosecuting the case, Hechler's office was out of the loop except to testify about his role in the initial investigations. This didn't stop an attack on one of Hechler's staffers, however. When Barbara Myers (then Starcher) went to testify, her car tires were slashed.[31] Interestingly, the local newspaper, the *Williamson News*, used more ink complaining about Hechler's actions than reporting the facts of the case, which dragged on for two more years. Once the grand jury brought a number of indictments, the paper's October 29, 1986, editorial complained, "We have heard all we want to hear from the self-appointed, pseudo-sanctimonious saviors that have swooped into our lives." Hechler returned fire, saying he wished the newspaper would lead the fight instead of ignoring the problem.[32]

No wonder the local newspaper turned a blind eye. By the time the investigation had untangled the web of illegal activities, former and current elected officials throughout the county were caught in it, and Hechler's old nemesis, Johnie Owens, appeared to be the chief spider. William Owens, Johnie's nephew, was charged in the Gilbert voting fraud case. Johnie Owens, who had served as the Mingo County sheriff, as well as the Democratic Executive Committee chairman, and was an ex-county commissioner, was charged with conspiracy to commit bribery in connection with allegations he accepted $15,000 to influence the outcome of an earlier murder case.[33] In May 1988, Owens was convicted and pled guilty to three counts of tax evasion as well. Sentenced to fourteen years in prison, Owens ultimately said the whole episode had made things better in Mingo County. "It worked pretty good for me for six or eight years. [But] it never lasts forever. There's always someone that wants to take over,"[34] he said. After his conviction, a statement from Owens led prosecutors to look into his charge that Arch had begged another man to take $10,000 of his money to buy votes.[35] The claim was only one of many in the investigation that resulted in Moore's 1990 conviction.

It had been a wild ride for Hechler so far. His discovery in Gilbert had led to uncovering vote buying, open drug dealing from the sheriff's office, bribery, jury fixing, widespread fraud in an antipoverty program, and a sheriff who bought his job for a $100,000 bribe.[36] It certainly wasn't the kind of activity Hechler was used to. According to Mary Ratliff, the job wasn't really the best fit for Hechler. "He made it the best fit it could be [by] using it as a bully pulpit and taking on the issues of campaign finance reform, election reform, and the things that were related to that office; but the administrative side of it was not a great fit for him. He's a policy wonk. That's what he loves and wants to work with."[37]

Nonetheless, Hechler's first four-year report shows that during his first term, he succeeded in making inroads on several policy issues that were dear to his heart. He drafted and, after two tries, got the state legislature to pass a law in 1986 establishing a three-hundred-foot campaign-free zone around polling places.[38] Previously, voters had to run a gauntlet of eager candidates, or their volunteers, poking campaign literature in their faces as they entered the polls. He said, "They call it literature because people throw it away and it litters the ground."[39] Hechler believed voters would be better able to vote their own consciences absent that gauntlet of politicians or political workers.[40] Moreover, he lengthened the absentee voting period, made it easier for military and overseas voters to register and request a ballot, and established emergency absentee voting for folks hospitalized just before an election. In further moves to clean up the election process, he prohibited anonymous contributions, required purging of the voter rolls based on obituaries, and increased the penalties for willful violation of campaign finance reporting requirements.[41] While these new laws no doubt slowed down corruption in West Virginia politics, it didn't disappear. Throughout his ensuing tenure in the office, he continued to investigate vote fraud in Wyoming and McDowell counties and the city of Parkersburg, among others.[42]

According to Judge O'Hanlon, Hechler didn't suffer fools or crooks gladly: "He just kept calling them out and calling them out."[43] Although improving the election process was top on his list of issues, Hechler's office was also tasked with rooting out unscrupulous or fraudulent charitable organizations as well as those that had never registered to solicit donations at all. In 1985, when he realized the Commission on Charitable Organizations had not met since 1979, he revived the board and mounted an aggressive campaign to draft new legislation to strengthen his office's power in stopping charity scams.[44] In his first term, he revoked, denied, or refused to grant licenses to eleven such deceptive or dishonest organizations, and forced the return of all collected money to their donors.[45]

In 1985, the United Mine Workers filed a complaint with Hechler about a security firm hired by the A. T. Massey Coal Company to provide guards during a strike at its Lobata mine in Mingo County. The complaint claimed the firm had a felon among the guards. Of course, this was against the law, so Hechler launched an investigation. At first, the company, Southeastern Security of Marietta, Ohio, refused to provide his office with a list of its employees. Hechler went to court and, after several appeals, won the right to the list, which revealed five more felons at Lobata on Southeastern's rolls.[46] He subsequently exercised his authority and revoked the security company's right to do business in the state. Massey took the matter back to court, claiming Hechler's actions were politically motivated, since he'd always been a strong supporter of the UMWA. The judge suspended Southeastern's revocation.[47] Hechler asked for a review by the state's supreme court of appeals. It was granted, and Hechler's actions were successfully defended.[48] In August, Southeastern Security was barred from doing business in the state.[49]

Hechler's ire toward dishonesty reached beyond charitable scams and dishonest corporations. In 1988, he received a report from the inspector general of the Department of Defense addressing Hechler's earlier allegations of waste and abuse in the repair and replacement of facilities at Camp Dawson, in Preston County. Badly damaged as a result of the November 1985 Cheat River flooding, it was slated for repair. The camp had been established in 1909 as a National Guard training facility, and was also used by active and reserve forces of other military branches.[50] As Armory Board members, Hechler, West Virginia auditor Glen Gainer, and Governor Arch Moore had oversight of all expenditures affecting the state's National Guard. In reviewing requests for project funding, they uncovered massive cost overruns to build and furnish plush officers' quarters at the camp, which could not be justified.[51] In a memo to Senator Robert Byrd, Hechler indicated that the funds, all $2,663,300 of it, had come from FEMA, but they constituted a 100 percent cost overrun nevertheless. However, not one penny came from flood relief funds, he was told.[52] As only the expenditure of National Guard funds was the Armory Board's purview, Hechler was satisfied that he had no further responsibility. He moved on to other issues.

When Hechler arrived on the state scene, his corporations division was in dire need of organizational help. Mail was answered in a haphazard manner, which often resulted in older mail piling up while newer requests for filing corporation papers were granted first. All records were on note cards, and there had been no microfilm backup for archival retrieval for two years. Normal turnaround for corporate requests was in excess of four business days.[53] Deputy Mary Ratliff dove in and quietly cleaned up the mess, without Hechler's knowledge or consent.[54]

She had met Hechler when she chaperoned some of his Week in Washington winners and had also kept in contact with him through the environmental group the West Virginia Highlands Conservancy. For her first ten years in Hechler's office, she managed relationships with county commissions and organized the elections, but behind the scenes she also started the computer revolution in the secretary of state's office. First she converted the existing film library to a more modern technology system, and then she began converting the index card system to a database. The process took about eighteen months and cost less than $100,000.

Following the conversion, which also included simplifying a number of forms, businesses typically received a response in twenty-four hours.[55]

One could argue that Hechler's most productive years as secretary of state were during his first term. A summary report showing the evolution of his office over all four terms outlines his continued success on several fronts: the ongoing updating of the computer system, the computerization of all the state regulations and the creation of its easily read index, the strengthening of laws to protect the public from scam charities, greater education of the public on the projects and responsibilities of his office, and his close scrutiny of the use of the state's Great Seal.[56] Though significant, these pale beside the major accomplishments of his first term.

While Hechler saw himself as an ombudsman for West Virginians seeking help on a wide range of issues, the statewide problems he could address didn't have the impact of those he'd handled on the national scene, like securing black lung benefits for miners. Nonetheless, he felt he'd succeeded in improving service in every area, and had brought fairness and thoroughness to the enforcement of the law. But once he'd tackled, to the extent of his official duties, the glaring problems of election fraud, cleaning up historical paper records and converting them to a computerized database, and ridding the state of scam charities, he may have grown bored. There was little else he could do that presented a challenge, and he thrived on challenges. During the next three terms, it seemed he simply kept the wheels turning, though not without a few hitches along the way.

19

THE PEOPLE'S OFFICE—THE REST OF THE STORY

Since Hechler had run unopposed in both the primary and general elections of 1988, shortly after his second term began in January 1989 he should have expected the next four years to run rather smoothly. Instead, he ran into a major stumbling block. The newly elected governor, Gaston Caperton, began to campaign to abolish Hechler's job, along with those of the secretary of agriculture and the state treasurer.

According to Caperton, the moves were part of his campaign promises to reorganize state government.[1] While both he and Caperton were Democrats, perhaps Caperton was in the same camp as those in the party who believed Hechler could be a liability. It was no secret that he couldn't be controlled; he never had toed the party line. Hechler was wildly popular with the people, but he didn't hesitate to trumpet his own accomplishments to the media, often embarrassing other politicians not as adept at media manipulation. And some would have shed no tears if he had been forced to drive his red Jeep away from the statehouse and into the sunset. Additionally, the last secretary of state, A. James Manchin, had done very little except travel the state lambasting its dirty streams. Perhaps Caperton felt Hechler was no different than Manchin and thus was expendable.[2] In fact, on one occasion, Caperton had said the secretary of state had one function only: protecting the use of the state's Great Seal.[3]

Therefore, in April 1989, Caperton proposed three constitutional amendments, one of which would eliminate the three department heads' positions. Another would have made the Department of Education answerable to him, instead of operating as an independent entity. Hechler heard about Caperton's move, not from the governor but from the media.[4] If enacted, all of Hechler's duties would have been scattered to other offices.

Caperton then formed a People for Better Government committee to fight for the amendments and raise $625,000 to support his cause in the election. Immediately Hechler criticized the effort.[5] "I discovered that to raise that [money] he was shaking down the bankers, the beer distributors, and anybody he could get to contribute $25,000," he said. "He would do this all downtown at the [Charleston] Marriott Hotel. All those contributors were then asked to come to dinner at the State House [Governor's Mansion], which I said was a corrupt use of the Governor's Mansion. Actually, the free meal was a reward for what they were doing."[6] Since Hechler had recently worked diligently to get the legislature to pass the state's first Governmental Ethics Act of 1989, no doubt Caperton's actions rankled Hechler deeply.[7]

In retaliation, Hechler published and distributed a statement entitled "Why West Virginia Needs a Secretary of State." He put up his own money to finance his own committee, We the People, to fight against the amendments on the ballot as well. He bought television time and crisscrossed the state to explain how the amendments would remove political power from the hands of the voters. He characterized Caperton's proposal as a power grab.[8]

He asked supporters to contact voters, address civic groups, register voters, and "do their own thing." They hoped to have 100,000 members by August and 400,000 by the special election in September 1989. According to a memo from Hechler, the election was going to cost over one million dollars. Hechler urged people to "write, phone, wire, and drive home to members of the legislature how foolish it is to squander over a million dollars when three constitutional amendments could just as easily be scheduled at the same time as the Nov 6, 1990, general election."[9] He further pointed out that passing these amendments would give the job of election control to an appointee of the governor. He reminded them that control over the election process is his most important function and required complete independence from the governor's influence,[10] and that the framers of the state constitution warned about giving the governor too much power. Hechler argued that in 1902, the constitution had been changed specifically to make his position an elected one.[11]

Fortunately for Hechler and the people of West Virginia, the amendments, which had required a two-thirds approval vote, failed overwhelmingly. Only 28 percent of the voters actually voted on September 9, but they were vociferous in their rebuke of Caperton's ideas. The third amendment, which would have eliminated Hechler's position, failed by 77 percent, and the other two by similar margins.[12] Some said the defeat spoke to voter antagonism toward the new governor, while others felt the amendments weren't well explained.[13]

Following the election, Hechler wrote a detailed memo to the commissioner of finance and administration reiterating his accomplishments during his first four years in office. He stated he had saved the state over $290,000 by cutting $70,000 in postage, cutting $81,000 in employee benefits, and reducing salaries when replacing staff who were retiring or simply leaving. He never charged for his own travel and spent $10,000 of his own money to buy West Virginia flags for groups, cities, and indigent individuals.[14]

In 1990, wounded perhaps by his recent battle with Caperton, Hechler took another stab at returning to Congress.

Ken Hechler campaign postcard, 1990 (Courtesy Ken Hechler)

It was an off year for his reelection, and according to the law, he did not have to relinquish his post to run against his old opponent, Nick Rahall, in the primary election. Though he'd retired from Congress twelve years earlier, he cited the current domination of political action committees as the reason he wanted to return and try to make a difference. He felt Congress was no longer representing the interests of average people. "The political landscape of this state is strewn with people who have corrupted public office and the public trust." His newest campaign jingle urged voters to elect him so they would have "a congressman with high moral standards again."[15]

During the campaign, Hechler and Rahall participated in at least one debate sponsored by the League of Women Voters, which was broadcast on public television. The league had laid out certain debate rules, one of which was that the candidates could not bring any props. Nevertheless, according to someone close to Rahall, Hechler brought in a huge boom box, reminiscent of the 1980s. At the end of the debate, Hechler told the audience he had something he wanted them to listen to and punched the tape player. It burst forth with his newest jingle. He had clearly violated the rules, but no one called him on it.[16]

Hechler recalls another detail from that debate's conclusion. He says the two agreed Hechler would have the last statement. But when the time came, and the moderator opened the floor for questions, Rahall jumped in and asked Hechler one last question, also violating the rules. He asked if Hechler was going to give up his current congressional pension if elected. "Of course, that was an impossible question to answer, but I should have said, 'If you'll give up your pay raise, I'll give up my pension.'"[17] Hechler then dodged a straight answer by playing the jingle instead. Suffice it to say, the two have always been "opponents." Just before the primary, the race was dubbed "too close to call"; and in the end, Hechler lost by less than nine thousand votes.[18] He returned to the statehouse to continue serving as secretary of state.

In his 1992 reelection race, the septuagenarian encountered strong opposition from Tom Susman of Daniels, West Virginia. In a nasty letter, Susman, who had accused Hechler of refusing to limit his campaign spending, ripped into him, saying, "Since you will not limit your campaign spending to $45,000, I am providing two money bags to make it easier for you to buy this election. I can provide more of these if you feel you need them."[19] This slap at Hechler's spending also questioned his integrity, although it was well known that Hechler had worked diligently to clean up vote buying in his first term. The two candidates had previously debated the use of political action committee money, which Hechler refused to use, saying, "I feel this is polluting the political wellsprings of democracy."[20] Despite Susman's negative attacks, Hechler beat the man 195,000 to 88,000.[21] But in a June 1 letter to a Swarthmore classmate and friend, Hechler admitted the primary election was bruising. With the endorsement of the UMWA,[22] Hechler then went on to win the general election over his Republican opponent and fellow Huntingtonian, Madalin Jackson, 417,893 to 182,203.[23]

Things got only a bit easier in 1996. That year, Hechler was unopposed in the primary election, but in the general, he faced another Huntington resident, Vernon R. Hayes Jr. While Hechler chose to refrain from criticizing Hayes if he brought up Hechler's age, which by then was eighty-two, the two often traded barbs on the subject. In back-and-forth correspondence over the summer, Hayes claimed Hechler had included a restriction of mentioning a candidate's age in the Code of Fair Campaign Practices for his own purposes, but Hechler denied it. Hayes felt that Hechler was unfairly using his office and the code to restrict discussion of the issue or Hechler's ability to do the job if reelected. Hechler responded that the clause was added after the passage of the Older Americans Act (in 1965) in order to comply with that law. He signed the letter, "Your Liberal Dinosaur Friend." After Hayes won his primary, Hechler offered to debate him anywhere, at any time. Hayes further reminded Hechler that when he had spoken to a Marshall University class three years earlier, he'd pledged to retire after his current term, or in January 1997.[24] When he learned that Hechler had also told a reporter he didn't plan to retire until 2012, when he would be ninety-eight, Hayes asked how he could justify breaking his word. He alleged if voters couldn't trust him on this, they wouldn't on other promises.[25] No record of Hechler's response exists.

Charlotte Pritt, who had previously served in the state legislature as both a delegate and a senator, ran for governor the same year against former Republican governor Cecil Underwood. In one campaign speech, she said of her opponent, "We don't need someone that takes naps in the afternoon and is too tired to get out and work for the state." This prompted Hechler's opponent, Hayes, to write to her, asking how she could make such a comment against the seventy-three-year-old Republican when her own candidate for secretary of state, Ken Hechler, was eighty-two. Hayes wanted Pritt to call Hechler out as being too old to serve as well.[26]

Later that month, Hechler challenged Hayes to a walk-a-thon at Princeton High School in support of a scholarship-granting foundation. Two walks were on the schedule: five miles and ten miles long. Sardonically, Hechler wrote, "Because of my advanced age, I will be making the ten mile hike instead of the five mile walk. I very much regret that you have not accepted my [earlier] challenge to five sets of tennis, or a five mile race." He then bet Hayes $100 that he would finish the ten-mile race ahead of Hayes in his shorter one. The loser had to contribute the money to the scholarship fund.

Two days later, Hayes responded that he had awoken with "incredible searing pain" in his right toe. He claimed he had been to the emergency room and was having an attack of gout and regretted he couldn't accept Hechler's challenge.[27] In November, after Hechler trounced the man by a 30 percent margin,[28] Hayes wrote to congratulate him.[29]

After sixteen years as secretary of state, in 2000 Hechler once again left a secure post to tilt at a national electoral windmill. As Mary Ratliff said, "Congress was the perfect fit for Ken." She understood why he wanted to return. She felt that Hechler saw people in the aggregate, as opposed to people individually. For him, they represented a situation, like miners working in unsafe conditions or the unemployed. On the national stage, he could again help resolve those broad problems. "He would not think so much about *that* individual person in *that* minimum wage job, but he had great empathy for people in that category and was interested in dealing with those types of issues," she said.[30]

By this time, Rahall was firmly ensconced in Hechler's old seat, but the elder statesman only saw that as a challenge, which he loved. Since Hechler's official residence was in Charleston, which was then in the 2nd Congressional District, he decided to try a return to Congress via the seat current congressman Bob Wise was vacating to run for governor. In a letter to Senator Robert Byrd, marked PERSONAL AND CONFIDENTIAL: FOR YOUR EYES ONLY, Hechler said he was definitely planning to file for the open seat. While he had often expressed opposition to the controversial Corridor H highway—which was to run from Elkins to the Virginia border[31]—on environmental grounds, he now pledged to vigorously support it.[32] True to his word, but after studying public opinion research, he released a statement on October 19, 1999, saying, "I have the strange and perhaps novel idea that public officials ought to listen to the people in making decisions. That's why God gave us two ears and only one mouth."[33]

In a letter to fellow Democrats, Hechler explained his reasons for entering the race. Reminding them of his ongoing trek, with veteran activist Doris "Granny D" Haddock, across the United States to gain support for campaign finance reform, he said, "This issue is very near and dear to my heart because I am working for a political system which will enable all candidates to campaign on a level playing field."[34] At a senior citizens fund-raising picnic in Dunbar, West Virginia, he said, "Life is a series of challenges, and I don't want to just coast along here." It wasn't just a challenge, however; Hechler wanted to address stronger controls on campaign financing, handgun control, and many other issues. Addressing the age issue, which at eighty-five he could hardly duck, he consistently reminded voters he played competitive tennis

Ken Hechler played a vigorous game of tennis until a hip replacement in 2007 (Courtesy of Ken Hechler)

four times a week, went white-water rafting in the summer, and was saving golf for his old age.

With a twenty-four-year-old Marshall University student by his side, Hechler spoke out about his age several times. "God will be setting my term limit," he said, "but I don't want to be known as the candidate of the seniors."[35]

As it turned out, Hechler lost the primary election to Jim Humphreys of Charleston by more than sixteen thousand votes.[36] In the general election, Humphreys lost to Republican Shelley Moore Capito, the daughter of former governor Arch Moore. Although it was a disappointing result because Hechler probably could have remained secretary of state for at least another term, he would not give up politics. As he had vowed, only God would set his term limit.

Even though Hechler's office was fully computerized by the time he resigned in 2000, he never took direct credit for the conversion. Therefore, when he ran to regain the office against Republican Betty Ireland in 2004 and she charged that he was technologically out of touch and that the office needed a computer system, he didn't dispute the allegation. As Hechler said, "I still had papers everywhere. All she had to do was take a picture of the huge number of loose papers on my desk and say she was going to computerize all that." Additionally, he didn't challenge Ireland, knowing the office's website was also out of date.[37] In contrast, hers was outstanding. She changed it every week, he said, but "I didn't spend any money [on mine], which I should have," he says. I should have realized a lot of young people look at your website to see how you stand on issues."

Hechler believes, however, that his defeat that year was more about breaking his own rules on campaign spending. As an avid supporter of campaign finance reform, when he violated his own pledge to limit spending, Ireland charged that he was trying to buy his way back into office. Reports that had him spending $1 million caused Ireland to say, "The reformer has turned against the reforms."[38] Hechler admits that his spending "made it very easy for Betty Ireland to point these things out."[39] However, Hechler reasoned that it was necessary. "These days television costs a great deal to buy a thirty second commercial," he countered.[40] Yet as he'd done in his many earlier campaigns, he also bought thousands of T-shirts and pens, sporting his red Jeep, to give away at campaign rallies, thinking the personal touch would work again.[41]

In spite of Ireland's frequent statement that the race was not about Hechler's age, he also refused to debate her, thinking it would be to her advantage. On the other hand, he insisted he knew people in their thirties who were over the hill, both intellectually and physically. In contrast, he was still physically active every day and was as mentally sharp as ever. He spoke without notes, and his memory was prodigious. When they did appear on stage together, however, it did display the discrepancy in their ages to her advantage. "At the end of the evening she would come over and extend her hand to help me get up. That was so obvious that she was the one helping me," he lamented.[42]

In the end, although Hechler had won the primary over a large field, he narrowly lost to Ireland in November. Now Hechler laughs about one letter he received following the election. His old enemy, the infamous Johnie Owens of Mingo County, wrote to say, "Yesterday was the happiest day of my life. No longer will your skinny ass be at the public trough." Hechler treasured the letter and distributed copies of it for years.[43] That statement would prove prescient, but not for lack of Hechler's several attempts to regain a national governmental seat.

20

WALKING WITH GRANNY D

From his days as a congressman, through those as secretary of state—the office he held from 1984 to 2000—Ken Hechler disdained raising money for political campaigns, especially his own. He loathed the idea that only the rich or those who owed their elections to big campaign donors could get elected. A consummate publicity hound, he sent out enough press releases to wallpaper his office. They kept him in the public eye and often served as his campaign statements. The media would run them at no cost, he reckoned, and he was often right. What reporter would ignore a candidate announcing his intention to run for office from the guardhouse of the governor's mansion? Most often, he spent his own money—and that, frugally, like when he encouraged his supporters to make signs on shirt cardboards and when he used his Jeep as his campaign headquarters.

Thus, it's no surprise that he espoused Theodore Roosevelt's view that campaigns should be financed publicly at both the state and the federal level. Hechler even disapproved of the one-dollar campaign finance check-off option on IRS tax forms. Advertising gimmicks like billboards and bumper stickers defaced the landscape, he said, and should be banned. In his ideal world, campaigning would be limited to three weeks, with free television and radio time reserved for debates, and voting would be mandatory.[1] He'd also do away with the Electoral College.[2] He said, "Three states . . . publically finance elections and it has worked very well to enable candidates to talk on the issues instead of dialing for dollars."[3] His wish that other states and the federal government would pass the same law led him to spend parts of 1999–2000 marching across the United States with avowed campaign finance reformer Doris Haddock, known to everyone as "Granny D."

Granny D lived in the small New Hampshire town of Dublin and belonged to an adult study group of nineteen women who called themselves the Tuesday Morning Academy. A lifelong activist, she had been involved in reform fights from her earliest years.[4] At eighty-eight, most thought she was through raising hell. But when she heard of the McCain-Feingold campaign reform bill and how it had stalled in Congress, she took the matter to her group. Her concern, she said, was that "our democracy was being purchased from under us." They studied the issue and then asked Doris what she planned to do about it. She said she'd think about it.[5]

Doris knew that after the Watergate scandal, Congress had begun to restrict campaign contributions, passing the Federal Election Campaign Act Amendments of 1974. But despite a Federal Election Commission ruling that donors' money could go only for party-building activities, the two major parties more often used it to support their candidates. Known as soft money, it became such a major source of campaign financing that a bill to restrict its use was passed in 1992, but President George H. W. Bush vetoed it. Under President Clinton, similar bills were introduced, but the two houses refused to agree on a joint one. In 1995, John McCain (R-AZ) and Russ Feingold (D-WI) introduced their own campaign finance reform bills. By 1998, a bill had reached the Senate, but a filibuster killed it for that Congress.[6] When Granny D learned that the House had added an amendment to one bill that would have allowed President Clinton to give a $50 million tax break to tobacco companies, she took on the fight.[7]

After training for a year in order to withstand carrying a backpack while walking ten miles a day, she set off by plane to

California, where she would begin her trek. Her goal? Washington, D.C., and the halls of Congress. After her local newspaper reported her intention to walk across the country to highlight the need for campaign finance reform, *USA Today* picked up the story, and others began interviewing Doris. When Hechler heard about her plans, he called her to say he thought it was a grand idea.[8] He then asked to walk with her. Although Granny D was unimpressed when Hechler told her he was West Virginia's secretary of state, she agreed but asked if he could afford to take care of himself.

On December 30, 1998, he flew to Pasadena, California, to join her as part of the Rose Bowl Parade. Though she'd previously gotten tentative permission to join the parade, when she called to find out what float she would ride on, the officials reneged. When she objected, they argued that if she rode, they'd have to let everyone else with a point of view, "like gays," do so. In fact, they said if she showed up, they would arrest her.[9] Knowing that hundreds of people traditionally took up a spot along the parade route on the day before the event, Hechler said he had an idea. He created a large sign saying, "Why ban Granny D from the Rose Bowl Parade?" and suggested they appear with it. Hechler carried it aloft, and when people asked her why she was being banned, they distributed petitions calling for campaign reform and asked people to sign them.[10] Granny D says she was a bit hesitant to approach people, but Hechler certainly wasn't. Afraid of no one, she says, he spoke to everyone, and with his big smile, they fell in love with him.[11]

Granny D described Hechler as a "tall, lean, charming man who always looked fit." She said he was "full of hat-tipping courtesy, and red-cheeked optimism, a deep, stirring voice, and a passionate command of political issues." No matter their ages—Hechler was eighty-four and Doris was eight-eight when

Ken Hechler with Doris "Granny D" Haddock, January 1999 (Courtesy of Ken Hechler)

they met—each may have developed a romantic crush on the other.

Knowing she loved chocolate, he once appeared with chocolate ice cream running down his arm and thereafter always brought her chocolate candy when he met her on the road.[12] Hechler later denied a romantic relationship, but not Granny D, who, perhaps wistfully, described them as walking through Los Angeles like a couple of teenagers. "I was not sure at first if his passion was for reform or for me, but at my age, whatever puts a little spring in your step is welcome," she wrote. On December 31, 1998, the pair walked the five-mile parade route and continued on, from Pasadena to Twenty-Nine Palms in the California desert. Amusingly, she thought it a long trek for an old man.[13]

On January 3, they attended a Friends meeting, where both Granny D and Hechler had the opportunity to speak about the march. In a handwritten note of that day, Hechler relates that most of the congregation kept their eyes closed and maintained absolute silence during the service. Shortly after it began, the clerk of the meeting, Richard Cooper, read from "Advices and Queries" in the Friends Book of Discipline. Hechler wrote, "Included among the Advices was this passage: 'We have regard for the worth of each person. We cannot be easy in our lives when others suffer indignity, injustice, or want.'" A few minutes later, Hechler—no stranger to Quaker meetings after his years at Swarthmore—stood to speak. He repeated Dr. Martin Luther King Jr.'s response upon being criticized for speaking out against the war in Vietnam: "injustice anywhere is a threat to justice everywhere." Following the formal service, they introduced Granny D to explain why she started this campaign. She in turn asked Hechler to elaborate his reasons for joining her. The pair then declined a lunch offer and struck out for Claremont, California.[14]

Because Hechler still held his full-time position as secretary of state, he couldn't walk continually, but he joined her throughout the next year for about a week at a time. Along the way, supporters and reporters joined the march for some miles, so Hechler was usually part of a larger entourage of mostly average citizens. He said they often felt compelled to join her, if just for a short distance, because they felt her efforts were for them.[15] In February, he learned that Dennis Burke, the eventual coauthor of her memoir of the journey, had borrowed a used van for Granny D to use for rest stops. It had to be returned, so Hechler offered to buy her one and outfit it with a bed. She accepted the offer, saying that by now, Hechler was a family friend, not a corporate sponsor.[16]

Throughout the following months, Hechler joined Granny D whenever he could and wherever she was. He'd fly out, spend a weekend or longer, walk ten miles each day, and then return to his duties in the statehouse. At the time, he was planning to run for his current post again in 2000, so perhaps it was a way for Hechler to feel he was still making a difference on the national stage, even though he had no official presence there. In a May interview conducted by Daniel Zwerdling for NPR's *All Things Considered*, Hechler introduced a parody he'd written for Granny D:

Oh, her name is Doris Haddock, and they call her
    Granny D.
She's fed up with big money in elections, don't you see?
She's walked across the country for campaign finance reform.
To win you have to sell your soul. They force you to conform.

While admitting his friends had said he could sing on key only in the shower, he belted it out for the broadcast to the tune of "McNamara's Band."[17]

Over and over, Hechler would appear along the route to join his reformer friend—the two slapping high-fives at the end of each ten-mile trek.[18] Near Phoenix they were told *Good Morning America* was coming to film an interview, so Hechler prepared to meet them. Although Granny D received a call late the evening before saying the segment had been canceled, she decided to wait until morning to tell the others. While Granny D had taken her preferred spot on the ground, Hechler was sleeping in the van. Oblivious to the cancellation, he rose at four in the morning, got dressed, and headed to the meeting place. After climbing over a few fences and avoiding cacti to get to the shoulder of the road, he headed to the church they'd agreed on for the interview. When no camera crew arrived, Hechler turned back in the predawn hours to find the campsite. Behind a barbed-wire fence in earshot of baying dogs, he wriggled under it. As he did so, he heard the sound of ripping fabric. Back at the camp, he examined his backside and was relieved to see that his trousers were merely scraped, not torn.[19]

Outside of Tucson, Hechler and Doris fell into a discussion of their many past romances and about their current situations. Granny D admitted to keeping company with a ninety-one-year-old gentleman back home, but Hechler made it clear there wouldn't be a similar relationship between them. Typical of him, who had often flirted with the opposite sex during his days overseas and on the campaign trail, only to leave them wondering why they couldn't land him, he said, "Not that I don't like you, Doris, but I seem to enjoy the company of young women." It was an astonishing admission—and one Granny D thought quite surprising for a politician. On another occasion, as she reached the Arizona border, there was Hechler, chocolates in hand. She felt flattered by his attention, "even if he did only like sweet young things," she wrote.[20] From his perspective, she was a great companion, one who enjoyed accompanying him in song as they walked.[21]

Despite their long-running mutual admiration society—Hechler admired her ability to quote Robert Frost; she loved his smile and the chocolates he brought—the pair had a heartbreaking falling out. In June, Hechler convinced the National Association of Secretaries of State to award Granny D the 1999 Margaret Chase Smith Award for her acts of political courage and selfless action in the realm of public service, and invited her to speak to the group. But in August, as the two were in Little Rock, Arkansas, their relationship began to fray a bit over her speaking style. Hechler thought she sounded more passionate when she spoke extemporaneously, but she preferred notes or, better yet, prepared speeches.

After her talk to the National Convention of Young Democrats, he was visibly disappointed that she hadn't used his ideas for the speech. She worried that his suggestions were not as much about campaign finance reform as about the two of them. However, she realized his long-standing reformation stance gave her own campaign credence; therefore, she was torn.[22] She also recognized that knowing who he was, the media did sometimes opt to speak with him instead of her.[23] By then, Hechler had changed his mind about trying to retain his current position and was running for Congress once again. He'd decided to run for the open West Virginia 2nd Congressional District seat recently vacated by Congressman Bob Wise, who was running for governor. Hechler said he was inspired to do so by Granny D's own acts of courage. He reasoned that if she could walk across America at eighty-nine, he could run for Congress again at eighty-four.[24]

In Little Rock, Hechler offered to rejoin the march on September 7 in Memphis, the place most associated with Martin Luther King Jr., thinking this would add strength to her campaign.[25] But at breakfast the next day, August 22, a heated discussion ensued. Another of Granny D's aides, John Anthony, suggested that Hechler only wanted to come to Memphis to gain publicity for his own congressional campaign, and that perhaps he should stay away this time. Anthony argued that Hechler was using the walk for his own purposes and had, on many occasions, sought personal publicity during the 330 miles he'd walked with Granny D. He also objected to Hechler's shirt, which proclaimed him as "Ken Hechler, Secretary of State," saying it drew the reporters' attention immediately to him.[26] Whether or not these were Anthony's only reasons is hard to determine. Perhaps he found Hechler's effusive nature too much to take, or he felt Hechler was trying to direct Granny D's campaign. In any case, she seemed to acquiesce to Anthony's assessment, even if she didn't agree.

According to Granny D, Hechler turned beet red with anger but managed to control his tongue by holding his head in his hands, as he had so often done in the past. Finally, he turned to Granny D and asked if she agreed. She struggled and then made the wrong decision, she says in hindsight. She told Hechler they needed to focus on the reform message more.[27] Anthony then reiterated his earlier statement, saying Hechler needed to stay away from Memphis in order to keep the focus exclusively on Granny D and her message. Hechler felt he'd "been handed his walking papers."[28] She says his face crumpled, as he took her response as a personal rebuke. Granny D saw him once more before he left. He was reading a book belonging to her, *The Healing of America*, which he said was just the right medicine. They smiled at each other, and she told him to take it with him. He reached into his pocket and pulled out a miniature chocolate box and handed it to her. "One of the three truffles had been raided, but the remaining two were delicious, filled as they were, with the milk of human kindness," she says.[29]

A few days later, Hechler wrote what he called an open letter to Granny D and several of the others who had been part of the marching party, including those who helped to oust him. In it he tried to defend himself, outlining at least nine major media markets he had purposely avoided in order to leave the spotlight for Granny D. Believing that a bit of levity would lighten his message, he started the letter by relating a phone call his office had received earlier in the week while he was in Arkansas but before he was "fired." A reporter spoke to Mary Ratliff to say, "There is an old man walking with Granny D down here in Arkansas who insists he is West Virginia's secretary of state. Could you verify for me who is the present secretary of state?"[30] She did. In addition to the humorous opening, Hechler added praise and appreciation for Granny D, her supporters, and the entire campaign, saying he felt honored to have been part of it for the past eight months.

Though Granny D replied with a handwritten note, which Hechler did not share, or keep,[31] because of its personal nature, he stayed away from the march. In it she did say she was "flabbergasted" at the argument that Sunday morning. But since she'd agreed with the sentiment Anthony expressed, he felt the remark was disingenuous.[32] Therefore, he responded in obvious resentment on August 30, "When you come to West Virginia, I have a very important mission to follow in running for Congress and will be unable to help or walk with you. The publicity for my campaign is so important that I certainly do not wish anyone else tainting that publicity."[33]

By November, Hechler regretted what he felt he'd done to create the rift. He wrote another open letter to Granny D and her supporters, saying that. "I hate myself. . . . I hate it that I was unable to discover that my over-enthusiasm so clouded my judgment that I was rapidly becoming persona non grata to the people and [the] cause I was working with all my might to support." While he again defended his actions, he reiterated his refusal to walk with her when she came to West Virginia the following month because it would be a reminder of their split. He says, "While I can endure physical pain . . . mental pain is deeper and more difficult to assuage."[34]

In a late November response to three pleas from Doris; her son, Jim; and Dennis to return to the march, Hechler outlined three non-negotiable conditions under which he would agree. One, he refused to give up the T-shirt Anthony had called "obnoxious"; two, he demanded a moratorium on discussing the August incident at Little Rock; and three, even though Dennis had asked him to participate in planning the appearance at the U.S. Capitol, he refused.[35] Regardless of his earlier protestations, Hechler relented. When Granny D crossed the Ohio River into Parkersburg, West Virginia, Governor Cecil Underwood, Parkersburg Mayor Jimmy Columbo, and Hechler were there to greet her. She'd written again asking Hechler to return, and both Dennis Burke and Jim Haddock had called to tell him he was greatly missed. She was wearing one of Hechler's campaign shirts. He greeted her with his toothy grin and a kiss. Granny D felt her family was back together again.

Later, when a producer from *60 Minutes* called Granny D, she learned the depth of Hechler's character. The producer had called to set up a Mike Wallace interview with Hechler about his political lone-wolf fight to stop mountaintop removal mining. As if to make amends, Hechler demurred, saying instead that Granny D's march would be far more interesting. Granny D was floored. "She [the producer] was calling me to get more information," she says, "but I was too amazed at the gallantry of my old friend to even try to hear much of what she was saying after that."[36]

As the new century dawned amid Y2K concerns about how dates in the new millennium would be displayed on computers around the world, Granny D marched on through rain and snow, sometimes with Hechler, sometimes without. He walked with her from Clarksburg, where he presented her with a one-year walking medal of his own design, to Fairmont.[37] And he met her, bundled like an Eskimo, along the path near Berkeley Springs, even though he was in the throes of campaigning.

On February 29, 2000, Granny D and an enormous crowd of supporters, including Hechler, arrived on the steps of the U.S. Capitol, where she spoke and then met with as many members of Congress as possible. At the lasagna dinner organized to thank her supporters, Granny D, with a plate of food in hand, went to find Hechler, but he was nowhere in sight. "He had quietly faded away, off in his inconspicuous red Jeep," she says, perhaps with a large dose of satire. Someone told her he'd returned home to continue campaigning. He had walked 530 miles of her 3,000-mile journey.

Granny D had kept a journal as she walked, and with fellow marcher Dennis Burke, she turned it into a book, *Granny D: Walking across America in My 90th Year*, which was published in 2001. Hechler figures prominently in her account. Yet there are places where they differ on certain incidents, particularly on the details of their rift. Hechler liked the book generally but felt compelled to write his versions of the stories to Dennis. Hechler asked him not to share them with Granny D, however, for fear she'd think he didn't like the book. Again, Hechler reiterated that his sole purpose in joining the march "was to show that a Chief Election Officer really believed in her issue and wanted to prove to the world that here was a brave woman who needed everybody's support."[38]

Granny D's march brought widespread attention to the issue of campaign finance reform, but the bill again stalled in Congress. When it didn't pass, Granny D returned to Washington in 2001. As the debate raged, she marched around the Capitol for two weeks and was arrested for reading the Declaration of Independence and the Bill of Rights in the "People's Hall," as she called the Capitol.[39] Finally, on April 2, 2001, the bill passed in the Senate. The House was about to let it die when the Enron scandal happened. Because its executives had given millions to members of Congress, many House members felt they needed to redeem themselves.[40]

At long last, on February 14, 2002, the Bipartisan Campaign Finance Reform Bill of 2002 (the old McCain-Feingold bill), which had been introduced in the House as the Shays-Meehan bill, passed Congress and was signed into law.

Hechler wasn't so fortunate. He lost the primary election of 2000, but that didn't stop him. Unlike old soldiers, Hechler didn't fade away. At eighty-six, during the last year of his stint as secretary of state, he'd begun fighting other battles: ending the coal mining practice of mountaintop removal and assisting the effort to preserve Blair Mountain, West Virginia, as a national historic site to commemorate the 1921 battle there between coal mine operators and miners. Additionally, he returned once again to the Marshall University classroom. He would not go gently into that good night.

21

——

FROM REBEL TO HELL-RAISER

——

Whether melancholia, boredom, or his advancing age prompted the idea is unclear, but while he was still secretary of state, Hechler began holding annual reunions of his former staffers and old friends. He'd learned that an old Swarthmore classmate, Sam Ashelman, owned Coolfont Resort in West Virginia's eastern panhandle town of Berkeley Springs, and that its occupancy the weekend after Labor Day was low.[1] So, in 1993, he invited his former congressional staffers, including Judy Roach Deegans, to an early September weekend gathering there. Using his old classroom parlor trick, Hechler asked each guest their favorite dessert and drink in preparation of having them on hand at arrival.[2] While personally and professionally frugal, Hechler's often surprising generosity now shone. He paid for everything: travel, lodging, meals, golf, spa visits, whatever they wanted to do—families included. For the first reunion, Deegans wanted sweatshirts made for the guests emblazoned with "Hechler's Angels." Hechler called that "over the top" and suggested "Hechler's Hecklers" instead. The name stuck. The weekend gave staff members the opportunity to retell their favorite anecdotes about one another, and especially about Hechler. This first sentimental gathering cost him $4,688.[3]

One year, Hechler's former public relations director, Dick Leonard, spoke of himself as the "humanizing factor" in Hechler's office. Hechler laughed, then responded, "Judy Roach said it more directly, and correctly. She said when I came in each morning to raise hell about something, Dick was the person who smoothed things over."[4] Hechler could always laugh at himself, and often was the one who told the joke. One year, standing in front of the group in a hooded sweatshirt and mock-serving a tennis racquet for illustration, he recalled his days at Marshall, saying, "When I was teaching my first class at Marshall thirty-eight years ago, I came in waving a tennis racquet and said, 'You'll be studying political science and all political science is a racquet.'"[5]

Each gathering focused on a specific serious topic as well. In 1995, his old cohorts Donald Rasmussen and Chip Yablonski attended.[6] That year, mountaintop removal mining (MTR) was front and center, but the general atmosphere was still relaxed and nostalgic. In 2000, after he'd marched with Granny D, both she and Dennis Burke attended. As they regaled the group with stories about their adventure, they urged them to continue fighting for publicly funded elections via campaign finance reform. In the course of her talk, Granny D said she initially thought Hechler was bossy. She even recalled replying, "Yes, sir," to one of his requests. She also praised him, however, for meeting her in all but two of the states she crossed and for marching with a twenty-five-pound backpack.[7]

That year, in a letter to those who were to be invited, Hechler said, "One of the joyfully wonderful aspects of losing an election is that now I have enough 'mazuma and moola' [Hechler's slang terms for money] to throw another big bash on the weekend after Labor Day. I had a bully platform as a congressman, which I won't have as a private citizen."[8]

While Hechler still had the secretary of state's bully pulpit, his enmity toward "King Coal" and its casual regard for the rights of others again appeared. In 1986, during his first term, the West Virginia legislature had proposed a bill that would have raised the weight limit of coal trucks by 30 percent. Hechler had asked Governor Moore to veto the bill if it landed on his desk. Concerned that the increase would exacerbate the destruction of roads already being damaged at the current weight limit, he implored, "It takes a Jeep like mine to negotiate many [WV] roads. In my travels, I have seen many coal trucks that have installed sideboards so they can carry even greater loads.[9] [I've] seen them avoid the current potholes they have previously made, swerving into the other lane to do so, almost hitting oncoming traffic, [and] talked with truck drivers who are running without 'Jake brakes.' "[10] He also argued that retaining the lower weight limits would increase the number of jobs in the industry, since coal operators would have to hire more drivers.[11] Although Moore heeded Hechler's plea and vetoed the bill,[12] the issue came up again under Governor Bob Wise. Hechler again fought it by running television ads asking the people to call their legislators to express their desire to limit hauling weights. And again in 2002, Hechler and the people won,[13] but the issue continued to be an ongoing battle through successive administrations.

While in Congress, Hechler had also tackled environmental issues through the legislative process. Now unable to use that method, he changed, as he said many times, from an "activist to an agitator, and then to a hell-raiser *extraordinaire*."[14] In 1993, officials of a company named Parsons and Whittemore announced plans to build a large pulp mill near Apple Grove in Mason County. Environmentalists opposed it on the grounds that the dioxin (a highly toxic pollutant formed as a result of industrial processes using chlorine) dumped into the Ohio River would kill or poison the fish there and thereby damage the food chain. The Ohio Valley Environmental Coalition (OVEC) fought the mill from 1993 to 1997 with protests and litigation. The company finally abandoned the project on March 1, 1997, after Judge Todd Kauffman had thrown out its building permit a few months earlier.[15] Once OVEC was successful in its efforts, Hechler allowed the group to announce the victory from his "people's room" in the secretary of state's office. According to OVEC staffer Vivian Stockman, it may have been the first time, but certainly not the last time, that Hechler supported the environmental organization.[16]

Hechler joined OVEC's efforts in 1999, instead of merely providing support. This time he wanted to help place the Blair Mountain battle site on the National Register of Historic Places. Until then, the site of the 1921 battle by union miners for better working conditions had no protection from mountaintop removal mining. Yet the site marked the spot of the only time the United States Army had declared war on its own citizens since the Civil War. The movie, *Matewan*, and the PBS documentary, *The Mine Wars*, depict the incident in detail. At that time, firearms and shell casings from the battle could still be found on the mountainside, leading preservation advocates to oppose mining on what they considered hallowed ground. While the Sierra Club and OVEC fought for Blair Mountain's preservation, the coal companies fought just as hard for permission to mine the tons of coal under it.

In August, the Blair Mountain Historical Organization and the Coal River Mountain Watch joined OVEC in sponsoring a small march to commemorate the original battle. Over several days, marchers retraced the original route from Marmet to Logan.[17] Because the historical recognition was about more than just formalities, opposition was strong. Angry miners, outnumbering the protesters four to one, pelted them with eggs and rotten tomatoes, shoved, kicked, and roughed up the small band of marchers, including Hechler. In his statement to the FBI, he says he heard shouts of "You son of a bitch; you shouldn't be here. You're a traitor." One man told Hechler, "If you value your life, you'll go home."[18] Art Kirkendoll, a Logan County commissioner, was among those who did the kicking. His actions later prompted

Hechler to protest when Governor Wise appointed Kirkendoll to the newly created position of Southern West Virginia economic development coordinator. Hechler appeared at an anti-Kirkendoll rally carrying a sign that read, "Kick ME and get a job with Bob Wise."[19] Shortly after the march, however, U.S. district court judge Charles H. Haden II issued a ruling saying that valley fills, in which debris, trees, and land dislodged by mountaintop removal explosions is shoved into the streams below, were illegal. While it was a win for the environmentalists, it didn't end the battle over Blair Mountain.

As the preservationists planned their next move to gain historic registry designation for Blair Mountain, other issues took the spotlight. In 2000, Hechler joined OVEC in planning and speaking at its Funeral for the Mountains, a protest against mountaintop removal mining. He'd long been opposed to it and had dubbed it "strip mining on steroids" after discovering that the 1977 bill curtailing strip mining contained a loophole that would allow the tops to be blown off the mountains in lieu of stripping the sides.[20] Hechler's opposition to MTR stemmed from his ongoing environmentalism, but it kicked up several notches after he became good friends with Larry Gibson. Gibson was a longtime West Virginia resident who had been fighting the coal companies' land-grabbing tactics. Once purchased, his neighbor's acreage had been devastated by mining practices that raped the land for its coal. Now they threatened to take and destroy his property, which had been in his family since the 1700s.

Born on Kayford Mountain, outside Charleston, West Virginia, Gibson had returned there following a workplace accident in a General Motors plant that forced his early retirement. When the large mining companies began buying out landowners in the 1980s in order to mine the land, Gibson used his home as a vivid demonstration of the destructive practice, since it overlooked a massive MTR site. His activism drew both national attention to the problem and the enmity of the mining companies. More than once his life had been threatened.[21]

Hechler first met Gibson—usually dressed in a day-glo green T-shirt and matching ball cap—when he worked at the Citizen Action Group office in Charleston. After Gibson formed the non-profit Keeper of the Mountains foundation, the two often traveled together, speaking out against MTR, and ultimately became best friends. Hechler recalls, "So we started just as good friends and then I, like every other person who listened to him describe the fact that this was land that was occupied and owned by his ancestors, it was a very easy process for me to join with Larry."[22] What Hechler doesn't mention is that he, along with OVEC founder Laura Foreman, also persuaded Gibson to go back to school to finish his education, which had ended many years earlier—at third grade. It paid off. Gibson later wrote the history of Kayford Mountain and of his family's life there.[23]

Aptly, on October 28, 2000, the day of the Funeral for the Mountains, clouds threatened in the Charleston sky. Mock tombstones, each one representing a mountain or stream lost to MTR, covered the east lawn of the West Virginia Capitol. Hechler had helped construct the tombstones. A troupe of bagpipers playing a mournful dirge led the somber funeral procession of black-clad marchers. They marched from the state Office of Surface Mining to the Capitol, where Hechler, also wearing black, gave this eulogy.

I think that I shall never see a dragline lovely as a tree.
Trees that look at God all day, and lift their leafy arms to pray.
A dragline towering toward the sky, its bucket filled with trees condemned to die.

> Close mountains blasted rocks and soil; valley fills that make
> me boil.
> The trees we honored at this wake can't be replaced, make no
> mistake.
> Mountaintop removal, don't you see, is just murder in the
> first degree.
> Bigger profits are their goal, but here's my message to Arch
> Coal.
> Draglines are made by fools like thee, but only God can make
> a tree.

He then apologized to Joyce Kilmer, whose poem he had parodied.

The following year, Hechler joined Larry Gibson at the kick-off of his walk from Harpers Ferry, in the eastern panhandle, to Huntington, in the southwestern cradle of the state, to bring further attention to the MTR issue. Gibson had been inspired by Granny D's march, and reminiscent of her first attempt to gain attention, his group had been forbidden to carry signs along the C&O Canal. Always eager to resolve a difficult situation, Hechler suggested they simply carry the mock headstones they had been given permission to display.[24]

Undeterred by the resistance he met on that first march on Blair Mountain and at other events where the opposition grew ugly, Hechler continued to join the supporters of that effort as well as those opposing MTR. Often the two issues dovetailed. After he left his secretary of state post in 2001, he was free to raise hell, and he did. Time and time again he appeared at rallies and marches, sometimes with his musician friend George Daugherty. The two would sing Hechler's parodies, and Hechler would speak, most often in the face of angry coal miners who believed abolishing MTR would also abolish their jobs. One parody inspired a bumper sticker still seen on West Virginia cars. Sung to the tune of John Denver's "Country Roads," he called it, "Almost Level, West Virginia."[25]

According to Janet Keating, the miners' animosity toward Hechler was ironic. "I think one of the saddest things in all of this is that it was Ken Hechler who helped get legislation and championed legislation for the coal miners' health and safety act. They turned on him. The young miners don't know the history," she said.[26] During the Mountain Justice Summer Kick-Off Rally and Concert in Charleston on March 31, 2005, Hechler harked back to those days when he was fighting for legislation to protect miners' health. Now, in an attempt to beat the coal operators again, he waved another hunk of bologna. This time it demonstrated what he thought of Big Coal's declaration that it can reclaim a decapitated mountain.[27]

On Earth Day, April 21, 2005, Hechler appeared with OVEC staffers to lobby once more for putting Blair Mountain on the National Register of Historic Places. In 2006, the site was nominated, but it took four more years before the registry listed it. Finally, on March 30, 2009, after nearly twenty years, WVU professor Dr. Barbara Rasmussen had succeeded in writing the winning application.[28] Despite the celebration that followed, the National Register inexplicably rescinded the designation four months later.[29] Most believed pressure on state officials from the coal industry caused the action.[30] Now Blair Mountain was merely "eligible" for the list. The fight for recognition resumed, but it became just another struggle in the ongoing fight against mountaintop removal mining. The environmentalists knew that both Massey Energy and Arch Coal had designs on Blair Mountain for that destructive practice. They'd seen valley fill kill the fish in the streams below and render the water undrinkable. And they'd seen the resulting poisonous sludge from coal processing plants stored in impoundment dams, usually near the mining site. They knew the cost to the environment and to people in the wake of MTR.

In 2009, one of these dams, the Brushy Fork impoundment, owned by Goal Coal, a subsidiary of Massey Energy, began to seep its toxic waste. Below it, just four hundred yards away, sat Marsh Fork Elementary School, in Raleigh County, West Virginia. Naturally, parents of the schoolchildren became alarmed, fearing another Buffalo Creek disaster. If the dam broke, they feared, the entire Coal River valley, including the school, would be flooded. Even if it didn't, parents were blaming the leaking toxins for the unusually high incidence of illness in their children. The parents alerted Coal River Mountain Watch and asked for its help in contacting governmental agencies.[31]

Back and forth the parents and watchdog groups fought through staged protests, letter-writing campaigns, and court petitions, but no governmental or corporate action was taken to protect the children. At one demonstration on May 23, 2009, at nearby Pettus, West Virginia, seventy-five environmentalists and parents picketed Massey Energy's Marfork Complex to protest the blasting only one hundred feet from the Brushy Fork sludge pond. Police arrested seven people who approached the entrance and refused to leave.[32] Hechler was there and tried to join the seven, but the police refused to arrest the well-known public figure.[33] Following the arrests, Hechler spoke, urging citizens to continue to stand up for their rights, which included nonviolent protesting.

Then, on June 23, a large group of parents, environmentalists, and MTR foes gathered at the school in an anti–mountaintop removal rally. NASA climatologist James Hansen; actress and activist Daryl Hannah; novelist Denise Giardina, author of *Storming Heaven*; George Daugherty dressed as Uncle Sam on stilts; and

Hechler were among the special guests. At the gathering, which had obtained the necessary assembly permits, Hechler spoke:

> We live in a free country and you can go up and down the streets swinging your arms as a free person, but if some-body comes along and you hit that person in the nose, your freedom ends where that person's nose begins. So I say to you here, the freedom of Massey is a clear and present danger to everyone that lives below Brushy Fork. [The sludge pond was at Brushy Fork, while the school below it was at Marsh Fork.] Their freedom ends because they have put thousands of people at risk [that] would be surely killed just the way the one hundred twenty-five were killed in 1972 on Buffalo Creek. The first three words of the constitution are "We the People," not "We the Corporations."[34]

After the speeches, the march to the Massey gates began. As the protesters walked, scores of Massey employees and their family members lined the route, holding signs aloft that proclaimed, "Tree Huggers Go Home" and "We Love Mountains That Produce Coal." Yelling "Massey, Massey," they shouted down the Gospel-singing marchers. Obscenities flew. Bikers revved their Harleys to add to the cacophony.[35] A group of twenty-nine protesters had previously decided to risk arrest by refusing to move from the road once they reached the Massey gates. The state police arrived and arrested thirty-one people, including Hannah, Hansen, Larry Gibson, and ninety-four-year-old Ken Hechler. It was the first time he'd ever been arrested. Even with the vitriol from the sidelines, the day ended peacefully, with none of the violence Hechler had experienced at the Blair Mountain march.[36]

Notwithstanding his arrest, Hechler wasn't sent to jail. He says it was because of his age-related infirmities. "I think one of the reasons that I didn't get sentenced after being arrested was because I can't walk at the speed that other people did. When I went up to the company headquarters to cross their property lines, I was walking or being transported by car. Since I couldn't walk as fast as the other people, I could argue in court and I could present photos to show I was not actually violating their property lines. That's the only way I avoided getting sentenced or was fined." In other words, Hechler believes he never made it to Massey's property line; but if he had, he says he'd gladly have gone to jail.[37]

On June 28, 2010, West Virginia's long-term senator, Robert Byrd, died, giving Hechler one more chance to throw his hat into national politics. On August 10, a ninety-five-year-old Hechler made the announcement. He reminded his audience that for years he'd used his classic Jeep in his campaign jingle. Although he planned to drive it across the state once more to campaign, he'd decided to drop the reference to it. "I want to narrow the issue. After all, they're not voting for a Jeep," he said. "They're voting for Ken Hechler and against mountaintop removal, which is my number-one issue, you know."[38] He really didn't expect to win, but he saw the election process as a way to bring national attention to the devastation of mountaintop removal mining.

While the timing of a special election was in question for a time, the West Virginia legislature eventually passed a compromise, for that year only, allowing a special primary election to be held on August 28, and a special general election on November 2, to coincide with the midterm elections.[39] Though garnering only 17 percent of the vote, Hechler came in second. Some said the votes he won, which he had declared would be a vote against MTR, embarrassed then governor Joe Manchin,[40] who did win the primary. Nevertheless, Hechler vowed to keep on fighting.

On September 8, Hechler held a press conference saying he thought he'd lost not because folks were against mountaintop removal mining but because they probably thought he might not live out the term. After all, Hechler *was* three years older than the man he had hoped to replace. At the announcement, his good friend Larry Gibson flanked Hechler's podium. Toward the end of the event, Hechler endorsed Mountain Party candidate Jesse Johnson for the senatorial seat he had originally tried to win. Johnson, Hechler pointed out, was young at fifty-one and a West Virginia native to boot. Given his recent primary thrashing, Hechler believed those qualifications gave Johnson a decided advantage.

But the elder statesman would not leave the spotlight easily. Before turning the podium over to Johnson, Hechler used the opportunity to speak his mind. First, he listed all the places he'd been during the steamy month of August to show he was still able to "rise each morning full of pee and vinegar, ready to do battle," as he said. He then blasted Governor Joe Manchin for claiming he wanted a balance between coal and the environment. Hechler said that position meant coal always wins and the environment always loses. He further pointed out his faithful participation in anti–mountaintop removal coal-mining rallies and protests, and credited Gibson for bringing international attention to the problem. Advocating placing Blair Mountain on the National Register of Historic Places, he noted that West Virginia Division of Culture and History director Randall Reid-Smith had submitted the objection that caused the designation to be withdrawn. He also said Manchin was ignoring the damage that drilling for Marcellus Shale oil was causing to the state's groundwater. He believed the state needed to follow the example of Pennsylvania in reining in the practice.[41] Despite Hechler's efforts and Johnson's candidacy, Manchin won the general election in 2010.

In a double defeat, the day after endorsing Johnson, Hechler discovered that someone had stolen his signature red Jeep, the fifth one he'd owned. It wasn't his first Jeep theft, however, but it would be the last. Although the 2008 Jeep Wrangler, sporting his "Ken Do" license plate was recovered,[42] at ninety-five, he finally gave up the driver's seat.

The following year, the battle to prevent mining operations on Blair Mountain again surfaced. Alpha Natural Resources, which had bought out Massey Energy, now owned most of Blair Mountain along with Arch Coal. That worried the environmentalists immensely. Along with labor groups, they were backing a lawsuit to restore its place on the National Register of Historic Places.[43] Plus, it had been ninety years since miners fought there for the right to unionize. This called for another march.

Dubbed the Second March on Blair Mountain, the June 2011 protest brought out such luminaries as environmental attorney Robert F. Kennedy Jr., singer and West Virginia native Kathy Mattea, Larry Gibson, and Hechler. Hundreds of concerned state, national, and international citizens joined them. Organizers hoped the expected media coverage would raise overall awareness of both the damage caused by MTR and the rights of laborers. The fifty-mile march took five days. Organizers had planned for the marchers to spend each night in a predetermined campground or park, but because of threats from the coal companies, owners withdrew their hospitality at the last minute. Volunteers subsequently drove the marchers back and forth from Marmet to the route each day. A rally at the foot of the mountain on Saturday, June 11, featured speeches by Kennedy, Mattea, Gibson, and others, including Hechler.[44] From his wheelchair, the feisty environmentalist urged the audience to keep fighting to preserve the mountains.

According to those at OVEC, Hechler was always there. "Ken has always been on the right side of the issues, environmental issues. . . . We could always count on Ken," said Janet Keating.[45] He even erected billboards near the coalfields that featured his

Ken Hechler and Larry Gibson on Kayford Mountain, 2007 (Photo by Mark Schmerling)

picture and the words, "My name is Ken. I'm 96 and a fighter. And I'm fighting to save our mountains." This may have been the fight Hechler was the most passionate about in his later years. He was as vehement about stopping mountaintop removal mining as he had been about improving miners' health and safety. Beyond participating in West Virginia protests, he traveled to several universities across the country with Larry Gibson to speak about the evils of the practice, and devoted much of his time writing or speaking to any group that would invite him, with or without his friend.

On September 9, 2012, at only sixty-six, Larry died of a heart attack on his beloved Kayford Mountain. Hechler had toured the mountain with him two days earlier.[46] He was devastated. Throughout his life, Hechler had met thousands of people, but until Larry, he referred to no one as his best friend once he grew to adulthood. There were colleagues, beloved staffers, and strong allies, but until late in life, he had hardly had any time to develop strong friendships. In Hechler's former Imperial Towers apartment in Charleston, a photograph of Larry, dressed in his "uniform" of day-glo green, hung on the living room wall. Beside it was a photo of the two men, Hechler's hands on Larry's shoulders, at the edge of Kayford's mountaintop removal operation, and another snapped of the pair during the Second March on Blair Mountain. Their friendship and respect for each other radiates from the images. Below the latter picture, Hechler placed these words, "Goodbye, my good friend, rest well, there's no MTR in heaven. We loved you."

According to Hechler, Larry had had chest pains and had gone to the hospital but didn't rest afterward, as the doctors recommended. "He immediately went back into the fight as though nothing had happened to his heart," Hechler said, "and that's what contributed to his death."[47] The following month, Hechler spoke at the memorial service for Gibson. Amid hearty applause from the audience at the Charleston Municipal Auditorium, Hechler was pushed in his wheelchair to the microphone. "Larry Gibson will live forever in our hearts," he said. "Larry expected us to stand up for the same principles he fought for. We promise you, Larry, we will never give up . . . never, never, never give up."[48] Without realizing it, Hechler was preaching a eulogy that could have become his own, for those words typify his spirit as well as Larry's.

22

INTO THE SUNSET

When Hechler walked out of the West Virginia statehouse in 2000, after resigning as secretary of state, he never won elected office again, though it wasn't for lack of trying. He ran that year to regain a seat in Congress, ran in 2004 to regain his post as secretary of state, and then, in 2010, ran for the United States Senate. Each time, he lost either in the primary or in the general election. By then, campaigning had changed, but Hechler still used his personal approach. And the people who had long supported him may have felt he had finally reached an age at which he was no longer effective. After all, he had long said politicians should stop serving at seventy—that is, until he reached that age.

Then again, if the voters didn't want him, higher education did. In his letter congratulating Hechler on his retirement, West Virginia State College president Hazo Carter also said, "We believe you still have much to offer to the region." He then offered to pay Hechler $10,000 to serve as a distinguished visiting scholar for the spring 2001 semester.[1] Hechler immediately accepted Carter's offer and subsequently taught two courses: The Life and Times of Harry Truman and Great American Political Personalities.[2] Once again, Hechler had returned to the classroom—his favorite haunt other than the halls of Congress. Both courses were similar to ones he'd taught previously at other institutions.

Marshall University wanted him, too. In 2001 and 2002, Martha Woodward—director of the Society of Yeager Scholars, the university's program for students with outstanding intellectual and leadership potential—invited the octogenarian to return to his old stomping grounds to teach an interdisciplinary seminar on President Truman. "I talked to him and he was really enthusiastic. How could you pass up a chance to expose young people to somebody like that?" Woodward said. "We had to turn people away; the class was oversold."[3] While Hechler had taught an undergraduate course on the politics of the Truman era at Marshall nearly twenty years earlier, this course focused more on the man himself. Hechler used David McCullough's Pulitzer Prize–winning biography, *Truman*, as his text, although he could have used his own memoir, *Working with Truman*. Though in a sense, he did. According to Hechler, "After they had read a particular passage in the [McCullough] biography, I would tell what the real inside story was."[4] As he had done in earlier classes, on the first day, Hechler asked the students to tell their names and something about themselves. He remembered it all throughout the class. Woodward says the kids loved him. "With Ken it was a relationship. A mutual admiration society."[5]

In order for his students to understand what made Truman the man he was, Hechler felt they needed to walk the streets of Independence, Missouri, the president's hometown. So he surprised them with instructions to be at Huntington's Tri-State Airport at 7 a.m. on a Saturday morning. Incredulous, they found two chartered jets waiting to transport them to Kansas City, Missouri, where a bus would meet them for the drive to Independence. Hechler had paid for it all.

"The mayor of Independence, the director of the Truman Library, and some surviving members of Truman's family came to a luncheon to regale the students with their very clear memories. We went to all the places that Truman had frequented as a youngster, including the drugstore where people who went to church on Sunday, and were religious, would put down a dime on the counter to get a shot of liquor,"[6] Hechler recalled with a laugh. In a thank-you letter to Hechler, one student called the experience "the mother of all field trips." According to another, "It was the greatest thing a professor has ever done for me. I learned so much more about Truman, and had a lot of fun as well. It's not everyday that you have a class where the professor has a first person account of that time in history, and the historical figures then."[7]

Hechler soon began to parlay this knowledge and his vast experiences into a one-man speakers bureau. He often traveled to Key West, Florida, to participate in an annual Truman Symposium at the Little White House. There he spoke on various topics surrounding the politics, the events, and the decisions of the former president. In 2011, he spoke on civil rights in Truman's era.[8] Two years later, he and Truman's grandson, Clifton Truman Daniel, presented a dialogue on the various military figures in Truman's era, including Douglas MacArthur and Truman's decision to relieve him of his duties.

Beyond the Truman Symposiums, he began appearing at other conferences, including a World War II conference in Sarasota, Florida, in 2007, where he spoke about his interviews with Herman Goering. As a guest speaker at a 2010 summer Chautauqua,[9] cosponsored by the Robert H. Jackson Center in Jamestown, New York, he told of his experiences at Selma with Dr. Martin Luther King. After Hechler's book, *Goering and His Gang*, gained significant attention upon its 2011 publication, he was invited to return to the Jackson Center in 2012. This time he shared his stories of interrogating Goering and other Nazi criminals before their Nuremberg trials.[10]

Accolades also began to accumulate after Hechler's retirement. Shortly after he had taken his Marshall students to Independence, the town fathers honored Hechler with the 2002 Harry S. Truman Public Service Award. Given to public servants who exemplify the qualities that distinguished Truman's career, the award has also

Ken Hechler at the Truman Symposium with Clifton Truman Daniel, 2013 (Photo by author)

been bestowed on John Glenn and Presidents Bill Clinton and Gerald Ford.[11] In 2006, he was inducted into the West Virginia Labor Hall of Fame for his congressional work on behalf of working people. He joined his idol, Mother Jones, in this honor. According to his cousin Arnold Schnobrich, who accompanied Hechler that day, many ordinary people came up to Hechler following the ceremony to thank him. They said they would have starved to death if it hadn't been for Hechler.[12] And, in 2010, Hechler was awarded the Martin Luther King Jr. Achievement Award by West Virginia University, primarily for walking with King at Selma.[13]

The Marshfield, Missouri, Cherry Blossom Festival honored Hechler for his lifetime achievements in April 2013. This festival has a history of inviting relatives, former employees, friends, and colleagues of the country's presidents. Hechler had previously attended to talk about his relationship with Truman. But this time, he was the one in the spotlight as he watched a video of his life, set to Frank Sinatra's "My Way," and heard several oral tributes. A twelve-year-old fiddler played what Hechler has often has called his theme song, "Don't Fence Me In," and followed it with "Country Roads." The evening concluded with a reception, complete with a giant birthday cake, even though his birthday was several months away.

Until he was one hundred, Hechler continued to travel for speeches, to speak in high schools and colleges, and to attend conferences, both inside and outside the state. At eighty-five he had undergone quintuple bypass surgery and returned to his job as secretary of state feeling fine.[14] It hadn't slowed him down at all. After this health scare, however, Hechler was afraid no one would preserve all his accomplishments in one place. Ever the teacher, he wanted a way to inspire future generations to dedicate their lives to public service, as he had done. Granted, Dr. Charles Moffat had written a biography in 1985, but that was fifteen years earlier, just at the start of his years as secretary of state. Hechler wanted something more.

He approached West Virginia filmmaker Steve Fesenmaier in 2005 for a recommendation about where to begin. Fesenmaier directed him to West Virginia Public Broadcasting's video documentary producer Russ Barbour. Barbour had long wanted to do a documentary on Hechler, but it had never worked out. Now Hechler was approaching him. "He was basically saying that he had had a health scare and he expected that he was going to be dying pretty soon," Barbour recalls. "He said, I've taken care of everything, I'm ready to go; but I want to be able to leave something."[15] After deciding to highlight those accomplishments that encompassed public service, Barbour set forth interviewing people across the country. Finding film highlights to match the comments wasn't difficult, since Hechler had a habit of going to the congressional recording studio to record anything he felt was important. During two long days of interviews with Hechler, which were filmed at the West Virginia Humanities Council office, Hechler's vanity made him refuse to wear his hearing aids, so Barbour had to yell the questions at him. Additionally, except for one shoot at the Truman Library in Independence, Hechler steadfastly refused to wear a coat and tie during the filming, saying, "I'm past all that."[16] Financed by Hechler and Marshall University, with support from the Humanities Council, *Ken Hechler: In Pursuit of Justice* was named West Virginia Film's 2008 Film of the Year.[17] It is still shown periodically on public broadcasting channels.

While his heart surgery didn't slow him down, the next surgery did. Even though he'd been a steady tennis player all his life, a hip replacement in 2007 ended that pastime. Hechler was disappointed. "He [his doctor] told me with this new hip I would be able to rush the net for every drop shot, but I did not find that to be the case," he said.[18] In order to maintain his fitness regime, Hechler took to swimming instead and could often be seen at the Charleston YMCA swimming laps. He continued to live in his Greenbrier Street apartment until June 1, 2012, when he moved across the Kanawha River to Imperial Towers. He could also be seen around the Capitol or at Shoney's lunching with former staffers or friends. According to Raamie Barker, Hechler's meals were often out of the ordinary but apparently ordered strictly for his health. One time he ate only a big plate of lima beans, and on another occasion he ate six oranges, which he cut in half. As the two ate, Hechler explained to Barker what each food did for the body.[19]

During his 2004 campaign to regain the secretary of state post, he met Anna Gayle Stevens, who was serving as a campaign volunteer. Shortly after he lost the election, Hechler hired her as his personal assistant and secretary. For the next few years, with her help, Hechler began amassing material for several books he planned to write. And he was prolific. In 2004 he self-published the nonfiction book *Hero of the Rhine: The Karl Timmerman Story*. It told the life story of the first American officer to cross the bridge at Remagen. Because Timmerman was born in Germany following World War I of an American soldier and his German war bride, Hechler had been fascinated with his story since writing his account of the Remagen battle. In 2007, he followed Timmerman's story with one about Sergeant Orland Jones, a United States Marine, which he called *Super Marine! The Sgt. Orland D. "Buddy" Jones Story*. After hearing of Jones from a fellow overnight bus passenger in 1944, Hechler wrote down the story. Sixty-two years later he painstakingly researched Jones's valiant fight on Iwo Jima through interviews, personal letters, and military documents, and wrote the book.[20] Turning to tales of bravery within his own family, in 2011 Hechler wrote the story of his own grandfather, George Hechler, in *Soldier of the Union*.

He followed these with selected memoirs from parts of his own past. In 2011, he published his account of the passage of the Mine Health and Safety Act and his relationship with Jock Yablonski, titled *The Fight for Coal Mine Health and Safety: A Documented History*. The same year, he wrote of his experiences interviewing Herman Goering and other Nazi war criminals in an introduction to the transcripts of all his interviews in *Goering and His Gang*. While the book topped 1,100 pages, he still had the time to publish a short book filled with his many parodies, called *Faith, Hope, and Parody*. This small volume displays Hechler's wit, as well as his often corny sense of humor. His last book, written in 2012, summed up his wisdom on *How to Be a Great Teacher*. With it, he hoped to give inspiration to those who spend their lives teaching the country's youth.

As he conducted the research for each book, Hechler reached back into his voluminous files, then stored at Marshall University. According to Nat deBruin, Marshall's Special Collections librarian, it was not surprising to get a call from Hechler asking for a specific letter he'd either written or received in the past, referring to it by a certain date. DeBruin says he Ken was rarely off by more than a few days in his recollection.[21]

23

TWILIGHT

Hechler's memory has always been remarkable, and his skill in predicting his own future wasn't bad either. He'd long said he'd marry before he died. In fact, when he was secretary of state, Hechler told his deputy, Mary Ratliff, he planned to do it before he was ninety. Despite this proclamation, she felt that might not be a wise move for him. "I did have a clear sense that he had much more empathy with people's situations in terms of their work life, and their public life, and community life, and so forth than he did with individual personalities."[1] She felt this would not bode well for marriage, especially for someone as set in his ways as Hechler.

Nevertheless, he marked that birthday, and several more, unattached. But it wasn't for lack of trying. Throughout his life, Hechler has had a great attraction to women, lots of women. But before he left for Swarthmore, his father warned him that if he "planted a seed," it would grow. This advice, along with his mother's admonition about a woman being an albatross around a man's neck, and his youthful inability to attract the opposite sex, caused Hechler considerable anxiety. Many coeds caught his eye, but his fears prevented him from learning how to succeed with any of them. When his best friend, Jimmy Hill, showed an interest in Ruth Mary Lewis, his Swarthmore love, Hechler had simply backed off. He still cared, though, and his heart was broken. Because he later regretted leaving town instead of escorting her mother down the aisle at Ruth Mary's wedding, in order to save himself from an emotionally devastating experience, Hechler wrote her to apologize for his behavior and to explain himself. "I thought the kindest thing to do was simply not probe into the depths of our wounds, but simply to cover them over quickly and slip away."[2]

Sadly, both Ruth Mary and her husband died young. Many years later, Hechler said he was glad he hadn't married her after all, for he'd have been left a heartbroken widower.[3] After Ruth Mary died, Hechler wrote to her daughter, Julie, in 1991, thanking her for returning the letters between him and Ruth Mary, whom he called "Reny." Delighted to know that returning them had been at Reny's behest, he said seeing the letters again allowed him "to recreate the wonderfully caring relationship I had with Reny over the years. If I have one regret . . . with Reny, it is that I always held back my inner feelings of affection, especially after my Swarthmore classmate, Jimmy, my good friend who usually sat near me in class, became involved. I was always apprehensive that [my] affection would be misinterpreted as interference."[4]

Things hadn't gone any better with his Barnard love, Jane Chippendale Stewart, either, regardless of their long courtship during World War II. When he realized his proposal had fallen on hesitant ears, he was so chagrined that he took back his mother's engagement ring and withdrew the proposal. These must not have been his only refusals, however, for he's claimed to have proposed five times to various women, but says he couldn't get any of them to marry him.[5]

After those two heartbreaking rejections, which only fueled his earliest insecurities, Hechler embarked on a certain behavior pattern toward women. He couldn't resist the fairer sex and was an unrepentant flirt, but once a girl fell in love with him, he backed off for fear of what he presumed would be another ultimate rejection. As he had said to Ruth Mary, "When you lose several times, your confidence evaporates and you give up the battle sooner."[6]

Love letter after love letter, from 1958 to 1980,[7] reveal the same scenario. Young women wrote pleading with Hechler to get together again, or call, or simply respond by letter. Obviously they'd had a relationship of some duration, whether an evening, a weekend, or an entire summer. It's clear that many of this bachelor's conquests included intimate relations. It's also clear that the women were much younger than Hechler. In 1969, one Marshall student anticipated marriage, yet she wrote, "Did you ever really propose to me? It seems to be a technicality we overlooked." Apparently he hadn't. Four years later, she married someone else.[8] One young lady went looking for him in Washington, not knowing he'd left Congress two years earlier. In another letter that looks as if it had been crumpled into a wad, Hechler describes, in poetic prose, his fascination with his date's breasts. He ends with, "I really didn't want to talk; I just wanted to look." Apparently he got his wish, for "Raving Rita" sent him a telegram wishing "Happy Fourth to the man who took away my independence."[9]

Yet Hechler's inability to solidify a loving relationship with women made him the driven man he became. While this flaw created a great personal loss for him, it gave the people a consummate public servant. In apologizing to Ruth Mary, Hechler spoke of his shortcomings and the sadness they had caused him. He knew he'd hurt her by ignoring her invitation to participate in her wedding and by ignoring many other invitations she'd extended in the ensuing years. In explaining, he said,

> When I try to be gentle, when I try to express my love, when I try desperately to be tender, when I try to give away all this love which is brimming over in my heart, I always stumble over a chair . . . bull over china . . . and what's worse, hurt the one I love. . . . All my life I've been a loser at love, and a winner in skin-deep superficial friendships. A loser in

one-on-one, a winner in giving and sharing love with hundreds. Therein lies the critical difference between love and politics. I can love people and my destiny is to help hundreds, thousands—groups, families, cities, ghettoes, programs, projects, human needs—but whenever I try to give the love in my heart to one person, I fail. It is almost as though God intended me to remain wed only to my job of helping, leading, accomplishing, working *for* others.[10]

This confession is similar to one he'd made many years earlier to Jane Stewart. To her, he'd written, "I'm not happy unless I have a cheering crowd on my side."[11]

Apparently Ruth Mary had wanted to renew their friendship, but Hechler declined, telling her that he had a tendency toward satyriasis,[12] and found it difficult to be around any female without making a pass at her. While he may have been exaggerating, he said he didn't want to make that mistake with her and refused to even meet, knowing a full relationship wasn't possible. He also admitted that he'd probably be polygamous all his life.

Knowing he couldn't have what he wanted once again, he also may have been dissembling. And in his letter to Julie, he blamed his parents for his flaws, though that, too, could be a rationalization. He wrote, "Their one negative was that they taught me to mask my feelings, to be guarded in overt expressions of love, to suffer inwardly without letting on when you're hurt, and to build a shell of phlegmatic thick-skinnedness [*sic*] against the world."[13] He had good reason to feel that way. He'd once received a birthday card from his mother signed "Your mother, Catherine Hechler."[14] But as he had said to Ruth Mary in the same apology letter, "that sublimation of love in an excessive amount of work, travel, and frenzied activity is very effective, good for digestion, and produces sound, deep sleep."[15]

Carlyle's great man theory is certainly working in Hechler's case. His early insecurities and his resultant flawed personality, not great events, created the man we know. Coupled with his childhood admiration for his parents' life of service, Hechler saw public service as a way to make people like him and formed the antidote to his inability to form intimate relationships. Consequently, Hechler's work, and frenzied activity produced the lifetime of public service for which he is revered—or, by some people, reviled. Looking back at his accomplishments, his fight for the passage of the Mine Health and Safety Act of 1969 brought the issue of black lung disease to the fore, and has provided financial benefits for thousands of miners since; his insistence on the importance of West Virginia's New River to the environment saved an ancient and wild river from destruction; his stand on civil rights placed him in a unique place in history as the only member of Congress to march at Selma with Dr. Martin Luther King Jr.; and his integrity and personal commitment to his constituents made him a public servant to be emulated.

But apparently this life didn't satisfy him as much as he said it did. Once, after speaking to Simon Perry's political science class at Marshall University, Hechler sat down to visit with his old friend. Perry recalls, "I said to Ken that in my view he'd had a great life, lots of freedom, plenty of time to reflect, to meet interesting people, and to write and travel. Then, I noticed sadness across his face. 'Simon,' Ken replied, 'I envy *you*. You have a wonderful wife and children. I deeply regret that this was not to be a part of my life.'" Hechler's remarks deeply touched Perry.[16] And given that Hechler was not known for introspection or for expressing his personal feelings, it was a rare revelation indeed.

In 2012, at Larry Gibson's memorial service, an old flame from Hechler's past, Carol Kitzmiller, reappeared. She had been one of Hechler's Week in State Government winners in the late 1980s, and despite their age difference, the two had become friends. After they had maintained their friendship for a few years, it became a full-fledged love affair that lasted a dozen more. When the relationship ended in 1999, bitter feelings remained, and the two hadn't seen each other for years. Carol had been Gibson's friend as well, and though she knew Hechler would be at the service, she didn't want to meet Hechler again.

Yet when she saw Hechler sitting in the hallway, greeting friends after the service, she felt sorry for him. He looked at her a few times, as if he knew her but was uncertain. "He didn't have his glasses on, and I've gained weight, so when there was no one there, I just went up and whispered my name in his ear," Carol recalls. "Tears came in his eyes and he took my hand and started kissing it. That was it. I melted."[17] It had been twelve years since the pair had split, but the reunion was immediate. Carol immediately promised she'd never leave him again. For Hechler, this vow may have freed him from his fear of rejection and allowed him to consider the commitment he had hinted at in his long-ago letter to Ruth Mary. In ending that letter, he had said, "This reservoir of dammed-up love will someday burst and someone will probably complain that she is being over-loved, over-protected, and has to deal with a schoolboy who has suddenly discovered a new toy."[18]

A few months later, Hechler and Carol were together after he and his assistant, Anna Gayle Stevens, had an acrimonious argument over her management of his finances, and they parted ways. Carol moved Hechler to Huntington, where he lived briefly with his old chief of staff, Bobby Nelson. From there he went to an assisted living facility, but he wasn't happy. He wanted to be with Carol and, by extension, her middle-school-age son, Josh. Serendipitously, his old Greenbrier Street apartment in Charleston was available, so he rented it and made some changes to accommodate his wheelchair. His idea was to spend time both in the capital city and on Carol's family farm. However, once the changes had been made, traveling back and forth became difficult, and he decided to abandon Charleston and Greenbrier Street. By April 2013, Hechler was living on the farm in Hampshire County. Though he still traveled and gave speeches to school groups of all ages, Carol went with him now. For a time, he also wrote a weekly newspaper column and had a radio program, as these he could do from home. Hechler was enjoying country living after so many years in busy cities.

For the next year, Hechler and Carol talked off and on of marriage, but Hechler always got cold feet and backed out. The fearful and gun-shy bachelor just couldn't commit, even at ninety-eight. As summer wound down, Hechler again asked Carol to marry him on Sunday, August 11, 2013. She thought he'd back out once more, but he fooled her. The next day, he rose raring to get married. He wanted to go across the border to Virginia because he wanted to keep it a secret. Carol called the Clark County Courthouse to see what papers they would need when they arrived, and she arranged for a 6 p.m. wedding at a park gazebo in Berryville, Virginia. They left that afternoon, but when they arrived, Hechler said, "Sweetheart, I don't want to." Carol thought he meant he was backing out, but what he really meant was that he didn't want to wait until 6 p.m. After getting their marriage license, Carol got a list of wedding celebrants, but learned they would have to be at Rev. Lance Orndorff's before 5 p.m. Unfortunately, Orndorff's chapel wasn't wheelchair accessible, and Hechler needed his wheelchair, so Rev. Orndorff suggested a picturesque setting in front of the old Frederick County Courthouse. They arranged to meet at the parking garage in the middle of town. When Orndorff arrived, Hechler again said, "Sweetheart, I don't want to." Now Carol was convinced he was reneging and asked, "What is it you don't want to do?"

Hechler replied, "I don't want to get married in front of the old courthouse. Can't we just do it right here?" They could, and they did. With Hechler in the passenger seat and Carol beside the truck, they were married in the Braddock Street parking garage in the middle of Winchester, Virginia, on August 12, 2013. According to Carol, her new husband wept. "Not because he didn't want to go through with the ceremony, but because he'd waited so long," she said.[19]

Afterward, Hechler swore he wanted to keep the big event quiet until his upcoming ninety-ninth birthday party in September, but he just couldn't. Two days later, at the Hampshire County Fair, he was at the Democratic booth doing a book signing. WELD radio was there, acting as the fair's announcer, and asked to interview Hechler. During the interview, he let his secret slip, and the marriage was announced to five counties. He told them that he'd intended to announce his recent marriage soon anyway, and that "all those other women who have been standing in line will just have to move to someone else's line."[20]

Since he'd spoiled the announcement he'd planned to make on his birthday, Hechler opted for another surprise for the crowd assembled at the South Branch Inn in Romney. He walked into the reception with the aid of his walker instead of riding in the wheelchair he'd been using for several years. He'd been exercising to strengthen his limbs, just so he could do this. And in a surprise for him, Carol presented him with a membership pin from Book and Key, the Swarthmore society he'd dreamed of joining as an underclassman. Even though that society had disbanded in 1962, the university decided to make an exception and allow him to join retroactively. They found an existing member who invited Hechler to the select group. He was delighted, for it finally erased his earlier exclusion—and one of his biggest regrets.

The room buzzed with conversations, speeches, and music. Hechler visited with old friends, including his army buddy Ed Martz, former secretary of state Helen Holt, and Bobby Nelson. Tributes and proclamations followed the spaghetti dinner from Jim's Steak and Spaghetti in Huntington, one of his favorite restaurants when he lived there years ago. At the end of the afternoon, Hechler invited everyone to return for his 100th birthday.

For the next year, Hechler dealt with several health issues, but by September, he was strong again and anticipating his 100th birthday. By 1 p.m. on Saturday, September 27, the Don Morris Room of the Marshall University Student Center was packed, awaiting Hechler's arrival. Old friends gathered in small groups to exchange stories, much as they had at Hechler's Coolfont reunions, but without Hechler. After an hour's wait, he arrived on his walker, again, unassisted. As he entered the room with Carol, a spotlight illuminated Hechler's smile. He paused and raised his hand in greeting, a gesture reminiscent of his campaigning days.

He headed for the seat designated for him to greet his guests, but the line formed too quickly, and he was forced to stop midway. Scores of well-wishers, old colleagues, former Week in Washington winners, former students, and admirers stood in line to wish him happy birthday or give him a small memento. Tributes from Eli Rosenbaum, chief prosecutor of war criminals at the U.S. Justice Department; Phil Carter, civil rights advocate and old friend; and Dr. Gerald Pops, former Air Force judge advocate and student of General George C. Marshall, captivated the crowd. Like a veteran politician, he welcomed the adulation, tiring only after several hours. But because he'd stopped in front of the band, the 1937 Flood, it was difficult for him to really hear what his guests were saying to him.

Ken Hechler arrives with his wife at his 100th birthday party in Huntington, WV (Courtesy of Carol Kitzmiller Hechler)

Exhausted, he asked to rest. Still, the crowds followed him to the lobby, where he sat with his feet up. Eventually, he returned to the reception and sat—head in hands, as he'd done so often—to listen to a tribute from his old political opponent, Nick Rahall, and a proclamation from Huntington's mayor, Steve Williams. The Huntington City Council had designated four blocks of the downtown area as Ken Hechler Government Way. With this decree, the blocks of Fifth Avenue that encompass the Cabell County Courthouse; Huntington City Hall, where he often held his open-air offices; the Federal Building, where he had his congressional office;

and the block where he lived became the only streets, bridges, or buildings ever named for him.

As the guests marveled at the cakes in the shape of Hechler's red Jeep and enjoyed a meal, one Marshall *Parthenon* writer approached Hechler with a microphone in her hand. Hechler perked up, as if he'd had a full night's sleep, and talked for another thirty minutes. Carol laughed, saying, "His jaws act like a generator; once he starts talking about his accomplishments, he gains strength."[21]

In the year after Hechler marked a century, several of his friends or contemporaries died: former West Virginia agriculture commissioner Gus Douglass; former secretary of state Helen Holt; former governor Arch Moore; and his old colleague, Donald Rasmussen. Hechler was distraught over each, but he was too frail to attend any of their services. Hechler was hospitalized several times that year, but the old fighter usually bounced back. However, the week before his scheduled 101st birthday party in Romney, he was hospitalized again. Once more, he rallied, and at his insistence, they released him the day before the party. Sadly, it was a mistake. He wasn't well, and those who greeted him saw a diminished Hechler. But at the end of the afternoon, he made sure to invite his guests to return for his 102nd. Over the next months, Hechler's health and stamina varied. Some days he felt well enough to sing "Happy Birthday" to Bobby Nelson via social media or to visit with old friends and colleagues, but on other days he didn't.

He's long said he planned to live to 105, and if determination can master the body, he may do it. Just before his 101st birthday, he and Carol bought a house in Romney, West Virginia. Nothing says optimism like a mortgage, and ironically, it's the first he ever signed. Until then, Hechler had lived his entire adult life in rented apartments. Finally, he had what he'd wanted for decades: a wife, a family, and a place to call home.

Regardless of Hechler's life span, he'll long be remembered for his accomplishments. Yet in spite of his many accolades and awards, he simply wants to be remembered for his efforts. Harry Truman once remarked on a tombstone he'd seen. It read: "He done his damndest." Hechler would be happy with that as well. An avowed hero-worshiper, Hechler is already a hero figure to scores. While luck may have played a part in putting him in the right place at the right time, Hechler worked hard to serve the people. Perhaps his ascetic lifestyle demonstrates this in part. Frugal in his dress, his home, and his office décor, he was unflinchingly generous to his constituents, students, and colleagues. More than once he showed his commitment to them or to a cause by spending his own money on it instead of on himself. Hechler once said he wanted people to remember "that I fought for average people, tried to stop exploitation and discrimination, tried to give every man, woman, and child an opportunity to get ahead and realize his or her greatest potential."[22] He'll get his wish.

NOTES

ABBREVIATIONS

Barbour	Russ Barbour, interviewer for documentary, *Ken Hechler: In Pursuit of Justice*, 2005
Barrett	Margy Minichan Barrett
Deegans	Judy Roach Deegans
Elsey, Elsey papers	George Elsey, Elsey Papers, Truman Library, Independence, MO
Haddock	Doris "Granny D" Haddock
CKH	Carol Kitzmiller Hechler
KH	Ken Hechler
Helme	Ned Helme
NJ, 1985	Niel M. Johnson, transcript of a 1985 tape-recorded interview, Truman Library, Independence, MO
Keating	Janet Keating
Nelson	Bobby Nelson
Ratliff	Mary Ratliff
Ryan, 2002	Barbara Haddad Ryan, former vice president of Swarthmore College at Coolfont Resort, WV
CTS	Carter Taylor Seaton
JS	Jane Chippendale Stewart, aka Jane Stewart Heckman
Stockman	Vivian Stockman

I. BEHIND THE WROUGHT IRON GATES

1 *Roslyn News*, September 11, 1903, 1.

2 "Katherine Duer Mackay, the First Mrs. Clarence Mackay, c. 1905," updated May 21, 2006, http://www.mackayhistory.com/2_mrs _mackays.html.

3 Richard Guy Wilson, *Harbor Hill, Portrait of a House* (New York and London: Society for the Preservation of Long Island Antiquities in association with W. W. Norton, 2008), 111.

4 Ken Hechler to Carter Taylor Seaton, Huntington, WV, January 26, 2013.

5 Wilson, *Harbor Hill*, 27.

6 Ibid., 3–5.

7 KH to CTS, Marshfield, MO, April 26, 2013.

8 KH to CTS, Huntington, WV, January 31, 2013.

9 KH to CTS, May 19, 2013, Key West, FL.

10 Letter from Catherine Hechler to KH, December 13, 1934, Hechler Collection, Special Collections, Marshall University, Huntington, WV, Accession 1977/01.0199, Addendum 2, Box 2. Note written in Ken's hand on the front of Folder 10.

11 KH to CTS, Key West, FL, May 18, 2013.

12 KH to CTS, Marshfield, MO, April 26, 2013.

13 KH to CTS, Key West, FL, May 17, 2013.

14 KH to CTS, Charleston, WV, December 12, 2012.

15 Myrna Sloam to CTS, June 11, 2013. Ms. Sloam is the archivist for the Hechler Collection at the Bryant Library, Roslyn, NY.

16 KH to CTS, Marshfield, MO, April 26, 2013.

17 KH to CTS, Key West, FL, May 19, 2013.

18 KH to Russ Barbour for the documentary *Ken Hechler: In Pursuit of Justice*, WVPB, Charleston, WV, July 21, 2005.

19 KH to Barbour, Charleston, WV, July 21, 2005.

20 KH to CTS, Charleston, WV, January 14, 2013.

21 KH to CTS, Charleston, WV, December 4, 2012.

22 Wilson, *Harbor Hill*, 149.

23 KH to CTS, Charleston, WV, December 27, 2012.

24 Unlabeled newspaper clipping, Acc. 1977, 2, Box 1, Folder 5.

25 KH to CTS, Huntington, WV, January 26, 2013.

26 KH to CTS, Charleston, WV, December 4, 2012.

27 Ken Hechler, *Soldier of the Union* (Charleston, WV: Pictorial Histories, 2011), 1–3.

28 Ibid., 243–246.

29 Ken Hechler's diary, Acc. 1977, 2, Box 1, Folder 7.

30 KH to CTS, Huntington, WV, February 9, 2013.

31 KH to CTS, Marshfield, MO, April 26, 2013.

32 KH to CTS, Key West, FL, May 19, 2013.

33 KH to CTS, Huntington, WV, January 26, 2013.

34 Acc. 1977, 2, Box 2, Note on front of Folder 12.

35 KH to CTS, Charleston, WV, December 13, 2012.

36 Wilson, *Harbor Hill*, 153–154.

37 KH to CTS, Key West, FL, May 19, 2013.

2. BIG MAN ON CAMPUS

1 Letter from Raymond Walters, dean of Swarthmore College, to KH, September 8, 1931, Acc. 1977, 2, Box 1, Folder 52.

2 Robert Brooks note on KH's paper for Political Motives course, undated 1933, Acc. 1977, 2, Box 1, Folder 29.

3 KH's 1931 Personal Budget and Account Book, Acc. 1977, 2, Box 1, Folder 10.

4 Remarks by Barbara Haddad Ryan, former vice president of Swarthmore, at Coolfont Resort, WV, 2002, Hechler's Personal Files.

5 Letter to KH from Charles Muldaur, *New York Times*, February 8, 1935, Acc. 1977, 2, Box 1, Folder 26.

6 KH note on folder dated November 1931–May 1932, Acc. 1977, 2, Box 1, Folder 17.

7 KH, Background Statement on Political Motives course, Acc. 1977, 2, Box 1, Folder 28.

8 KH Memoir, undated from the Hechler Collection, Special Collections, Marshall University, Huntington, WV, Personal & Family Series, Accession 2010/05.0777, Series IIc, Box 8, Folder 18.

9 From his earliest campaign in 1958, Ken listed his name as Ken Hechler or Dr. Ken Hechler, but he didn't legally change it until

required to do so after he became secretary of state. WV Code paragraph 3-5-7 (d) (3) requires a person who is a candidate for public office to file a certificate of announcement which contains "the legal name of the candidate and the exact name the candidate desires to appear on the ballot." Ken wrote, "Petitioner desires to file in the future such a certificate of announcement in the name of 'Ken Hechler.'"

10 KH to Barbour, Charleston, WV, July 21, 2005.

11 Ibid.

12 Catherine Hechler to KH, undated, Acc. 1977, 2, Box 2, Folder 2.

13 KH, Background Statement on Political Motives course, Acc. 1977, 2, Box 1, Folder 28.

14 KH to CTS, Charleston, WV, January 26, 2013.

15 Post cards, Acc. 1977, 2, Box 2, Folder 49. (One student stated that the only instruments he played successfully were the Victrola [phonograph] and the radio.)

16 *Phoenix*, October 10, 1933, 6, http://triptych.brynmawr.edu/cdm /compoundobject/collection/SC_Phoenix/id/9321/rec/92.

17 Remarks by Ryan, 2002, Hechler's Personal Files.

18 KH to Catherine Hechler, June 2, 1933, Acc. 1977, 2, Box 2, Folder 27.

19 KWINK is the name of the organization; it is not an acronym.

20 Remarks by Ryan, 2002, Hechler's Personal Files.

21 KH to CTS, Charleston, WV, December 6, 2012.

22 KH to CTS via telephone, September 9, 2013.

23 Remarks by Ryan, 2002, Hechler's Personal Files.

24 Swarthmore College, 1935, *Halcyon*, p. 67, Acc. 1977, 2.

25 Ken Hechler to Niel M. Johnson, transcript of a 1985 tape-recorded interview, Truman Library, Independence, Missouri, 18.

26 Class papers for various political science classes, 1933–1935, Acc. 1977, 2, Box 2, Folders 32–38 and 40–50.

27 KH to NJ, 1985, 18.

28 Ken Hechler, *How to Be a Great Teacher* (Missoula, MT: Pictorial Histories, 2012), 5.

29 KH to CTS, Franklin, PA, August 4, 2013.

30 Judy Roach Deegans to CTS, Lewisburg, WV, January 18, 2013. Ms. Deegans was in charge of Ken's congressional office in Huntington,

WV, from 1971 to 1977. In some chapters, she is referred to by her previous married name, Judy Roach.

31 KH, summary of part-time jobs at Columbia, July 12, 1984, author's files.

32 Robert Brooks to KH, August 8, 1935, Acc. 1977, 2, Box 2, Folder 21.

33 KH, "Will Roosevelt be Re-elected: A Prognostic Analysis of Faces, Factors, and Figures in the 1936 Presidential Election," preface master's thesis, submitted May 1, 1936, Acc. 1977, 2, Box 4, Folder 10.

34 KH, master's thesis, p. 345, Acc. 1977, 2, Box 4, Folder 11.

35 *Wikipedia*, s.v. "*The Literary Digest*," accessed September 11, 2013, http://en.wikipedia.org/wiki/The_Literary_Digest.

36 KH, master's thesis, p. 92, Acc. 1977, 2, Box 4, Folder 10.

37 KH to CTS, Key West, FL, May 19, 2013.

38 KH to Barbour, Charleston, WV, July 22, 2005.

39 KH course description, Great American Political Personalities, Columbia University, 1938, Acc. 1977, 2, Box 3, Folder 17.

40 KH to CTS via email, November 25, 2013.

41 "Dementia praecox is a chronic, deteriorating psychotic disorder characterized by rapid cognitive disintegration, usually beginning in the late teens or early adulthood." *Wikipedia*, s.v. "Dementia praecox," last modified September 23, 2016, https://en.wikipedia.org/wiki/Dementia_praecox.

42 KH to CTS, Franklin, PA, August 2, 2013.

43 KH to CTS, Key West, FL, May 18, 2013.

44 Ibid.

45 KH to CTS via email, November 25, 2013.

46 KH to NJ, 1985, 33.

47 KH to CTS, Huntington, WV, January 26, 2013.

48 Acc. 1977, 2, Box 3, Folder 25.

49 Hechler, *How to Be a Great Teacher*, 10.

50 Ibid.

51 KH to Barbour, Charleston, WV, July 22, 2005.

52 KH to CTS, Charleston, WV, April 30, 2013.

53 KH to Barbour, Charleston, WV, July 22, 2005.

54 The Payne-Aldrich Tariff Act of 1909 lowered certain tariffs on goods entering the United States. It greatly angered Progressives,

who began to withdraw support from President Taft, and the debate over the act split the Republican Party. *Wikipedia*, s.v. "Payne–Aldrich Tariff Act," accessed December 4, 2013, http://en.wikipedia .org/wiki/Payne–Aldrich_Tariff_Act.

55 Joseph G. Cannon served as Speaker of the United States House of Representatives from 1903 to 1911, and many consider him to be the most dominant Speaker in United States history, with such control over the House that he could often control debate. *Wikipedia*, s.v. "Joseph Gurney Cannon," accessed December 4, 2013, http://en .wikipedia.org/wiki/Joseph_Gurney_Cannon.

56 KH to NJ, 1985, 27.

57 KH to Barbour, Charleston, WV, July 22, 2005.

58 KH to NJ, 1985, 25.

59 KH to Yale administration, June 12, 1939, Acc. 1977, 2, Box 4, Folder 12.

60 KH to NJ, 1985, 49.

61 KH to CTS, Charleston, WV, April 28, 2013.

62 KH to Barbour, Charleston, WV, July 21, 2005.

63 KH to CTS, Charleston, WV, April 28 and April 30, 2013.

64 *Wikipedia*, s.v. "Winter War," accessed October 23, 2013, http://en .wikipedia.org/wiki/Winter_War.

65 Hechler, *How to Be a Great Teacher*, 13.

66 Ibid, 13–22.

67 Handwritten note by KH on Waldorf Astoria letterhead, November 1, [1939,] no year included, Acc. 1977, 2, Box 3, Folder 39.

68 KH to Robert Brooks, November 6, 1939, Acc. 1977, 2, Box 2, Folder 21.

69 KH's undated notes on the visit to Hoover, Acc. 1977, 2, Box 3, Folder 39.

70 KH to CTS, Key West, FL, May 17, 2013.

71 KH to NJ, 1985, 35–42.

72 KH to CTS, Key West, FL, May 17, 2013.

73 KH to NJ, 1985, 40–41.

74 KH to CTS, Charleston, WV, October 4, 2013.

75 KH to CTS, Charleston, WV, December 4, 2012.

76 KH to CTS, Charleston, WV, December 6, 2012.

77 *New York Times*, January 31, 1941, Acc. 1977, 2, Box 4, Folder 3.

78 1-B classification before Pearl Harbor meant available, fit only for limited military service, accessed December 4, 2013, http://www.armchairgeneral.com/forums/showthread.php?t=81909.

79 KH to CTS, Charleston, WV, October 4, 2013, and by telephone, October 22, 2013.

80 KH to CTS, Charleston, WV, December 4, 2012.

81 Grayson Kirk to KH, September 16, 1941, Acc. 1977, 2, Box 4, Folder 13.

82 KH to CTS via telephone, October 22, 2013.

3. OVER THERE!

1 KH to NJ, 1985, 52.

2 *Wikipedia*, s.v. "Office for Emergency Management," accessed December 6, 2013, http://en.wikipedia.org/wiki/Office_for_Emergency_Management. The office was disbanded in 1942 and replaced with the Division of Information of the Office for Emergency Management.

3 KH to CTS via telephone, October 22, 2013.

4 KH to Barbour, Charleston, WV, July 22, 2005.

5 KH to CTS, Charleston, WV, October 4, 2013.

6 KH to NJ, 1985, 39.

7 Letter from Harold Smith, June 15, 1942, and response from KH, Acc. 1977, 2, Box 6, Folder 1.

8 KH to CTS, Charleston, WV, February 16, 2013.

9 "This Day in Truman History," accessed December 6, 2013, http://www.trumanlibrary.org/anniversaries/nationalguard.htm.

10 KH to CTS, Huntington, WV, February 16, 2013.

11 KH to CTS, Charleston, WV, October 5, 2013.

12 KH to Barbour, Charleston, WV, July 21, 2005.

13 KH to Barbour, Charleston, WV, July 22, 2005.

14 KH speech to Southern Illinois University, Carbondale, IL, 1998, KH Personal, File labeled "S. Illinois U—Personal Reflections, 1998."

15 KH to NJ, 1985, 52.

16 KH speech to Southern Illinois University, Carbondale, IL, 1998, KH Personal, File labeled "S. Illinois U—Personal Reflections, 1998."

17 KH to Dr. Pendleton Herring, KH Personal, Folder labeled "Fort Knox in OCS." Dr. Herring held several positions in Washington during and after World War II, advising President Roosevelt and President Truman on matters including the unification of the military services within the Department of Defense. He later served as president of the American Political Science Association, when Ken worked there.

18 Jack Kelly to KH, May 10, 1943, Hechler Collection, Acc. 2010, Series IIc, Box 8, Folder 17.

19 KH to CTS, Charleston, WV, April 30, 2013.

20 KH notes dated March 2, 2006, KH Personal, File labeled "Fort Knox Tough Talk in OCS."

21 KH's recollection of the weekend in Huntington, July 24–25, 1943, undated document, Acc. 1977, 2, Box 9, Folder 1.

22 KH to NJ, 1985, 55.

23 KH to CTS, Charleston, WV, December 4, 2012.

24 KH to Barbour, Huntington, WV, August 10, 2005.

25 KH to CTS, Charleston, WV, April 30, 2013.

26 Letter from Brigadier General S. G. Henry, February 20, 1943, Acc. 1977, 2, Box 6, Folder 3.

27 KH to General S. G. Henry, March 12, 1943, Acc. 1977, 2, Box 6, Folder 3.

28 KH to Barbour, Huntington, WV, August 10, 2005.

29 KH to NJ, 1985, 57–59.

30 KH to CTS, Charleston, WV, April 30, 2013. The chanting was also in defiance of British Authority, according to Ken. In opposition to Neville Chamberlain, President de Valera advocated neutrality for Ireland in the coming war and opposed conscription.

31 KH to CTS, Huntington, WV, February 9, 2013.

32 SLA Marshall to KH, April 19, 1945, KH Personal, File labeled "Combat Historian."

33 KH to CTS, Key West, FL, May 19, 2013.

34 KH to NJ, 1985, 65.

35 KH to Barbour, Huntington, WV, August 10, 2005.

36 KH to CTS, Charleston, WV, April 30, 2013.

37 Ken Hechler, "How to Interview," undated, Acc. 1977, 2, Box 6, Folder 20.

38 KH to NJ, 1985, 63–64.

39 KH's military record, Acc. 1977, 2, Box 6, File 4.

40 KH's speech at the Remagen Reenactment, Tidioute, PA, August 3, 2013.

41 Ken Hechler, *The Bridge at Remagen*, 6th rev. ed. (1957; reprint, Missoula, MT: Pictorial Histories, 2004), ix.

42 KH note, December 12, 1983, Acc. 1977, 2, Box 6, Folder 6.

43 KH to CTS, Charleston, WV, April 30, 2013.

44 KH's military record, Acc. 1977, 2, Box 6, File 9.

45 Undated, unattributed citation, Acc. 1977, 2, Box 6, File 9.

46 Hechler's U.S. Army military records, author's personal files.

47 Censorship report dated September 13, 1944, Acc. 2010, Series IIc, Folder 3.

48 KH to Jane Chippendale Stewart, November 11, 1943, KH Personal, File labeled "Army Ground Forces Trip West to? & California—Letters to Penny, 1943."

49 JS to KH, March 14, 1944, KH Personal, File labeled "Jane Stewart Gives KH Hell, Early 1944."

50 KH to JS, March 17, 1944, KH Personal, File labeled "Jane Stewart Gives KH Hell, Early 1944."

51 KH to JS, November 11, 1943, KH Personal, File labeled "Army Ground Forces Trip West to? & California—Letters to Penny, 1943."

52 Acc. 1977, 2, Box 7, Folder 16.

53 *Wikipedia*, s.v. "Buchenwald concentration camp," last modified September 14, 2016, http://en.wikipedia.org/wiki/Buchenwald_concentration_camp.

54 KH to CTS, Charleston, WV, January 14, 2013.

55 KH to NJ, 1985, 84–85.

56 KH to CTS, Franklin, PA, August 3, 2013.

57 KH to NJ, 1985, 88.

58 *Wikipedia*, s.v. "Camp Ashcan," last modified September 27, 2016, http://en.wikipedia.org/wiki/Camp_Ashcan.

59 Ken Hechler, *Goering and His Gang* (Missoula, MT: Pictorial Histories, 2011), 1–2.

60 KH to Barbour, Huntington, WV, August 10, 2005.

61 KH to CTS, Charleston, WV, January 14, 2013.

62 KH at the Robert H. Jackson Center, Jamestown, New York, November 13, 2010.

63 Hechler, *Goering and His Gang*, 4–5.

64 Ibid., 7.

65 "Hermann Göring (1893–1946)," Historical Boys' Clothing, last modified April 2, 2012, http://histclo.com/bio/g/bio-goer.html.

66 *Wikipedia*, s.v. "Hermann Göring," last modified September 28, 2016, http://en.wikipedia.org/wiki/Hermann_Göring.

67 KH to CTS, Charleston, WV, December 13, 2012.

68 Excerpts from Walter Warlimont's testimony at the Nuremberg trials, June 21, 1948, http://www.und.nodak.edu/instruct/calberts/Nuremberg/Warlimont.html.

69 KH to CTS, Charleston, WV, January 14, 2013.

70 KH to NJ, 1985, 83.

71 KH to Barbour, Huntington, WV, August 10, 2005.

72 KH to CTS, Charleston, WV, January 14, 2013.

73 KH to CTS, Charleston, WV, December 12, 2012.

74 Hechler, *Goering and His Gang*, 6.

75 Ed Martz to CTS, Romney, WV, September 22, 2013.

4. PRINCETON'S PROFESSOR OF POLITICS

1 KH to NJ, 1985, 93–95.

2 KH to CTS, Key West, FL, May 19, 2013.

3 KH to CTS, Huntington, WV, February 9, 2013.

4 JS to Barbour, July 29, 1005, Chicago, IL.

5 KH to NJ, 1985, 95–97.

6 Letter from Patterson H. French to George A. Graham, November 27, 1946, Acc. 1977, 2, Box 7, Folder 1.

7 George Graham to KH, February 20, 1947, Acc. 1977, 2, Box 10, Folder 1.

8   KH to CTS via e-mail, February 10, 2014.

9   Class syllabi, Acc. 1977, 2, Box 8, Folders 24–26.

10   List of KH's expenses 1947–48, Acc. 1977, 2, Box 7, Folder 18.

11   "Education by Long Distance Phone," *New Jersey Today*, undated article, Acc. 1977, 2, Box 8, Folder 21.

12   Milton Lehman, "Person-to-Person Professors," *Saturday Evening Post*, undated article, Acc. 1977, 2, Box 8, Folder 23.

13   Various letters, Acc. 1977, 2, Box 8, Folders 24–26.

14   KH to CTS via telephone, February 21, 2014.

15   "Education by Long Distance Phone."

16   Letters, Acc. 1977, 2, Box 7, Folder 19.

17   "Education by Long Distance Phone."

18   KH to Barbour, Charleston, WV, July 22, 2005.

19   Hechler's handwritten notes, Acc. 1977, 2, Box 7, Folder 13.

20   Telegram dated October 16, 1948, from McCaney to Robert Hagy, *Time*, for article that appeared November 15, 1948, Acc. 1977, 2, Box 8, Folder 22.

21   Memorandum to George Elsey, December 12, 1948, in preparation for his talk to KH's Princeton class, Elsey papers, Truman Library, Box 102.

22   KH to CTS via email, February 10, 2014.

23   "Education by Long Distance Phone."

24   Wayne Morse was elected to the United States Senate as a Republican; he became an Independent after Dwight D. Eisenhower's election to the presidency in 1952. He later joined the Democratic Party. *Wikipedia*, s.v. "Wayne Morse," last modified June 4, 2016, http://en.wikipedia.org/wiki/Wayne_Morse. John Carroll was elected as a Democratic representative from January 3, 1947, to January 3, 1951, and served as a special assistant to President Truman from 1951 to 1952. He served in the U.S. Senate from January 3, 1957, to January 3, 1963. *Wikipedia*, s.v. "John A. Carroll," last modified August 16, 2016, wikipedia.org/wiki/John_A._Carroll.

25   Undated letter from Peter Bunzel, Acc. 1977, 2, Box 7, Folder 4.

26   KH to CTS via email March 1, 2014.

27   Elsey to KH, December 6, 1948, Elsey papers, 102.

28 KH to NJ, 1985, 99–101.

29 Letter from Amherst, dated December 8, 1947, Acc. 1977, 2, Box 7, Folder 2.

30 Letter from Roland Young, October 20, 1947, Acc. 1977, 2, Box 7, Folder 3. "Founded in 1903, the American Political Science Association is the leading professional organization for the study of political science." www.apsanet.org/ABOUT/About-APSA.

31 Undated, handwritten draft of resignation letter from KH to George Graham, Acc. 1977, 2, Box 7, Folder 4.

32 KH to CTS via telephone, February 21, 2014.

33 KH to NJ, 1985, 107.

34 Judge Sam Rosenman to Clark Clifford, September 16, 1949, Elsey papers, 102.

35 Elsey to KH, September 9, 1949, Elsey papers, 102.

36 KH to Russ Barbour, Charleston, WV, July 26, 2005.

37 KH to Elsey, November 27, 1949, Elsey papers, 102.

38 KH to NJ, 1985, 111–115.

39 KH to Elsey, December 13, 1949, Elsey papers, 102.

40 KH to Barbour, Independence, MO, July 26, 2005.

41 Clark Clifford to Harry S. Truman, December 22, 1949, Elsey papers, 102.

42 KH to NJ, 1985, 120–121.

43 Ken Hechler, *Working with Truman: A Personal Memoir of the White House Years* (Columbia & London: University of Missouri Press, 1982), 130–132.

44 KH to NJ, 1985, 123–126.

45 KH to NJ, 1985, 128.

46 KH to Judge Sam Rosenman. Charles A. Moffat, *Ken Hechler, Maverick Public Servant* (Charleston, WV: Mountain State Press, 1987), 74.

5. THE TRUMAN WHITE HOUSE

1 "About Blair House: A Step into History," accessed May 20, 2014, www.blairhouse.org/about.

2 KH to CTS, Charleston, WV, December 27, 2012.

3 "The Blairs," accessed May 20, 2014, www.blairhouse.org/history /the-blairs.

4 KH, Hechler Files, Boxes 5–9, Truman Library.

5 KH to Barbour, Independence, MO, July 26, 2005.

6 KH to NJ, 1985, 127.

7 George Elsey quote regarding Hechler, Elsey papers, 102.

8 *Economist* 158 (1950): 1167.

9 Ken Hechler, *Working with Truman*, 143.

10 Ibid., 145.

11 KH to NJ, 1985, 135.

12 Ibid., 143.

13 Ibid., 149.

14 " 'Enemies from within,': Senator Joseph R. McCarthy's Accusations of Disloyalty," accessed April 18, 2014, http://historymatters.gmu .edu/d/6456.

15 *Wikipedia*, s.v. "Alien and Sedition Acts," last modified September 22, 2016, http://en.wikipedia.org/wiki/Alien_and_Sedition_Acts.

16 Hechler, "A Study of 'Witch-Hunting' and Hysteria in the United States," KH Personal, File labeled "Witch-hunting—A study by KH for Truman."

17 Hechler, *Working with Truman*, 184–186.

18 "Have You No Sense of Decency?," June 9, 1954, http://www.senate .gov/artandhistory/history/minute/Have_you_no_sense_of_decency .htm.

19 "Senate Resolution 301: Censure of Senator Joseph McCarthy (1954)," http://www.ourdocuments.gov/doc.php?flash=true&doc =86.

20 "Harry S. Truman: Life in Brief," accessed May 21, 2014, http:// millercenter.org/president/truman/essays/biography/print.

21 *Wikipedia*, s.v. "Attempted assassination of Harry S. Truman," accessed May 21, 2014, http://en.wikipedia.org/wiki/Truman _assassination_attempt#Attack.

22 Ken Hechler, "The 1950 Attempt on President Truman's Life," Hechler Files, Addendum 2, Box 6, Truman Library.

23 KH to NJ, 1985, 183–184.

24 Ibid.

25 *Wikipedia*, s.v. "United States elections, 1950," accessed May 22, 2014, http://en.wikipedia.org/wiki/United_States_elections,_1950.

26 KH to CTS, Huntington, WV, January 26, 2013.

27 George Elsey quote regarding Hechler, Elsey papers, 102.

28 Elsey to KH, December 26, 1950, Elsey papers, 102.

29 Hechler, *Working with Truman*, 167.

30 KH to CTS, Charleston, WV, December 27, 2012.

31 Harry S. Truman, *Memoirs*, vol. 2, *Years of Trial and Hope: 1946– 1952* (Garden City, NY: Doubleday, 1956), 442.

32 KH to CTS, Charleston, WV, December 13, 2012.

33 http://www.history.com/this-day-in-history/lincoln-removes -mcclellan. Accessed October 19, 2016.

34 Hechler, *Working with Truman*, 179.

35 KH to CTS, Charleston, WV, December 13, 2012.

36 Dennis Wainstock, *Truman, MacArthur and the Korean War* (West- port, CT: Greenwood Press, 1999), 124.

37 Harry S. Truman, quoted in Merle Miller, *Plain Speaking: An Oral Biography of Harry S. Truman* (New York: Berkley, 1973), 211.

38 Log of Truman's Tenth Visit to Key West, November 8–December 9, 1951, Truman Library, http://www.trumanlibrary.org/calendar /travel_log/.

39 Tour Guide, Little White House, Key West, FL, May 17, 2013.

40 KH to CTS, Key West, FL, May 19, 2013.

41 Truman's Travel Log, 62–68.

42 KH to CTS, Key West, FL, May 19, 2013.

43 Hechler, *Working with Truman*, 243–244.

44 Truman's Travel Log, 62–68.

45 KH to CTS, Key West, FL, May 19, 2013.

46 KH to CTS, Charleston, WV, December 27, 2012.

47 KH to CTS, Charleston, WV, January 14, 2013.

48 KH to CTS, Charleston, WV, December 27, 2012.

49 KH to CTS, Marshfield, MO, April 26, 2013.

50 "1952: Saluting Eisenhower," *New Hampshire Union Leader*, May 3, 2011, http://www.unionleader.com/article/99999999/NEWS0605 /110509970.

51 Hechler, *Working with Truman*, 242–248.

52 Handwritten notes by Hechler, April 3, "Some Notes, April 1–4, 1952," Truman Library.

53 *Wikipedia*, s.v. "1952 Democratic National Convention," accessed April 22, 2014, http://en.wikipedia.org/wiki/1952_Democratic_National_Convention.

54 Memo from KH to Elsey, July 3, 1952, Elsey papers, 102.

55 "The President's Day," Harry S. Truman's appointment calendar, September 1952, Truman Library.

56 Hechler, *Working with Truman*, 251.

57 KH to CTS, Charleston, WV, December 27, 2012.

58 KH to NJ, 1985, 162–163.

59 Hechler, *Working with Truman*, 251–252.

60 Neustadt later became an advisor to Presidents Kennedy and Johnson, and a distinguished professor at both Columbia and Harvard. "Richard Neustadt Remembered as Guiding Force at KSG" *Harvard Gazette,* November 6, 2013, http://news.harvard.edu/gazette/story/2003/11/richard-neustadt-remembered-as-guiding-force-at-ksg/.

61 KH to CTS, Charleston, WV, December 27, 2012.

62 KH to Barbour, Independence, MO, July 26, 2005.

63 Hechler, *Working with Truman*, 269.

64 Bonnie K. Goodman, "Overviews and Chronologies: 1952," http://presidentialcampaignselectionsreference.wordpress.com/overviews/20th-century/1952-overview.

65 KH to NJ, 1985, 158.

66 Hechler, *Working with Truman*, 273.

67 KH to NJ, 1985, 180–181.

68 KH to Elsey, Elsey papers, 102.

69 George Elsey quote regarding Hechler, Elsey papers, 102.

70 Hechler, *Working with Truman*, 279.

71 KH to NJ, 1985, 185–186.

6. THE ROAD TO CONGRESS WINDS THROUGH WEST VIRGINIA

1 KH to NJ, 1985, 195.

2 Bernard Grun, ed., *The Timetables of History*, 3rd ed. (New York: Simon & Schuster, 1991), 535–536.

3 Hechler's appointment letter from Dr. Edward Litchfield, April 15, 1953, Acc. 1977, 2, Box 9, Folder 1.

4 KH to NJ, 1985, 188.

5 Kenneth Holland, president of the Institute of International Education, to KH, March 22, 1955, Acc. 1977, 2, Box 9, Folder 4.

6 Letter from the Sheraton Corporation, May 21, 1954, Acc. 1977, 2, Box 9, Folder 2.

7 "History of the Congressional Fellowship Program," http://www.apsanet.org/PROGRAMS/Congressional-Fellowship-Program/History-of-Congressional-Fellowship-Program.

8 Frederick Clark to KH, July 10, 1980, Acc. 1977, 2, Box 9, Folder 5.

9 Jeffery Biggs to CTS via email, June 17, 2014.

10 Hechler's notes for Stevenson, Acc. 1977, 2, Box 9, Folders 18–30.

11 KH to NJ, 1985, 191.

12 Hechler's notes for Stevenson, Acc. 1977, 2, Box 9, Folder 32.

13 KH to CTS, Charleston, WV, December 13, 2012.

14 KH to NJ, 1985, 166.

15 KH to CTS, Charleston, WV, December 27, 2012.

16 KH to NJ, 1985, 190.

17 Ken Hechler, "Adlai E. Stevenson," undated but written for a speech after his election to Congress in 1958, Acc. 1977, 2, Box 9, Folder 38.

18 Ibid.

19 KH to Barbour, Independence, MO, July 26, 2005.

20 Marshall University is now the second largest university in the state, with an annual enrollment of approximately fifteen thousand in 2015–16.

21 KH to CTS, Huntington, WV, January 31, 2013.

22 KH to CTS, Charleston, WV, December 4, 2012.

23 Conley Dillon to KH, November 28, 1956, Acc. 1977, 2, Box 9, Folder 2.

24 J. F. Bartlett to KH, December 20, 1956, Acc. 1977, 2, Box 9, Folder 2.

25 KH to NJ, 1985, 199.

26 Hechler's fare stub, Acc. 1977, 2, Box 9, Folder 3.

27 Simon Perry to CTS, telephone interview, Huntington, WV, April 9, 2013.

28 KH to Barbour, Independence, MO, July 26, 2005.

29 KH to Barbour, Huntington, WV, August 13, 2005.

30 KH to CTS, Charleston, WV, December 6, 2012.

31 Carl Leiden to Ken Hechler, letter dated July 12, 1957, Acc. 1977, 2, Box 9, Folder 27.

32 Marshall College publications, Acc. 1977, 2, Box 9, Folders 4–5.

33 KH to CTS, Charleston, WV, December 6, 2012.

34 Ann Dexter to CTS, telephone interview, May 8, 2013.

35 Letter from Dean Bartlett to David Steindler, manager of C&P Telephone, February 14, 1957, Acc. 1977, 2, Box 9, Folder 2.

36 A. Michael Perry to CTS, Huntington, WV, February 26, 2013.

37 KH to CTS, Huntington, WV, January 31, 2013.

38 A. Michael Perry to CTS, Huntington, WV, February 26, 2013.

39 KH to Barbour, Independence, MO, July 26, 2005.

40 Margy Minichan Barrett to CTS, telephone interview, March 5, 2013.

41 KH to Barbour, Independence, MO, July 26, 2005.

42 Class syllabus, Acc. 1977, 2, Box 9, Folder 8.

43 Class assignment, Acc. 1977, 2, Box 9, Folder 10.

44 Barrett to CTS, telephone interview, March 5, 2013.

45 KH to CTS, Charleston, WV, December 4, 2012.

46 Student papers, Acc. 1977, 2, Box 9, Folders 11 and 14.

47 David Haden to CTS, telephone interview, February 28, 2013.

48 Hechler's notes, Acc. 1977, 2, Box 9, Folder 17.

49 Student evaluations, spring semester 1957, Acc. 1977, 2, Box 9, Folder 17.

50 Barrett to CTS, telephone interview, March 5, 2013.

51 "Harold E. 'Hal' Greer," http://www.hoophall.com/hall-of-famers /hal-greer/.

52 KH to CTS, Huntington, WV, January 31, 2013.

53 *Wikipedia*, s.v. "Hal Greer," last modified September 26, 2016, http://en.wikipedia.org/wiki/Hal_Greer.

54 KH to CTS, Huntington, WV, January 31, 1013.
55 KH in a paper, "Working for Colorado Senator John A. Carroll," Acc. 1977, 2, Box 9, Folder 39.
56 Hechler, *The Bridge at Remagen*, x–xi.
57 Pay stub receipt from WHTN, Acc. 1977, 2, Box 11, Folder 46.
58 KH to Barbour, Huntington, WV, August 13, 2005.
59 KH to CTS, Charleston, WV, December 27, 2012.
60 Richard Tyson to Barbour, Huntington, WV, September 20, 2005.
61 KH to CTS, Huntington, WV, January 31, 2013.
62 KH to Barbour, Huntington, WV, August 13, 2005.
63 Bobby Nelson to CTS, Huntington, WV, April 8, 2013.
64 Ibid.
65 Ibid.

7. ROGUE CAMPAIGN

1 "West Virginia: Political Parties," Worldmark Encyclopedia of the States, accessed July 21, 2014, http://www.city-data.com/states/West-Virginia-Political-parties.html.
2 Hechler, undated draft of his 1958 primary campaign announcement, Acc. 1977, 2, Box 12, Folder 2.
3 Helen Holt to CTS, September 22, 2013.
4 Student invitation, Acc. 1977, 2, Box 12, Folder 3.
5 KH to Nor VA Jal Music Co., April 30, 1958, Acc. 1977, 2, Box 12. Folder 41.
6 Helen Holt to CTS, September 22, 2013.
7 Letter from Hulett C. Smith, West Virginia Democratic Executive Committee Chairman, to Luther H. Carson, Chairman, Kanawha County Democratic Executive Committee, December 20, 1957, Acc. 1977, 2, Box 11, Folder 4.
8 Nelson to CTS, Huntington, WV, April 8, 2013.
9 Ibid.
10 KH to NJ, 1985, 208.
11 KH to CTS, Charleston, WV, January 23, 2013.
12 KH to CTS, Marshfield, MO, April 26, 2013.
13 Nelson to CTS, Huntington, WV, April 8, 2013.

14 Hechler's "Information for Campaign Workers," Acc. 1977, 2, Box 12, Folder 13.

15 Ann Dexter to CTS, telephone interview, May 8, 2013.

16 Charles Hechler to KH, May 27, 1958, Acc. 1977, 2, Box 12, Folder 5.

17 S.L.A. Marshall to KH, July 15, 1958, Acc. 1977, 2, Box 12, Folder 39.

18 Hubert Humphrey to KH, May 22, 1958, Acc. 1977, 2, Box 12, Folder 19.

19 Undated handwritten letter from Armour Adkins of Huntington, WV, to the *Parkersburg News*, Acc. 1977, 2, Box 12, Folder 10. Apparently it was written as a letter to the editor, as it addresses "Fellow Democrats."

20 KH to NJ, 1985, 206.

21 KH to Barbour, Huntington, WV, August 13, 2005.

22 Clark Clifford to KH, July 2, 1958, Acc. 1977, 2, Box 12, Folder 21.

23 KH to Mr. & Mrs. Homer Peyton, May 9, 1958, Acc. 1977, 2, Box 12, Folder 5.

24 *Parkersburg News*, July 20, 1958, Acc. 1977, 2, Box 12, Folder 10.

25 Acc. 2010, Series VIIIb.2, Box 29, Folder 19.

26 Hechler's "Information for Campaign Workers," Acc. 1977, 2, Box 12, Folder 13.

27 Transcript of August 4, 1958 radio speech, Acc. 1977, 2, Box 12, Folder 16.

28 Acc. 1977, 2, Box 12, Folder 44.

29 KH to CTS, Charleston, WV, January 31, 2013.

30 Campaign expenditure report, Acc. 1977, 2, Box 12, Folder 45.

31 Nelson to Barbour, Huntington, WV, September 21, 2005.

32 Sam Mallison to KH, September 5, 1958, Acc. 2010, Series VIIIb2, Box 29, Folder 2.

33 A. Michael Perry to CTS, February 26, 2013.

34 KH to CTS, Charleston, WV, December 6, 2012.

35 Letter from Miles Stanley, dated September 9, 1958, Acc. 1977, 2, Box 12, Folder 36.

36 Nelson to CTS, Huntington, WV, April 8, 2013.

37 Bryan Ward, "Battleground West Virginia: Electing the President in 1960," accessed July 28, 2014, www.wvculture.org/history/1960presidentialcampaign/article.html.

38 Speeches, 1932–1960, Folder 7, Papers of Raymond Moley, Hoover Institution Archives, Stanford University.

39 KH to CTS, Charleston, WV, December 6, 2012.

40 KH to CTS, Charleston, WV, January 26, 2013.

41 Betty Ireland defeated Ken in his 2004 bid to again become secretary of state.

42 Hechler to Cabell County Democratic Executive Committee, August 29, 1958, Acc. 1977, 2, Box 13, Folder 1.

43 Robert Byrd to KH, August 15, 1958, Acc. 1977, 2, Box 13, Folder 20.

44 KH to CTS, Charleston, WV, December 6, 2012.

45 Hechler's "Information for Campaign Workers," Acc. 1977, 2, Box 12, Folder 13.

46 Acc. 1977, 2, Box 13, Folder 21.

47 KH to Barbour, Huntington, WV, August 13, 2005.

48 Results of voter survey, Acc. 1977, 2, Box 13, Folder 17.

49 KH to Barbour, Huntington, WV, August 13, 2005.

50 *Point Pleasant Register*, October 31, 1958, Acc. 1977, 2, Box 13, Folder 24.

51 KH to CTS, Charleston, WV, December 6, 2012.

52 1958 general election results, Acc. 1977, 2, Box 13, Folder 25.

53 Harry W. Ball, *Charleston Gazette*, November 7, 1958, KH Personal, File labeled "Election, 1958."

54 KH to Barbour, Huntington, WV, August 13, 2005.

55 Adlai Stevenson to KH, November 25, 1958, Acc. 1977, 2, Box 13, Folder 38.

56 David Lloyd to KH, November 10, 1958, Acc. 1977, 2, Box 13, Folder 38.

57 Harry Truman to KH, November 13, 1958, Hechler Papers, Truman Library, Independence, MO, Box 5, Folder labeled "Personal Correspondence."

58 Nelson to Barbour, Huntington, WV, September 21, 2005.

8. YOUR SERVANT IN CONGRESS

1 Dorothy McCardle, "Kenneth Hechler among Washington's Bachelors," *Washington Post*, North American Newspaper Alliance, KH Personal, File labeled "Bachelor in DC in 1959!"

2 Deegans to CTS, Lewisburg, WV, January 18, 2013.

3 Various romantic letters, 1958–1979, Hechler Collection.

4 KH to CTS, Charleston, WV, December 12, 2012.

5 Ibid.

6 Hechler congressional letterhead 1965, Acc. 2010, Series IXa, Folder 1.

7 KH to CTS, Charleston, WV, January 14, 2013.

8 Ned Helme to CTS, telephone interview, April 30, 2013.

9 Nelson to CTS, Huntington, WV, April 8, 2013.

10 KH to CTS, Huntington, WV, January 26, 2013.

11 KH to CTS, Charleston, WV, January 14, 2013.

12 Deegans to CTS, Lewisburg, WV, January 18, 2013.

13 KH to CTS, Huntington, WV, March 4, 2013.

14 Nelson to CTS, Huntington, WV, April 8, 2013.

15 KH to CTS, Huntington, WV, January 26, 2013.

16 Nelson to CTS, Huntington, WV, April 8, 2013.

17 Raamie Barker to CTS, telephone conversation, April 5, 2013.

18 Deegans to CTS, Lewisburg, WV, January 18, 2013.

19 Nelson to Barbour, Huntington, WV, September 21, 2005.

20 KH to CTS via telephone, April 26, 2013.

21 Helme to CTS, telephone interview, April 30, 2013.

22 *Wikipedia*, s.v. "Twenty-Sixth Amendment to the United States Constitution," last modified August 27, 2016, http://en.wikipedia .org/wiki/Twenty-sixth_Amendment_to_the_United_States _Constitution#Background.

23 Nelson to Barbour, Huntington, WV, September 21, 2005.

24 Senator Robert Dole to Barbour, Washington, DC, September 26, 2005.

25 Nelson to Barbour, Huntington, WV, September 21, 2005.

26 Senator George McGovern to Barbour, Mitchell, SD, September 12, 2005.

27 David Tyson (1971 Hechler Page) to CTS, January 14, 2013.

28 Dr. Alan B. Gould to CTS via telephone, January 28, 2016.

29 Mrs. Bos Johnson to CTS, Huntington, WV, May 22, 2013.

30 Dr. William Cobb to CTS, Charleston, WV, January 12, 2013.

31 Charles Frisbey to CTS, telephone interview, April 3, 2013.

32 Dave Ball to CTS, Huntington, WV, January 1, 2013.

33 Mrs. Bos Johnson to CTS, Huntington, WV, May 22, 2013.

34 KH to President Gerald Ford, July 27, 1976, Acc. 2010, Series IXn, Box 42, Folder 2.

35 KH to congressional colleagues, June 20, 1975, Acc. 2010, Series IXn, Box 42, Folder 3.

36 *Wikipedia*, s.v. "Chuck Yeager," accessed July 17, 2015, https://en .wikipedia.org/wiki/Chuck_Yeager.

37 "Rep. Kenneth Hechler," www.govtrack.us/congress/members /kenneth-hechler/405304#.

38 KH to CTS, Charleston, WV, January 14, 2013.

39 KH to CTS, Huntington, WV, February 16, 2013.

40 CTS to Ned Helme, telephone interview, April 30, 2013.

41 Deegans to CTS, Lewisburg, WV, January 18, 2013.

9. CONGRESSIONAL CAMPAIGNING, HECHLER STYLE

1 Nelson to Barbour, Huntington, WV, September 21, 2005.

2 Bob Brunner, *Bob Brunner's Reporter's Recollections* (WV: Self-published, 2012).

3 Bosworth Johnson to CTS, Huntington, WV, May 22, 2013.

4 Ibid.

5 Correspondence between KH and Ned Chilton, March and April 1970, Acc. 1977, 1, Box 37, Folder label, "Letters."

6 KH note, undated, Acc. 1977, 1, Box 35, Folder labeled "WV Subject 1960 Campaign—Opponents."

7 Letter from KH to Clyde Pinson, August 25, 1960, Acc. 1977, 1, Box 35, Folder labeled "WV Subject 1960 Campaign—Opponents."

8 Pinson Flyer, Hechler Collection, Acc. 1977, 1, Box 35, Folder labeled "WV Subject 1960 Campaign—Opponents."

9 Victor K. Heyman, report on West Virginia Congressional Reapportionment, 1961, Acc. 1977, 1, Box 35, Folder labeled "Reapportionment."

10 Pinson, quoted in *U.S. News and World Report*, November 21, 1960, Acc. 1977, 1, Box 35, Folder labeled "WV Subject 1960 Campaign—Opponents."

11 Leroy Clyde Hardy, "The Practice and Theory of Reapportionment," paper prepared for the 1960 Annual Meeting of the American Political Science Association, 4.

12 Victor K. Heyman, report on West Virginia Congressional Reapportionment, 1961, Acc. 1977, 1, Box 35, Folder labeled "Reapportionment."

13 "Welcoming Opposition," *Washington Post*, October 1, 1961, Hechler Collection, Acc. 1977, Box 324, Folder 7.

14 Correspondence between Daniel Dahill and KH, September 23–25, 1961, Acc. 1977, 1, Box 35, Folder labeled "1962 Campaign Election results."

15 George McClung to Robert Kennedy, March 25, 1962, Acc. 2010, Series VIIIb2, Box 29, Folder 1.

16 "Statement by Ken Hechler in reply to charges made in the Democratic Primary Political Campaign," undated press release, Acc. 1977, 1, Box 35, Folder labeled "1962 Campaign Election results."

17 Letter dated April 18, 1962, from "Pete" to KH, Acc. 1977, 1, Box 35, Folder labeled "Opponents."

18 Undated press release by KH, Acc. 1977, 1, Box 35, Folder labeled "Opponents."

19 KH to CTS, Charleston, WV, January 14, 2013.

20 Letter from George McClung to various labor leaders dated March 12, 1962, with polygraph report attached, Acc. 1977, 1, Box 35, Folder labeled "Opponents."

21 *Charleston Gazette*, March 17, 1962, Acc. 1977, 1, Box 35, Folder labeled "Newspaper articles."

22 KH to CTS, Charleston, WV, October 4, 2013.

23 1962 Primary election return report from the Secretary of State's office, Acc. 1977, Box 324, Folder 42.

24 KH to CTS via message from Carol Kitzmiller Hechler, September 23, 2014.

25 KH to CTS via telephone from CKH, September 20, 2014.

26 George Lantz to KH, undated note, Hechler Collection, Acc. 1977, 1, Box 36, Folder labeled "1964 Campaign Administrative notes."

27 Bill Francois to KH, October 30, 1964, re Robert Fletcher, Acc. 1977, 1, Box 36, Folder labeled "1964 Campaign Letters."

28 Thomas Stafford, column, *Charleston Gazette*, March 1, 1964, KH Personal, File labeled "Campaign 1964."

29 Thomas Stafford, column, June 7, 1964, and Ken's June 14 response, Acc. 1977, 1, Box 36, Folder labeled "1964 Campaign–Newspaper Articles."

30 Jack Miller telegram to KH, October 13 and 15, 1964, Acc. 1977, 1, Box 36, Folder labeled "1964 Campaign Opponents."

31 1964 official election returns, Secretary of State's office, Acc. 1977, 1, Box 36, Folder labeled "1964 Campaign Election results."

32 *Herald Advertiser*, November 10, 1964, Acc. 1977, 1, Box 36, Folder labeled "1964 Campaign–Newspaper Articles."

33 Acc. 1977, 1, Box 36, Folder labeled "1966 Speeches."

34 Acc. 1977, 1, Box 36, Folder labeled "1964 Campaign Election results."

35 Katherine Hechler, undated letter, Hechler Collection, Acc. 1977, 1, Box 36, Folder labeled "Publicity."

36 Dave Peyton, column, *Huntington Advertiser*, October 30, 1968, Acc. 1977, 1, Box 36, Folder labeled "Newspaper Articles."

37 Secretary of State's Official Election Results, Acc. 1977, 1, Box 36, Folder labeled "1968 Election Results."

38 Hechler undated press release, Acc. 1977, 1, Box 36, Folder labeled "Press Releases."

39 Acc. 1977, 1, Box 36, Folder labeled "1968 Hechler/Miller Project."

40 Acc. 1977, 1, Box 36, Folder labeled "1968 Campaign Canvassing."

41 KH to Dorothy Govern, July 30, 1968, Acc. 1977, 1, Box 36, Folder labeled "Letters."

42 KH to CTS, Huntington, WV, January 31, 2013.

43 *Wikipedia*, s.v. "Twenty-Sixth Amendment to the United States Constitution," last modified August 27, 2016, http://en.wikipedia.org/wiki/Twenty-sixth_Amendment_to_the_United_States_Constitution.

44 Hechler press release, November 6, 1970, Acc. 1977, 1, Box 37, Folder labeled "Press Releases."

45 Study of Hechler's election results by Richard Rector, CTS personal files.

46 Hechler press release, November 6, 1970, Acc. 1977, 1, Box 37, Folder labeled "Press Releases."

47 Hubert Humphrey to KH, December 4, 1970, Hechler Collection, Acc. 1977, 1, Box 37, Folder labeled "Letters."

48 Nelson to CTS, Huntington, WV, May 9, 2013.

49 Letters and documents, Acc. 1977, 1, Box 37, Folder labeled "Letters."

50 KH to CTS, Charleston, WV, April 28, 2013.

51 Editorial, *Charleston Gazette*, January 24, 1972, Acc. 1977, 1, Box 37, Folder labeled "Publicity."

52 KH to Jennings Randolph, February 23, 1972, Acc. 1977, 1, Box 37, Folder labeled "Letters."

53 Jennings Randolph to KH, March 2, 1972, Acc. 1977, 1, Box 37, Folder labeled "Letters."

54 Hechler Press Release, March 10, 1972, Acc. 1977, 1, Box 37, Folder labeled "Press Releases."

55 Nelson to CTS, Huntington, WV, May 9, 2013.

56 Editorial, *Beckley Post Herald and Register*, March 19, 1972, Acc. 1977, 1, Box 37, Folder labeled "Administrative Notes."

57 Jim Dent undated cartoon, *Charleston Gazette*, Acc. 1977, 1, Box 37, Folder labeled "Newspaper Articles."

58 League of Conservation Voters, April 1972 Newsletter, Acc. 1977, 1, Box 37, Folder labeled "Newsletters."

59 *Bluefield Daily Telegraph*, May 1, 1972, Acc. 1977, 1, Box 37, Folder labeled "Newspaper Articles."

60 Undated press release, Acc. 1977, 1, Box 37, Folder labeled "Press Releases."

61 Ken Hechler's Newsletter, December 1973, Acc. 1977, 1, Box 39a, Folder labeled "Letters."

62 KH undated press release, Acc. 1977, 1, Box 39a, Folder labeled "Press Releases."

63 Pineville West Virginia newspaper, January 11, 1974, Acc. 1977, 1, Box 39a, Folder labeled "Newspaper Articles."

64 Proclamation from Governor Arch Moore to KH, Acc. 1977, 1, Box 39a, Folder labeled "Election Results."

65 KH to NJ, 1985, 228.

66 Hechler Collection, Acc. 1977, 1, Box 39a, Folder labeled "Administrative Notes #5."

67 Ken Hechler press release, March 12, 1976, Acc. 1977, 1, Box 39a, Folder labeled "Administrative Notes #4."

68 Nelson to CTS, Huntington, WV, May 9, 2013.

69 Stratton Douthat to CTS, telephone interview, May 7, 2013.

70 Analysis by John Womack, Political Science 652, October 12, 1977, Acc. 1977, 1, Box 39a, Folder labeled "1976 Analysis of Election."

71 Undated notes of suggested statements, Acc. 1977, 1, Box 39a, Folder labeled "Administrative Notes #4."

72 Deegans to CTS, Lewisburg, WV, January 18, 2013.

73 Nelson to CTS, Huntington, WV, May 9, 2013.

74 Study of Hechler's election results by Richard Rector, CTS personal files.

75 Deegans to CTS, Lewisburg, WV, January 18, 2013.

76 KH to CTS, Charleston, WV, December 6, 2012.

77 James Casto, former *Herald Dispatch* editorial page editor, to CTS, Huntington, WV, October 14, 2014.

78 Undated and unsigned handwritten notes, Acc. 1977, 1, Box 39a, Folder labeled "Administrative Notes #1."

79 Helme to CTS, telephone interview, April 30, 2013.

80 Ibid.

10. SPACE . . . WHERE HECHLER DIDN'T EXPECT TO GO

1 Undated draft by Ken Hechler to unnamed person (presumably House Majority Leader John McCormack), Acc. 2010, Series IXb, Box 40, Folder 7.

2 *Herald Dispatch*, October 5, 1957.

3 *Herald Dispatch*, November 4, 1957.

4 Edwin B. Haakinson, Washington, DC, AP report, *Herald Dispatch*, October 5, 1957.

5 Robert C. Albright, *Washington Post*, October 20, 1957.

6 Ken Hechler, *Toward the Endless Frontier: History of the Committee on Science and Technology, 1959–79* (Washington, DC: U.S. House of Representatives, 1980), 3.

7 Ibid.

8 Cong. Rec. of the 85th Congress, May 29, 1958–June 13, 1958, remarks by Congressman McCormack.

9 Hechler, *Toward the Endless Frontier*, 28.

10 Ibid., 39.

11 Ken Hechler, Cong. Rec., February 17, 1960, vol. 106, Part 3, p. 2941, KH Personal, File labeled "Eisenhower and Presidential Leadership."

12 KH to CTS, Key West, FL, May 19, 2013.

13 Ibid.

14 Nelson to CTS, May 9, 2013.

15 KH to CTS, Key West, FL, May 19, 2013.

16 KH to NJ, 1985, 237.

17 Congressman James Symington to Barbour, Washington, DC, September 8, 2005.

18 "History of Green Bank and the NRAO," last modified May 18, 2014, https://science.nrao.edu/facilities/gbt/facilities/gbt/green-bank -local-area-information/history-of-green-bank-and-the-nrao.

19 Hechler, *Toward the Endless Frontier*, 215.

20 "TIROS," May 22, 2016, http://science.nasa.gov/missions/tiros/.

21 Hechler, *Toward the Endless Frontier*, 250.

22 Presidential Chief of Staff Sherman Adams, quoted by Hechler, *Toward the Endless Frontier*, 5.

23 John F. Kennedy, "Inaugural Address," January 20, 1961, http://www .presidency.ucsb.edu/ws/?pid=8032.

24 KH to CTS, Key West, FL, May 19, 2013.

25 Hechler, *Toward the Endless Frontier*, 62.

26 *Dominion News*, Morgantown, WV, July 15, 1969.

27 Hechler, *Toward the Endless Frontier*, 91.

28 Senator Tom Harkin to Barbour, Washington, DC, September 28, 2005.

29 Ken Hechler, "Accidents Teach Us Grim Lessons," *Charleston Gazette*, February 12, 1986, Acc. 2010, Series IXb, Box 40, Folder 9.

30 Ken Hechler in a public address, July 19, 1969, quoted in Moffat, *Ken Hechler: Maverick Public Servant*, 149.

31 Undated Hechler remarks to Congress after the moon launch, Acc. 2010, Series IXb, Box 40, Folder 7.

32 NASA memo release No. 69–83F, July 13, 1969.

33 Pearlman, Robert Z., "Search for States' Missing Apollo 11 Moon Rocks Continues," July 25, 2013, http://www.space.com/22108-states -missing-apollo-moon-rocks.html.

34 William Hutchinson to CTS, telephone interview, February 27, 2013.

35 Senator Tom Harkin to Barbour, Washington, DC, September 28, 2005.

36 KH to CTS, Key West, FL, May 17, 2013.

37 Undated draft notes of remarks by Ken Hechler, Acc. 2010, Series IXb, Box 40, Folder 7.

38 Hechler, *Toward the Endless Frontier*, 684.

39 KH to CTS, Key West, FL, May 17, 2013.

40 KH to CTS, Huntington, WV, February 16, 2013.

41 Congressman James Symington to Barbour, Washington, DC, September 8, 2005.

42 Bob Kittle, Dateline Washington (column), *Charleston Daily Mail*, July 24, 1978, Acc. 2010, Series IXb, Box 40, Folder 8.

43 Letter by Ken Hechler, August 2, 1978, Acc. 2010, Series IXb, Box 40, Folder 2.

44 KH to CTS, via telephone, November 13, 2014.

II. WIN SOME, LOSE SOME

1 Various notes to and from Hechler, Hechler Collection, Acc. 1977, Box 327, Folders 1–32, Hechler Collection, Marshall University Special Collections.

2 Ken Hechler, Undated Personal Biography, Hechler Collection, Acc. 2010, Series XVIIb—Box 85, Folder 2.

3 "Bill Summary & Status Search Results," Items 1 through 71, THOMAS, Library of Congress, accessed June 8, 2015.

4 Various notes to and from Hechler, Hechler Collection, Acc. 1977, Box 327, Folders 1–32, Hechler Collection, Marshall University Special Collections.

5 Letter from Ken Hechler to Hershel "Woody" Williams, Congressional Medal of Honor holder from West Virginia, April 28, 1960, Hechler Collection, Acc. 1977, Box 166, Folder 3. Hechler states that he voted for that bill on July 20, 1959.

6 Wilbur J. Cohen, "The Forand Bill: Hospital Insurance for the Aged," *American Journal of Nursing* 58, no. 5 (May 1958).

7 KH to NJ, 1985, 207.

8 KH to various constituents, Hechler Collection, Acc. 1977, Box 163, Folder labeled "1960 Letters."

9 Andrew Glass, "President Johnson Signs Medicare Bill on July 30, 1965," This Day in Politics, *Politico*, July 30, 2007.

10 Various letters from Hechler to constituents, 1960, Acc. 1977, Box 166, Folder 3.

11 Hechler to Frank Fowler Sr. of Parkersburg, WV, February 8, 1960, Acc. 1977, Box 166, Folder 3.

12 Ken Hechler to M. Eugene Lathey, Dunbar, WV, et al., 1974, Acc. 1977, Box 336, Folder labeled "WV Subject File—Textbook Controversy."

13 Ken Hechler to Matt Wolfe, Huntington, WV, 1975, Acc. 1977, Box 336, Folder labeled "WV Subject File—Textbook Controversy."

14 The congressional franking privilege, which dates from 1775, allows members of Congress to transmit mail matter under their signature without postage. Congress reimburses the U.S. Postal Service for franked mail.

15 Various letters from Hechler to constituents, 1960, Acc. 1977, Box 164, Folders 18–19.

16 "Postage Rates for Periodicals: A Narrative History," accessed June 10, 2015, https://about.usps.com/who-we-are/postal-history/periodicals-postage-history.htm.

17 "Hooray for Mr. Hechler," flyer dated April 3, 1967, Acc. 1977, Box 164, Folder 19.

18 KH to Alan Rabinowitz, June 19, 1967, Acc. 1977, Box 164, Folder 19.

19 Various letters from Hechler to constituents, 1960, Acc. 1977, Box 164, Folders 21 and 23.

20 Letter from Hechler to a constituent, May 25, 1960, Acc. 1977, Box 166, Folder 3.

21 Various clippings and letters from Hechler to constituents, 1960, Acc. 1977, Box 164, Folders 2, 3, and 17.

22 *Wikipedia*, s.v. "Gun Control Act of 1968," accessed June 8, 2015, http://en.wikipedia.org/wiki/Gun_Control_Act_of_1968.

23 "The Vietnam War Timeline of Important Dates," accessed June 13, 2015, www.shmoop.com.

24 Acc. 1977, Box 166, Folder 23.

25 KH to CTS, Huntington, WV, January 26, 2013.

26 Ken Hechler, "An Unwritten Chapter in the History of the Marshall University Medical School," July 8, 1985, Acc. 2010, Series XIIId, Box: MU Med School, Folder 2.

27 Hechler, "An Unwritten Chapter."

28 *Marshall Magazine*, Fall 1982, Acc. 2010, Series XIIId, Box: MU Med School, Folder 8.

29 Dave Lavender, *Herald Dispatch*, "First Dean of the Marshall University Medical School Dies," December 14, 2015, 1 & 4a.

30 Ken Hechler, "The Battle for Midway Airport," *Pathway*, January 1971, 6–9, Acc. 1977, Box 329, Folder 17.

31 *Herald Advertiser*, February 23, 1967, Acc. 1977, Box 339, Folder 2.

32 "We Can Grow Faster," *Herald Dispatch*, February 28, 1967; "Joint Charleston-Huntington Jetport Aired as Fund-Saver," *Charleston Gazette*, February 25, 1967, Acc. 1977, Box 339, Folder 2.

33 Letters to the FAA from Kentucky senators Morton and Cooper, March 1, 1967, and from Kentucky congressman Carl Perkins, Acc. 1977, Box 339, Folder 1.

34 Nelson to CTS, Huntington, WV, April 8, 2013.

35 Dick Leonard to KH, October 10, 1966, Acc. 1977, Box 339, Folder labeled "WV Subj. File Midway Airport (Documents and Correspondence) Oct. 1966."

36 Jim Casto, "It's Time to Stop Playing with Our Future," *Huntington Quarterly*, Summer/Autumn 2001.

37 Various letters and articles, Acc. 1977, Box 342, Folder labeled "Open Letters by Jennings Randolph (1968–1971)"

38 Hechler, "Battle for Midway Airport."

39 KH to John Slack, undated, Acc. 1977, Box 342, Folder labeled "WV Subject—Midway Airport, Letters & Direct Mail Outs to Voters."

40 KH to CTS, Charleston, WV, January 14, 2013.

41 The Kanawha County Airport was renamed Yeager Airport in 1985, honoring West Virginia native Brigadier General Chuck Yeager.

42 KH to CTS via email, July 18, 2015.

12. MARCHING TO SELMA

1 Ken Hechler, "Prelude to Selma," undated handwritten notes, Acc. 2010, Series IXa, Box 40, Folder 7.

2 Hechler campaign leaflet put together by his staff to distribute to black voters in Kanawha County, 2003, KH Personal, File labeled "Civil Rights."

3 Hechler undated notes for an upcoming speech, Acc. 2010, Series IXa, Box 40, Folder 23.

4 Ibid., 2013.

5 KH in a paper, "Working for Colorado Senator John A. Carroll," Acc. 1977, 2, Box 9, Folder 39.

6 George McGovern to Barbour, Mitchell, SD, September 12, 2005.

7 KH to CTS, Huntington, WV, February 16, 2013.

8 George McGovern to Barbour, Mitchell, SD, September 12, 2005.

9 Philip Carter to Barbour, Huntington, WV, September 22, 2005.

10 Ibid.

11 Philip Carter, "Statement," Acc. 2010, Series IXa, Box 40, Folder 23.

12 Philip Carter to Barbour, Huntington, WV, September 22, 2005.

13 KH in an article in the *Wirt County Journal*, July 11, 1963, Acc. 2010, Series IXa, Box 40, Folder 18.

14 KH in an article in the *Parkersburg Times*, July 11, 1963, Acc. 2010, Series IXa, Box 40, Folder 18.

15 Hechler's 1988 speech draft, Acc. 2010, Series IXa, Box 40, Folder 23.

16 Hechler's handwritten notes, Acc. 2010, Series IXa, Box 40, Folder 24, Note 1.

17 KH to CTS, Charleston, WV, December 27, 2012.

18 Hechler's handwritten notes, Acc. 2010, Series IXa, Box 40, Folder 24.

19 Hechler's typed undated notes, Acc. 2010, Series IXa, Box 40, Folder 7.

20 Hechler's handwritten notes, Acc. 2010, Series IXa, Box 40, Folder 24.

21 Hechler's 1990 draft of a speech given to commemorate King's birthday, Acc. 2010, Series IXa, Box 40, Folder 7, p. 4.

22 Ibid., p. 6.

23 Hechler's handwritten notes, Acc. 2010, Series IXa, Box 40, Folder 24, Note 1.

24 KH to CTS, Charleston, WV, December 27, 2012.

25 Hechler's handwritten notes, Acc. 2010, Series IXa, Box 40, Folder 24, Note 2.

26 Hechler's 1990 draft of a speech given to commemorate King's birthday, Acc. 2010, Series IXa, Box 40, Folder 7, p. 6.

27 KH to CTS, Key West, FL, May 17, 2013.

28 "Selma to Montgomery March (1965)," http://mlk-kpp01.stanford .edu/index.php/encyclopedia/encyclopedia/enc_selma_to _montgomery_march/.

29 KH to CTS, Charleston, WV, December 27, 2012.

30 Ibid.

31 Various letters to and from KH on Selma, Acc. 2010, Series IXa, Box 40, Folders 1–3.

32 Brandon Rottinghaus, "Reassessing Public Opinion Polling in the Truman Administration," Northwestern University, 2003, http:// www.politicalscience.uh.edu/faculty/rottinghaus/Publications /PUBLISHED%20WORK/HST%20and%20Polls%20(PSQ) /Psq252325.pdf.

33 Various letters to and from KH on Selma, Acc. 2010, Series IXa, Box 40, Folders 1–3.

34 "Voting Rights Act," http://www.history.com/topics/black-history /voting-rights-act.

35 Joan Browning's account of MLK Award, January 23, 2010, op-ed column in West Virginia University's *Mountain Messenger*, Browning's files.

13. FIGHTING FOR MINERS' LIVES

1 Cong. Rec., 90th Cong., 2nd Sess., vol. 114, September 12, 1968.

2 Ken Hechler press release, November 22, 1968, KH Personal.

3 Brit Hume, *Death and the Mines: Rebellion and Murder in the United Mine Workers* (New York: Grossman, 1971), 8.
4 "This Week in Mining History," *Mining Accident News No. 1101*, January 2011, 2, http://ioqnz.co.nz/wp-content/uploads/Mining -Accident-News-No-1101.pdf.
5 Hume, 15–16 passim.
6 Ken Hechler, *The Fight for Coal Mine Health and Safety* (Charleston, WV: Pictorial Histories, 2011), 75.
7 Hume, *Death and the Mines*, 17.
8 Hechler press release, November 22, 1968, Hechler personal files.
9 Hume, *Death and the Mines*, 82.
10 Hechler, *Fight for Coal Mine Health and Safety*, 90.
11 Hume, *Death and the Mines*, 74–75 passim.
12 Ibid., 82–83 passim.
13 Ralph Nader to Stewart L. Udall, March 23, 1968, report in the U.S. Senate, Committee on Labor and Public Welfare, 90th Cong., 2nd Sess., 527.
14 UMWA, *Proceedings*, 1968, vol. 1, pp. 316, 320, 313–321 passim.
15 Hume, *Death and the Mines*, 104.
16 Donald Rasmussen to Barbour, Pinch, WV, August 14, 2005.
17 Hechler, *Fight for Coal Mine Health and Safety*, 85–90.
18 *Charleston Gazette*, January 16, 1969.
19 Hechler, *Fight for Coal Mine Health and Safety*, 91–93 passim.
20 Hume, *Death and the Mines*, 82.
21 Ibid., 79.
22 KH to CTS, Huntington, WV, February 9, 2013.
23 Hechler, *Fight for Coal Mine Health and Safety*, 100.
24 Cong. Rec., 91st Cong., 2nd Sess., vol. 116, May 15, 1969, pp. 3718–3722.
25 Hechler, *Fight for Coal Mine Health and Safety*, 102–104 passim.
26 "Tough Mine Rules Proposed," *Charleston Gazette*, February 7, 1969.
27 Hechler, *Fight for Coal Mine Health and Safety*, 104–106 passim.
28 KH to CTS, Huntington, WV, February 9, 2013.
29 Hume, *Death and the Mines*, 128–129 passim.
30 Ibid., 134–135 passim.
31 KH to CTS, Charleston, WV, January 31, 2013.

32 Hume, *Death and the Mines*, 134–135 passim.

33 KH to CTS, Huntington, WV, February 9, 2013.

34 Paul Nyden to CTS via email, May 25, 2016.

35 Hechler, *Fight for Coal Mine Health and Safety*, 134.

36 Ibid., 149.

37 Nelson to CTS, Huntington, WV, February 13, 2013.

38 Hechler, *Fight for Coal Mine Health and Safety*, 155.

39 KH to CTS, Huntington, WV, February 9, 2013.

40 Hechler, *Fight for Coal Mine Health and Safety*, 155–156.

41 Ibid., 157.

42 Hume, *Death and the Mines*, 31, 45 passim.

43 Ibid., 161–168 passim.

44 Hume, *Death and the Mines*, 153–157 passim.

45 Joseph A. "Chip" Yablonski to Barbour, Washington, DC, September 5, 2005.

46 Hume, *Death and the Mines*, 173.

47 Joseph A. "Chip" Yablonski to Barbour, Washington, DC, September 5, 2005.

48 Cong. Rec., 91st Cong., 2nd Sess., vol. 116, June 9, 1969.

49 Hechler, *Fight for Coal Mine Health and Safety*, 179.

50 Ibid., 189.

51 Hume, *Death and the Mines*, 220.

52 KH to CTS, Charleston, WV, January 26, 2012.

53 Hechler, *Fight for Coal Mine Health and Safety*, 171.

54 KH to CTS, Charleston, WV, January 26, 2012.

55 Joseph A. "Chip" Yablonski to Barbour, Washington, DC, September 5, 2005.

56 Acc. 2010, Series X, Box 048, Taxation and Coal, Folder 3, Newspapers.

57 Hechler, *Fight for Coal Mine Health and Safety*, 247.

58 Ibid., 216–217.

59 Hume, *Death and the Mines*, 234.

60 Hechler to Richard Nixon, October 31, 1969, Acc. 2010, Series X, Box 049, Taxation and Coal, Folder 1.

61 KH to CTS, Charleston, WV, January 26, 2012.

62 Hechler, *Fight for Coal Mine Health and Safety*, 269.

63 KH to CTS, Charleston, WV, January 31, 2013.

64 Hechler press release, "Behind the Scenes on the Mine Safety Bill," January 5, 1970, KH Personal.

65 Ken Hechler, "Hechler Says He's Lucky to Be Here," *Charleston Gazette*, December 31, 1994, KH Personal, File labeled "Joseph Yablonski."

66 Donald Rasmussen to Barbour, Pinch, WV, August 14, 2005.

67 Gilly and Vealey were sentenced to death, but Martin avoided execution by pleading guilty and turning state's evidence.

68 KH to CTS, Huntington, WV, February 9, 2013.

69 Hechler, "Hechler Says He's Lucky to Be Here."

70 *Sunday Gazette-Mail*, June 5, 2011, 4c.

71 Paul Nyden, *Charleston Gazette* reporter, to Barbour, Charleston, WV, September 22, 2005.

72 Donald Rasmussen to Barbour, Pinch, WV, August 14, 2005.

73 KH, November 30, 1969, Acc. 2010, Series X, Box 049, Folder 3, Reports.

14. HECHLER VS. BIG COAL—ROUND TWO

1 Correspondence between constituents and Ken Hechler, Acc. 1977, Box 330, Folder 17.

2 Hechler letter, April 11, 1970, Acc. 1977, Box 328, Folder 18.

3 Acc. 1977, Box 328, Folder 20.

4 Ken Hechler to Senator Williams, Acc. 1977, Box 331, Folder 2.

5 Hechler to Walter Hickel, April 22, 1970, Acc. 1977, Box 328, Folder 18.

6 Hechler to Jim Rentch, Manchester, KY, April 27, 1970, Acc. 1977, Box 328, Folder 18.

7 Acc. 1977, Box 328, Folder 18.

8 "Coal Fatalities for 1900 through 2015," United States Department of Labor, http://arlweb.msha.gov/stats/centurystats/coalstats.asp.

9 Acc. 1977, Box 330, Folder 20.

10 Jim Haught, "Revisiting the UMWA Cleanup," *Charleston Gazette*, March 22, 2005.

11 Miners for Democracy Collection, accessed March 24, 2015, www.reuther.wayne.edu/files/LR000589.pdf, p. 1.

12 Nathaniel deBruin, Marshall University Special Collections, to Carter Seaton, March 26, 2015.

13 Arnold Miller to Ken Hechler, August 3, 1973, Acc. 1977, Box 331, Folder 22.

14 Hechler to Joseph Finley, Philadelphia, December 26, 1972, Acc. 1977, Box 331, Folder 22.

15 Hechler statement, February 18, 1971, Acc. 1977, Box 328, Folder 19.

16 Editorial, *Washington Post*, June 29, 1971, Acc. 1977, Box 328, Folder 20.

17 Hechler statement, July 2, 1971, Acc. 1977, Box 328, Folder 19.

18 Hechler, *Washington Post*, July 3, 1971, Acc. 1977, Box 328, Folder 20.

19 Cecil Roberts to Barbour, Merrifield, VA, September 29, 2005.

20 Constituent letter to Ken Hechler, December 7, 1970, Acc. 1977, Box 327, Folder 56.

21 Hechler handwritten note, Acc. 1977, Box 329, Folder 1.

22 "House Bill Asks Strip Mining Ban," *Wilkes-Barre Record*, February 19, 1971, Acc. 1977, Box 329, Folder 7.

23 Jay Rockefeller, quoted in a news article, April 17, 1971, Acc. 1977, Box 329, Folder 10.

24 Ken Hechler, "How Congress Enabled Mountaintop Removal," in *Coal Country: Rising Up against Mountaintop Removal Mining*, ed. Shirley Stewart Burns, Mari-Lynn Evans, and Silas House (San Francisco: Sierra Club Books, 2009).

25 "House Bill Asks Strip Mining Ban," *Wilkes-Barre Record*, February 19, 1971, Acc. 1977, Box 329, Folder 7.

26 KH to supporter, Acc. 1977, Box 329, Folder 7.

27 Ned Helme to CTS, telephone interview, April 30, 2013.

28 Reprint from November 20, 1970, Acc. 1977, Box 329, Folder 2.

29 Hechler, "How Congress Enabled Mountaintop Removal."

30 Ned Helme to CTS, telephone interview, April 30, 2013.

31 Constituent congressional testimony, November 29, 1971, Acc. 1977, Box 329, Folder 8.

32 Hechler, "How Congress Enabled Mountaintop Removal."

33 Ibid.

34 Uday Desai, "The Politics of Federal-State Relations: The Case of Surface Mining Regulations," *Natural Resources Journal* 31, no. 4 (1991): 788.

35 Hechler, "How Congress Enabled Mountaintop Removal."

36 WV Department of Culture and History, "Buffalo Creek," accessed April 16, 2015, http://www.wvculture.org/history/buffcreek/buff1 .html.

37 KH to Barbour, Huntington, WV, August 13, 2005.

38 KH to CTS, Huntington, WV, February 9, 2013.

39 "Hechler Cites 'Gob' Pile Danger, *Logan Banner*, July 7, 1969, Acc. 1977, Box 323, Folder 6.

40 KH to Barbour, August 13, 2005.

41 WV Department of Culture and History, "Buffalo Creek."

42 Paul Nyden to CTS, May 25, 2016.

43 The study was part of a long-range program made possible by Citizens for Environmental Protection, Inc. Slide show available in Acc. 2014, Series VI, Artifacts, Box 6, 1973 Mountaintop Removal Slide Show Scripts.

44 Ned Helme to CTS, telephone interview, April 30, 2013.

45 Ibid.

46 James M. McElfish Jr. and Ann E. Beier, *Environmental Regulation of Coal Mining: SMCRA's Second Decade*, ELI Monograph Series (Washington, DC: Environmental Law Institute, 1990), 18–19.

47 Hechler to Florida resident, Acc. 1977, Box 329, Folder 32.

48 Acc. 1977, Box 330, Folders 1–7.

49 Hechler Statement, November 23, 1973, Acc. 1977, Box 170, Folder 19.

50 Hechler, OVEC public statement, February 27, 2008, accessed March 15, 2015, http://ohvec.org/issues/mountaintop_removal/misc /2008_02_27.html.

51 Hechler, "How Congress Enabled Mountaintop Removal."

52 Ibid.

53 Various statements, Acc. 1977, Box 170, Folder 19.

54 Desai, "The Politics of Federal-State Relations," 789.

55 Hechler to all members and staff, March 11, 1975, Acc. 1977, Box 171, Folder 5.

56 Gerald R. Ford, "Veto of a Surface Mining Control and Reclamation Bill," May 20, 1975, http://www.presidency.ucsb.edu/ws/?pid=4928.

57 421 members were present and voting. Two-thirds or 281 could have overridden the veto. The vote was 278–143. *All Bill Information (Except Text) for H.R.28—Surface Mining Control and Reclamation Act (1975)*, https://www.congress.gov/bill/94th-congress/house-bill /28/all-info.

58 Hechler statement, undated, Acc. 1977, Box 170, Folder 19.

59 Hechler, "How Congress Enabled Mountaintop Removal."

60 Ned Helme to CTS, telephone interview, April 30, 2013.

61 Hechler, "How Congress Enabled Mountaintop Removal."

62 KH to CTS, Charleston, WV, January 14, 2013.

63 Ibid.

64 Hechler, "How Congress Enabled Mountaintop Removal."

15. SAVING THE NEW RIVER

1 Stephen L. Neal, *Neal Seeking Support to Save New River*, undated flyer, Acc. 1977, Box 166, Folder 6.

2 KH to Barbour, Huntington, WV, August 13, 2005.

3 Ibid.

4 KH notes for a press conference dated September 26, 1972, Acc. 1977, Box 166, Folder 13.

5 KH, draft public statement on New River National Park, undated, Acc. 1977, Box 166, Folder 7.

6 Doug Yarrow, "Local Men Argue for River," *Raleigh Register*, June 2, 1974, Acc. 1977, Scrapbook 1974.

7 KH to the National Parks and Recreation Subcommittee, House Interior and Insular Affairs Committee, June 3, 1974, Acc. 1977, Box 166, Folder 7.

8 Arnold Miller letter to U.S. Representatives, December 17, 1974, Acc. 1977, Box 166, Folder 4.

9 KH statement to the House Committee on Rules, December 11, 1974, Acc. 1977, Box 166, Folder 7.

10 "Hechler Blasts Moore in Tabling of Blue Ridge Bill, *Welch Daily Mail*, December 12, 1974, Acc. 2010, Box 048, Folder 1.

11 Chuck Goddard, "Last Rites Held for 250 Million-Year-Old River," *Raleigh Register*, December 16, 1974, Acc. 2010, Series, Xi, Box 048, Folder 2.

12 Neal, *Neal Seeking Support to Save New River*.

13 Release from Ken Hechler, January 9, 1975, Acc. 2010, Series, Xi, Box 048, Folder 3.

14 Jay Wild, "History of the Management Plan for the South Fork of the New River in N.C.," accessed August 4, 2015, http://www.nps.gov/parkhistory/online_books/symposia/newriver-84/sec15.htm.

15 Sam J. Ervin, foreword to *The New River Controversy: A New Edition*, by Thomas J. Schoenbaum (Jefferson, NC: McFarland, 2007).

16 Ken Hechler, "The New River . . . Like It Is," statement dated May 20, 1976, Acc. 1977, Box 166, Folder 5.

17 Acc. 1977, Box 166, Folder 7.

18 Hechler press release notes, Acc. 1977, Box 166, Folder 19.

19 KH to Barbour, Huntington, WV, August 13, 2005.

20 Hechler, "The New River . . . Like It Is."

21 John Vaughan, *Hearings before the Subcommittee on the Environment and Land Resources of the Committee on Interior and Insular Affairs*, May 20–21, 1976, http://babel.hathitrust.org/cgi/pt?id=uiug.30112052639298;view=1up;seq=3, p. 38.

22 Ibid., 126–128.

23 Senator Metcalf, *Hearings before the Subcommittee on the Environment and Land Resources of the Committee on Interior and Insular Affairs*, May 20–21, 1976, http://babel.hathitrust.org/cgi/pt?id=uiug.30112052639298;view=1up;seq=3, p. 38.

24 Ervin, foreword to *The New River Controversy*.

25 Senator Sam Ervin, Sr., *Winston Salem Sentinel*, June 22, 1976, Acc. 1977, Box 166, Folder 19.

26 *CQ Almanac*, 1976, p. 152, Hechler Collection, Acc. 2010, Box 048, Folder 4.

27 KH to CTS, Charleston, WV, December 13, 2012.

28 KH to CTS, Charleston, WV, December 6, 2012.

29 KH to Barbour, Huntington, WV, August 13, 2005.

16. HECKLING CONGRESS

1 Senator George McGovern to Barbour, Mitchell, SD, September 12, 2005.

2 KH to CTS, Huntington, WV, February 16, 2013.

3 KH text of a speech, "WV Getting Short Changed," Cong. Rec., July 16, 1959, Hechler Collection, Acc. 2010, Series IX, Box 042, Folder 11, labeled "1959–1965 Congressional Record."

4 Ken Hechler, *Faith, Hope, and Parody* (Missoula, MT: Pictorial Histories, 2011).

5 Senator Tom Harkin to Barbour, Washington, DC, September 28, 2005.

6 KH remarks, Cong. Rec., September 15, 1965, Acc. 2010, Series IX, Box 042, Folder 11, labeled "1959–1965 Congressional Record."

7 Thomas Stafford, *Charleston Gazette*, June 7, 1964, Acc. 2010, Series IXi, Box 042, Folder 5.

8 KH notes, Acc. 2010, Series IXi, Box 042, Folder 13.

9 *Wikipedia*, s.v. "Salaries of Members of the United States Congress," accessed August 19, 2015, https://en.wikipedia.org/wiki/Salaries_of _members_of_the_United_States_Congress.

10 *Parkersburg News*, February 15, 1969, Acc. 2010, Series IXi, Box 042, Folder 13.

11 Ken Hechler, "Why I'm Against Federal Pay Increases Now," November 16, 1973, Acc. 2010, Series IX, Box 042, Folder 16.

12 Acc. 2010, Series IXi, Box 042, Folder 3.

13 Acc. 2010, Series IXi, Box 042, Folder 4.

14 Document dated 6/1/76–6/30/76, Acc. 2010, Series IX, Box 042, Folder 16.

15 Acc. 2010, Series IXi, Box 042, Folder 3.

16 Ibid.

17 Ibid., Folder 5.

18 Congressional Record, January 4, 1965, https://www.gpo.gov/fdsys /pkg/STATUTE-79/pdf/STATUTE-79-Pg1422.pdf.

19 Judy Schneider, Christopher M. Davis, and Betsy Palmer, *Reorganization of the House of Representatives: Modern Reform Efforts*,

October 20, 2003, http://archives.democrats.rules.house.gov /archives/RL31835.pdf.

20 *Beckley Post Herald/Raleigh Register*, January 13, 1973, 8.

21 KH to CTS, Key West, FL, May 17, 2013.

22 Dr. Simon Perry, professor emeritus, Marshall University, to CTS, April 9, 2013.

23 KH to Simon Perry, February 22, 2007, courtesy of Dr. Simon Perry, CTS Files.

24 Simon Perry to CTS, April 9, 2013.

25 KH to CTS, Huntington, WV, January 14, 2013.

26 Hechler Work Record Log, Acc. 2010, Series IX, Box 042, Folder 2.

27 KH to CTS, Huntington, WV, January 14, 2013.

28 Deborah Baker, "Hechler Is Farmer for a Day," *Raleigh Register*, August 21, 1975, accessed February 19, 2013.

29 "Congressman Goes Home, Finds Work and Some Humility," *Chicago Tribune*, September 17, 1975, Acc. 2010, Series IX, Box 042, Congressional Recess, Folder 1.

30 Ibid.

31 *Charleston Gazette*, December 8, 1969.

32 KH letter to Barbara Jenkins, Charlton Heights, WV, August 27, 1973, Acc. 1977, Box 348, Folder WV Subject—Watergate/Impeachment letters.

33 KH letter to Leon Anderson, January 28, 1974, Acc. 1977, Box 348, Folder WV Subject—Watergate/Impeachment letters.

34 Lauralyn Bellamy, Capitol Hill News Service, press release, November 25, 1973, Acc. 2010, Series IX, Box 042, Folder labeled "Capitol Hill News Service #12/2 IMPEACHMENT."

35 *Charleston Gazette*, September 8, 1973, Acc. 1977, Box 348, Folder WV Subject—Watergate/Impeachment letters.

36 "Most of House Members Queried Still Undecided about Impeachment," *Nashua Telegraph*, January 28, 1974, 14.

37 KH to Mary Lou Taylor, Bluefield, WV, December 3, 1973, Acc. 1977, Box 348, Folder WV Subject—Watergate/Impeachment letters.

38 KH to Cabell County Democratic Women, 1974; in Moffat, *Ken Hechler, Maverick Public Servant*, 272.

39 Hechler, *Courier-Express*, Dubois, PA, September 17, 1974, 9.

40 Hechler, *Princeton Times*, August 15, 1974.

41 Senator Tom Harkin to Barbour, Washington, DC, September 28, 2005.

42 Senator Robert Dole to Barbour, Washington, DC, September 26, 2005.

43 Senator George McGovern to Barbour, Mitchell, SD, September 12, 2005.

44 KH to CTS, Huntington, WV, February 16, 2013.

17. THE INTERREGNUM

1   KH undated press release, Hechler Collection, Acc. 1977, 1, Box 39a, Folder labeled "Press Releases."

2   KH to CTS, Charleston, WV, December 6, 2012.

3   Ibid.

4   Flyer for volunteers, 1976 Gubernatorial Campaign, Hechler Collection, Acc. 2010, Series VIIIa.1, Box 28, Folder 1.

5   Acc. 2010, Series VIIIa.1, Box 28, Folder 2.

6   Chuck Goddard, "Ken Hechler Opens Campaigning Headquarters at Parking Meter," *Beckley Register*, March 26, 1976, Acc. 2010, Series VIIIa.1, Box 28, Folder 12.

7   Acc. 2010, Series VIIIa.1, Box 28, Folder 4.

8   Acc. 2010, Series VIIIa.1, Box 28, Folder 3.

9   Acc. 2010, Series VIIIa.1, Box 28, Folder 8.

10 *Beckley Post-Herald*, June 25, 1976, Acc. 2010, Series VIIIa.1, Box 28, Folder 11.

11 *Beckley Register*, October 26, 1976, Acc. 2010, Series VIIIa.1, Box 28, Folder 11.

12 Hechler, *Toward the Endless Frontier.*

13 *Spokesman Review*, November 12, 1976.

14 1977–1978 letters to KH from Robert Miller, Acc. 2010, Series VIIIb.2, Box 29, Folder 7.

15 *Charleston Gazette*, February 5, 1978, Acc. 2010, Series VIIIb.2, Box 29, Folder 8.

16 *Glenville Democrat*, May 25, 1978.

17 Nick Rahall Sr. to KH, November 7, 1978, Acc. 2010, Series VIIIb.2, Box 29, Folder 13.

18 KH notes for speech at the Radisson Hotel, Huntington, WV, Acc. 2010, Series IIIg, Box 13, Folder 15.

19 Hillary Harper to KH, September 17, 1980, Acc. 2010, Series IIIg, Box 13, Folder 15.

20 Hechler, *Working with Truman*, 299.

21 Editorial reviews, *Working with Truman*, https://www.amazon.com /Working-Truman-Ken-Hechler/dp/0399127623/ref=tmm_hrd _swatch_o?_encoding=UTF8&qid=&sr=.

22 Acc. 2010, Series VIIc, Box 26, Folder 5.

23 Madge Patterson, Putnam Publishing Group, to KH, March 1, 1984, Acc. 2010, Series VIIc, Box 26, Folder 8.

24 Karen Caplinger Marketing Manager, University of Missouri Press, to KH, March 18, 1996, Acc. 2010, Series VIIc, Box 26, Folder 8.

25 KH to Warren Wade, North Park College, Chicago, IL, March 25, 1981, Hechler Collection, Acc. 2010, Series IIIh, Box 013, Folder 4.

26 Undated newspaper clipping, Acc. 2010, Series IIIh, Box 013, Folder 1.

27 Acc. 2010, Series IIIh, Box 013, Folder 1.

28 Acc. 2010, Series IIIh, Box 013, Folder 14.

29 KH to Professor Evelyn Harris, Political Science Department, University of Charleston, July 29, 1982, Acc. 2010, Series IIIg, Box 013, Folder 15.

30 *Parthenon*, August 12, 1982, Acc. 2010, Series IIIg, Box 013, Folder 15.

31 Alan B. Gould to Ken Hechler, September 3, 1983, Acc. 2010, Series IIIg, Box 013, Folder 8.

32 Acc. 1977, 2, Series IX, Box 9, Folder 36.

33 Acc. 1977, 2, Series IX, Box 9, Folder 37.

34 Acc. 2010, Series IIIg, Box 013, Folder 6.

35 Acc. 2010, Series IIIg, Box 013, Folder 7.

36 Acc. 1977, 2, Series IX, Box 9, Folder 37.

37 Hechler campaign release, March 21, 1984, Acc. 2010, Series VIIIc, Box 31, Folder 23.

38 *Parthenon*, Acc. 2010, Series VIIIc, Box 31, Folder 22.

39 Donald Rasmussen to the Appalachian Pulmonary Laboratory Inc. Council, April 16, 1984, Acc. 2010, Series VIIIc, Box 31, Folder 5.

40 KH to Chris Sowards and Chuck Smith, May 15, 1984, Acc. 2010, Series VIIIc, Box 31, Folder 7.

41 Campaign brochure, Acc. 2010, Series VIIIc, Box 31, Folder 20.

42 *Charleston Daily Mail*, June 6, 1984, Acc. 2010, Series VIII c, Box 31, Folder 22.

43 "Sparks Fly between Hechler, Owens Due to Rally Remarks," *Williamson Daily News*, October 30, 1984, Acc. 2010, Series VIIIc, Box 31, Folder 22.

44 *Parthenon*, undated article, Acc. 2010, Series VIIIc, Box 31, Folder 22.

18. THE PEOPLE'S OFFICE—THE FIRST TERM

1 Allen H. Loughry, II, *Don't Buy Another Vote, I Won't Pay for a Landslide* (Parsons, WV: McClain, 2006), 131–132.

2 KH to Fred Vinson, August 31, 1967, Acc. 2010, Series XIIb, Box 53, Folder 3.

3 KH letters, November 20, 1984, Acc. 2010, Series VIIIc., Box 31, Folder 8.

4 Barbara Myers to CTS, April 27, 2013.

5 Barbara Myers to Barbour, September 1, 2005.

6 Paul Nyden to Barbour, September 22, 1005.

7 Judy Cooper to CTS, October 15, 2015.

8 Mary Ratliff to CTS, Lewisburg, WV, January 18, 2013.

9 *Charleston Gazette*, August 6, 1985, Acc. 2010, Series XIb, Box 53, Folder 4.

10 Jim Wallace, *A History of the West Virginia Capitol: The House of State* (Charleston, SC: History Press, 2012), 120.

11 Ratliff to CTS, Lewisburg, WV, January 18, 2013.

12 KH to CTS, Charleston, WV, December 6, 2012.

13 Ratliff to CTS, Lewisburg, WV, January 18, 2013.

14 Judy Cooper to CTS, October 15, 2015.

15 Week in State Government papers, Acc. 2010, Series XIp, Box 56, Folder 9.

16 Phil Hancock to Barbour, September 2, 2005.

17 *Charleston Daily Mail*, October 24, 1986, Acc. 2010, Series XIa, Box 53, Folder 1.

18 Chronology of Charleston City Workers Case, Acc. 2010, Series XIa, Box 53, Folder 18.

19 Testimony, January 24, 1986, Acc. 2010, Series XIa, Box 53, Folders 7–17.

20 *Charleston Daily Mail*, October 24, 1986, Acc. 2010, Series XIa, Box 53, Folder 1.

21 Chronology of Charleston City Workers Case.

22 *Charleston Gazette*, September 4, 1985, Acc. 2010, Series XIa, Box 53, Folder 1.

23 Loughry, *Don't Buy Another Vote*, 481.

24 Judge Dan O'Hanlon to CTS, Huntington, WV, October 2, 2015.

25 "Arch Moore Jr., . . . Dies at 91," *Washington Post,* January 8, 2015, https://www.washingtonpost.com/politics/arch-moore-jr -charismatic-wva-governor-convicted-of-corruption-dies-at-91 /2015/01/08/e5857798-974d-11e4-927a-4fa2638cd1b0_story.html.

26 Undated statement from the secretary of state's office, Hechler Collection, Acc. 2010, Series XIb, Box 53, Folder 2.

27 Hechler statement, July 20, 1985, Acc. 2010, Series XIb, Box 53, Folder 2.

28 *Williamson Daily News*, June 2, 1986, Acc. 2010, Series XIb, Box 53, Folder 10.

29 Hechler, "Keeping Elections Clean," *Mountain Messenger*, January 12, 1988, http://mms.stparchive.com/Archive/MMS/MMS 01121988P04.php.

30 Judge Dan O'Hanlon to CTS, Huntington, WV, October 2, 2015.

31 Barbara Myers to CTS, Huntington, WV, April 27, 2013.

32 Hechler news release, November 6, 1986, Acc. 2010, Series XIb, Box 53, Folder 2.

33   Associated Press, undated article, Acc. 2010, Series XIb, Box 53, Folder 4.

34   *Williamson Daily News*, undated article, Acc. 2010, Series XIIIb, Box 53, Folder 22.

35   Loughry, *Don't Buy Another Vote*, 142.

36   KH to CTS, Charleston, WV, December 6, 2012.

37   Ratliff to CTS, Lewisburg, WV, January 18, 2013.

38   Hechler, "Four-Year Report," December 30, 1988, Acc. 2010, Series XId, Box 53, Folder 11.

39   KH to CTS, Charleston, WV, December 12, 2012.

40   Barbara Myers to Barbour, Morgantown, WV, September 1, 2005.

41   Hechler, "Four-Year Report."

42   Acc. 2010, Series XIb, Box 53, Folders 3–5.

43   Judge Dan O'Hanlon to CTS, Huntington, WV, October 2, 2015.

44   Hechler, "Why West Virginia Needs a Secretary of State," undated, Acc. 2010, Series XIg, Box 55, Folder 23.

45   Hechler, "Four-Year Report."

46   Hechler, "Why West Virginia Needs a Secretary of State."

47   *Williamson Daily News*, September 19, 1985, Acc. 2010, Series XIc, Box 53, Folder 8.

48   Richard A. Brisbin Jr., *A Strike Like No Other Strike: Law and Resistance during the Pittston Coal Strike of 1989–1990* (Baltimore: Johns Hopkins University Press, 2002), 107.

49   Hechler, "Why West Virginia Needs a Secretary of State."

50   "History of Camp Dawson," accessed November 10, 2015, http://www.wv.ngb.army.mil/campdawson/Form2.aspx?MP=Mg==&P=Mg==.

51   Correspondence regarding Camp Dawson, Acc. 2010, Series XIh, Box 54, Folder 2–3.

52   KH to Robert C. Byrd, July 27, 1988, Acc. 2010, Series XIi, Box 54, Folder 1–2.

53   Hechler, "Four-Year Report."

54   KH to CTS, Key West, Florida, May 17, 2013.

55   Hechler, "Four-Year Report."

56   Hechler, "West Virginia Secretary of State's Report, 1985–2000," KH Personal, Folder labeled "WV Secretary of State."

19. THE PEOPLE'S OFFICE—THE REST OF THE STORY

1 "West Virginia Votes to Keep Independent State Board, Superintendent," September 20, 1989, http://www.edweek.org/ew/articles/1989/09/20/09050031.h09.html.

2 Bob Robinson, "Hechler's Fight for the Constitution," *Parkersburg News*, March 19, 1989, Acc. 2010, Series XIg, Box 54, Folder 1.

3 KH to CTS, Charleston, WV, December 4, 2012.

4 KH to Gaston Caperton, September 25, 1989, Acc. 2010, Series XIc, Box 54, Folder 1.

5 *Charleston Gazette*, July 27, 1989, Acc. 2010, Series XIg, Box 54, Folder 1.

6 KH to CTS, December 6, 2012.

7 Letter from Robert Hall, Dean of Social Sciences, WV State College, December 3, 1977, to Daniel Fleming, Blacksburg, VA, Acc. 2010, Series XIo, Box 56, Folder 1.

8 *Pt. Pleasant Register*, May 18, 1989, Acc. 2010, Series XIg, Box 54, Folder 30.

9 Hechler press release, March 26, 1989, Acc. 2010, Series XIg, Box 54, Folders 13–14.

10 Undated memo to the committee, Acc. 2010, Series XIg, Box 54, Folder 16.

11 KH to campaign supporters, undated, Acc. 2010, Series XIg, Box 54, Folder 28.

12 Acc. 20107, Series XIg, Box 54, Folder 18.

13 *Charleston Daily Mail*, September 12, 1989, Acc. 2010, Series XIg, Box 54, Folder 1.

14 KH to Commissioner of Finance and Administration, undated, Acc. 2010, Series XIg, Box 54, Folder 19.

15 Maralee Schwartz, "Hechler Returns to West Virginia Fray," *Washington Post*, May 6, 1990.

16 Kent Keyser, assistant to Nick Rahall, to CTS, telephone interview, May 5, 2013.

17 KH to CTS, Key West, FL, May 19, 2013.

18 "1990 Primary Election—Official Returns of the Democratic Party," West Virginia Secretary of State website, accessed November 11,

2015, http://www.sos.wv.gov/elections/history/electionreturns/Documents/1990/1990%20Primary%20Election%20-%20Official%20Returns%20of%20the%20Democratic%20Party.pdf.

19 Tom Susman to Ken Hechler, April 17, 1992, Acc. 2010, Series VIIIc, Box 31, Folder 12.

20 Ken Ward, *Charleston Gazette*, April 17, 1992, Acc. 2010, Series VIIIc, Box 31, Folder 21.

21 KH to Swarthmore friend, June 1, 1992, Acc. 2010, Series VIIIc, Box 31, Folder 10.

22 Ken Ward, *Charleston Gazette*, August 17, 1992, Acc. 2010, Series VIIIc, Box 54, Folder 6.

23 "1992 General Election—Official Election Returns," West Virginia Secretary of State website, accessed November 11, 2015, http://www.sos.wv.gov/elections/history/electionreturns/Documents/1992/1992%20General%20Election%20-%20Official%20Election%20Returns.pdf.

24 KH to reporters, January 12, 1999, during his first march with Granny D, Acc. 2010, Series XIIb, Box 62, Folder 7.

25 KH to Vernon Hayes, and VH to KH, various dates, Acc. 2010, Series XIc, Box 54, Folder 6.

26 Vernon Hayes to Charlotte Pritt, September 1, 1996, Acc. 2010, Series XIc, Box 54, Folder 7.

27 Correspondence between KH and Vernon Hayes, September 25–27, 1996, Acc. 2010, Series XIc, Box 54, Folder 7–8.

28 "1996 General Election—Official Election Returns," WV Secretary of State website, accessed November 10, 2015, http://www.sos.wv.gov/elections/history/electionreturns/Documents/1996/1996%20General%20Election%20-%20Official%20Election%20Returns.pdf.

29 Correspondence between KH and Vernon Hayes, September 25, 27, 1996, Acc. 2010, Series XIc, Box 54, Folder 8.

30 Ratliff to CTS, Lewisburg, WV, January 18, 2013.

31 Kim Baker, former Hechler 2000 congressional campaign chair, to CTS, Huntington, WV, May 5, 2013.

32 KH to Senator Byrd, undated, Acc. 2010, Series XIj, Box 54, Folder 2.

33 Hechler statement, October 19, 1999, Acc. 2010, Series XIIb, Box 62, Folder 12.

34 KH to fellow Democrats, undated letter, Acc. 2010, Series XIIb, Box 62, Folder 12.

35 Frances X. Clines, "West Virginia, Home of the Gray in America," *New York Times*, July 17, 1999.

36 "2000 House of Representatives Primary Results," West Virginia Secretary of State website, accessed November 11, 2015, http://www .sos.wv.gov/elections/history/electionreturns/Documents/2000 /2000%20House%20of%20Rep%20Pri.pdf.

37 KH to CTS, Key West, FL, May 17, 2013.

38 Clayton Sandell, "90-Year-Old Running for W.Va. Executive Office," ABC News, October 26, 2004, http://abcnews.go.com/WNT /Vote2004/story?id=196261&page=1.

39 KH to CTS, Charleston, WV, December 6, 2012.

40 Sandell, "90-Year-Old Running for W.Va. Executive Office."

41 KH to CTS, Charleston, WV, December 6, 2012.

42 KH to CTS, Huntington, WV, January 26, 2013.

43 Johnie Owens to KH, as told by KH to CTS, Charleston, WV, December 6, 2012.

20. WALKING WITH GRANNY D

1 KH notes, Hechler Collection, Acc. 1977, 1, Box 37, Folder labeled "Campaign Financing."

2 KH to CTS, Huntington, WV, February 9, 2013.

3 KH to CTS, Huntington, WV, February 16, 2013.

4 Doris "Granny D" Haddock to Barbour, Dublin, NH, August 20, 2005.

5 Bill Moyers, foreword to *Granny D: Walking across America in My 90th Year*, by Doris Haddock with Dennis Burke (New York: Villard, 2001), ix–x.

6 *Wikipedia*, s.v. "Bipartisan Campaign Reform Act," accessed November 30, 2015, https://en.wikipedia.org/wiki/Bipartisan_Campaign _Reform_Act.

7 Kevin Wilborne, "Granny D Promotes Voting, Activism," *Parthenon* 105, no. 35, clipping in a personal copy of *Granny D: Walking across America in My 90th Year*.

8   Haddock, *Granny D*, 15.

9   Haddock to Barbour, Dublin, NH, August 20, 2005.

10 KH to CTS, Charleston, WV, December 4, 2012.

11 Haddock to Barbour, Dublin, NH, August 20, 2005.

12 Ibid.

13 Haddock, *Granny D*, 18–19.

14 Ken Hechler, Acc. 2010, Series XIb, Box 62, Folder 5.

15 Hechler at the opening of Doris Haddock's collection of papers at Keene State College, September 23, 2011, "College Preserves Legacy of New Hampshire Activist, Granny D," http://www.syracuse.com /news/index.ssf/2011/09/college_preserves_legacy_of_ne.html.

16 Haddock, *Granny D*, 35.

17 KH Parody, Acc. 2010, Series XIff, Box 61, Folder: Parodies.

18 "Granny D's 90th Birthday, Cumberland, MD," *Good Morning America*, January 24, 2000, Acc. 2010, VT 601.

19 Haddock, *Granny D*, 50.

20 Ibid., 63, 67.

21 KH to CTS, Charleston, WV, December 4, 2012.

22 Haddock, *Granny D*, 173.

23 Haddock to Barbour, Dublin, NH, August 20, 2005.

24 Haddock, *Granny D*, 105. Hechler was actually 85 when he filed to run for Congress in 1999.

25 KH to Doris Haddock, John Anthony, Dennis Burke, Matt Keller, et al., August 26, 1999, Acc. 2010, Series XIIb, Box 62, Folder 12.

26 Haddock to Barbour, Dublin, NH, August 20, 2005.

27 Haddock, *Granny D*, 173.

28 KH to Haddock et al., August 26, 1999, Acc. 2010, Series XIIb, Box 62, Folder 12.

29 Haddock, *Granny D*, 173.

30 KH to Haddock et al., August 26, 1999, Acc. 2010, Series XIIb, Box 62, Folder 12.

31 Since he kept and placed in the archives all his other documents, including love letters, I assume he did not keep the letter.

32 KH open letter to Haddock et al., November 9, 1999, Acc. 2010, Series XIIb, Box 62, Folder 12.

33 KH to Haddock, August 30, 1999, Acc. 2010, Series XIIb, Box 62, Folder 12.

34 KH to Haddock, November 9, 1999, Acc. 2010, Series XIIb, Box 62, Folder 12.

35 KH to Haddock et al., November 24, 1999, Acc. 2010, Series XIIb, Box 69, Folder 12.

36 Haddock, *Granny D*, 225–226.

37 Ibid., 229.

38 KH to Dennis Burke, May 9, 2001, KH Personal, Folder labeled "Granny D."

39 Kevin Wilborne, *Parthenon* 105, no. 34, clipping in a personal copy of *Granny D: Walking across America in My 90th Year.*

40 "Granny D Goes to Washington," PBS special, produced by the Corporation for Public Broadcasting, Acc. 2020, VT 626.

21. FROM REBEL TO HELL-RAISER

1 KH to CTS, Huntington, WV, January 31, 2013.

2 KH to Coolfont guests in 2002, KH Personal, Folder labeled, "Marshall U 'Hechler's Hecklers' 2002."

3 Invitations and bills from the 1993 reunion, Acc. 2010, Series Xvi, Box 76, Folder 3.

4 Acc. 2010, VT 450.

5 Acc. 2010, VT 455.

6 Letters to invitees, Hechler Collection, Acc. 2010, Series XVi, Box 76, Folder 5.

7 Granny D's speech at Coolfont, August 26, 2000, Acc. 2010, VT 444.

8 KH to Bonni _____, May 16, 2000. Acc. 2010, Series XVi, Box 76, Folder 7.

9 Sideboards are extensions to increase the carrying capacity of coal trucks and to minimize spillage of smaller loads.

10 A Jake brake is an engine compression release brake used especially for steep downgrades. The lack of one increases the chances of the driver losing control of the vehicle because he or she can't slow it down sufficiently. The Jake brake turns a power-producing engine

into a power-absorbing air compressor, thus slowing the truck. Jake is short for Jacobs, the company that invented the brake system.

11 KH to Governor Arch Moore, March 17, 1986, Acc. 2010, Series Xj, Box 48, Folder 5.

12 Chris Knap, "Moore Vetoes Major Bills, Plans May Session," *Charleston Gazette*, March 27, 1986, library.cnpapers.com, accessed 12/21/15.

13 Vivian Stockman, "The People Win Round 1 in Coal Truck Weight Battle," *OVEC Newsletter*, November 2002, http://ohvec.org /newsletters/woc_2002_11/article_07.html.

14 KH, "Keeper of the Mountains" fund-raising plea, December 19, 2011, YouTube video, https://www.youtube.com/watch?v=TaJRkQZj1PM.

15 Janet Fout, "Apple Grove Pulp Mill Update—On the Water (Permit) Front," *OVEC Newsletter*, July 1997, ohvec.org/newsletters/enotes_97 -01_pdf/enotes_1997_07.pdf.

16 Stockman to CTS, Huntington, WV, March 13, 2013.

17 Beth Wellington, "The Second March on Blair Mountain," *The Writing Corner* (blog), September 3, 2006, https://bethwellington .wordpress.com/2006/09/03/the-second-march-on-blair -mountain/.

18 KH statement to FBI, Acc. 2010, Series Xm, Box 49, Folder 2.

19 Laura Foreman, "Art Kirkendoll—An Un'Wise' Appointment in Charleston," *OVEC Newsletter*, May 2001, http://ohvec.org /newsletters/enotes_97-01_pdf/enotes_2001_05.pdf.

20 KH to CTS, Charleston, WV, December 13, 2012.

21 *Wikipedia*, s.v. "Larry Gibson," last modified July 18, 2016, https://en .wikipedia.org/wiki/Larry_Gibson.

22 KH to CTS, Charleston, WV, December 13, 2012.

23 Janet Keating to CTS, Huntington, WV, March 13, 2013.

24 Stockman to CTS, Huntington, WV, March 13, 2013.

25 Hechler, *Faith, Hope, and Parody*, 24–25.

26 Keating to CTS, Huntington, WV, March 13, 2013.

27 Stockman to CTS, Huntington, WV, March 13, 2013.

28 Sierra Club, "Spring 2009: Blair Mountain Added to National Register of Historic Places!" press release, March 31, 2009, http://www .pawv.org/news/blairrelease.htm.

29 Associated Press, "Blair Mountain Coming Off Historic Register," press release, July 6, 2009, http://www.pawv.org/blairdelist.htm.

30 Travis Crum, "Marchers Scale Blair Mountain," *Charleston Gazette*, June 11, 2011.

31 "Marsh Fork Elementary," Coal River Mountain Watch, October 2010, http://www.crmw.net/projects/marsh-fork-elementary .php.

32 "March 5, 2009: Activists Protest Mountaintop Removal, Pettus, WV," sourcewatch.org, http://www.sourcewatch.org/index.php /Nonviolent_direct_actions_against_coal:_2009#March_5.2C _2009:_Activists_protest_mountaintop_removal.2C_Pettus.2C _WV.

33 Sparki Ran, "Hooray for the Riff Raff," *The Understory* (blog), Rainforest Action Network, May 27, 2009, http://www.ran.org/hooray _for_the_riff_raff.

34 KH at Massey gates, reported by Jeff Biggers for the *Huffington Post*, "Hechler to President Obama: Time for a Harry Truman Moment in the Coalfields," July 6, 2009, http://www.huffingtonpost.com/jeff -biggers/rep-hechler-to-president_b_211996.html.

35 Acc. 2010, VT 505.

36 Jeff Deal, "News for the Marsh Fork Elementary School Rally of June 23rd, 2009," *Appalachian Voices Newsletter*, July 26, 2009, http://appvoices.org/2009/06/26/2391/.

37 KH to CTS, Charleston, WV, December 13, 2012.

38 Jared Hunt, "Hechler Ready for Rough Terrain," *Charleston Gazette*, August 12, 2010.

39 *Wikipedia*, s.v. "United States Senate special election in West Virginia, 2010," accessed December 28, 2015, wikipedia.org/wiki /United_States_Senate_special_election_in_West_Virginia, _2010.

40 Peter Slavin, "A Vote for Ken Hechler Is a Vote against Mountaintop Coal Removal Mining," *Swarthmore College Bulletin*, October 2010, http://bulletin.swarthmore.edu/bulletin-issue-archive /archive_p=523.html.

41 Ken Hechler press conference, Charleston, WV, September 8, 2010, www.youtube.com.

42 "Hechler's Jeep recovered after apparent theft," *Charleston Gazette*, September 13, 2010, http://www.wvgazettemail.com/policebrfs/201009130836.

43 Travis Crum, "Marchers Scale Blair Mountain," *Charleston Gazette*, June 11, 2011.

44 Chuck Belmont Keeney, "The Second Battle of Blair Mountain: Mountaintop Removal Is Destroying Our Heritage," June 8, 2011, http://thinkprogress.org/climate/2011/06/08/239896/the-second-battle-of-blair-mountain-mountaintop-removal-is-destroying-our-heritage/.

45 Keating to CTS, Huntington, WV, March 13, 2013.

46 Arnold Schnobrich, Ken Hechler Tribute, Cherry Blossom Festival, Marshfield, MO, April 26, 2013.

47 KH to CTS, Charleston, WV, December 13, 2012.

48 Ken Hechler at Larry Gibson's memorial service, October 14, 2012, YouTube video, https://www.youtube.com/watch?v=ujPYOM4__mo.

22. INTO THE SUNSET

1 Hazo W. Carter Jr. to KH, October 10, 2000, KH Personal, Folder labeled "WV State College—KH Teaching."

2 Ibid.

3 Martha Woodward to CTS, Huntington, WV, April 11, 2013.

4 KH to CTS, Huntington, WV, April 30, 2013.

5 Woodward to CTS, Huntington, WV, April 11, 2013.

6 KH to CTS, Huntington, WV, January 31, 2013.

7 University Honors Fall 2002 Evaluations, Acc. 2010, Series IIIg, Box 13, Folder 9.

8 "Ken Hechler on Civil Rights in the Truman Administration," 2011: The Civil Liberties Legacy of Harry S. Truman, http://www.trumanlittlewhitehouse.com/key-west/harry-truman-symposium/harry-truman-symposiums.htm.

9 An adult education movement in the United States, highly popular in the late nineteenth and early twentieth centuries. Named after Chautauqua Lake, in western New York, where the first one was

held, Chautauqua assemblies expanded and spread throughout rural America until the mid-1920s. *Wikipedia*, s.v. "Chautauqua," last modified October 24, 2016, https://en.wikipedia.org/wiki/Chautauqua.

10 "Ken Hechler on Goering," Robert H. Jackson Center, https://www.youtube.com/watch?v=naTLLwohK3Q.

11 Harry S. Truman Public Service Award, Independence, Missouri, City Council website, http://www.ci.independence.mo.us/CityCouncil/TrumanAward.

12 Arnold Schnobrich, Ken Hechler Tribute, Cherry Blossom Festival, Marshfield, MO, April 26, 2013.

13 "Hechler wins MLK Award," *Charleston Gazette*, January 19, 2010.

14 "Hechler Back at Work Following Bypass Surgery," *Charleston Daily Mail*, June 29, 2000, https://www.highbeam.com/doc/1P2-18968255.html.

15 Barbour to CTS, Huntington, WV, March 2, 2013.

16 Ibid.

17 http://wvpublic.org/post/producer-profile-russ-barbour.

18 KH to CTS, Charleston, WV, April 30, 2013.

19 Raamie Barker to CTS, telephone interview, April 5, 2013.

20 Ken Hechler, *Super Marine! The Sgt. Orland D. "Buddy" Jones Story* (Missoula, MT: Pictorial Histories, 2007), x.

21 Nat deBruin to CTS, Huntington, WV, December 10, 2012.

23. TWILIGHT

1 Ratliff to CTS, Lewisburg, WV, January 18, 2013.

2 KH to Ruth Mary Lewis, no date, Hechler Collection.

3 KH to CTS, Key West, FL, May 19, 2013.

4 KH to Julie _____, May 7, 1991, Hechler Collection. (Last names of women Hechler dated either unknown or purposely omitted.)

5 KH to Barbour, November 13, 2005.

6 KH to Ruth Mary Lewis, no date, Hechler Collection.

7 Various letters, Hechler Collection.

8 Becky_____ to KH, July 22, 1969, Hechler Collection.

9 KH about Rita _____, and a telegram to KH from Rita _____, July 4, 1956, Hechler Collection.

10 KH to Ruth Mary Lewis, no date, Hechler Collection.

11 KH to Jane Stewart, no date, KH Personal, File labeled "Fort Knox, Armored? Love Letters."

12 Defined as an unusual male sex drive.

13 KH to Julie _____, May 7, 1991, Hechler Collection.

14 Deegans to CTS, January 18, 2013.

15 KH to Ruth Mary Lewis, no date, Hechler Collection.

16 Simon Perry to CTS, Huntington, WV, April 9, 2013.

17 CKH to CTS, Huntington, WV, April 11, 2013.

18 KH to Ruth Mary Lewis, no date, Hechler Collection.

19 CKH to CTS, via telephone, August 13, 2013.

20 CKH to CTS, via telephone, August 20, 2013.

21 CKH to CTS, Huntington, WV, September 27, 2014.

22 KH, undated answers to autobiographical questions, KH Personal, File labeled "Biography."

BIBLIOGRAPHY

ARCHIVAL SOURCES

George Elsey's Papers, Truman Library—Elsey Papers.

Hechler Collection, Special Collections, Marshall University, Huntington, WV, Accession 1977/09.0199, Addendum 1—Acc. 1977, 1, Box #, Folder #.

Hechler Collection, Special Collections, Marshall University, Huntington, WV, Accession 1977/09.0199, Addendum 2—Acc. 1977, 2, Box #, Folder #.

Hechler Collection, Special Collections, Marshall University, Huntington, WV, Accession 2010/05.0777—Acc. 2010, Series #, Box #, Folder #.

Hechler Collection, Special Collections, Marshall University, Huntington, WV, Accession 2010/05.0777, Video Tape Collection—Acc. 2010, VT #.

Hechler Collection, Special Collections, Marshall University, Huntington, WV, Accession 2014/10.0802—Acc. 2014, Series #, Box #, Folder #.

Hechler's Personal Files—KH Personal.

Log of Truman's Tenth Visit to Key West, November 8–December 9, 1951, Truman Library—Truman's Travel Log.

SOURCES

Brisbin, Richard A., Jr. *A Strike Like No Other Strike: Law and Resistance during the Pittston Coal Strike of 1989–1990.* Baltimore: Johns Hopkins University Press, 2002.

Brunner, Bob. *Bob Brunner's Reporter's Recollections.* WV: Self-published, 2012.

Ervin, Sam J. Foreword to *The New River Controversy: A New Edition*, by Thomas J. Schoenbaum, 1–6. Jefferson, NC: McFarland, 2007. First published 1979 by John F. Blair.

Grun, Bernard, ed. *The Timetables of History.* 3rd ed. New York: Simon & Schuster, 1991.

Haddock, Doris, with Dennis Burke. *Granny D: Walking across America in My 90th Year.* New York: Villard, 2001.

Hechler, Kenneth W. *The Bridge at Remagen.* 1957. 6th revised printing. Missoula, MT: Pictorial Histories, 2004.

———. *Faith, Hope, and Parody.* Missoula MT: Pictorial Histories, 2011.

———. *The Fight for Coal Mine Health and Safety: A Documented History.* Charleston, WV: Pictorial Histories, 2011.

———. *Goering and His Gang.* Missoula, MT: Pictorial Histories, 2011.

———. "How Congress Enabled Mountaintop Removal." In *Coal Country: Rising Up against Mountaintop Removal Mining*, edited by Shirley Stewart Burns, Mari-Lynn Evans, and Silas House, 63–70. San Francisco: Sierra Club Books, 2009.

———. *How to Be a Great Teacher.* Missoula MT: Pictorial Histories, 2012.

———. *Insurgency.* New York: Russell & Russell, 1964.

———. *Soldier of the Union.* Charleston, WV: Pictorial Histories, 2011.

———. *Super Marine! The Sgt. Orland D. "Buddy" Jones Story.* Missoula, MT: Pictorial Histories, 2007.

———. *Toward the Endless Frontier: History of the Committee on Science and Technology, 1959–79.* Washington, DC: U.S. House of Representatives, 1980.

———. *Working with Truman: A Personal Memoir of the White House Years.* Columbia & London: University of Missouri Press, 1982.

Hume, Brit. *Death and the Mines: Rebellion and Murder in the United Mine Workers.* New York: Grossman, 1971.

Loughry, Allen H., II. *Don't Buy Another Vote, I Won't Pay for a Landslide.* Parsons, WV: McClain, 2006.

McElfish, James M., Jr., and Ann E. Beier. *Environmental Regulation of Coal Mining: SMCRA's Second Decade.* ELI Monograph Series. Washington, DC: Environmental Law Institute, 1990.

Miller, Merle. *Plain Speaking: An Oral Biography of Harry S. Truman.* New York: Berkley, 1973.

Moffat, Charles H. *Ken Hechler, Maverick Public Servant.* Charleston, WV: Mountain State Press, 1987.

Moyers, Bill. Foreword to *Granny D: Walking across America in My 90th Year,* by Doris Haddock with Dennis Burke, ix–xv. New York: Villard, 2001.

Truman, Harry S. *Memoirs.* Vol. 2, *Years of Trial and Hope: 1946–1952.* Garden City, NY: Doubleday, 1956.

Wainstock, Dennis. *Truman, MacArthur and the Korean War.* Westport, CT: Greenwood Press, 1999.

Wallace, Jim. *A History of the West Virginia Capitol: The House of State.* Charleston, SC: History Press, 2012.

Wilson, Richard Guy. *Harbor Hill, Portrait of a House.* New York and London: Society for the Preservation of Long Island Antiquities in association with W. W. Norton, 2008.

INDEX